Love Light

By

Ana Corman

ISBN: 1-4140-0851-1 (e-book)
ISBN: 1-4140-0850-3 (Paperback)

Library of Congress Control Number: 2003097676

This book is printed on acid free paper.

Printed in the United States of America
Bloomington, IN

1stBooks – rev. 02/23/04

To My Catherine, I dedicate this book to you.

I'm eternally grateful for the day you walked into my life and the years you have contributed to my dreams. You alone fuel my imagination and feed my heart. You unconditionally fill my life with love and light. Catherine, you are my greatest treasure and my love light.

"The first time I saw you sitting at your mother's bedside, holding her hand after that first seizure, you looked so scared, yet so strong and brave and very angry. I just wanted to reach out and take all your worries away. At the time, you would have just bit off my hand, and that made you all the more alluring.

"Then I found myself just aching to see you, talk to you, and comfort you. I haven't wanted a woman like this since Laura. Then I would think about her, and I would miss her so much. I wasn't ready to let her go when she died, Adrianna, but I thought I was managing pretty well. Instead, what I was doing was cocooning in my grief and hoping

never to feel the things I felt for Laura. Then I saw you there beside your mother, and you took my breath away. Your eyes, your face, your grief, your anger. I wanted to explore it all and understand everything about you."

Chapter 1

She reached for the doorknob and hesitated. The single pane of frosted glass obscured the view of the family within the quiet room. She never understood why they called it the quiet room. Even in the silence you could hear and feel the screams of anguish, shock, and disbelief. She took a deep breath as she tightened her grip on the doorknob. This was the one part of her job she hated. A part she knew all too well.

She stepped into the large, bright, single room and gently closed the door. Even the floor to ceiling mural depicting an underwater scene seemed out of place in this tension-filled room. The middle-aged couple stood together with their hands tightly clasped and their tears streaked down their cheeks, staring so fiercely as if hoping to will away the words they knew were coming.

"Mr. and Mrs. Kirkland?"

The gentleman placed his hand on his wife's lower back. "Yes. I'm James, and this is my wife Madeleine."

Erica extended her hand. "I'm Dr. Erica Beaumont, your daughter's neurosurgeon." Both parents nodded their heads in silent acknowledgment and cautiously shook her hand. Erica gestured toward the couch. "Please, have a seat, so we can talk. I understand you just arrived in town." Erica sat on the edge of the coffee table, directly facing both parents.

Mr. Kirkland looked at his wife before turning to Erica. "We live just outside of San Diego. We've been driving for six hours. We just got in our car and started driving after we received the phone call from the police last night about Nicole's accident. When we arrived at the hospital, they told us she was in the neurosurgical intensive care unit. The security guard brought us here to this waiting room. The charge nurse, Sarah, said you wanted to speak to us before we went in to see our daughter. How is she, Dr. Beaumont? How badly hurt is she?"

Erica clasped her hands together before leaning forward and resting her elbows on her thighs. "The news is not good, and I'm going to be totally honest and straightforward with you. Your daughter suffered a massive head injury in the car accident last night. The damage that was done to her brain is permanent and irreversible." Mrs. Kirkland clutched at her chest and blinked in disbelief.

Mr. Kirkland looked from his wife to Erica. "What does that mean, permanent and irreversible? She's still alive, isn't she? She's going to be okay, isn't she? Isn't there something we can do, surgery or medication or something? For God's sake, she's our only child. She called us just before she was heading to the library last night. How can this be happening?"

2

Erica reached forward and laid her hand on Mr. Kirkland's arm. "I'm sorry. I'm so sorry to have to tell you this, but there is nothing we can do. Your daughter is brain dead. We did an EEG this morning, and there is absolutely no brain activity. The CAT scan shows the gross extent of her brain injury. We have Nicole on a ventilator, and without it your daughter would not be breathing."

Mrs. Kirkland released an anguished gasp as she leaned into her husband's arms. "Oh, God! She's gone. God has taken our baby girl from us. How are we going to go on without her? This isn't supposed to happen. She's not supposed to die before us."

Mr. Kirkland rocked her gently in his arms as tears coursed down his face. He tried valiantly to calm his sobbing wife as he struggled with the insanity of this news.

Erica fought to swallow past the lump in her throat as she handed them more tissues from her lab coat pocket. Mrs. Kirkland accepted the tissues and watched Erica struggle with her own emotions.

Erica took Mrs. Kirkland's hand and held it tight. "I'm so sorry."

Mrs. Kirkland clutched at the tissue and held it to her trembling lips. "The policeman said Nicole was hit head on by a drunk driver. She was such a good girl. She's an honor student at her university. She wanted to go to med school and be a doctor like you, Dr. Beaumont. Now all her hopes and dreams are gone. Her precious young life is wasted because of a drunk driver."

"What has happened to your daughter is a horrible tragedy. I wish there was something we could do to

3

help her, but there is nothing within our means to fix what has been done. Sadly, there is nothing we can do to help Nicole, but your daughter may be able to help others."

Mrs. Kirkland clutched at her husband's hand and struggled to contain the sob in her chest. "What do you mean?"

"This may be too early for you both to even think of this, but you may want to consider your daughter being an organ donor. I don't know if you have ever talked about this as a family or if Nicole has shared her thoughts with you on this. I can tell you that she has a signed organ donor card in her wallet. She has a donor sticker on the back of her license consenting to donate her organs if this should ever happen to her." Erica allowed the parents to absorb their shock and thoughts.

"I'm only asking you to think about this possibility. I know this is an extremely difficult time for both of you. What I'm asking of you is one of the hardest things I could ever ask of you as parents, and I truly wish I did not have to put you through this." Erica hesitated long enough to let them process the information.

"I don't expect you to make a decision now. Take all the time you need to talk about this together. I will be here to answer any of your questions when you're ready. If and when you want more information on organ donation, I will arrange for a representative from the Organ Donor Network to come and spend some time with you. In the meantime, I want you to spend as much time as you need with your daughter. The nursing staff and I are here to answer any of your questions and concerns."

Mrs. Kirkland pressed the tissue to her mouth before drying her tears. "Thank you, Dr. Beaumont. We need time to think. What we need to do first is see our daughter."

"Of course. I just want to prepare you for what you're going to see when you walk into your daughter's room. As I mentioned earlier, Nicole is on a ventilator, so she has a breathing tube in her mouth. She also has a large dressing around her head and some bruising on her face. She has an intravenous in her right arm. Other than that, she looks like she's sleeping. If you wish to see the hospital chaplain, just let the charge nurse, Sarah, know, and she will be happy to arrange that for you."

"Is she in pain, Dr. Beaumont? I don't want my daughter to feel any pain," Mr. Kirkland said, choking back tears.

"No, sir, your daughter is not in any pain. Come with me and I will take you to see her." They all stood together as Erica watched them gather their things. "I'll leave you with your daughter for a few hours, and then I will come back to answer any questions you may have."

Erica held the door open for them and guided them down the hall to the large double doors labeled Neurosurgical Intensive Care Unit. She punched her four-digit security code into the panel on the wall and guided the Kirklands through the automatic doors.

She led them around the u-shaped nurses' station, past several individual rooms separated only by glass walls. The Kirklands could see the nurses busy in each room with patients attached to all kinds of beeping, blinking machinery. Erica stopped outside the doorway of room five. She gestured inside. "This is your daughter's room."

James and Madeleine Kirkland stood just inside the doorway staring at the motionless figure lying in the bed. Madeleine turned her face into her husband's chest and sobbed painfully. She cried, "Why," over and over again as she clutched his chest with her fist. He tried to silence her pleas as the tears ran down his tormented face. They held each other tight for several minutes before venturing farther in the room.

Erica stepped back and stood outside the glassed-in room and watched James and Madeleine tentatively stand on either side of their daughter's bed. They set their things down in an empty chair and stared at her lifeless form for several seconds as the hiss of the ventilator echoed loudly in the room.

Madeleine's tears coursed down her face as she touched her daughter's swollen, bruised cheek. "We love you, baby. We will always love you. You have been such a wonderful daughter. We don't want to lose you, but God needs you now. That is the only sense we can make of this. We can't fight what we don't understand. We just want you to know that you have been the most wonderful daughter we could ever have asked for. We want you to be in peace and free of pain. If God is calling, then we want you to go. Till that moment happens, we will be right here with you. You're not alone, sweetheart. Your dad and I are here with you."

Erica felt a familiar tightening in her chest. She watched the Kirklands lean into their daughter and rest their heads against hers. She slowly slid the glass door closed and allowed the family the privacy they needed.

These were the times she felt so inadequate as a physician. All of the knowledge, skills, and technology at her fingertips, and she could do nothing to help young Nicole Kirkland. She often wondered why these tragedies struck such innocent people.

Erica turned and saw the charge nurse, Sarah, watching her from the center of the nurses' station. Sarah had been a charge nurse in the neurosurgical ICU for twenty years after immigrating from London, England, at the tender age of twenty-one. Sarah stood out among the others. Her intelligence and skills shone above and beyond anyone Erica had ever worked with during her residency. She had been infinitely patient with Erica as she grew from an intense, insecure, inexperienced resident, teaching her so much about the patients they both cared for.

Sarah walked toward Erica and laid her hand on her shoulder. "We'll take care of them, Erica. Are you all right?"

Erica blinked away her tears. "I'm okay, Sarah. It's just been a really lousy morning." Erica reached down for the pager vibrating against her hip and pulled it from her belt. "It's the E.R."

"It's probably Dr. Thomas. He called up here when you were in the quiet room with the Kirklands. I asked him to give you about twenty minutes. He said there was a patient down there he wanted you to see. He said he would page you when the patient's CAT scan was done."

"I'll go down and see Michael then. I'll see what he has for us." Erica turned back and looked through the glass wall of room five. She watched Mrs. Kirkland take her daughter's hand to her lips and kiss

7

her gently. Erica rested her hand on Sarah's arm. "Make sure they have everything they need. I promised them I would come back and talk to them. They're from San Diego, Sarah, so maybe we can see if there is a room available for them in the family hostel in the hospital so they can stay close to Nicole."

"Good idea. I'll call the nursing supervisor and see what's available for them."

"That would be great. They just need some time right now. Page me if you need anything, okay?"

"I will, Erica. Don't worry. Call me if you need a bed for that patient in the E.R. We only have two open beds."

"I will. Thanks, Sarah."

Erica headed out of the double doors and down the hall to the E.R., wondering when she could take a badly needed vacation. She felt reassured that Sarah would take good care of the Kirklands and always felt at ease when Sarah was in charge of the patients in the unit. She was an extremely intelligent and caring nurse, and Erica respected the way she took care of the patients and their families. Erica always saw Sarah as the matriarch of the NICU. They had become close friends over the ten years they had worked together, and Erica treasured that friendship as much as their professional working relationship.

Erica walked down several hallways before she emerged into the midst of the chaotic emergency room. She was instantly swallowed up by the buzz of activity and the annoyingly loud noise level. She felt like she had spent her life in this emergency department, yet could never get used to the feeling of emotional tension and urgency that hung in the air.

She watched as the nurses moved in fast-forward as they completed ten tasks at once. An ambulance crew brushed past her with a patient in full cardiac arrest. A mother carried a sobbing child with a huge gash on his forehead. A man assisted another emaciated man into a wheelchair and bent down to talk to him softly as he wrapped him in a warm blanket. Erica watched them as tears slid down the cheeks of the man in the wheelchair and the man kneeling before him lovingly wiped them away and kissed him softly. Erica was so moved by their warmth that she didn't notice Michael till he laid his hand on her back.

"Welcome to my insane world. I was trying to get your attention from the nurses' station, but you were pretty lost in thought."

Erica squeezed Michael's hand. She had adored him from the moment he flew a paper airplane into her hair during a male anatomy class with a message stating, "You might try to look not so disgusted. You're giving yourself away." They had become dear friends since that inaugural paper flight, and that bond had only strengthened throughout the years.

Michael stared deeply into her coral green eyes. "Hey, are you okay?"

"I'm fine, Michael. I was just wondering if you wanted to trade your insane world for mine for the rest of the day."

"Not a chance, Erica. You're the absolute best at what you do. I couldn't fill your shoes even if there were ten of me. Now, come with me, darling. I have a CAT scan I want you to see."

Dr. Erica Beaumont and Dr. Michael Thomas stood side by side before the view box, studying the CAT scan before them. Michael explained the patient's symptoms as Erica listened carefully and absorbed the information before her with focused, intelligent eyes.

They discussed their findings for several minutes before Erica snapped the CAT scans off the view box and slipped them back into their manila envelope.

Michael handed Erica the patient's chart and gently squeezed her arm. "Thank you for seeing her, Erica. She's a lovely lady, and I don't like what I see on her CAT scan. I know that her best chance to fight this is in your capable hands."

Erica blushed slightly and looked into the steely gray eyes of her longtime friend and colleague. Those eyes held a great depth of knowledge and warmth; his chiseled features and short, wavy chestnut hair gave many women cause to take a good long look and sigh with appreciation. Erica took his hand and squeezed it tight. "Thanks for the vote of confidence, Michael. That means a lot to me."

"Come on, Erica. You're the best neurosurgeon I've ever worked with, and I'm just grateful to have you as a friend." Michael couldn't resist toying with a stray chocolate-brown ringlet that cascaded like a waterfall over Erica's shoulders. "However, I would be much happier if you would just marry me and give up this futile search for this mythical perfect woman that you seem to have a burning desire to find."

Erica burst into laughter and loved the grin softening Michael's usually serious expression. "I promise you that I will seriously consider your marriage proposal in another lifetime, okay? I've dedicated this lifetime to the full pursuit of my lesbian dreams."

Michael shook his head in defeat and shoved his hands in the pockets of his pleated gray trousers as he followed Erica out of the x-ray room. "Man, how am I supposed to compete with that?"

Erica laughed and shook her head as Dr. Abigail Cooper stepped into the hallway. Erica smiled into the glowing light, brown eyes of her med school roommate.

Michael took the opportunity to pluck Abby's pager off her lab coat pocket. He slipped the back cover off and dropped the batteries into the palm of his hand. "Well, would you look at that. This thing actually has working batteries in it."

Abby gave Erica a confused look before turning back to Michael. "Dr. Thomas, may I ask you what you're doing dismantling my pager?"

"I'm just checking to see if this thing is actually real and not just a toy. I've been paging you for the last hour, Abigail. Your cardiac patients are filling up my E.R. beds faster than I can go through a jar of gourmet jelly beans."

Abby rolled her eyes and scooped her pager and its parts back from the palm of Michael's hand. "Some of us have been really busy this morning, Michael. And I would appreciate it if you would stop dismantling my toys."

Erica burst into laughter. "I'll leave you two to slug it out while I go see my new patient."

Michael squeezed Erica's arm. "Good luck with Mrs. Taylor, Erica. Let me know what happens."

"I sure will." Erica smiled and turned to Dr. Cooper. "Hey, Abby, Michael's looking for a bride if you're interested."

Abby clipped her pager back onto her lab coat pocket and gave Michael a thorough looking over. "I hate to have to turn down such an outstanding opportunity, Erica, but I already explained to Michael that I learned in grade two that men were nothing but trouble when Tommy Jameson stuck that big wad of gum in my hair at recess."

Michael raised his eyebrows. "Isn't that the kid you gave a black eye?"

Erica burst into laughter. "It sure is. I was standing right beside the guy when Abby unloaded on him. I bet he never stuck a wad of gum in a girls hair after that."

"After an experience like that, it's no wonder I'm a lesbian."

Erica burst into laughter and waved good-bye.

Abby blew Erica a kiss and guided Michael toward the nurses' station. "Come on, Michael. Guide me to my patients that I'm sure you have taken excellent care of in my absence."

"You owe me a jar of gourmet jelly beans for clogging up my E.R., Dr. Cooper."

Erica could hear Abby's infectious laughter as she headed down the hall and stood in the doorway leading to the observation rooms. She stared at the chart in her hands and felt concerned for the symptoms of this sixty-eight-year-old woman. She knew this day was only going to get worse before it ever got any better.

Erica pushed the door open and headed toward observation room two. As she rounded the corner, she saw the drapes partially pulled around a woman lying on a stretcher. Her silver-streaked hair cascaded around her face. The wrinkles at her eyes creased with

12

the smile she gave the distinguished man sitting on a stool, gently caressing her flowing hair and talking to her softly. Erica was touched by their warmth and smiled as she approached them.

The gentleman stood as he saw Erica approach. The lady on the stretcher turned to face Erica with bright blue eyes and a tired smile.

Erica extended her hand to the patient on the stretcher. "Hello. Are you Mrs. Carolyn Taylor?"

The patient's lovely blue eyes smiled as she took Erica's hand. "Yes, I am. And this is my husband, David."

Erica turned and shook his hand. "Hello. I'm Dr. Erica Beaumont. I'm a neurosurgeon. Dr. Thomas asked me to see you."

Mr. and Mrs. Taylor both looked shocked. They turned and smiled at each other before bringing their attention back to Erica. "I must admit to you, Dr. Beaumont, we did not expect to see a woman when Dr. Thomas told us that he was going to have a neurosurgeon come to see me. And certainly not one as young and as beautiful as yourself."

Erica blushed as she smiled and thought of the hundred times that patients had looked at her this way when she introduced herself as their neurosurgeon.

Mrs. Taylor looked up at Erica and saw a truly beautiful woman. She figured she must be in her mid-thirties and obviously a very highly skilled and highly intelligent woman. Her unusual teardrop eyes, the color of a green coral sea, were framed by a mass of flowing, dark brown, untamed ringlets. She probably stood five feet, eight inches tall with a slender, strong, athletic figure. She exuded confidence, intelligence, and warmth, and Mrs. Taylor really liked that about her. Mrs. Taylor guessed that this Dr. Erica Beaumont probably left an impression on many people whose lives she touched. Dr. Thomas had said she would be seeing one of the best, most highly respected neurosurgeons at University Hospital, and Mrs. Taylor had a gut instinct that she was in good hands with Dr. Erica Beaumont.

Mrs. Taylor touched Erica's arm. "We didn't mean to make you feel uncomfortable, dear. You're just not what we expected to see in a neurosurgeon. We had visions of an older, balding man, possibly close to retirement."

"The way I feel today, retirement sounds awfully nice, but I might be a little ways off from balding with this head of hair."

Mrs. Taylor kept her hand on Erica's arm and squeezed gently. "You have absolutely beautiful hair, my dear, and we hope that you don't seriously consider retirement yet. At least not till you take care of whatever it is that's causing my annoying headaches."

"I would really like to do that for you. Mr. Taylor, why don't you take a seat, and we can begin." Erica leaned her hip against the side of the stretcher. She laid the chart on the foot of the stretcher and pulled out her penlight, pen and notebook. "Mrs. Taylor, tell me when your headaches began."

Mrs. Taylor settled back into her pillows and looked directly into Erica's sea-green eyes. "I would really like you to call me Carolyn."

Erica smiled and looked into her blue eyes. "Okay, Carolyn."

Carolyn smiled, and the creases at the corners of her eyes smiled with her. "I've suffered from migraines for approximately ten years, but I never let them slow me down." She turned to her husband, who took her hand. "We have two daughters, and three weeks ago we went out to dinner with our older daughter. I felt this excruciating headache during dinner that I had never felt before. It was different than my usual migraines."

"Where specifically was the headache?"

Carolyn placed one hand over both her eyes. "It was concentrated mostly behind my eyes, but I felt like my head was about to explode."

"What happened then?"

Carolyn placed her hand in her lap and looked up into Erica's eyes. "Well, I became really nauseated and couldn't stand it any longer, so David and our daughter took me home. I took some pills and went straight to bed. The next morning I felt a lot better, but this headache has not really gone away completely. It has been a very annoying presence behind my eyes for three weeks now."

Erica watched intently as Carolyn shared her story. "Tell me what happened this morning."

Carolyn turned to her husband. "David would be better able to tell you about this morning. It's mostly a blur to me."

Mr. Taylor squeezed his wife's hand and looked at Erica with troubled eyes. "Carolyn's headaches these past three weeks are only the tip of the iceberg. Ever since that excruciating headache that one night, she has had a tough time concentrating on simple tasks. She has been vague at times when I have been talking to her and inattentive to things that she always took care of. She's normally a very emotional woman, and the past three weeks she has been very flat, almost depressed. I've never, in the fifty years that we have been married, seen her like this."

Erica gave him a minute to compose himself.

"This morning was a nightmare. It was six o'clock, and I was awakened by Carolyn making these strange gurgling noises like she was choking. I turned toward her and saw her eyes roll to the top of her head, and she started shaking all over. I was terrified and I tried to talk to her and the shaking wouldn't stop so I grabbed the phone and dialed 911. Within minutes an ambulance crew was there, and Carolyn finally stopped shaking. They told me that she had had a seizure and brought her here immediately."

Erica placed her hand on his shoulder to comfort him. Erica turned to Carolyn and saw the tears in her eyes.

"Has this ever happened before? Has she ever had a seizure before this morning?"

He looked sad and exhausted. "No, never. This is the first time this has ever happened."

Erica looked at her watch and over at Carolyn. "It's nine o'clock in the morning now. It's been three hours since that seizure. How do you feel?"

Carolyn watched her husband and frowned. "I feel very tired, and the headache behind my eyes is worse. My right arm doesn't feel like it belongs to me, and at times I have difficulty finding the words that I want to say. I've also been having problems with urinary incontinence and that's really embarrassing."

Erica set the chart, her pen and notebook down on the counter. She stepped away and pulled the curtain completely around Mrs. Taylor's stretcher, giving them what little privacy they could have to do a full neurological assessment.

"Carolyn, if you don't mind, I'd like to examine you at this time."

"That would be fine, Dr. Beaumont."

"David, you're more than welcome to stay if you would like."

"Thank you, Dr. Beaumont. I'd like that."

Erica gently lowered Carolyn's gown and placed her stethoscope on her chest when she noticed the small scar on her breast. "Did you have surgery on your right breast, Carolyn?"

"I was diagnosed with breast cancer four years ago and treated with a lumpectomy and radiation. As far as we know, I have not had any recurrences since then."

Erica nodded and proceeded to spend thirty minutes thoroughly assessing Carolyn and making a mental note of all her findings. Erica stepped before the sink and washed her hands as they continued talking.

Mrs. Taylor's nurse peeked around the curtain. "I'm sorry for interrupting, Dr. Beaumont, but Mrs. Taylor's daughter is here. I was wondering how long I should tell her to wait before I bring her in?"

Erica looked at David and Carolyn. "That must be our younger daughter, Leah," Carolyn said.

The nurse stepped closer to Mrs. Taylor's stretcher. "She's a very nice lady, and she's really worried about you. I believe her husband is with her."

"That's right. That would be our son-in-law, Grant."

"They're welcome to come back here if you both would like that, then I can talk to all of you together."

"I would really like that, Dr. Beaumont."

Erica turned and asked the nurse to bring the family into the room.

Erica turned back to Carolyn and David. "You mentioned you have two daughters. Are you expecting your other daughter as well?"

David sighed and said, "I called our daughter Adrianna in New York this morning and she was going to hop on the first plane out. She should be here in a few hours."

Erica slipped her pen and penlight back into her pocket. "Does she live in New York?"

"David and Adrianna are both lawyers." Carolyn smiled at her husband. "Adrianna lives here in Phoenix, but her law firm does quite a bit of work in New York, so she divides her time between both cities. She doesn't particularly like all the traveling and time away from us but …"

David interrupted and ended her sentence, "She goes where the action is. I offered her work in my law firm ever since she graduated from Stanford ten years ago, but she has made it clear that we are just not big enough or sensational enough for her restless spirit."

Erica was intrigued by their description of their spirited daughter and the animosity between father and daughter.

"Adrianna is so much like her father."

David tried unsuccessfully to suppress a smile.

"Admit it, David. You idolize each other, but you are both too bull-headed and stubborn to see each other's points of view."

David shook his head and was saved by the arrival of their younger daughter.

Erica stepped back and watched as a beautiful woman with Carolyn's eyes engulfed her mother in an emotional hug. David turned to Erica. "Dr. Beaumont, I would like you to meet our daughter, Leah, and her husband, Grant. Grant and Leah, this is Dr. Erica Beaumont. She's your mother's neurosurgeon."

Erica shook Leah's hand and felt drawn to the concern in her light blue eyes. She gripped Erica's hand tightly as her eyes searched for answers. Erica squeezed her hand in comfort before turning to Grant and shaking his hand. Grant was very handsome with sharp, rugged features, chestnut brown eyes, and the physique of a man who prided himself on staying in shape.

Grant looked at Erica with that same stunned look of surprise. "Wow! A female neurosurgeon. I'm impressed."

Leah turned and poked him in the ribs with her elbow. "Watch it, mister! There's no reason why we women can't dominate any career you men have possessed for centuries."

Erica touched her arm and leaned close. "Thank you. I thought I might have to kick his shins, but you handled that wonderfully for me."

Both women smiled at each other, forging an instant bond with their eyes as Grant rubbed his injured ribs.

David laid his hand on Grant's shoulder and laughed softly. "Watch it, son. We're outnumbered by these strong, intelligent women."

Leah playfully glared at her husband then stepped toward her mother and took her hand. "How are you feeling, Mom?"

Erica's pager vibrated at her hip as she looked down at the display screen. "If you will all just excuse me for a few minutes, I'll go answer this page from the ICU. When I get back, we will talk about my findings." Carolyn nodded her head. Erica slipped behind the curtain and headed toward the nurses' station, allowing the Taylor family some private time.

Erica returned fifteen minutes later. "I'm sorry for that interruption."

Everyone was standing around Carolyn's stretcher. Carolyn reached for Erica's hand and pulled her closer. She squeezed her hand gently and frowned. "Well, Dr. Beaumont, what exactly is happening to me?" Carolyn tilted her head. "Since the moment we have been fortunate enough to meet you, you have had this deeply concerned look in your eyes, and I wish to know what is behind that look. I expect you to be up front and honest with us. We want to know everything so that we can make the appropriate decisions together. We think you are an exceptional woman, Dr. Beaumont, but you wear your heart on your sleeve and are terrible at covering up your sadness."

Erica blushed. "I didn't think I was that obvious."

Carolyn gave Erica's hand a gentle squeeze. "You're a pure and gentle soul, Dr. Beaumont. Now, talk to us. I want to know what is happening."

Erica took a deep breath and looked directly at Carolyn. "I reviewed your CAT scan before I came to see you, and it shows that you have a brain tumor." Erica paused as the family took this in. "It is located in your frontal lobe, right behind your forehead, and that explains your headaches, inattentiveness, poor concentration span, and vagueness. Erica stopped as she watched Carolyn take a deep breath. "In my assessment I noticed that your short-term memory is affected. Your right arm is weaker than your left, and you mentioned that you have experienced urinary incontinence over these past three weeks." Erica paused long enough to allow this information to sink in. "These are all symptoms of your frontal tumor." Erica squeezed Carolyn's hand and watched her tears tumble onto her cheeks. Erica felt an uncomfortable constriction in her chest as she took a deep breath. "I'm sorry, Carolyn. I wish this was not happening to you."

Carolyn squeezed Erica's hand and wiped away her tears. "Don't apologize, Dr. Beaumont. We're finally finding the cause of my headaches after all these years." Carolyn bit at her lower lip in an attempt to curb her tears. She accepted tissues from her husband and stared intently into Erica's eyes. "What next? What are our options?"

Erica slowly rubbed her forehead and allowed Carolyn time to dry her tears. "We need to remove the tumor. I would like the opportunity to do that for you. From what I saw on your CAT scan, your type of tumor looks like a meningioma. A meningioma is a benign brain tumor that develops from the protective lining of the brain. It is extremely rare for these types of tumors to be malignant. We will biopsy the tumor, and that will give us more information. Its position and size indicate that it will be relatively easy to remove surgically, but I will know more once we expose the tumor." Erica paused as she watched the emotions in Carolyn's eyes. "After the surgery we can discuss the possibility of radiation or chemotherapy."

Carolyn immediately raised one hand toward Erica and closed her eyes. "Absolutely not, Dr. Beaumont. I had radiation for my breast cancer, and I've never been the same since. That was a horrible experience, and my brain tumor can even be metastatized from my breast cancer, which means we went through all that for nothing."

Erica frowned as Carolyn looked away.

"The way I feel right now, I would opt for surgery, and that is as far as this will go. But I will discuss this further with my family." Carolyn reined in her anger as she saw the look on Erica's face. "Stop frowning, Dr. Beaumont. I've heard your professional opinion, and I appreciate everything you have shared with us. I will always listen to what you have to say, but you must also respect my wishes, which I don't sense will be a problem. Am I correct?"

Erica couldn't help but smile at Carolyn's tenacious spirit. "Yes, ma'am," she replied.

"Good. Now, when do you expect we can do this surgery?"

Erica looked around the room at the other distraught family members, then back at Carolyn. "I would like to do it this afternoon. I would be able to schedule you into the operating room at three o'clock."

Carolyn exhaled deeply. "Wow, that soon." Carolyn reached for David's hand and held it close. "I guess we need some time to talk."

Erica collected Carolyn's chart and hugged it close. "Carolyn, I'm going to admit you into the neurosurgical intensive care unit so the nurses can watch you carefully for any further seizure activity. I'll order you medication to help prevent that from happening again. We need to make sure we have your seizures under control. Your brain tumor is not life threatening at this point, but your seizures can be. I want them completely under control before we take you to the operating room.

"I'm also going to have the nurses do more blood work and order a chest x-ray and EKG. I'm going to ask that you not eat or drink anything, and I'll order you some Demerol for your headache. I'm going to ask your nurse here in the emergency department to give you a dose through your intravenous before they transfer you upstairs to the ICU." Erica looked around at everyone's concerned faces. "I'll get the nurses to transfer you into the unit as soon as possible, so you can have several hours together to discuss the information that I've given you."

Carolyn placed her hand on Erica's arm. "Do you think it's important to do the surgery today?"

"Yes. I think that we need to remove your tumor as soon as possible. Waiting any longer will only put you at risk for other complications, and I'm not willing to sit back and watch that happen to you."

Carolyn smiled at the look in Erica's eyes "If you feel it's important to move on this, then I guess we will. I'll just need to spend some time with my family."

Erica smiled and touched Carolyn's hand. "I'll see you in the ICU in a few hours. Then we can discuss the surgery in greater detail. I'll explain all the complications to you and have you sign the consent form along with David."

"Our daughter Adrianna should be here by then, and we will discuss this with her. If she has any further questions, I will get her to direct them to you."

"That would be perfectly fine," Erica said, as she squeezed Carolyn's hand. She gave her a warm smile as she stepped toward the curtain and looked back at everyone. "I'm sorry I could not have given you better news, but I'm glad that you're here, so we can take care of this for you. I'll see you all in a couple of hours. I'll be doing my rounds and then spending some time with another family in the ICU. If you have any further questions or need me for anything, please don't hesitate to have the nurses page me."

Erica was about to step away as she heard Carolyn say, "Dr. Beaumont."

Erica looked back into those warm, blue eyes. "Yes?"

"Thank you for everything. Especially your kindness."

"Don't thank me till we have successfully completed your surgery and you're feeling better and heading home with your lovely family. Then and only then will I say, 'You're welcome.'"

Erica waved good-bye and headed toward the nurses' station as she felt a constriction around her heart.

David dropped the side rail on his wife's stretcher and took her in his arms. "She's a true gem."

Carolyn leaned her forehead against his. "She's a true angel."

Ana Corman

Chapter 2

Erica was standing at the nurses' station of the neurosurgical ward, surrounded by her residents. They were discussing the case of a forty-five-year-old man who had fallen off his ladder at work and suffered a subdural hematoma ten days before.

Erica was listening intently to her senior resident, Peter, explain the patient's neurological deficits. He was one of Erica's brightest residents, and she really enjoyed working with him and watching him learn and grow. He had an insatiable appetite for knowledge and truly loved the field of neurosurgery. His boyish good looks and the spiked bangs of his short dark hair made him appear ten years younger than his age of thirty. His lanky frame added to his youthful appearance, but his mature personality and bright mind made him stand out among the rest.

Peter was reviewing the patient's medications when Erica's pager sounded. She looked up at her residents, "You guys go ahead and see the rest of the patients while Peter and I answer this page from the ICU."

Peter looked at her with concern as they hurried down the hall and into the ten-bed neurosurgical intensive care unit.

Sarah saw Erica and Peter walk through the doors and stepped around the nurses' station to meet them. "Erica, it's Mrs. Taylor. She had a grand mal seizure. We gave her two milligrams of Ativan, and the seizure lasted thirty seconds. Unfortunately, her family was in the room with her at the time, and they're very upset. I know you wanted to be paged right away if she had another seizure."

Erica took a deep breath and ran her fingers through her hair. "Thanks for paging me, Sarah. I was hoping that this would not happen."

"Is this the new patient with the frontal brain tumor you were telling me about?" Peter asked.

"Yes. Mrs. Carolyn Taylor. We loaded her with Dilantin. I was hoping we would have her seizures under control so we could take her to the operating room."

"They're in room two, Erica." Erica and Peter followed Sarah toward the Taylor family.

Erica stood in the doorway of room two and saw everyone standing around Carolyn's sleeping form. The tension in the room was as thick as the fog on a seaside autumn morning. Erica scanned the room and noticed a woman that she had not met before. She was sitting beside Carolyn's bed and gently caressing her cheek, as she talked to her in a soft whisper. Her thick, flowing, dark brown hair framed her delicate face. Erica was drawn to her distraught oval-shaped, sapphire-blue eyes. Her long, rich eyelashes continually battled to hold back the tears welling in those exquisite eyes.

Sarah stepped into the room and rechecked Carolyn's vital signs. David turned and saw Erica in the doorway.

He stepped toward her and touched her arm. "Thank God you're here, Dr. Beaumont."

Everyone turned and looked at Erica as she took David's hand. "Sarah paged me right away. I'm sorry you all had to witness that seizure."

The woman sitting at Carolyn's bedside groaned in disgust. "Give me a break! You can't possibly be my mother's neurosurgeon."

David was appalled and practically shouted, "Adrianna! I can't believe you just said that!" He glared at the woman who had not taken her eyes off Erica and turned toward Erica. "That is our other daughter, Adrianna. She arrived just as her mother started to have a seizure."

Erica looked into those beautiful, oval, sapphire-blue eyes clouded with fear and was awestruck by her intensity and despair. She was humming with barely controlled anger that was threatening to spring loose. Erica was shaken by this stunning woman's fierce emotions. She felt stung by the woman's contemptuous attack and decided this was not the place to explain herself. She forced herself to bring her attention back to Carolyn.

Erica turned to Sarah and struggled to clear her vision of those sapphire eyes. "Tell me about Carolyn's seizure and her vital signs."

Sarah answered all of Erica's questions as she continued to make Carolyn comfortable. Another nurse gently readjusted her oxygen mask as Carolyn stiffened and arched her back. She gasped and gurgled her next breath as her eyes rolled to the top of her head and her arms and legs simultaneously flailed against the padded side rails. Carolyn was having another grand mal seizure as the entire family stood watching.

Erica, Peter, and Sarah automatically stepped into action. Erica looked up at the faces of the Taylor family. "Please, go out to the waiting room." She watched them take several steps toward the doorway, their eyes riveted on Carolyn.

Erica turned her attention back to Carolyn. "Sarah, get me another two milligrams of Ativan, now." Peter grabbed a Lardol bag and began to administer a higher flow of oxygen to Carolyn. Erica helped to position Carolyn farther on her side. Sarah quickly administered the Ativan intravenously. Erica timed the seizure on her watch and looked up to see the Taylor family watching from the doorway.

Adrianna caught her eye and stepped closer to the bed. "Do something to stop this, Dr. Beaumont! Why the hell can't you control these seizures? Why are you standing by and watching this happen to my mother?"

Erica was beginning to lose her patience as she turned to David. "Please get her out of here, now."

Sarah stepped toward the Taylor family to guide them to the waiting room.

Adrianna brushed her father's hand away from her arm. She stepped closer to Erica with sheer terror in her eyes. "I want someone in here that can help my mother! I can't stand to watch her go through this, and you obviously are not doing anything to help her."

Erica felt raw anger burning in her stomach as she looked deeply into those intense sapphire eyes. "I'm here to help your mother, believe it or not. I have no time to deal with your anger and ignorance, so I'm going to tell you to leave this room immediately or I will have security come and physically remove you. You're not helping in here, and I need to focus my efforts on your mother and not you."

Erica saw the fire in those sapphire eyes engulf this enraged woman as she watched her move one step closer.

"I don't see that you're being any more helpful in here than I am."

Sarah turned to Erica and touched her arm. "It's stopped. The seizure has finally stopped." They all looked at Carolyn's flaccid body lying very still in the bed. Erica looked at her watch and back at Carolyn.

Erica turned sharply back to Adrianna. "You have really tried my patience. I have no time for this emotional warfare. I understand that you're upset about your mother, but I will not tolerate your childish behavior in our unit."

Erica's anger slipped from her control as she stood tall and found herself totally captivated by Adrianna's emotional sapphire-blue eyes. "Now get out of my face so we can both cool off before I say things I might regret later. I need to spend my time and energy with your mother, not butting heads with you."

Adrianna glared fiercely at Erica. She slowly stated something in a language Erica did not understand, then turned abruptly and headed out the door with tears in her eyes.

Erica felt her heart pounding from their exchange as she watched Adrianna walk away. She closed her eyes as she was strangely blanketed by Adrianna's incredible, emotional strain. Erica opened her eyes and saw David leaning over Carolyn caressing her silver hair. "I'm afraid to ask what Adrianna said to me on her way out."

Leah stepped in from the doorway and stood at the foot of her mother's bed, carefully watching her. "Adrianna spoke to you in Italian, Dr. Beaumont. What she said to you roughly translates into, "You and I are far from finished where it concerns my mother's medical care." Leah turned and looked at Erica with saddened eyes. "I left a few colorful adjectives out to spare you the grief. I'm so sorry, Dr. Beaumont. Adrianna's not usually that ill tempered, and you didn't deserve any of what she said."

Erica looked into Leah's eyes as she ran her hand through her hair in frustration. "You don't have to apologize for Adrianna. I think I understand where she's coming from. It's very stressful to watch someone you love go through a seizure, as you all know."

Erica watched Grant move in beside Leah and place his arm around her shoulders, bringing her in tight to him. David bent down and gently kissed Carolyn's face before looking up at Erica.

"I'm sorry you all had to witness that. I'm going to assess Carolyn again and give her more medication to control these seizures. She's going to be totally out of it for the rest of the day as a result of the seizure. We call it the postictal phase. I'm going to postpone her surgery till we can get her seizures under control. If she is seizure free throughout the night, then I may consider doing the surgery tomorrow morning."

David nodded his head in agreement and looked back at his wife.

Erica turned to Sarah in the doorway. "Sarah, please show the Taylor family to the quiet room."

Sarah waited while David bent down and kissed his wife on the cheek. She gently took him by the elbow.

Erica touched his arm. "I'll come and talk to you in there as soon as I'm done reassessing Carolyn."

David nodded his head and whispered, "Thank you." Erica squeezed his hand and watched as Carolyn's family headed out of the ICU behind Sarah.

Erica leaned against the doorframe in frustration and thought of Adrianna and her uncontrolled anger. She was baffled by her own need to reach out to that woman and comfort her even after their emotional sparring. She wanted to strangle her one minute and hold her in her arms the next. She felt badly that she could not have handled the situation better, but those intense, sapphire-blue eyes and harsh words instantly put her on the defensive and ignited her own temper. Adrianna was fighting for control in unfamiliar territory, and that made her very vulnerable. Erica chastised herself for losing her cool and knew that she owed Adrianna an apology. Erica knew that Adrianna must be feeling lost and frightened and felt the undeniable urge to comfort her. Erica could not believe she was so lost in thought about that ill-tempered woman as she turned back to Carolyn and went about reassessing her.

****

Sarah unlocked the quiet room as Leah looked across the hall toward the massive glass wall showcasing a thick, colorful garden. Beyond the lush greenery, Leah could barely see Adrianna sitting on a wooden bench with her face buried in her hands. Leah turned to her father and husband. "I'm going to talk to Adrianna."

Sarah pointed down the hall to a set of glass doors. "Those are the doors leading into the gardens. You're welcome to sit in there any time. It's a really beautiful place."

"Thank you."

Leah watched Sarah walk away and reached for Grant's hand. "I'll see you both in a little while."

Grant gripped Leah's hand and looked at her with years of warmth and tenderness. "Are you going to be okay?"

"I'll be fine, Grant. I just want to spend some time with Adrianna." Leah leaned up on her toes and kissed her husband softly. "I love you. Please don't worry. I'll be back with Adrianna in a little while."

Grant and David watched Leah head down the hall and walk into the green oasis.

Leah heard Adrianna sobbing into her hands. She settled on the bench beside her and wrapped her arms around her. Adrianna looked up at her younger sister and leaned into her arms.

They both struggled to control their tears as Adrianna clung to Leah. "We can't lose her. We can't let her die."

"We're not going to lose her, Adrianna. She's tougher than this. She's going to fight this just like she has been fighting her breast cancer. You know Mom. She's made of tough Italian stock. She's never going to let something like this brain tumor knock her down."

Adrianna pulled some tissues out of the pocket of her pleated slacks and handed one to Leah. "I love her so much. I can't believe this is happening. This is so unfair. Mom doesn't deserve any of this."

"I know. I think we're all in shock. At least we finally found a doctor that could identify the problem and tell us what we're dealing with."

Adrianna glared at her sister and dried her eyes. "Yeah, well, I have a problem with this Dr. Erica Beaumont."

"We all noticed that, Adrianna. Would you care to share with me what it is that made you completely lose it back there?"

Adrianna rose from the bench in a flurry of anxiety and stood before her sister. "I want the best for Mom, Leah. I believe that's what we all want for her. I want her to have the best medical care possible. What kind of experience does Dr. Beaumont have? How long has she been a neurosurgeon? For God's sake, she looks like someone that should be on the cover of *Vogue* magazine, not a highly skilled, knowledgeable neurosurgeon."

Leah tried to stifle a laugh as she stood before Adrianna and took her hands. "Those are questions you're going to have to ask her yourself, big sister. What I can tell you is that I feel a tremendous sense of peace knowing that Mom is in her hands."

"Yeah, well, you were always easier to please than I was, and I doubt the fiery Dr. Erica Beaumont is in much of a frame of mind to answer any of my questions in the near future."

Leah laughed as she squeezed Adrianna's hands. "What do you expect? You both behaved like a pair of feuding alley cats back there in Mom's room."

"Well, I'm glad we established that I was not the only one who behaved poorly."

"I agree. I don't think that either one of you will look back on that incident with pride."

Leah pulled Adrianna close and hugged her tight. "Come on, Addie. Let's go inside and talk about Mom with Dad and Grant."

The sisters linked arms as they headed back in through the glass doors.

"I think that Dad is ready to send me to the time-out corner."

Leah laughed as she squeezed Adrianna's hand. "You'll be lucky if he doesn't send you into orbit after that little fiasco. You both seem to feel very differently about doctors."

"Yeah, well, I have my reasons to be leery."

"I know, Adrianna, but I think this time you're going to have to put down your sword and give our Dr. Beaumont a chance to prove herself."

"I'll think about giving her a chance but rest assured I'll keep my sword handy."

❇❇❇❇

One hour later Erica stood in the open doorway of the quiet room and saw the Taylor family sitting together on one of the soft cream couches, talking softly. All except Adrianna. She was sitting in a chair near them, staring out a window, lost in her own thoughts. Erica instantly felt her pain and anguish and was jolted by her overwhelming need to reach out to this total stranger. Erica admired Adrianna's beautiful, flowing dark brown hair and slender, regal figure. Her face was as delicate and flawless as a porcelain doll's. Thick dark eyelashes gave her a glow of youthful innocence and accentuated her huge, oval blue eyes. An innocence Erica was sure she lost a long time ago by the intensity of that heated temper and sharp-edged tongue. Erica wondered if the intensity of that seething anger was any indication of the passion that this breathtaking woman was capable of.

She watched Adrianna aimlessly play with a button on her white blouse and admired the way her fashionable, gray tweed slacks fit her slender figure perfectly. Her fingers trembled ever so slightly, and Erica wanted to take that elegant hand in her own till her fear subsided.

David was the first to notice Erica in the doorway and stood to greet her. "Dr. Beaumont. How's Carolyn?"

He quickly brought Erica back to reality as she stepped into the room. "She's resting comfortably at the moment. Please, David, have a seat." Erica slipped into the nearest empty chair.

Erica made herself comfortable and took a deep breath as she felt Adrianna's intense eyes bore into her.

Erica leaned forward and looked at each family member. "Carolyn is breathing on her own, and we have given her more medication for her seizures.

She's more awake now but will remain pretty drowsy for some time. She's resting comfortably, and the nursing staff will be monitoring her very closely for any further signs of seizure activity. As I said before, I will postpone the surgery till tomorrow morning if we manage to control Carolyn's seizures overnight."

Erica explained her findings and the effects the seizure would have on Carolyn for the rest of the day. She answered all their questions and let them express their fears and concerns. Throughout the entire conversation, Adrianna had not said a word, and Erica found herself acutely aware of her penetrating eyes.

Erica turned to her. "Adrianna, is there anything you want to say or ask? You have my undivided attention."

Everyone looked at Adrianna as the depth of Erica's emerald-green eyes mesmerized her. She was totally amazed by Erica's strength and self-confidence and couldn't seem to take her eyes away from this unique woman who infuriated her for so many reasons. Half of which Adrianna was not sure she understood. Adrianna paused and felt the warmth and compassion flowing from Erica's beautiful eyes. She really wished she wouldn't look at her with such genuine concern. It made battering her with anger so much harder.

"Do you seriously want to hear what I have to say?"

Erica leaned forward in her chair, decreasing the space between them and making Adrianna feel increasingly unsure of her own emotions.

"Of course I want to hear what you have to say. It couldn't possibly be as bad as the insults you hurled at me in your mother's room, in English and in Italian."

Adrianna felt acutely embarrassed by her behavior earlier as she felt the heat rise in her cheeks. She was a captive of Erica's intense emerald eyes as she marveled at this woman's tenacity and felt soothed by her sweet voice. She thought to herself, "Figures my mother would end up with a neurosurgeon with as much willpower as herself." Adrianna gathered up her courage and leaned toward Erica with a serious look in her eyes. "I want a second opinion."

The entire Taylor family was stunned and began to argue with Adrianna. The noise level in the room climbed dramatically, and Erica couldn't stand to see the fighting among them.

Adrianna was attempting to defend herself to her father when Erica raised her voice and shouted, "Stop it, everyone! Right now!"

Silence fell in the room as everyone looked at Erica.

Erica closed her eyes and took a deep breath, attempting to regain her own composure. She lifted her head and looked around at everyone. "Adrianna is making a perfectly reasonable request. I will ask the head of the neurosurgical department to review Carolyn's case and ask him to come and share his findings with you. Then you can decide, as a family, whether or not you wish for me to continue caring for Carolyn."

David leaned toward Erica with anger blazing in his eyes. "That's not necessary, Dr. Beaumont. We know that you're quite capable of caring for Carolyn. Don't let Adrianna ..."

Erica raised her hand and interrupted him. "David, it's important to me that you all feel comfortable with my diagnosis and plan of care. If Adrianna wants a second opinion, then I will arrange for that to happen this afternoon. I do not feel professionally insulted by Adrianna's request. I feel quite confident in my diagnosis and plans for Carolyn. Adrianna only wants the best for her mother, and I respect that."

David leaned back in the couch.

Erica looked over at Leah and Grant. "Do you guys have any other questions for me or any concerns you want to discuss?" They both shook their heads.

Erica looked at Adrianna for the first time since she had made her request. Their eyes met in a war of wills. Erica struggled to understand the incredible emotions tumbling in Adrianna's eyes and sensed her struggle to gain some sort of control in this situation. "You, Adrianna Taylor, are determined to make this as difficult for me as possible, and that doesn't intimidate me if that is what you're trying to do. I will arrange for Dr. Worthy to give you a second opinion, and then you can have me paged when you want to talk to me about his findings. Meanwhile, I will continue to care for your mother in the best way I know how. I understand that you are scared and very concerned about your mother. You have every right to be. This is very serious, and I will do my best to control her seizures till we can get her to the operating room. I'm sorry that you all had to watch her go through that." She stopped and felt engulfed by the sadness in Adrianna's eyes as she watched her struggle valiantly to control her tears.

Erica had to fight the urge to reach out and touch Adrianna's trembling hands. "We need to get something straight before we go any further. I will not tolerate the behavior you displayed in your mother's room earlier. You were rude and very nasty, and I refuse to work in that kind of an environment. If you need to vent like that again, then I would appreciate it if you and I could do that in private, instead of disrupting the entire unit and upsetting the rest of the patients and their families. I would also ask if we could communicate in English, since I don't speak Italian. From now on, I expect you to be on your best behavior when you are in visiting with your mother. Carolyn needs her rest and does not need to deal with your outbursts and temper tantrums while she's here. I can handle your anger, but I will not have you interfere in my work again. Have I made myself perfectly clear?"

"Yes, perfectly clear," Adrianna answered quietly.

Erica smiled softly as she leaned closer. "Good, then. Let's call it a truce, and I'll arrange to fulfill your request for a second opinion."

Erica rose from her chair and looked around at everyone. "You can all go back in and be with Carolyn whenever you feel ready. I'll go and talk to Dr. Worthy and arrange for him to see Carolyn this afternoon. I'll also be around to keep a close eye on Carolyn."

David slowly rose from his chair. "We will have you paged when we have spoken to Dr. Worthy."

Erica smiled at David's warmth and felt instantly angry with Adrianna for causing her family such unnecessary grief. She bid them good-bye and headed out the door.

Adrianna watched Erica leave in numb amazement. She could not help but be overwhelmed by her unflappable courage. She watched her walk out with the grace and rhythm of an athlete. Adrianna was stunned how that tall, sensual woman left this volatile situation with her head held high and her dignity and dedication intact.

She chastised herself for being caught up in this woman's emotional and physical beauty and found herself visualizing those glowing emerald eyes seething with anger and compassion. Her full, voluptuous lips enhanced her sensuality, and Adrianna could clearly visualize those beautiful ringlets bouncing softly around her ravishing face.

Adrianna shook her head as if to clear her thoughts of the captivating Dr. Erica Beaumont. She turned toward her family and knew by the looks on their faces that she was about to get an earful.

Chapter 3

Erica stood before the bank of elevators and hit the up button. She had completed her rounds with her residents and was heading into her office to meet with Dr. Mark Worthy. She massaged her tired neck and looked at her watch, already five-thirty in the evening. Her stomach was certainly aware of the time but she was not in much of a mood to eat. She badly needed a break from this emotional day.

The nearest elevator chimed as Erica stepped in with a crowd of people all vying for space among helium balloons, perfumed flowers, and the pharmacy technician's cart loaded with intravenous antibiotics waiting to be delivered. Everyone called out their floor as Erica settled into a back corner with her thoughts. She was concerned that she had not heard from the Taylor family. She did feel relieved that Carolyn had not suffered any further seizures and was slowly coming around.

Erica worked her way out of the elevator on the fifth floor and headed down the hall. She stepped into her plush office and stood in the open doorway. Sitting at her antique mahogany desk was Dr. Mark Worthy, with his feet comfortably perched on an open drawer and an issue of *Sport Fishing* magazine open before him.

Erica had been one of Dr. Worthy's residents in the early years of her neurosurgical residency and had learned so much from him. She felt blessed for being asked to join his neurosurgical team at University Hospital, a team that was world renowned for its work and research in the area of trauma and spinal cord injuries. They had worked together as colleagues for five years now, and Erica's respect and admiration for him had grown with the years. He had recently celebrated his sixtieth birthday, and Erica prayed he would stay as the head of the neurosurgical department for many years to come.

Erica closed her office door behind her. Dr. Worthy's salt and pepper head popped out of his magazine. He gave Erica his engagingly handsome grin and leaned back in her black executive leather chair.

"Get those size ten boy feet off my desk, you big lug."

Dr. Worthy rocked back and enjoyed the sound of the rich leather giving way beneath his weight. "Now, is that any way to speak to the man who went out of his way to see one of your patients and her family today, Dr. Beaumont?"

Erica smiled as she slipped out of her lab coat and hung it in her closet.

Dr. Worthy rolled the magazine in his hands and gestured around Erica's office. "Have I told you lately what a beautiful office you have, Erica? And how did you get these great magazines in your waiting room? My waiting room has nothing but *Readers Digest, People* magazine, *Martha Stewart Living,* and *Oprah.* Nothing but women's magazines."

Erica stepped toward her desk and swatted at Dr. Worthy's feet. They landed with a thud on the floor as she closed her top drawer and perched herself on the edge of her desk. "Thank you. I really like my office, and I have no idea how some fishing magazine got in my waiting room. It certainly isn't my subscription. Now, stop with the idle chitchat and tell me what you think of Carolyn Taylor's case."

"Oh, my. Did someone get up on the wrong side of the bed this morning?"

Erica laughed as she dropped her chin to her chest. "I'm sorry, Mark. It's just been one lousy day."

Dr. Worthy leaned forward in the chair. "I've seen you deal with some pretty horrific experiences without letting it upset you like this, Erica. What happened today?"

Erica looked down at her polished Italian loafers and sighed. "It started off when I had to tell James and Madeleine Kirkland that their daughter was brain dead and would they please consider donating her organs. Then I admit Carolyn Taylor, and her family witnesses her seizure in the NICU. I walk in after the seizure, and their daughter rips my face off and questions my medical integrity and demands a second opinion. Wouldn't a day like that upset you?"

Dr. Worthy leaned back in the plush leather chair and tapped his chin with the rolled magazine. "Yes, I would say that would rank right up there in my ten least favorite days as a neurosurgeon. When I was in the NICU, Sarah told me about Nicole Kirkland. By the sounds of it, you handled the situation with your usual heartfelt compassion and outstanding professionalism. As a matter of fact, the representative from the Organ Donor Network was in with the Kirklands when I was there. Those are always heart-wrenching cases, Erica. You obviously handled it beautifully.

"The Taylor family are wonderful people, and Mrs. Taylor is a sweetheart. I reviewed her CAT scan and read through her chart and all of your notes as you had requested. You were flawless, Erica. Your assessment, diagnosis, and treatment regime for Mrs. Taylor is impeccable. But I didn't need to tell you that. You're one of the best neurosurgeons in the field, and I told the Taylors that. You specialize in Mrs. Taylor's types of tumors, and I told them they were in good hands with you. The daughter, Adrianna, is a very fiery, intelligent woman, and she asked some excellent questions. She even seemed pleased with my assessment of your work."

"Thanks, Mark. That means a lot coming from you. Thank you for taking the time to talk to the Taylor family and ease their concerns. Or ease Adrianna's concerns, shall we say. I just want the entire family to feel comfortable with my care and plans for Carolyn."

"The entire family adores you, Erica. Adrianna just needed some reassurance. For some reason, you didn't offer her any today when she needed it most."

"Yeah, well, Adrianna has tried my patience today."

Dr. Worthy watched Erica shift on her desk as he scratched his chin. "She's scared, Erica. We both know that when people are scared they transfer it into anger. Along with her fear and anger, Adrianna has a strong personality, and she's an incredibly beautiful woman. I'm sure you noticed that well before I did." Mark watched the smile touch the edges of Erica's eyes. "She's likely to challenge every fiber of your being, professionally and personally. She needs you just as much as Mrs. Taylor needs you right now. She'll probably demand more of you than any other family member. Are you going to be able to be there for both of them within a professional scope?"

Erica looked away from Mark's concerned eyes and slipped off her desk. She stepped toward her large picture window and stared out at the dry South Mountain range oblivious to the beautiful view before her as visions of Adrianna's anguished eyes filled her mind. Erica could not get her off her mind all afternoon and felt increasingly worse for the way she had handled her. She couldn't believe how that woman could evoke such emotions within her in a matter of seconds. Erica was becoming confused by her intense reaction to Adrianna. She slipped her hands into the pockets of her black pleated slacks and turned back to Mark. "I'll be there for both of them, Mark. I'll give Carolyn my best, and I'll try to be more understanding of where Adrianna's coming from. She stirs something in me that I don't quite understand yet, but I can promise you that I will get them both through this."

Mark rose from the leather chair and stood before Erica. "I have no doubt in my mind that you will give

47

that family your best, Erica. You always do. Prepare yourself, though. Adrianna is going to be your biggest challenge in this case. Compared to her, Carolyn's tumor will be a walk in the park."

Erica laughed. "If today is any indication, I think you might be right."

"Now, if you're done with me, Dr. Beaumont, I'm going home to my lovely wife."

Erica reached out and touched his arm. "Thank you for everything, Mark. I really do appreciate your time with the Taylor family."

"I was glad to help. You've been there for me in similar situations, and I've always appreciated your medical input. Now, go and talk to that family before you go home. I told them I was going to see you in your office after I met with them. They're in the quiet room."

"Thanks, Mark. I'll go see them now."

Mark touched Erica's chin with the edge of the magazine. "You're very welcome. Hey, can I keep the magazine?"

Erica laughed. "Be my guest. Just don't let it distract you from the time you should spend with that lovely wife of yours."

Mark headed for the door and stopped before stepping out. "I wouldn't dream of it." He waved with the magazine before heading down the hall.

Erica leaned against the window and rested her head against the window frame. She felt the need to clear the air with Adrianna and let her know that she was there for her if she needed someone to talk to. Erica's mind was filled with Adrianna's pain as she opened her closet and slipped into her tailored, double-breasted gray suit jacket. She checked her appearance in the long mirror behind the door and tidied her white blouse. She closed the closet door and headed for the elevators.

Erica entered the quiet room and was greeted warmly by David, Grant, and Leah. She noticed immediately that Adrianna was not in the room. David took Erica's hand and thanked her for coming to see them.

"I missed you guys. I thought you had traded me in for an older, balding, retiring neurosurgeon."

They all laughed together. David shook his head. "Not a chance. We finished talking to Dr. Worthy, and he had nothing but the highest praise for you. He completely agrees with your diagnosis and plan of care. He said you have been very thorough and appropriately aggressive in your treatment. He said you specialize in these types of tumors and that we have the best person for the job."

Erica smiled at David's kind words.

"We apologized for wasting his time because we already knew everything he had told us about you."

Erica gently squeezed his arm. "You're very kind, David."

David smiled at Erica and squeezed her hand. "Does that mean you'll stay on Carolyn's case?"

Erica looked at him in disbelief. "I never had any plans of handing over this lovely family or my favorite patient to anyone else. Carolyn and I are going to see this thing through to the bitter end, regardless of her feisty daughter who is determined to give me gray hair."

David looked relieved. "I'm so glad to hear you say that. We were afraid that Adrianna had driven you away from us."

Erica laughed softly. "I've got pretty tough skin, and I think I can learn to handle Adrianna."

Leah stepped closer to Erica. "I'm sorry about the way Adrianna has been treating you. She normally is such a lovely, caring, kind person. She's just used to always being in control, and this brain tumor has really sent her for a loop. She's very close to Mom, and for some reason she has chosen you to vent all her anger and frustration on. You don't deserve to be the target of her wrath, and we all feel badly for her behavior."

Erica squeezed Leah's hand. "Don't feel badly. Adrianna is just hurting, and we need to help her vent more constructively because I'm getting tired of being her punching bag."

They all laughed.

Erica looked around the room. "Speaking of Adrianna, where is the temperamental Tasmanian devil?"

"She had gone home to shower and change her clothes because she decided she would spend the night here with Mom. We have a four-year-old daughter at home, and Adrianna knows that we need to get home and spend some time with her. Dad is also pretty exhausted, and we would like to see him get some sleep. So Adrianna just kicked us out for the night and assigned herself the night shift. She also said she didn't think you needed all of us to tell you how wonderful you are and that Dr. Worthy said you were the best neurosurgeon we could ask for."

"I bet she cringed as she heard Dr. Worthy say all those things about me. She must have been ready to spit nails when she realized she was stuck with me."

Leah shifted her purse strap over her shoulder. "Actually she didn't look one bit surprised by Dr. Worthy's assessment of your work. Adrianna is an excellent judge of people, and I know she sees your ability and dedication without anyone having to describe it to her."

Erica smiled as Leah watched her blush. "We think she's actually a little intimidated by you. Nobody handles Adrianna like you did today, and we were all very impressed by your emotional strength. Nobody matches Adrianna's personal drive like you do, and I think she admires that in you. You know how to handle her, and we know she doesn't like that one bit."

Erica looked down at her hands. "I could have been a little more gentle with Adrianna today. I don't usually handle people so harshly when they are under such emotional stress. I owe Adrianna an apology for being so hard on her."

Leah gently squeezed Erica's arm. "Funny, Adrianna also feels she owes you an apology. We told her she owes you more than an apology. She feels really badly about the way she behaved today, and she even apologized to all the nurses and ordered them several boxes of pizza to show our appreciation for everything you guys have done for Mom."

Erica put one hand over her heart and looked shocked. "Be still, my heart. I don't know if I can handle this gentler, kinder Adrianna. I think I liked it better when she had her claws in my screen door."

Grant moved closer and placed his hand on Leah's back. "Adrianna has settled down and come to her senses after we talked to Dr. Worthy this evening. She told us to make sure you knew there was pizza in the nurses' lounge and to help yourself to some."

"Adrianna is emotionally distraught, and we feel she just needs to spend some time with her mother," David explained.

Erica smiled at David and squeezed his hand. "You guys should go home and get some rest. I hope to perform Carolyn's surgery tomorrow, so it could be a long day for everybody."

"You get some rest too, Dr. Beaumont, and we look forward to seeing you tomorrow morning. We're just going to go in and say good-bye to Carolyn before we leave."

Erica walked the Taylor family into the neurosurgical intensive care unit. She waved good-bye as she watched them head to Carolyn's room.

Erica approached Nicole Kirkland's room and stepped inside. Nicole lay peacefully on her side, the blinds drawn to block the strong rays of the setting sun.

Sarah stepped into the room and hung a new IV bag. "The Kirklands stepped out to get a bite to eat. I told them that we had a residency building right next to the hospital and that one whole floor of rooms was used for families that are from out of town. I told them I arranged a room for them in the family hostel as you had requested. They were really pleased to be able to stay near their daughter tonight without having to find a hotel room."

"How were they doing, Sarah? I spent some time with them just before lunch. Dr. Worthy told me that a nurse from the Organ Donor Network came in to see them."

"They seem to be hanging in there. They're very strong people. The Organ Donor Network nurse did come in this afternoon to speak to them. They seemed at peace with their discussion. They said they needed to speak to other family members before they made their decision."

Erica reached down and pulled the crisp white linen sheet higher over Nicole's shoulder, a comforting measure that soothed Erica more than the patient. "They're really lovely people. Such a sad waste of a precious young life. If they need to speak to me this evening, don't hesitate to page me. I'll be home this evening."

"Okay, Erica. I'll pass that on to the night shift."

Sarah handed Erica the nursing flowsheet for the day documenting Nicole's vital signs and watched her scan the information. Sarah flipped open Nicole's chart and held it before Erica. "These are the lab results from the blood work you ordered this afternoon."

Erica took the chart from Sarah. "Thank you." She absorbed the numbers and flipped through several other test results. She closed the chart and handed it back to Sarah. "Thanks, Sarah. All her numbers look fine."

Erica took one last look at Nicole. "I'm going to check on Carolyn Taylor before I head home."

Sarah hugged the chart to her chest. "Oh, how I'd love to be a fly on that wall."

Erica looked out through the glass wall and watched the Taylor family leave the unit. "Is Adrianna in with her mother?"

"She was the last time I checked in on Carolyn. She's settled down, Erica. She was asking to speak to you. She really swallowed her pride this afternoon and apologized for her behavior. That took a lot of guts, and I respect her for that."

"Well, I guess it's my turn to swallow some pride." Erica touched Sarah's shoulder as she stepped out of the room and headed for room two.

The lights in the unit had been dimmed, and all the lights were out in Carolyn's room to diminish any stimulation that might induce another seizure. Erica stood in the doorway and allowed her eyes to adjust to the soft light. She could see Carolyn sleeping peacefully on her side. Erica looked up at Carolyn's cardiac monitor and took in the vital signs continually registering across the screen. Erica was absorbing this information as she heard that distinct, sultry voice float toward her.

"You can come in. I promise not to bite," Adrianna whispered.

Erica followed her voice to the other side of Carolyn's bed and saw Adrianna sitting in a high-back chair beside the bed, holding her mother's hand. She smiled as she saw the soft shadows of the sunset gently illuminate Adrianna's stunning features. Erica realized that this was the first time she had seen Adrianna smile. She admired her slender figure, dressed in a silky, powder blue blouse and navy blue slacks.

Erica slipped her hands into her pockets and stared into Adrianna's eyes. "I absolutely refuse to step into this room unless you promise to play nicely. Otherwise, I'm just going to ban you from ever playing in my sandbox again." Erica loved the rich sound of Adrianna's laughter. She carefully entered the room and walked to the foot of Carolyn's bed. She focused on Adrianna's shimmering eyes, her smile.

"I promise to be kinder and I'll even bring my own pail and shovel if you let me play in your sandbox."

Erica was deeply charmed by this woman's sense of humor as she smiled. "This sounds like a better start than where we began this afternoon. If we could only stop throwing sand at each other, then maybe we could help each other and Carolyn through this ordeal." Erica was acutely aware of the deep sadness in Adrianna's eyes. She wished she could somehow ease her pain.

Adrianna laid her hand on the chair beside her. "Would you like to sit for a few minutes, Dr. Beaumont, or are you on your way home?"

Erica carefully made her way toward the chair in the darkened room and felt Adrianna's hand at her elbow guiding her into the chair. Adrianna let her fingers linger on Erica's arm, sending a surge of heat roaring throughout Erica's body, intensifying her awareness of how close they sat.

Erica leaned back into the comfortable chair and crossed her legs. "Thank you for the chair, and yes, I am on my way home. I just wanted to stop by and check on Carolyn before I left and ..." Erica's voice trailed off as she shifted in her chair and looked directly into Adrianna's intensely captivating eyes. "I was hoping to find you so I could apologize for my behavior earlier."

Adrianna leaned closer to Erica and felt the energy between them. "You don't owe me an apology, Dr. Beaumont."

Erica felt determined to express her feelings as she sat up taller. "Yes, I do. So please be quiet and let me finish."

Adrianna leaned back in her chair and smiled.

"You were under immense emotional stress today, and I was not very understanding of your pain. I usually don't treat people as badly as I treated you, but you certainly made me feel very angry today at your behavior in here. However, that does not excuse the way I treated you, and for that I am sorry. I will try my best to be more understanding of where you're coming from as long as you try your best to talk to me instead of yelling at me. Preferably in English. I'm not used to being yelled at, and it's not something I wish to experience again, Ms. Taylor." Erica paused long enough to enjoy the beautiful smile curling the corners of Adrianna's soft, full lips. "I hope you can forgive me and that we can possibly find some way of working together to get your mother through this."

Adrianna was sitting with her legs crossed and her hands entwined on her knee, looking intently at Erica. "Are you finished?"

"Yes, I am."

Adrianna smiled and leaned closer. "May I speak now?"

Erica tried unsuccessfully to stifle a laugh. "Certainly. You may now take the podium."

Adrianna cleared her throat dramatically as if to make a formal announcement. "Dr. Beaumont ..."

Erica quickly interrupted her. "Erica. Please call me Erica."

Adrianna's smile lit up the room as she leaned even closer. "I'd like that. Thank you, Erica. Now, please be quiet and let me finish."

They both smiled as Erica forced herself to move away from this woman's magnetic sensuality.

"Of course I forgive you. I would like to apologize for the horrible way I treated you all day. You've been terrific with my mom, and I can see that you have a true passion for your work. I regret all the insults I slapped you with, English and Italian, and I feel totally ashamed of the way I challenged you and your ability to do your job." Adrianna looked down at her own hands. "Dr. Worthy said that we have the best neurosurgeon looking after my mom, and I really didn't need him to tell me that from what I saw in you today." Adrianna looked back into Erica's emerald eyes.

"I was totally freaked out when my family told me that my mother had a brain tumor. I was with them three weeks ago at dinner when she suffered that horrible headache, and I feel terrible for not pushing her to go to the hospital that night. I feel somehow responsible for all this, and I feel so angry and confused by what this all means. To make matters worse, I walked into my mother's room when she was having that horrible seizure. You walked in after that, and I wanted someone who looked like Santa Claus and could instantly make everything better."

Erica watched the intensity in Adrianna's eyes as she fought her tears and swallowed her pride. Erica leaned close enough to Adrianna to make her heart skip a beat and encompass her in incredible warmth. "Adrianna, didn't anyone ever tell you that Santa Claus doesn't exist?"

Both women broke into soft laughter. "Don't tell my mother that. She still gives us Christmas gifts from Santa."

Erica laughed. "Are you serious?"

"Yes, I'm serious. Ask Leah." They both laughed as they leaned back in their chairs. They contentedly stared into each other's eyes and enjoyed the deep connection forming between them.

Adrianna smiled warmly at Erica and broke their comfortable silence. "Well, Dr. Erica Beaumont, have I been forgiven for my bad behavior, or would you like to discuss some sort of punishment that you feel is suitable?"

Erica gave Adrianna a mischievous smile and folded her arms across her slender abdomen. "I do believe that a punishment is in order. I have no intention of letting you off the hook easily, so I believe that once we get your mother out of the hospital we will discuss the possibility of you making me dinner to make up for the torture you put me through today."

Adrianna's smile warmed Erica's soul as she extended her hand. Erica gently took it in an intimate connection, and Adrianna firmly shook her hand.

"You have a deal. Punishment accepted." The electricity in that handshake jolted them both, so they hesitantly removed their hands and fidgeted in their seats.

Adrianna cleared her throat. "Speaking of food, did you get some of the pizza we had delivered into the unit?"

"No, I didn't. My stomach has been a little unsettled all day, and I know if I eat some pizza I'll really feel sick. But that was very kind of you to do that. I'm sure the nurses really appreciated your kind gesture."

Adrianna gracefully uncrossed her legs. "What's upsetting your stomach?"

Erica looked away from the intensity in Adrianna's eyes and watched Carolyn sleep peacefully. "My stomach is usually where I feel my emotional stress. It gets really sensitive, and I have a hard time eating when a certain family member of my favorite patient torments me endlessly and tries to break me." Erica saw Adrianna look away.

"I'm sorry I upset your stomach today."

Erica leaned close enough to Adrianna to smell her soft peach scent. "You upset more than my stomach today, Ms. Taylor. You completely disrupted my world, and I did not appreciate that."

Adrianna looked into Erica's eyes. "I'm really sorry for the way I treated you today, Erica. I promise you that it will not happen again, and I hope that you can find it in your heart to forgive me."

"I'm putting you on probation tomorrow. You have to prove to me that you can be the sweet, wonderful person that your family claims you are before I decide if I'm going to forgive you or drag on your torture as you did to me today."

Adrianna wore a shocked expression. "You're giving me one day to prove what a wonderful person I can be? Wow, you're really a tough warden."

Erica leaned toward Adrianna and placed her hand on her knee. "It took you fifteen seconds today to

59

prove to me that you can be an absolute pain in the ass, and you think I'm being hard on you to give you one full day to prove otherwise? Who's being unreasonable here?"

Erica reluctantly removed her hand from Adrianna's knee and saw the intense warmth deepen her eyes to a coral blue.

"Okay, I'll do my best tomorrow to prove to you that I'm not a total pain in the ass."

Erica smiled triumphantly. "That a girl. Now, that wasn't so hard, was it?" Erica enjoyed the warm energy flowing between them as she leaned toward Adrianna. "You said earlier that you felt badly for not pushing your mom to come to the hospital the night she suffered that horrible headache. Don't feel badly, Adrianna. People who suffer from migraines know the best way to control their pain. Unfortunately, in some cases like your mother's, it will mask the symptoms of a brain tumor. Carolyn's tumor has been there a lot longer than three weeks, so I don't want you to feel responsible for not taking action that one night."

Adrianna's face grew serious as she absorbed Erica's words. "I'm glad you explained that to me because all day I've been feeling like I could have prevented this if I had brought my mother in here that night."

Erica felt Adrianna's guilt as she watched her struggle to control her tears. "Well, now you know you could not have prevented any of this, so I don't want you to feel responsible in any way." Erica saw the tension leave Adrianna's face and luxuriated in her smile. "See how easy it is to have your fears and questions answered instead of stomping your little foot all day and demanding a second opinion?"

Adrianna blushed and looked down at her hands. "Was I really all that bad?"

Erica chuckled and leaned close. "Worse than a bear with a thorn stuck in its paw."

"Wow, that's pretty awful."

They both laughed as they heard Carolyn's sweet voice. "Is that my angel, Dr. Beaumont?"

Adrianna rolled her eyes and leaned back in her chair. "Oh, brother. You really have won this family over today, haven't you, Dr. Beaumont?"

Erica leaned closer to Carolyn and took her other hand. "The whole family minus one member. But I figure once I'm able to remove the thorn from her paw, then we might be able to be friends."

Adrianna's smile illuminated the room. She watched Erica turn to her mother and was warmed by the fresh apple scent of her hair and a subtle hint of a light perfume, scents so refreshing and real compared to the antiseptic smell of the hospital.

"I'm right here, Carolyn. How are you feeling?"

Carolyn struggled to keep her eyes open and focused on Erica and Adrianna.

"I feel really tired, and my headache is still there. Other than that, I'm okay and very happy to see you two getting along. Adrianna was telling me about everything that happened today. I'm really sorry for everything that Adrianna and I put you through."

Erica smiled at Carolyn's loving face. "Please don't apologize for your seizures today. I'm just sorry that you and your family had to go through that. As for Adrianna, she was absolutely awful to me, and I'm punishing her by making her cook dinner for me some day when you're feeling a lot better."

Adrianna rolled her eyes at Erica. Carolyn smiled at their warmth. "Adrianna is normally a lovely person, Erica. Please forgive her and give her a chance to show her true colors when she's not so bothered by my illness."

Erica smiled at Adrianna and gently squeezed Carolyn's hand. "Some of those true colors are starting to filter through now, Carolyn. I was just beginning to enjoy her company."

"You're both so similar in so many ways. I know that you'll become very good friends."

Erica and Adrianna exchanged a smile.

"Now, Dr. Beaumont, it's been a very long day for you today, and if you plan on mucking around in my brain tomorrow, I would like you to get a good night's sleep."

Erica gave Carolyn an indignant look as she placed one hand on her own chest. "Mrs. Carolyn Taylor, I do not muck around in people's brains. What I do is the fine art of neurosurgery, and I would appreciate it if you would not use that term again when referring to my chosen profession."

"Well, excuse me," Carolyn said.

Adrianna's laughter warmed Erica's soul as she turned and glared at her.

Adrianna failed to stifle her laughter. "I'm just glad I'm not the one you're chastising for a change."

They all laughed. Carolyn yawned and squeezed Erica's soft hand. "Erica, there must be a fine young man waiting for you at home, so get going before he retires to your bed without you."

Erica blushed as she looked from Adrianna's curious eyes to Carolyn. "There is no man in my bed, and I prefer it that way. The only thing keeping my bed warm is my teddy bear, and he never expects anything from me." Erica blushed as she attempted to avoid Adrianna's eyes. Erica turned to Carolyn. "Are you being nosey about my personal life, Carolyn?"

"Absolutely. You know everything there is to know about me, so why shouldn't I know all about you?"

Erica shook her head and laughed.

"Adrianna is used to this. We've had many discussions about her personal life, haven't we, dear?"

Adrianna rolled her eyes and sighed. "Mother! I don't think that we need to be discussing my personal life right now."

Erica looked at Adrianna with a mischievous look in her eyes. "Why not? Why should you be spared from this conversation?" Erica squeezed Carolyn's hand. "Don't worry, Carolyn, you can tell me all about Adrianna's personal life when we have a moment alone." Adrianna looked at Erica with a look of shock in her eyes. "That's not fair. You guys wouldn't do that to me, would you?"

Erica laughed at Adrianna's displeasure. "Why not, Adrianna? Do you have something to hide?"

Adrianna slapped Erica's knee. Erica grimaced and pretended to be injured.

Carolyn yawned again and pulled her covers up higher. "Oh, I think you two will be sharing a lot of things in the future. Soon there will be no more secrets."

Erica and Adrianna looked at each other in stunned silence as they tried to understand the weight of her words.

Sarah stepped into the room and turned on a dimmer light. "Hello, everyone. Adrianna, it's seven o'clock and we're going to be changing shifts. Would you mind stepping out for about an hour so the night nurse can get report and have some time to assess Carolyn?"

"Not at all. I didn't realize what time it was."

Erica and Adrianna rose together. Erica reached out and squeezed Carolyn's hand. "Sleep well tonight, Carolyn. I'll see you bright and early in the morning."

"I'll be here, Erica. Get yourself a good night's sleep with that teddy bear of yours."

Erica walked to the doorway with Sarah. Sarah looked at Carolyn over her shoulder and smiled. "You're going to have to tell me about this teddy bear, Carolyn."

Adrianna laughed as she leaned over her mother and kissed her softly. "I'll be right back, Mom. Be good while I'm away."

"Not much of a chance of being otherwise in this place, darling. I'll see you shortly."

Adrianna grabbed her purse, blew her mother a kiss and stepped past Erica through the doorway. Erica watched Adrianna slip her purse strap over her shoulder.

Sarah touched Adrianna's arm. "I'm sorry to have to ask you to step out, Adrianna. It's our policy to restrict visitors during shift change."

"Don't apologize, Sarah. I understand. I'll use the time to retrieve my messages from the office and return my clients' phone calls."

Erica watched the unease flit across Adrianna's eyes as she peeked back at her mother. "There's a garden across from the unit where you can sit and get caught up with your work. I'm sure Sarah explained that you can't use your cell phone in the unit because it interferes with our cardiac monitors."

Adrianna looked at Sarah and smiled. "She sure did. I've gotten more exercise walking out of this unit to answer my cell phone than I care to discuss. I finally called the office and asked my secretary to take messages and not call me unless it was an emergency. My cell phone has been blissfully quiet all afternoon."

Sarah laughed. "I'd always know when Adrianna's cell phone had gone off because I would hear her say something in Italian and I knew it couldn't be good."

Erica loved the coy smile on Adrianna's face. "I can just imagine. I certainly got an earful of Italian this afternoon. Are you going to tell me what it was exactly that you said or do I need to buy a translation guide?"

A blush slowly crept up Adrianna's cheeks. "I don't think you'll find what I said in any translation guide. Besides, I think you should stick to Leah's interpretation if you and I are going to share the same sandbox."

Erica and Sarah laughed.

Erica slipped her hands into the pockets of her pleated, black slacks. "How did you become so fluent in Italian?"

"My grandparents would only speak to us in Italian so we could learn the language. I loved them for it. They passed away several years ago. I really do miss them, especially at times like this."

Erica touched Adrianna's elbow. "They sound like they were wonderful grandparents. If you would like to sit in the garden, I would be happy to take you there."

Adrianna looked from Sarah to Erica. "Actually, I was there with Leah today. It really is a beautiful place. Do you both think Carolyn will be okay if I sit out there?"

Erica smiled at Adrianna's warmth toward her mother. She pointed at the cell phone on Adrianna's belt. "If you give Sarah your number, they'll call you if Carolyn needs you."

Sarah grabbed Carolyn's chart. "Go ahead and give me your cell phone number, Adrianna. I'll record it in your mother's chart so everyone knows where to find it."

Adrianna finished giving Sarah her number as Erica touched her elbow. "Come on, I'll walk you out there. I'll be heading home soon, Sarah. Please tell the night staff not to hesitate to page me if they need anything or if Mrs. Taylor's condition changes."

"I will, Erica. Good night. I'll see you in the morning."

"Good night, Sarah. See you tomorrow."

Erica led Adrianna out of the unit. They walked down the long corridor and out onto the beautiful, well-lit cobblestone walkway. They walked side by side as Adrianna looked around at the lush greenery in awe. Majestic towering California fan palm trees lined their path as they approached a circular water fountain in the center of a massive courtyard dotted with a dozen umbrella tables. Lush gardens filled with birds of paradise, century plants, white and purple vinca, paleface delphinium, lavender and white creeping phlox, pink evening primrose, morning glory, zinnias, rosebushes of all colors, and cascading purple and white alyssum lined the courtyard.

Erica stopped beneath an arbor completely embraced by an orange Cape Honeysuckle vine as she looked back into Adrianna's astonished eyes. "Beautiful, isn't it?"

Adrianna looked at her enshrouded by the gorgeous orange blossoms and thought she had never seen anything so beautiful in her entire life as the woman standing before her. "Breathtaking."

"A little farther down the path is a much more private area. Through here there are benches and tables nestled among the palm trees. Come and see."

Adrianna followed Erica through the arbor and down the path.

Erica stepped into a clearing with a wooden bench and a wrought iron table for two. "This is my favorite spot." She slipped her hands into her pockets and looked up at the full moon. "The moon is beautiful tonight."

Adrianna stood beside Erica and looked up at the shining globe. "I think that the moon, sunsets, and sunrises lose their appeal unless you have someone to share them with."

Erica was shocked by her answer. She turned to see the sadness in Adrianna's beautiful eyes. "You need to appreciate them for yourself before you can share them with anyone else."

Adrianna looked away from those intense, emerald eyes and turned her back to her. "This place is beautiful. I had no idea it was this lush and vast when Leah and I were out here earlier."

Erica smiled and looked around at the surrounding beauty. "It's a place of healing. The hospital created this area so people can come here and feel at peace with their emotions. I love coming out here and just sitting by myself. I find it so peaceful, especially when I feel really stressed and need to collect my thoughts."

Adrianna turned and watched Erica admire the moon. A gentle breeze toyed with a stray ringlet at her forehead. Adrianna ached to brush it from her shimmering eyes. The courtyard lights cast a soft shadow across Erica's high cheekbones and tiny nose as she tilted her head slightly. Her full, sensuous lips parted slightly. Adrianna wondered what it would feel like to taste those lips with her own.

Erica looked down from the moon and saw the intense look in those mesmerizing sapphire eyes.

Adrianna cleared her throat and felt an unusual tingling heat caressing her skin. She placed her hand over the fluttering sensation in her belly. "Did you come out here today?"

Erica looked at Adrianna's perplexed expression and gave her a look. "At least a dozen times."

Adrianna looked down at the ground.

Erica stepped toward Adrianna and gently touched her chin, raising her eyes to meet her own. "I didn't bring you out here to talk about our behavior today. I brought you out here so you could feel at peace. I wanted to show you a place where you can feel more comfortable letting your guard down and releasing your tears." Erica brushed her fingertips across Adrianna's chin and slowly removed her hand.

Adrianna inhaled sharply and moved one cautious step back. "What makes you think I have any desire to let my guard down?"

"Because contrary to popular belief, I think that lawyers are human, and I have watched you struggle with your tears all day. I thought this might be a place where you could let your guard down and release your constant desire to be in total control of your emotions."

Erica walked away and sat down on the wooden bench. She patted the spot beside her and invited Adrianna to join her.

Adrianna hesitated briefly before taking the seat beside Erica. She set her purse down beside her and mindlessly wrapped the strap around her hand. She wound and unwound the strap from one hand to the other as she shifted in her seat and stared up at the luminous moon.

Several more minutes passed as Erica looked over at Adrianna. Her thick, dark brown hair flowed gently over her delicate shoulders. Adrianna mindlessly tucked a loose strand behind her ear. Her diamond earring twinkled in the soft lighting. Erica ached to reach out and touch the precious gem perched on that tiny ear. Her long, rich eyelashes blinked several times over her exquisite oval-shaped eyes, fighting to maintain her emotional control. Adrianna's olive skin gleamed in the moonlight, giving her face porcelain perfection. She moistened her bottom lip with the tip of her tongue and sent a geyser of heat and desire soaring through Erica's entire being. Erica had to momentarily close her eyes to control the emotions threatening to spiral out of control. She slowly opened her eyes and saw the tiniest tremor of Adrianna's bottom lip before she clenched it with her teeth.

"Adrianna, stop fighting your feelings. You have every right to be scared and upset." Erica watched Adrianna lower her head as her pent-up emotions won the battle and her tears squeezed past her closed eyes. Erica reached into her jacket pocket and handed her several tissues.

Adrianna took them and whispered, "Thank you."

Erica could not fight the urge any longer, so she placed her hand on Adrianna's back and gently comforted her.

Adrianna wiped her eyes and took a deep breath. She looked into Erica's eyes and gently slapped her thigh. "Look what you've done to me."

Erica lightly rubbed Adrianna's back, feeling her arch slightly into her touch.

Adrianna closed her eyes and sighed. "Thank you. That feels so comforting. I'm not ready to lose her, Erica. I love my mother very much, and she has always been one of my dearest friends. I had a tough time dealing with her breast cancer and now this." Adrianna slowly shook her head.

Erica gently squeezed Adrianna's shoulder. "If this surgery is successful, Adrianna, then your mother will have many good years left. We have to keep our fingers crossed and hope for the best tomorrow. That, or you and I could step into a church and do a lot of praying."

"I haven't been in a church in a long time, Erica. Now might be a good time to reaffirm my faith."

Erica brushed a loose strand of hair over Adrianna's shoulder and watched her take several deep breaths.

"I'm scared, Erica. I'm really scared."

"I know. You have every right to be scared. But I want you to take comfort in the fact that your mom is a fighter. She's an incredible woman, and she has proven that through her fight with breast cancer and her years of struggling with her migraines." Erica slid her hand across Adrianna's silky back and squeezed her shoulder. "I can only pray that your mother's neurosurgeon gives you a small degree of faith, but I don't think she has quite earned that yet in your eyes."

Adrianna smiled sheepishly and stared down at her hands entwined in her lap. "It doesn't help that my mother's neurosurgeon looks like she should be sauntering down some catwalk in New York City modeling evening wear rather than in a pair of surgical scrubs performing a highly skilled surgical procedure that I always thought was reserved for much older, more experienced doctors."

Erica leaned her head back and laughed. "Well, that's quite a compliment, Adrianna. I think." Erica smiled at Adrianna's discomfort and slowly floated her hand through the thick flowing hair cascading down her back. "I've operated on lots of these tumors, Adrianna, but somehow I don't think that gives you any comfort unless I fly in on Rudolph and walk into the operating room wearing the jolly old fellow's red suit."

Adrianna burst into laughter and leaned back against Erica's shoulder. "Would you do that for me, Erica? Would you don Santa's suit to make me feel better?"

Erica looked into those huge, teary sapphire eyes and felt herself sinking deep into their emotional depth. She was tumbling into a place she had not been in two years and was shaken by the intensity of the moment. In that one instant, she knew she would do anything for this spirited beauty sitting much too close. She leaned back slowly and took a deep breath. "I would do anything to give you a measure of faith in my ability to take care of your mother."

Adrianna leaned forward and laid her hand on Erica's knee. "I do have faith in you, Erica. My gut instinct tells me that my mother is in the best hands possible, and my gut is never wrong."

"I'll do everything I can to strengthen your faith in me and your gut instinct."

Adrianna gave Erica a glowing smile. "I don't doubt that for one minute."

Erica watched Adrianna lean back into the bench and fold her hands into her lap. The heat on her knee from Adrianna's touch tingled uncomfortably as Erica slowly crossed her legs. "Since the diagnosis of your mother's breast cancer, have you and Leah gone for a mammogram?" The dark cloud of sadness cascading across Adrianna's eyes stunned Erica.

Adrianna took a deep breath and looked down at her hands. "Leah has had one done every year, but I put it off till exactly one year ago when I started having pain in my right breast. We were all terrified that I also had breast cancer but after an agonizing week of waiting for the results they finally told us that I had two large cysts that they felt needed to be surgically removed. It was a huge relief, and I went ahead with the surgery. I was really sore for a long time after that, and now I go for mammograms every six months, which reminds me, I need to make that appointment soon."

Erica watched Adrianna with wonder. "I'm so grateful it was just cysts, but I'm sorry you had to go through all that."

Adrianna smiled and stared intensely into Erica's loving eyes. "I would like to have known you at the time. It would have been nice to talk to you about all this medical stuff. It makes my head spin."

Erica smiled at Adrianna's vulnerability. "Well, you know me now, so don't ever hesitate to ask me any questions about anything."

Adrianna leaned back in the bench and fought her desire to reach for this astonishing woman. "I'm really glad that we had this opportunity to talk. It's been a real pleasure getting to know you this evening."

Erica couldn't help but tease Adrianna as she leaned intimately close. "You're lucky that I'm even speaking to you. In English, no less."

Adrianna smiled as she tugged on the lapel of Erica's jacket. "Who are you trying to kid? You refused to give up on me all day. You tried so hard to reach me and comfort me, and that infuriated me even further." Adrianna enjoyed watching Erica blush a beautiful crimson red. "You were terrific with me today, Erica, even though I was such a bear to you. I admire how you handled me and didn't let me interfere in the way you cared for my mother. I really do believe that we are blessed to have you as my mother's neurosurgeon." Adrianna enjoyed the intense warmth in Erica's eyes as she placed her hand on her knee. "Now, as my mother would say, go home and get some sleep if you plan on mucking around with her brain tomorrow."

"You must have gotten your Italian spirit from Carolyn."

"We sure did. Carolyn's pure Italian, and David is pure Texas cowboy. They met in college. David likes to say she lassoed him and there was no looking back."

Erica smiled as they both rose.

Adrianna slipped the strap of her purse over her shoulder. "I had to laugh when you said you prefer a teddy bear in your bed to a man."

Erica blushed. She guided Adrianna down the cobblestone path and moved aside so she could pass through the arbor first. "And you, Ms. Taylor, what do you prefer in your bed? A teddy bear or a man?"

Adrianna smiled and stopped on the other side of the blossoming arbor. She turned and looked up into Erica's glimmering emerald eyes. "I've never had a man in my bed, so I guess I would have to answer teddy bear." Adrianna turned away from those expressive, jubilant eyes and led the way back to the hospital entrance. Adrianna stopped before the large glass double doors and reached out and touched the lapel on Erica's gray jacket. "Now, please go home and take care of your stomach for me."

Erica looked at this exceptional woman before her. "Are you trying to get rid of me, Ms. Taylor?"

Adrianna toyed with a slate-gray button on Erica's jacket as she admired the stunning deep purple amethyst stone framed by a slim gold triangle at her chest. "I don't want you to go, Dr. Beaumont, but I do want you to be your best for my mother's surgery, so that means you need to go home and get a good night's sleep. If you don't go soon, I'll have security escort you to your car."

Erica laughed, enjoying Adrianna's exhilarating company.

"That feels so good, to threaten you with that after you threatened to have me physically removed from my mother's room earlier today."

Erica stepped in front of Adrianna and smelled the light scent of her peach hand cream. "You were so close to being the first woman I've ever had to physically remove from the unit. You're also the first woman that I've ever had the undeniable urge to want to spank."

"You wouldn't dare."

Erica leaned into Adrianna as Adrianna wisely backed herself up against the glass doors. Erica was mesmerized by the stormy intensity in Adrianna's eyes. She moved one step closer and felt embraced by the sensuality of their chemistry. They both stared intently and never lost eye contact. The air seemed to crackle and sizzle between them.

"Don't push me, Ms. Taylor. You're on probation, remember? I highly recommend you practice being the model of decorum for the rest of your mother's stay with us."

Adrianna had to force herself to look away from those full, moist lips. "I'll do my part if you promise to do your best work with my mother."

Erica watched the concern and fear darken Adrianna's eyes, and she could feel the depth of her love for her mother. She touched her arm. "One thing I will promise you, Adrianna, is that I will do the best I can for your mother."

Adrianna blinked several times, swallowing hard. "That's all I would ask of you, Dr. Beaumont."

Erica leaned back slightly to create some space between herself and this woman whom she wanted to take in her arms and whose anguish she wanted to ease. She reached beside Adrianna and opened the glass door for her, following her wordlessly to the entrance of the neurosurgical intensive care unit.

Adrianna stopped before the big double doors and stood before Erica. "You should go home, Dr. Beaumont. I don't exactly cherish the idea of you leaving, but you have a big day ahead of you tomorrow."

"All right, I'm going. Try to get some rest tonight if you can, and I'll see you in the morning. Don't hesitate to page me if anything changes with Carolyn."

"I will. Tell me, Dr. Beaumont, do you always give this much of yourself to your patients?"

Erica smiled as she reached into her pocket for her keys. "Your mother told me I wear my heart on my sleeve. I try to be emotionally strong, but I can't help feeling for the patients I care for. That's just who I am. I'm hoping that with practice I'll be able to tuck my heart into a sleeve or pocket for safety. Otherwise, someday I'll start looking like Santa Claus."

Adrianna smiled as she touched her fingers to Erica's heart. "Don't stop being who you are, Dr.

Beaumont. You're a unique gift as a woman and a doctor."

Adrianna removed her hand and took one step back. "Good night, Erica."

"Good night, Adrianna." Erica turned to walk away and gave Adrianna a gentle wave as she disappeared around the corner.

Adrianna stood frozen in her spot, overwhelmed by this incredible woman who had stormed into her life only a few hours before.

✳✳✳✳

Adrianna rested her weary head against her chair as she watched her mother sleep and gently caressed her hand. She smiled as she thought of her mother's unconditional love and constant support of all of her choices in life. Her mother could always lift her spirits with a simple phone call, and now she lay helpless in a hospital bed, awaiting the moment that a skilled surgeon would attempt to remove the source of her constant headaches.

Adrianna's tears blurred her vision as she heard the soft musical chime of her cell phone. She wiped away her tears and leaned down beside her chair for her purse. She waited for the caller to leave a message. A soothing warmth spread across her chest as she read the displayed message. "Hi, I'm home," and a phone number printed below the message. Adrianna reached for her mother's bedside phone and dialed Erica's home number. Adrianna hugged the phone close as she heard the familiar sweet voice.

"Hello there. I thought I would just call you and check on Carolyn before I turned in for the night."

"Well, isn't this a lovely surprise, Dr. Beaumont. My mother's doing really well. She seems to drift off into short naps and wakes up with lots to talk about."

"I'm not surprised. Encourage her to get as much sleep as she can, Adrianna. She needs her rest. You both do."

"That's easier said than done. My mother never runs out of interesting things to talk about. Speaking of interesting things, how did you get my cell phone number?"

"I memorized it when you gave it to the Sarah this evening."

"Well, I'm impressed, Dr. Beaumont. Now, will you please try and eat something to soothe your stomach before you go to sleep."

"I will, and you try and get some rest. It'll be close to impossible to sleep in that chair, but close your eyes for a while."

They shared a few seconds of gentle silence as Adrianna curled her leg under her and reached for Carolyn's hand. "I'll get some sleep tomorrow while you operate on my mom, so I should be okay. Besides, I don't know how anybody could get any sleep around here with the constant activity and noise in this unit."

"It is incredibly noisy, isn't it, but I'm sure the nurses will keep you entertained all night, and they will certainly appreciate your company."

Adrianna smiled sheepishly and looked out toward the nurses' station. "No offense against the nurses here, but I would rather be entertained elsewhere."

"Really. Where would you rather be entertained at this very moment, Ms. Taylor?"

Adrianna blushed and fidgeted in her chair. "I can think of a few places, Dr. Beaumont. Now go away." Erica's laughter filled Adrianna's soul. "Thanks for calling to check up on my mother, Erica. That was really nice."

"It was my pleasure, and it was nice to talk to you. Good night, Adrianna."

"Sweet dreams, Erica. Sweet dreams," Adrianna whispered, as she gently hung up the phone.

✳✳✳✳

The nurses had finished giving Carolyn a bed bath and helped to reposition her onto her side. Adrianna thanked them and pulled the covers snuggly around her mother's shoulders. Adrianna bent down, kissed her mother's forehead, and whispered, "I love you."

Carolyn reached up and touched her daughter's face. "I love you too, sweetheart."

Adrianna leaned her forehead against her mother's. "Now, it's five fifteen in the morning. It's early, so try and close your eyes and get some more sleep."

Carolyn stifled another yawn and turned to kiss Adrianna's hand. "You won't get any argument from me."

Adrianna slipped into the chair beside her mother's bed as Carolyn watched her intently. "You're very special to me, Adrianna. I just want you to know that."

Adrianna felt the tears in her eyes. "You're very special to me too, Mom. Now, stop trying to make me cry and go to sleep."

79

Carolyn smiled as she touched Adrianna's chin. "Speaking of special people, isn't that Dr. Beaumont something?"

Adrianna looked deeply into her mother's eyes. "Gee, Mom, I never noticed." Adrianna glared at her mother. "Will you please stop trying to find me a woman, Mother?"

Carolyn reached out to caress Adrianna's hair. "Dr. Beaumont is no ordinary woman, Adrianna. I can feel the chemistry between the two of you from across the room. You both share a special warmth, and I love to watch the two of you together. You care about each other, and I feel that you both are beginning a friendship that will last for all time. Enjoy that, Adrianna, because friendships like that only come along once in a lifetime. It would be even more exciting if you could develop your friendship into something more fulfilling for both of you."

Adrianna smiled at her mother's insight. "Mother, you were so bad the way you were probing Erica for information about her personal life last night. Besides, I don't even know if Erica's a lesbian."

Carolyn scoffed as she gave Adrianna a shocked look. "Oh please, Adrianna. Give me a break. I knew she was a lesbian the moment I met her."

Adrianna was shocked. "Mother! How can you say that? You act like an expert on gay women!"

Carolyn laughed at Adrianna's surprised expression. "I am an expert. You gave me a lifetime of experience in raising a gay daughter." Carolyn caressed Adrianna's cheek. "Now, stop being so protective of our dear Dr. Beaumont and go for it. As you said to me once when you were in hot pursuit of some woman, go and rock her world."

Adrianna's laughter filled their room as Carolyn kissed her cheek and settled back into her pillows.

Adrianna was stunned by her mother's insight and shook her head. "I wonder what Erica would say if she could have heard this discussion."

Carolyn covered her mouth with her hand and yawned. "She would blush beautifully like she does when we embarrass her."

Adrianna laughed as her mother yawned again and drifted off into a light sleep.

Adrianna leaned her head back and closed her eyes.

She must have just drifted off to sleep for a few minutes when she heard the chime of her cell phone. She grabbed it from her purse and waited for the message. She wondered who would be calling her at five thirty in the morning. Adrianna smiled deeply as she read the message: "Good morning. Have you seen the sunrise?"

Adrianna felt intense warmth encompass her entire being as she picked up her mother's bedside phone and dialed Erica's number. She carried the phone over to the window and held the phone close as she heard that sweet voice.

"Are you looking out your mother's window?"

Adrianna was mesmerized by her gentle, soothing tone. "Yes," she answered softly.

"What do you see?"

Adrianna peered between the partially opened blinds and leaned against the window frame. "Early morning traffic, garbage piled on the curbs, flashing police lights, a newspaper delivery boy."

Erica's sweet laughter interrupted Adrianna's observations. "No, Adrianna. The sunrise. Look at the sunrise."

Adrianna unsuccessfully attempted to conceal her laughter. "Oh, that. What about it, Dr. Beaumont?"

Erica released an exasperated sigh. "Close your eyes, Adrianna."

Adrianna was enjoying toying with Erica's early morning patience. "First you ask me to look at the sunrise, then you tell me to close my eyes. Please make up your mind, Dr. Beaumont."

"Adrianna, are you always this feisty in the morning?"

"Don't tell me you're Sally Sunshine when you haven't slept all night, Dr. Beaumont."

"Sleepless nights come with the job, Ms. Taylor. I have had lots of practice perfecting my Sally Sunshine mode."

"Were you born with that halo and pair of wings, or did you sprout them during med school?"

"If you asked your family, I bet they would say I was born with them."

"Oh, brother. How nauseating." Adrianna loved the sound of Erica's laughter.

"Please stand in front of the window and close your eyes, Adrianna. Do it for me."

Adrianna closed her eyes and listened to Erica's gentle breathing.

"Are those beautiful sapphire eyes closed?"

"Yes," Adrianna answered softly.

"Good. Now, don't open them till I tell you to."

Adrianna leaned her forehead against the cool glass. "Okay, but hurry up, or the sunrise will no longer be a sunrise."

"You hate relinquishing the tiniest bit of self-control, don't you, Adrianna? You probably have had to be in total control your whole life, and you find it difficult to have someone else take care of you. I know you feel very vulnerable standing there with your eyes closed, yet you trust me enough to let me guide your thoughts."

Adrianna was mesmerized by Erica's insight and caressing voice.

"Don't let it frighten you, Adrianna, because you're beautiful when you're vulnerable and not totally in control."

Adrianna was filled with warmth as she continued to close her eyes and listen to Erica's voice.

"Now, slowly open your eyes and look into the horizon and tell me what colors you see."

Adrianna obediently opened her eyes and stared out the window. "A soft red that's caressing the mountains as it slowly fills the morning air with its warmth. A brilliant yellow sun that's peeking its face beyond the horizon, teasing us with promises of a sunny day. And white, fluffy clouds, gently tickling the top of the White Tank Mountains."

"When you watch a view like that, what is the one emotion that you feel the strongest?"

"Well, I feel all kinds of things but ..."

"No, Adrianna, I don't want an intellectual explanation. I want you to think with your heart right now and tell me what is the one single emotion you feel when you look out that window? One emotion, one word."

Adrianna was engulfed by the spectacular view and Erica's caressing voice. "Peace. I feel at peace."

"Good girl. Now, that wasn't so hard to enjoy, was it?"

Adrianna smiled as stepped back from the window. "You, Dr. Beaumont, are incredible. Now, tell me where you are at this very moment while you share this view with me?"

"I'm sitting on my back deck, eating breakfast."

Adrianna pulled the blinds closed and slipped back into her chair. "I hope that means that your stomach is feeling better this morning."

"Much better, thank you. Speaking of breakfast, have you had anything to eat?"

"No. I'll probably eat something when I go home this morning."

"How was Carolyn's night?"

"It was uneventful and restful. She slept for a few hours here and there, and the most important thing is that she didn't have any more seizures. The nurse said that her vital signs were very stable. So overall we had a very good night."

"That's really good news."

"How did you sleep last night, Erica?"

"Fine, except I had this dream about this beautiful, blue-eyed maiden taking me captive on her pirate ship and threatening to feed me to the sharks if I didn't control her mother's seizures. Isn't that the strangest dream? I've been racking my brain trying to think of the significance behind that dream."

Adrianna tried to stifle her laughter. "Are you saying you dreamt about me last night, Dr. Beaumont?"

"All I'm going to tell you is that you were on my mind when I laid my head on my pillow."

Adrianna felt a heightened sensitivity throughout her body. "What were you doing up at three in the morning?"

"How did you know I was up at that hour?"

Adrianna smiled and leaned back in her chair. "The nurse came in and told us that you called in to check on Carolyn and that you even asked about me."

"Nothing is sacred around that place. If you must know about my nightly habits, my bladder woke me up at three o'clock. Since I was up, I thought I'd call the unit and see how you were both doing."

"Does your teddy bear get up to pee in the middle of the night as well?"

"At least four or five times. I'm starting to get really worried about him. I was thinking about getting his prostate checked out."

Adrianna burst into laughter, hugging the phone close. "You have an incredible sense of humor, Erica."

"It's really nice to hear you laugh, Ms. Taylor. I should be heading there shortly. Can I bring you anything?"

Adrianna smiled at Erica's kindness. "Only you and your skilled, surgical hands so that you can make my mother all better."

"I'm going to do the best I can for your mother, Adrianna."

"I count on that, Erica. Drive carefully coming in to work. I'll see you soon."

"Yes, you will. See you soon."

Adrianna hung up the phone and placed it back on the bedside table.

Carolyn opened her sleepy eyes and readjusted her pillow. "Who was on the phone?"

Adrianna smiled and settled back in her chair. "Santa Claus."

Chapter 4

Erica waved to the hospital parking garage attendant as she waited for the arm to fully rise. She drove past the kiosk and maneuvered her midnight black Lincoln Navigator into her assigned parking spot on the first level. She opened the back door and grabbed her burgundy leather computer bag. She set it on its wheels and secured her purse on top. As she closed the doors and locked her SUV, her cell phone chimed on her waist. Erica grabbed the phone and smiled at the number displayed on the screen. "Hello, Mom."

"Hello, sweetheart. Where are you?"

"I'm just getting on the walkway from the parking garage to the hospital. What are you and Dad doing?"

"Darling, it's only six o'clock in the morning. Your dad and I have just gotten out of bed and are sitting on the back deck sipping our coffee. We were talking about you and knew you were probably on your way to work, so we thought we would call. I have to tell you, Erica, I'm happy not to be walking across that walkway at this ungodly hour any more."

Erica stepped through the automatic glass doors and hit the up button on the service elevator. "Oh, come on, Mom. How could you miss all those years of catching catnaps between traumas and raising a family at the same time?"

Erica loved her mother's rich laughter. "Darling, I'm much happier getting caught up on catnaps with your dad and watching my babies flourish in their chosen professions."

Erica stepped onto the service elevator and hit the button for the fifth floor. "You may be happier, Mom, but the day you retired was a huge loss to the trauma surgery team in this hospital. You are still sorely missed even five years later."

"That's really sweet, darling, but I know they will continue to be the best trauma team even without me. After all, they are blessed to have you. What more could I have left them but a daughter who is one of the best neurosurgeons in the country?"

Erica stepped off the elevator and headed down the hall to her office. "Now who's being sweet? What are you and Dad doing today?"

"We were going to go horseback riding this morning and then head to the Phoenix Art Museum this afternoon."

"Now that sounds like a really rough day. I wish I could join you."

"I wish you could too, sweetheart. How does your day look?"

"I have a patient scheduled for the O.R. this morning to remove her frontal tumor. I pray that all goes well."

"Is she a difficult case?"

"No, the surgery should be pretty straightforward. Pressure from the tumor is causing her to have seizures, so I'm anxious to get the surgery done. She's a real sweetheart, and her family is wonderful. I just want the best results for them."

"They have you as their surgeon, Erica. That gives your patient the best chance she could ask for."

Erica parked her computer bag beside her office door and slipped her key into the lock. "Thanks, Mom. That mean's a lot to me that you feel that way."

"Is there something about this case that troubles you, Erica?"

Erica slipped into her office and closed the door behind her. "Nothing surgical. The eldest daughter and I started off practically dueling to the death, but now we've learned to communicate in a much more civil manner. She's really worried about her mom. I want everything to go well as much for my patient as I do for her."

"This sounds like a story I want to hear from the very beginning. I know you need to start your rounds. Will you call me tonight when you get home?"

"I sure will, Mom. I'll fill you in on all the details."

"Will we see you on Sunday as usual?"

"Absolutely. I wouldn't miss a Sunday with the family."

"We'll see you then, sweetheart, and I'll talk to you tonight."

"Sounds great, Mom. Give Dad a big hug and kiss for me. I love you both."

"We love you too, sweetheart. Have a good day and I'll talk to you tonight."

"Okay, Mom. I love you." Erica clicked off her phone and slipped it back into its leather case on her belt. She quickly slipped out of her khaki double-breasted jacket, hung it in her closet, and slipped into her lab coat.

※※※※

Erica entered the neurosurgical intensive care unit and stopped at the nurses' station to use the phone.

Adrianna felt her presence before she even saw Erica out of the corner of her eye. She sensed the change in atmosphere in the ICU and was mesmerized as she watched her. Each nurse made a point of greeting her, and Adrianna noted the respect and warmth they shared for this elegant woman.

Erica was dressed in a pair of khaki pleated slacks and a midnight-black sleeveless turtleneck under her crisp white lab coat. The slacks brought out the emerald in her eyes, and that mane of bouncing ringlets astounded Adrianna. She watched Erica talk on the telephone and reach across the counter to sign a chart a nurse had put in front of her. Her slender frame moved fluidly and gracefully.

Carolyn poked Adrianna in the ribs to bring her back to reality. "Gee, I wonder who has captivated your attention in that nurses' station?"

Adrianna blushed as Carolyn leaned closer to her daughter. "It must be our favorite non-lesbian doctor," Carolyn whispered playfully in Adrianna's ear.

Adrianna gave her mother a stern look, then rose from her chair to receive a steaming cup of black coffee from her father.

David smiled at them. "What are you two whispering about?"

Erica entered the room and spared Adrianna from answering that question.

Erica walked around the room and shook hands with David, Leah, and Grant.

David gestured toward the crowded over-bed table by Carolyn's window. "Can I offer you a coffee and a carrot muffin, Dr. Beaumont?"

"No, thank you, David. I had breakfast, but that was very kind."

Adrianna remained standing with her back against the wall as she watched Erica interact with her family. Their eyes finally met. "Good morning, Dr. Beaumont. Where's your red suit?"

Erica smiled at Adrianna as she walked around Carolyn's bed. "Good morning to you, Ms. Taylor. I believe it must be at the cleaners. I couldn't find it in my closet this morning. I couldn't find any of the reindeer either. It's so hard to get good transportation these days."

Adrianna burst into laughter. She watched Erica sit on the edge of her mother's bed and take her hands.

"And good morning to you, Mrs. Taylor. It's so wonderful to see you sitting up in bed and looking so bright."

"Good morning, my angel. What in the world are you and Adrianna talking about? I've heard nothing but talk of Santa Claus since you called here this morning."

"Adrianna would rather see Santa Claus do your surgery, but I think she's starting to get used to the idea that she's stuck with Ms Claus instead."

Everyone laughed together as Erica held Carolyn's hands. "Are you ready for today?"

"I don't think I have much of a choice, so I guess I'm as ready as I'll ever be."

"Have faith, Carolyn. We'll get you through this. Now, let's talk about the surgery and possible complications."

Erica spent the next twenty minutes explaining the procedure to the entire Taylor family. She answered all of their questions and then had Carolyn and David sign the consent form.

Erica handed the consent form to Sarah. Sarah turned to Carolyn and went through the pre-operative checklist with her.

Erica stood before Adrianna and Leah. Her nearness ignited a caressing heat in Adrianna's belly. Adrianna placed her hand over the tingling sensation. She had not felt this intensity and arousal from another woman in a very long time. She was mesmerized by her, and she didn't know if she liked being an emotional captive of this alluring woman.

Adrianna looked at Erica over the rim of her coffee cup. "Are you sure you're not supposed to be at some photo shoot today?"

Leah burst into laughter, and Erica looked from one woman to the other in absolute bewilderment.

"What is she talking about, Leah?"

"Adrianna thinks you belong on the cover of *Vogue* magazine rather than the cover of the *American Journal of Medicine.*"

Erica smiled. "*Vogue* hasn't called me yet, but I have made the cover of the *American Journal of Medicine.*"

"Oh, brother. That figures." Adrianna looked past Erica and squeezed her arm. "Did you hear that, Mom? Your neurosurgeon's a cover girl."

"I wouldn't doubt it. She's such a beautiful woman. A true angel."

Adrianna rolled her eyes, and Leah laughed and headed over to the table for a cup of coffee.

Erica watched her walk away and turned back to Adrianna. "You must be exhausted this morning."

"I do feel tired, but I received this amazing early morning phone call that totally invigorated my soul."

Erica's smile was breathtaking as she stared deeply into Adrianna's glimmering eyes. "Anyone I know?"

Adrianna gazed into Erica's emerald eyes. "I think so. You might have met her on a pirate ship last night."

They both laughed. Erica looked down into the cup of coffee in Adrianna's hand. "Is that coffee going to help or hinder your sleep today?"

Adrianna looked down into her cup. "Probably hinder. I rarely drink coffee. I much prefer tea, but this morning anything with caffeine will do."

Erica carefully took the full cup of black coffee from Adrianna's hand, lightly brushing against her fingers and electrifying her soul as she headed toward the sink.

Adrianna was instantly upset with Erica for moving away from her and taking her coffee. "Hey, what're you doing, Dr. Beaumont?"

Erica looked back at her sheepishly as she poured half the coffee into the sink.

Erica wiped the side of the coffee cup with a paper towel and walked back to Adrianna, placing the cup back in her hand. "I only poured out half of your drink. I want you to be able to sleep today, and coffee's not good for you anyway."

Adrianna looked at her with disbelief and watched her toss the paper towel into the nearest trashcan. "Don't you drink coffee, or would that tarnish your halo?"

"Actually, I have never acquired a taste for it."

Adrianna brought the coffee cup to her full lips and took a sip. "What else have you never acquired a taste for, Dr. Beaumont?"

"Men."

Adrianna spluttered into her coffee and began coughing.

Erica took her coffee cup from her hand. Adrianna tried desperately to control the coughing. Erica put the coffee cup down and gently rubbed Adrianna's back and watched her finally catch her breath.

Everyone in the room was looking at them. Carolyn turned to Erica. "Dr. Beaumont, what are you doing to my daughter?"

"Nothing, Carolyn, we were just discussing men."

Carolyn laughed and sat up higher in bed. "Oh, really, a subject that you're both experts in."

The entire room burst into laughter, and Erica blushed deeply.

Adrianna squeezed her arm. "You set yourself up for that one."

Erica hesitantly moved away to get her a drink of water.

Adrianna gladly accepted the glass of water from her. "Thank you."

"Are you okay?"

"Much better, thank you. Remind me not to discuss men with you when we're eating or drinking, okay?"

They laughed together as Sarah came back into the room. "Dr. Beaumont, Dr. Michael Thomas is calling from the emergency department. He said he has a question for you if you have a minute."

"I'll be right there." Erica turned and saw the startled look in Adrianna's shining eyes. She reached up and touched her shoulder. "Are you all right?"

Erica watched something dark and troubled play across Adrianna's eyes before she expertly tucked it away behind a strong façade.

"I'm fine, just tired." Adrianna quickly broke eye contact with Erica and reached onto the table to take a carrot muffin. A muffin Erica was sure she was in no mood to eat.

Erica stored Adrianna's reaction away for future thought and looked at the muffin in her hands. Erica pulled off half of the top and headed toward the door.

"Hey, that's my favorite part of the muffin!"

Erica stopped and looked back at Adrianna and winked seductively. "Mine too." Erica waved at everyone and walked out the door, popping a piece of the muffin into her mouth.

Adrianna stared after her and watched her take her phone call in the nurses' station.

✳✳✳✳

Erica and her residents had completed their rounds of all the other patients in the intensive care unit. They were all standing around Carolyn's bed as Erica asked them questions about Carolyn's type of tumor and the significance of her symptoms. The Taylor family had pulled their chairs back from Carolyn's bed and sat listening to Erica with her residents.

Erica had involved Carolyn in the discussion as much as possible and smiled as she watched Carolyn articulately describe her symptoms and answer the residents' questions.

Adrianna was spellbound watching Erica with her residents.

Sarah stood in the doorway. "I'm sorry for interrupting, Dr. Beaumont, but the operating room is ready for Mrs. Taylor. They said they would be down in fifteen minutes to get her."

"That's good. Thank you, Sarah."

The residents all wished Carolyn luck with her surgery and left the room.

Erica stood in the doorway, watching the Taylors as they gathered around Carolyn to say good-bye. Their distraught faces touched Erica as she quietly stepped back into the room. "The quiet room is open if you guys want to relax in there during the surgery. I'll come and talk to all of you right after we're finished."

Erica took Carolyn's hand and gently squeezed it. "Are you okay, Carolyn?"

"I'm okay, Erica. Just be careful when you're in there mucking around with my brain. Don't erase my memory of how to make my famous homemade apple pie."

Everyone burst into laughter as Erica squeezed her hand. "There's absolutely nothing about you that I would want to erase or change when I am mucking around in your brain this morning. However, if I could get inside Adrianna's brain, I would definitely turn down her Italian temper gauge a few notches."

The sound of laughter in the room was infectious as Adrianna playfully stuck her tongue out at Erica.

"Let's get this show on the road, Dr. Beaumont."

"I'm going to get changed, so I'll see you in the operating room."

David stood at Carolyn's bedside and wrapped her hand in his. "Take care of her for me, Dr. Beaumont."

"I will do my best, David."

"That's all we could ever ask of you."

Erica smiled as she said good-bye to everyone and stepped toward Adrianna, guiding her out of the room by her elbow.

They stood outside Carolyn's room together as Erica looked into Adrianna's moist eyes and watched her look down at her own hands.

Adrianna struggled to control her emotions as she looked up into Erica's eyes. "I wish you luck in performing your fine art of neurosurgery on my mother's brain, Dr. Beaumont."

Erica took Adrianna's shaking hands in her own and felt their incredible connection as she fought the urge to take this woman into her arms and hold her tight.

Adrianna looked down at their entwined hands as she rubbed her thumbs across the backs of Erica's hands. "I know that my mother is in good hands with you. I just wish I could be there with both of you to offer moral support."

Erica smiled and squeezed Adrianna's soft hands. "Your support would be greatly appreciated, but you need to go home and get some sleep."

They momentarily locked onto each other's eyes. Erica luxuriated in the warmth of Adrianna's hands. "Adrianna, would you do me a favor today?"

"Of course. What is it?"

Erica reached for Adrianna's chin and tilted her head. "Will you book that mammogram appointment and let me know when it is? I would like to go with you to that appointment."

Adrianna had to just stare at her in wonder. "Okay. I'll take care of that today."

"That would be great. Now, drive safely going home, and when you lay your beautiful head down on your pillow and dream about me, try to find the compassion that I know you possess not to throw me off that pirate ship and feed me to the sharks."

Adrianna smiled beautifully as her eyes filled with mischief. "No, I think I would like to keep you around just a little while longer. But watch yourself, Dr. Beaumont, because if you threaten to spank me one more time, I wouldn't hesitate to feed you to those hungry sharks."

Erica leaned closer to Adrianna. "Such empty threats. Please make that appointment today, and I look forward to seeing you later."

Adrianna watched her intently and knew this woman was going to rock her world.

❊❊❊❊

Six hours later, Erica untied the mask that was dangling around her neck and tossed it into the nearest trashcan. She slipped off her hair cap and left her hair tied back in a ponytail. She read through the orders she had written on Carolyn's chart and signed beneath the last order. She closed the chart and handed it to the recovery room nurse.

"I'm going to talk to the Taylor family. Page me if you need anything. Mrs. Taylor should be ready to be transferred back into the ICU in about an hour."

The nurse went over all of Erica's orders with her and promised to keep Carolyn comfortable.

Erica walked out of the recovery room and headed to her office to change back into her khaki dress slacks and sleeveless black turtleneck before talking to the Taylor family.

She stood in the doorway of the quiet room and found David anxiously pacing the carpeted floor. Leah and Grant sat close together on the couch with their hands entwined, lost in their own thoughts. Adrianna tore at Erica's heart. She was leaning against the window frame staring out at the afternoon traffic. She hugged her arms across her slender belly and rocked herself gently.

Erica stepped into the room. "You can all stop looking so worried. Carolyn's surgery was a huge success."

They moved in unison toward Erica and started bombarding her with questions. Erica held up her hand to halt the onslaught. "Wait a minute. Let me try and answer one question at a time."

Erica had them take a seat. "Yes, I removed the entire tumor, and it was a benign meningioma as I had suspected. It was well encapsulated, and there was no evidence of spreading of the cells. It was so well encapsulated that it was easy to remove without causing too much stress to the surrounding structures and tissue."

Erica leaned back in her chair and enjoyed everyone's relieved sighs. "I'm thrilled at how easily Carolyn woke up after the surgery. Once we removed the breathing tube, she started mumbling something about having to change her babies' diapers. I told her that Adrianna and Leah had progressed nicely through potty training."

Everyone burst into laughter as Erica leaned forward on the edge of her chair. "She looked at me like I had three heads for a moment and then started giggling that sweet laughter of hers. She said, 'You're going to tell my girls I said that aren't you, Dr. Beaumont?' I of course told her I couldn't wait to tell you what she had said."

Erica was pleased to feel the tension ebb from each family member. "Carolyn has not shown any signs of further neurological deficits, and I'm really excited about that. As we talked about before the surgery, she could develop some brain swelling. She could bleed at the surgical site and develop a blood clot on her brain; these are all things we will watch for very carefully over the next twenty-four to forty-eight hours. As part of our regular procedure, I sent off a biopsy of the tumor, and we should get the pathology results within the next three days. I expect the pathologist to confirm that it is a benign tumor."

Erica looked around at everyone as they absorbed this information. She continued to answer their questions for the next thirty minutes.

Adrianna leaned forward in her seat. "When can we see my mother, Erica?"

"She should be back in the ICU in an hour. Once the nurses get her settled and hooked up to the monitor, you guys will be free to be with her. My question for you, Ms. Taylor, is what are you doing here? You should be at home sleeping."

Adrianna looked down at her hands. "I couldn't sleep. I wanted to be here."

"I'm sure your mother will be thrilled to know you're here. You all mean the world to her. I'm going to go into the unit to spend some time with another family. I'll come and see you all when Carolyn is settled back in her room. I'll let Sarah know that you're all waiting. She will come and get you when Carolyn is settled."

They all rose with Erica. David took her hand in his. "Thank you for everything, Dr. Beaumont. I really mean that."

"Your love and family support have provided Carolyn with her strength and success, David. Together, I knew we could all get Carolyn through this."

Erica squeezed his hand and headed out the door. She stopped in the hallway and watched Grant take Leah in his arms and hug her tight. Adrianna melted into her father's arms as David held her close and slowly caressed her hair. Regardless of their professional differences, there was no question of the depth of love between father and daughter.

Erica punched in her four-digit security code and walked into the neurosurgical intensive care unit. She entered Nicole Kirkland's room and found her parents speaking to the hospital chaplain. They all turned when they saw Erica.

"I'm sorry for interrupting. I just wanted to come in and see how you were doing."

Madeleine Kirkland stepped before Erica. "You're not interrupting, Dr. Beaumont. We were just going to say a prayer with Father Lawson. Would you care to join us?"

"I'd love to."

Everyone joined hands at the bedside and bowed their heads as Father Lawson led them through the Lord's Prayer. They stepped back and watched him lean over Nicole Kirkland's still form and give her the last rites. He blessed Nicole's parents and then quietly left the room.

James took a seat beside Nicole as Madeleine stood over her daughter and gently brushed her fingers across her warm cheek. "Dr. Beaumont, do you think that Nicole can hear us when we talk to her?"

"I believe she hears you. Because of her head injury, she's not able to express in any way that she acknowledges what you're saying. But I don't think that should stop you from telling her everything you want to say."

Madeleine nodded her head and stroked her daughter's forehead. "That's what we think." She moved a chair in beside Nicole and sat close as she took her lifeless hand in hers. "We've talked to everyone in our family, and we've decided to honor Nicole's wishes of donating her organs. It's what she wanted. She gave so much to others in her short lifetime, and this would be what she would want to give in her death. The Organ Donor Network nurse said that Nicole is so young and healthy that many people could benefit from her organs. They're no use to her now, so we might as well see other people benefit from this tragedy."

Erica moved to the foot of Nicole's bed. "That would be a very loving thing to do. If you would like, I will contact the Organ Donor Network and inform them of your decision."

James looked back. "Thank you. We would appreciate that. My wife and I would rather let Nicole rest in peace than have her life supported by all this machinery. She would not want this. We don't want this for her. This is no way for anyone to live."

"No, it's not. I'm sorry there isn't more we could have done."

"I'm sorry, too, Dr. Beaumont. But we do appreciate everything you have done for us. You've all been very kind and taken excellent care of our daughter."

"It's the least we could do."

James stroked his daughter's arm and looked up at Erica. "We also decided we're going to contact a lawyer about the accident. The person who did this will not go unpunished. We just don't know how to go about it. We've never been in this situation before, and we feel lost being so far from home. We talked to Adrianna Taylor in the waiting room and she told us she was a lawyer. We were thinking of asking her for her advice."

"I'm sure that Adrianna would be happy to help you in any way she can."

Madeleine took Nicole's hand in her own and stroked her fingers. "The three of us were in the waiting room alone last night and shared our stories. That's when we found out she was a lawyer. She's been so kind and supportive. We would like to talk to her about this if she's able to help us."

"I'm sure Adrianna would love to help you. I'll mention it to her when I see her."

"Thank you, Dr. Beaumont. We really need to speak to someone who can answer our legal questions."

Erica squeezed his shoulder. "I'll go ahead and contact the Organ Donor Network, and I'll let you know when they'll be arriving. You're welcome to spend the night with Nicole as they go through the process of matching her organs to potential recipients. The transplant team will probably not take her to the operating room till the morning. They'll keep you informed every step of the way."

Madeleine rose from her chair and stood before Erica. She reached out and took her hands. "Thank you. We would like to spend what little time we have with our daughter."

Erica took her into her arms and hugged her close. "What you're doing is one of the greatest gifts you could ever give."

"No, Dr. Beaumont. Our daughter was the greatest gift. It's only natural that she would want this."

Erica squeezed her hands and stepped back. "I'll go make that phone call. Let us know if you need anything."

Madeleine nodded and headed back to take her seat at her daughter's bedside as Erica stepped out of the room.

Ana Corman

Chapter 5

Carolyn had been back in the neurosurgical intensive care unit for two hours when Erica walked into her room and found Leah, Grant, and David sitting at her bedside.

Erica walked in just as Grant said, "If we had known things were going to be this serious, Carolyn, we would have written a larger life insurance policy for you."

Leah punched Grant in the arm and delivered a short, sharp tirade in Italian.

David and Carolyn laughed as Erica stepped in behind their chairs. "It looks like both Taylor daughters prefer to speak Italian when they are slightly irate."

They all laughed as Leah turned to Erica. "He deserved it, Dr. Beaumont. Did you hear what he said?"

"I did. Do you want me to have security remove him from the building like I threatened Adrianna?"

Leah turned back to her husband. "No. I'll fix him when we get home."

Grant cautiously slid his arm around the back of Leah's chair. "I was just trying to make Carolyn laugh, babe. It worked, didn't it?"

Leah fixed her husband with an evil stare. "We'll see who will be left laughing."

Erica made her way around David's chair and stood at Carolyn's beside. "Carolyn, how am I going to make your daughters understand that you need a peaceful, calm environment so you can rest and get better?"

Carolyn smiled. "They're Italian, Erica. They feel everything passionately. It makes them very interesting women."

Erica did not miss Carolyn's mischievous smile as she leaned closer and gently checked her head dressing for any signs of bleeding. "How's my favorite patient in the whole world feeling?"

Carolyn reached up to touch her head dressing. "I feel really groggy and tired, but my headache is tremendously better, and my right arm feels stronger already. I'm just thrilled to have that surgery behind us."

"I'm so pleased at how well you've done, Carolyn."

Carolyn slipped her hand from David's and touched Erica's cheek. "How can I ever thank you for what you've done for me?"

"That smile on your face is all the thanks I need."

Erica discussed the surgery for a few minutes with Carolyn and her family to make sure Carolyn grasped everything she had said to her in the recovery room.

"Everything went so well, but there was one very interesting thing that happened when I was mucking around in your brain."

Carolyn looked at her. "What was that?"

Erica pulled out an index card from her lab coat pocket. "I found this recipe for your world-famous apple pie."

The family burst into laughter as Carolyn reached for the index card. "Hey! That's mine. Give that back to me."

Erica laughed and moved the blank index card out of Carolyn's reach. "Not so fast, Carolyn. I will return this recipe to you only if you promise to bake this pie for me someday."

"It would be an absolute pleasure to have you join us for dinner, Dr. Beaumont. I would definitely bake my apple pie for you."

"I accept your invitation for dinner."

"I will have Adrianna coordinate both your schedules so that we can pick a night where we can all be together. Speaking of Adrianna, she should be here in a couple of hours. Just in case you were wondering."

Everyone laughed as Erica blushed. "I haven't given that feisty, argumentative, stubborn, fascinating woman a thought all day."

Leah smiled up at Erica. "Speaking of Adrianna, she asked me to pick this up for you." Leah reached under her chair and pulled out a shiny gold gift bag and handed it to Erica. "We call it the Taylor family survival kit."

Erica set the bag on the foot of Carolyn's bed and reached inside among the gold tissue paper and pulled

109

out a large manual. She laid it flat in her hands and read, "The Complete Idiot's Guide to Learning Italian. Second Edition." They all burst into laughter. "This is great. Now, I'll be able to translate all the bad words I've heard over the past several days."

"Adrianna thought you would get a kick out of that. There's also something else she had me put in the bag."

Erica reached deep inside and pulled out a jumbo size bottle of tropical assorted fruit Tums, extra strength. She held the bottle up for everyone to see. "What more could I ask for from the Taylor family. A book to help me translate the insults and Tums to ease the stress those insults cause my stomach."

They all laughed together. "Now I know why Adrianna asked me to get both. She would have picked those things up for you herself but she needed to go by her law office to check on things and pick up some work. She plans on spending another night here with Mom. It's hard to slow her down. Adrianna feels she has to be everywhere and do everything. When we try to take some responsibility from her, she feels hurt. She strives to be perfect at all times, and we try hard to encourage her to slow down and not feel that she has to take care of everything and everyone before herself."

"Why does none of that surprise me about Adrianna?"

"It shouldn't."

They laughed.

"It's nice that you are both able to be here with Carolyn and David."

Grant smiled at Leah. "This is where we want to be. Leah and I have our own insurance company so that allows us the freedom to be here. It pays to be the bosses at times like this."

"You're a special family. I wish all my families were as supportive and close as you guys are." Erica's pager shattered their peace. Erica moved her lab coat aside and looked down at the display screen. "It's the emergency department. I should go and see what they need. I'll come back in a few hours and check on you, Carolyn. In the meantime, continue on this stellar road of recovery."

"Are you kidding? If I could get my family to stop talking to me, I might be able to catch a nap."

Erica took Carolyn's hand. "I'm not sure who I should have Adrianna slap with a gag order, Carolyn. You or them?"

Carolyn squeezed Erica's hand. "Whose side are you on, anyway?"

"Your side, Carolyn. I'm always on your side."

Carolyn gave her a smile as she watched Erica place her gifts back in the gift bag. She waved as she stepped out of the room and headed to the nurses' station to return the page from the emergency department.

Erica hung up the phone in the nurses' station just as the overhead page called out: "Dr. Erica Beaumont to postpartum, stat. Dr. Erica Beaumont to postpartum, stat." Peter held the unit door open for her as they both ran for the nearest stairwell.

✳✳✳✳

Erica and Peter stepped off the elevator on the first floor and moved down the hall to the emergency room.

111

They stepped through the large automatic double doors and were greeted by the security guards. They walked past the crowded waiting area and headed toward the area that contained the four large glassed-in trauma rooms. Erica and Peter stepped into the only trauma room that was bustling with activity and saw Dr. Michael Thomas clip a cervical spine x-ray onto the view box. Erica and Peter stood beside him.

"Hey, guys. What was that stat call to postpartum all about?"

Erica checked her pager once more before clipping it back on her lab coat. "It was awful. You know it always is when we get stat-paged to postpartum. It was a twenty-eight-year-old who had delivered her first child six hours ago. She had been complaining of a terrible headache since the delivery, and her blood pressure had been slowly creeping upward. When the nurse went in to check on her, she was really drowsy and lethargic. The nurse noticed her right arm was completely flaccid at her side and when she went to check her pupils, she saw that one pupil was fixed and dilated."

"Wow. How dramatic. Did she blow a blood vessel in her brain?"

"She sure did. We did a CAT scan of her head, and she has a subarachnoid hemorrhage. Peter and I just finished admitting her into the unit. We'll watch her really closely overnight."

"Man, that's awful."

"It sure is. Sorry it's taken us a while to get down here. What do you have for us?"

"I actually have two patients for you to see." He gestured toward the films. "Take a look at these x-rays first. Pretty impressive, don't you think?"

Peter squinted and looked closer. "Jesus! What happened to this guy? He doesn't look like he has many bones left intact."

"What we have here is a thirty-five-year-old man who was trimming a forty-foot palm tree this afternoon. What he failed to see was the huge beehive nestled in the palm fronds on his way up. Our patient is allergic to bees. When he got to the top and heard that ear-splitting hum of several hundred angry bees, he freaked out, lost his balance, and fell right out of the tree."

"Jesus. It's a wonder he's still alive."

"My sentiments exactly, Peter. Right now, I think he wishes he were not alive. He's in a lot of pain. Orthopedics has seen him, and they want to take him to the operating room to set his broken arms and legs." Michael tapped the x-ray with his pencil. "But this guy is not going anywhere till you guys have a good look at his spine x-rays and clear him for surgery."

Erica leaned in closer and scanned the series of spinal x-rays very carefully. "Is he able to wiggle his fingers and his toes, Michael?"

"He sure can. He wisely chooses not to at this time, but it seems he has no neurological deficits from my findings. But of course, I would leave that final judgment to your brilliant neurosurgical minds."

Erica squeezed Michael's arm. "What's the second patient?"

"This kid is really interesting. He's sixteen years old, and his parents say that for the last three days he's

113

been complaining of headaches, sleeping a lot more than usual, and not eating much at all. He stayed home from school today, and when they got home from work, they could barely wake him up, so they brought him in. His temperature is 103°F. He's restless, irritable, and confused in his conversation. He has a very stiff neck, and he wasn't too happy with me when I asked him to flex it for me."

Peter looked at Erica. "Sounds like meningitis."

"It sure does. He sounds pretty sick. Let's go have a look at the trauma patient first; then we'll take a look at the sixteen-year-old."

Erica laid her hand on Michael's arm. "You should consider being a neurosurgeon, Michael. You just might be able to make it to our intellectual level."

Michael glared at Erica until she quickly moved to the other side of the trauma room and grabbed a pair of gloves.

Peter laughed as he followed Erica.

Michael folded his arms across his chest as Erica looked back at him and blew him a kiss.

Michael mouthed, "Smart-ass."

Chapter 6

Erica rubbed her eyes and checked the wall clock in the nurses' station, already five thirty in the afternoon. She signed her name to the completed progress note on the sixteen-year-old with meningitis. "I think we're done for the day, Peter. Why don't you go on home? I'll check on the patients in the NICU before I leave."

Peter signed his name on the note on the trauma patient. "That would be great, Erica. I've been here for thirty-six hours, so it would be great to actually reintroduce myself to my own bed."

"I'm sure it would be. You deserve an evening to yourself. You've done an excellent job caring for our patients, Peter. You should be proud of yourself. I certainly enjoy working with you."

Peter leaned back in his chair and slipped his small leather-bound daily planner and Cross pen into the pocket of his lab coat. "That means a lot to me that you feel that way, Erica. Your program is widely known in academic circles as one of the best and one of the toughest. You have the same high expectations for me as you do for yourself, and that just makes me want to work harder. You challenge me to be the best I can be and I couldn't ask for more from any teacher."

They both stood and tucked their chairs into the long u-shaped counter of the nurses' station.

"Well, thank you, Peter. It's always a pleasure to work with someone that really enjoys what we do."

Peter saw Michael step into the nurses' station behind Erica. "I really do. Besides, Dr. Thomas told me to start with the compliments early if I expected to make it through your program."

"Oh, he did, did he?"

Michael slid a chart onto the chart rack beside Erica. "I heard my name being used in vain."

"Michael, are you teaching the residents to suck up to me?"

"Heck, ya. How else are they going to survive your grueling program?"

Peter laughed as he gathered their notes. "I'll take these to the unit, Dr. Beaumont, and check on the patients we just admitted."

"No, Peter. Go home. You've put in two long days and you deserve this evening to yourself." Erica took the papers from his hands and tucked them under her arm. "I'll take care of these and check on all the patients in the unit before I go home. Now, get out of here, and I'll see you at seven A.M. sharp."

"Good night, Dr. Beaumont. See you in the morning."

Michael set his hand on Peter's shoulder. "See what some good sucking up will do for you, Peter? Keep up the good work."

Michael and Peter laughed as Peter headed for the residents' room.

Erica turned to Michael. "You think you're cute, don't you?"

Michael gave Erica a grin. "That's what the girls keep telling me."

Erica rolled her eyes.

Michael took the papers from her hands and set them down on the counter. "Come sit in the garden with me for a minute, and I'll buy you a cold drink."

"That would be wonderful, big spender."

Erica followed Michael down the hall and waited at the entrance to the garden as he dropped a handful of change into the soda machine and pulled out two ice-cold Pepsis.

Erica held the glass door open for him as they stepped into the balmy evening sun. They found a shaded wooden bench beneath a group of towering palm trees and settled in side by side.

Michael loudly popped the tab on one Pepsi and handed it to Erica.

"Thanks, Michael."

He ripped open his tab and clanked his can against hers. "You're very welcome, my dear. Cheers."

He propped his arm across the back of the bench and took a big sip of his soda. He set the can on his knee and looked up at the sun filtering through the swaying palm fronds. "I've been meaning to ask you what happened with Mrs. Taylor and her frontal tumor."

"We just got out of surgery this afternoon, and she's doing great. I have a really good feeling about her. I think she's going to do really well. As for her daughter, she has certainly been a handful."

Michael looked at her. "The daughter that was in the E.R. with her?"

"No, that's the good daughter. Her older daughter arrived later, after I transferred her to the NICU. She's the wicked daughter."

Michael crossed his long legs and took a big sip of soda. "This sounds like a story I want to hear."

"She started off as the family member from hell, and since then I've been able to get to know her and understand her better. She was just scared, and we somehow set each other off, and it turned into a disaster. Things are much better now. She's a really fascinating woman."

Michael watched Erica stare into her soda and run her thumb around the damp lip of the can. He leaned forward and set his hand on her shoulder. "Fascinating as in a good thing or a bad thing?" He watched Erica shift in her seat.

"Good thing. I find I'm thinking about her a lot. I have this deep need to reach out to her. She's so strong-willed and stoic, yet I see a soft, vulnerable side to her. I just feel I want to be there for her, I guess."

Michael took another sip of his soda and rested the can back on his knee. "When are you going to ask her to move in?"

Erica looked at him and smacked his hand. "It's not like that, Michael. How can you say that? You know I'm not like that at all. I just care about her. That's all there is to it. Besides, you know I swore I would never date patients or their family members. Professionally I'm telling myself I just want to help her through this, and personally I'm a little confused by what I feel."

Michael took Erica's hand in his. "Some rules are just meant to be broken, Erica. I haven't seen you look this lost about a woman in years. If you enjoy her company, then enjoy it. Don't throw away an opportunity with someone special just because you met her at work. That would be such a waste."

Erica ran her thumb across Michael's knuckles. "Her mother is the priority right now, Michael. I just want to help them both through this. That's all that matters right now."

"That's right, Erica. That is the priority right now. But when you send Mrs. Taylor home and she is no longer your patient, are you going to still be thinking about her daughter?"

"I don't know. I'll have to wait and see what happens. Besides, I don't even know what her preference really is. All I know is that she has never had a man in her bed, and that could mean she's just not found the right one yet."

Michael shook his head and stared at Erica. "How in the world did that come up in conversation already?"

"It was just a teddy bear question. Teddy bear or man? She said she would prefer a teddy bear since she has never had a man in her bed."

Michael ran his hand through his wavy chestnut hair and groaned. "For God's sake, Erica, why didn't you just come right out and ask the woman if she was a lesbian?"

Erica leaned back and frowned. "Because that would be inappropriate, Michael. It was just an innocent question at the time. A question that has been driving me nuts since then."

Michael laughed at his friend's frustration. "Erica, I love you so much, and you know that. I just want to see you happy in a relationship again. It's been a long time since that horrible night. Don't be afraid to step out and start dating again. You have so much to offer someone. Be brave. Why shouldn't you be happy?"

Erica leaned back into Michael's outstretched arm. "I wish it could be that easy, Michael. I wish I could be that brave."

Chapter 7

Erica checked on the 16-year-old boy with meningitis and was pleased at how he was responding to his medication. She spent time with the husband of the woman who had the subarachnoid hemorrhage after delivering her baby. She was not waking up, and Erica felt deeply concerned. She returned several phone calls and checked on all the rest of the patients in the NICU before walking into Carolyn's room. She stopped in the doorway as she caught sight of Adrianna hugging a beautiful woman and kissing her softly on the lips. Mystery solved. Both women turned and looked at Erica. Erica blushed and managed to find her voice. "I'm sorry. I didn't mean to interrupt."

The other woman looked from Adrianna to Erica and back to Adrianna as she sensed something between them. "That's okay. We were just saying good-bye. You must be the infamous Dr. Erica Beaumont that Carolyn and Adrianna have been raving about." The woman extended her hand to Erica. "I'm Shannon Simms. I'm Adrianna's ex-girlfriend."

Question answered. Erica took her hand and shook it firmly. Shannon turned to Adrianna and gave her a quizzical look.

"It's nice to meet you, Shannon."

"It's a pleasure to meet you, Erica. I wish I could stay and chat, ladies, but I have a plane to catch." Shannon stepped toward Carolyn's bed and leaned forward to give her a hug.

Carolyn took her face in her hands and kissed her softly. "Thanks for coming by, Shannon. Give your parents our love when you get to Boston."

"I will, Carolyn. This is a combined business and pleasure trip but I will be in Boston for about a month so I should be able to spend some quality time with the folks."

"Make sure you spend more time with your parents than pursuing those big investment clients of yours."

Shannon smiled. "I hear you, Carolyn. You get well and get yourself home. I'll call you next week to see how you're doing."

Carolyn hugged her close. "That would be great."

Adrianna took one step closer to Erica and smiled.

Shannon said good-bye to Carolyn and gathered her purse and briefcase. Adrianna touched her arm. "Come on, Shannon, I'll show you the way out."

"Good-bye, Dr. Beaumont. Please take care of Carolyn. She's a special lady."

"She sure is special, Shannon. I promise to take good care of her."

Erica watched them walk away and couldn't help appreciating what a beautiful couple they made. She didn't like the sinking feeling in her gut as she wondered how Adrianna still felt about Shannon. A thousand questions careened through her mind about their relationship and what happened. She knew she had no right to question anything about Adrianna's personal life as much as Adrianna had no right to captivate her heart as she did.

Carolyn's laughter brought Erica back. "Come and sit here with me, Dr. Beaumont, and try not to let your deep displeasure with Shannon show all over your face."

Erica shoved her hands into the pockets of her lab coat. "Am I that obvious, Carolyn?"

Carolyn laughed as Erica sat on the edge of her bed. "You're as obvious as a flashing neon sign."

Carolyn and Erica laughed together. "You'd like Shannon. She's a lovely person. Adrianna and Shannon ended their relationship five years ago. It was quite sad at the time because they had been together for three years when they realized they were growing in different directions. They have remained good friends through the years, and Shannon will always be special to us."

"Why does she have to be so charming and beautiful?"

Carolyn laughed. Adrianna walked back into the room. She gently brushed her hand across Erica's back, sending a surge of heat coursing through Erica's body. She slipped into her chair and faced Erica and her mother.

Erica did not like the grin on her face one bit. "I'd like to thank you for my Taylor family survival kit."

Adrianna burst into laughter. "I thought you would appreciate being on the same playing field. The Tums are to soothe your stress."

"To be on the same playing field, you should have inserted post-it notes on the pages that would tell me what you said to me after Carolyn had that seizure."

"If I did that, we wouldn't be playing at all. Besides, I believe someone conveniently tore those few pages out."

Carolyn laughed. "Good move, Adrianna. I always knew you were a smart girl."

Erica glared at her and Adrianna.

Erica folded her arms across her chest and glared at Carolyn. "Stop encouraging her, Carolyn." Erica turned to Adrianna. "And you, Ms. Taylor, did you not read the sign on the door of this unit?"

"What sign is that?"

"The one that says you're not allowed to kiss any former girlfriends in my unit."

Carolyn and Adrianna burst into laughter. "But, Dr. Beaumont, she's such a good kisser."

Erica rolled her eyes and dropped her face as Carolyn turned to her beaming daughter. "I think our dear Dr. Beaumont is a wee bit jealous, Adrianna. What do you think?"

Adrianna looked at her mother with a smile. "I think you might be right, Mom."

Adrianna looked at Erica. "You're so beautiful when you're jealous, Dr. Beaumont."

Erica blushed. "Oh, will you two please stop picking on me?"

"Shannon certainly thought you were rather beautiful and charming. She asked if you were single and if I would give her your phone number."

Erica smiled shyly, captivated by Adrianna's glowing, sapphire blue eyes.

124

"I told her all I knew about your personal life is that you sleep with a teddy bear. I told her she couldn't pay me enough to give her your phone number." They all laughed as Adrianna leaned closer to Erica. "She accused me of keeping you for myself. Imagine that."

Adrianna's seductive wink drew Erica deeper into that sapphire depth.

Carolyn laid her hand on Erica's arm. "So tell us, Erica, why is there not a special woman in your life right now?"

Erica looked at her hands.

Adrianna reached forward and touched her knee. "Don't feel you have to answer my mother's nosy questions."

Erica felt the warmth in Adrianna's eyes and in her gentle touch. She took a deep breath and looked away from Adrianna. "Her name was Laura," Erica said quietly. "She was an orthopedic surgeon, and we met one night in the trauma room. We were both called to assess a man badly injured in a hang-gliding accident." Erica smiled. "I thought she was very abrasive and had her priorities all screwed up, and she thought I was obnoxious and overbearing. Can you imagine?"

Carolyn and Adrianna laughed softly. "We argued in that trauma room like cats and dogs. The next day we both walked into that patient's room at the same time and agreed to disagree. We talked throughout the next week and then one night we went out to dinner. We ended up being together for the next ten years."

Erica looked down at her hands and tugged mindlessly at the cuff of her blouse. "Two years ago, I had spent almost forty-eight hours straight here in the hospital. Half of that time I was in the operating room, so by the time I was ready to go home, I was totally exhausted and incapable of driving. It was two o'clock in the morning, and I wanted to call a cab but Laura insisted on coming to get me. She was two minutes from the hospital when she was hit head-on by a drunk driver."

Adrianna placed her hand on her chest and leaned closer. "Oh, my God, Erica."

Tears clouded Erica's eyes as she looked away from Adrianna. "They brought her into our emergency department, and my friend, Dr. Michael Thomas, and the entire trauma team tried valiantly for two hours to save her life. She had such massive internal injuries that she hemorrhaged to death. I held her hand the whole time and felt her slip away."

Adrianna pulled her chair closer to Erica and laid her hand on her knee as she watched Erica wipe her eyes. "Erica, that is such a nightmare."

Carolyn and Adrianna were speechless. Adrianna finally took Erica's hands and held them gently. "Erica, I'm so sorry."

Erica nodded her head. Carolyn wiped her own tears and touched Erica's arm. "Laura must have been very special, Erica."

"She really was. You guys would have liked her. That was two years ago, and it feels like it was just yesterday."

Adrianna handed her a tissue from Carolyn's bedside table. "You must have been beside yourself with grief."

"I was a basket case for months. I totally immersed myself in my work and tried to hide from the grief and despair that continually shadowed me. If it wasn't for my family and my closest friends, Trina and Abby, I don't think I would have been able to pull myself together. I will always carry the guilt of not convincing Laura to stay home instead of coming to the hospital to get me that horrible night." Erica stared down at her hands as she balled the tissue in her fist. "For the past two years, I've tried to deal with the loss of Laura and painfully learned to go on without her. There has not been anyone in my life since Laura, and I know I have purposefully avoided getting involved with anyone because of my fear of feeling this deep sense of loss again."

"Erica, you have grieved for Laura for two years now. You're such an exceptional woman, and you have your whole life ahead of you. I know that there's somebody out there that you could find true happiness with again. I believe that Laura would want you to be happy with someone, as you would if the roles were reversed," Carolyn said. "Open your heart to love again, Erica. Allow yourself the true happiness you deserve."

Erica leaned closer to Carolyn and kissed her cheek. "Carolyn, you're a darling."

Adrianna stood before Erica, placing her hands gently on her shoulders. Erica ached to pull her in closer, as she admired her black and gray pinstriped slacks and gray silk blouse. Their eyes met and locked, as Erica saw a profound depth of compassion flow from Adrianna's eyes.

Adrianna brushed away a ringlet from Erica's forehead and let her touch linger along her damp cheek. "Are you okay, Erica?"

"I'm okay. Sorry for all the tears."

Adrianna cupped Erica's chin and held her still. "Don't ever apologize for that. That was one of the most heart-wrenching stories I've ever heard. I'm so sorry for your loss of Laura. As my mother said, you're an exceptional woman, and I'm totally amazed at how well you've fared through such an enormous tragedy. Thank you for sharing that part of your life with us. That meant a lot to me that you felt comfortable enough to open your heart and share your painful memories."

Sarah stepped into the room and smiled at Adrianna and Erica. She stood beside Carolyn's bed and set her pills on the bedside table. "I've got your medicine for you, Carolyn." She refilled Carolyn's water glass. "Are these two exhausting you?"

"They've worn me out, Sarah." Carolyn winked at Adrianna and sat up higher in bed. "Ladies, I'm going to have Sarah help me into the bathroom, and then I'm going to have a nap after I take my pills. David should be back in a little while to visit with me. Why don't you both go visit for a while, and I'll catch up on my beauty sleep."

Adrianna bent down and kissed her mother's forehead. "I love you. I'll be back in a little while."

"Okay, sweetheart."

Erica and Adrianna stepped out to the doorway, while Erica pulled the curtain across the glass wall.

Adrianna looked into her eyes. "Are you okay?"

Erica looked into Adrianna's gleaming sapphire eyes and squeezed her arm. "I'm fine. Thanks for asking. How are you feeling? You certainly didn't sleep very much today. You must be beat."

"I don't feel too bad. I'm just so grateful that my mother is doing so well. It was well worth the lack of sleep to be here for her. Now, are you finished for the day, Dr. Beaumont?"

"Yes, I am."

"Have you had a chance to eat any dinner yet?"

"No, I haven't. Have you?"

"No, I haven't either. I brought a few of my mother's favorite foods, and I also made several chicken salad sandwiches and a spinach salad. I was wondering if you would like to share some with me."

Erica raised her eyebrows. "You made me dinner?"

"Yes, I did. And don't look so shocked. I do believe that was my penance. Unless of course you had plans with your teddy bear."

"No plans with Teddy. Looks like I'm free this evening."

"Good. Come with me, Dr. Beaumont. I reserved a table for us in the garden."

"Should I bring my new Complete Idiot's Guide to Learning Italian?"

Adrianna's smile brightened her eyes to a deep sapphire blue. "Not unless you plan on making me really angry."

Erica laughed as Adrianna touched her elbow and guided her toward the ICU doors. She stopped long enough to get her square cooler bag from the patients' fridge.

They headed down the hall together, and Erica reached for the glass door to the garden, opening it for Adrianna. Erica followed her through the door and stopped. She looked between the towering palm trees and saw the huge red ball of sunshine slowly descend toward the mountain peaks. A gentle warm breeze caressed her face.

Adrianna watched her tilt her face upward. "It's really beautiful out here. I see and feel something different each time I come out."

Erica slowly closed her eyes and allowed the balmy heat to flow through her. "I feel the same way. It's truly an ethereal place." Erica opened her eyes and enjoyed the look of contentment and peace on Adrianna's face.

Adrianna touched Erica's wrist and guided her through the arbor to Erica's favorite spot nestled among the dwarf palm trees.

Adrianna pulled out a chair for Erica at the wrought iron table, then spread a small red and white-checkered tablecloth. Next, she set out two place settings, two bottles of water and served their spinach salads and chicken salad sandwiches.

Erica sat back in her chair with her arms folded across her chest.

Adrianna took her seat, looked up into Erica's eyes, and spread her own napkin across her lap.

"You're truly amazing, Adrianna Taylor. This is a beautiful spread, and I'm totally flabbergasted that you went through all this trouble to bring this romantic meal to me."

Adrianna blushed and tucked in her chair. "I was thrilled to do this for you. I would have brought wine and candles, but I didn't think that you should be seen drinking wine at work. I didn't want to tarnish your Mother Teresa image."

Erica tilted her head back and laughed.

"Besides, I feel responsible for the well-being of your stomach these days. I thought I would try and get a decent meal in you before you had to start popping those Tums." Adrianna picked up her fork and toyed with her spinach salad before looking up at Erica. "We're all ecstatic at how well my mother's surgery went, Erica. Dig into your salad and tell me all about the surgery from the very beginning and don't leave out any details."

"Are you sure you want to discuss her surgery over dinner?"

"Of course. Medical stuff always fascinates me, and this is my mother we're talking about. So feel free to share all the details, as long as it doesn't bother you."

Erica picked up her fork and explained Carolyn's surgery in great detail and answered all of Adrianna's questions. They finished their salads and moved on to their sandwiches as they talked about Laura, their careers, their educations, their families, and their dreams.

Erica thoroughly enjoyed her chicken salad sandwich and was overwhelmed when Adrianna pulled out bakery fresh lemon poppy seed muffins.

Adrianna tossed their paper plates into the nearest trashcan and placed the leftover food back into the cooler bag.

Erica leaned across the table, feeling her heart race and heat surge throughout her body with their close proximity. "That was an incredible meal, Adrianna, and the company was equally wonderful. I don't know how you found the time but you, young lady, can cook for me anytime." Erica forced herself to move back

131

slightly to control the emotions catapulting through her entire being.

"I haven't enjoyed a picnic like this in a long time. Thank you."

"Thank you for making this picnic possible for us."

Erica sensed Adrianna's attempt to relax. She desperately wanted to know everything about this lovely creature. "Shannon was really sweet. It was nice to meet her."

Adrianna set the cooler bag down on the ground beside her and leaned her elbows on the table. "She is sweet, and the look on your face when you walked in on that kiss was priceless."

Erica lowered her head and attempted to hide her embarrassment. Adrianna leaned across the table and touched her chin with her fingertips, raising her eyes to meet her own. "My mother is so right about you when she said you wear your heart on your sleeve. You looked instantly unhappy when you saw me with Shannon." Adrianna let her fingers linger along Erica's chin and struggled to look away from her full, moist lips.

"I was unhappy." Erica loved the way Adrianna's smile lit up her eyes.

"Shannon and I are just friends, Erica. We never let the end of our relationship affect our friendship, and that meant a lot to me."

"That's great that you could maintain your friendship. I really mean that, Adrianna. She does seem like a doll, and it's always hard to appreciate the friendship once the relationship ends." Erica enjoyed the warmth in Adrianna's eyes. "I was wondering, Adrianna, do you have Shannon's phone number? I was going to call her and get her to show me just how good a kisser she really is."

Erica could hardly contain her laughter at the look of total disbelief in Adrianna's eyes. She watched as Adrianna leaned closer across the table with fire in those sapphire-blue eyes.

"No, I will not give you Shannon's phone number, and if you don't want to hear me spew my thoughts in Italian, you will not ask me again. You're just going to have to take my word for it that she's a good kisser, okay?"

Erica tilted her head back and laughed. "At least now I have my Idiot's guide to help me translate."

Adrianna leaned closer. "You're far from an idiot, Erica, and I don't want you to have to flip through that manual to understand me. Hear me loud and clear in English. No, I will not give you Shannon's phone number. Understood?"

Erica stared at Adrianna's sensuous, full lips. "Understood."

They both enjoyed the intensity between them as Adrianna gently shook her head. "You should have heard the barrage of questions I had to fight off about you when I walked Shannon to her car. Shannon is very particular about her women, and she was very partial to you. I'm serious, Erica. You have this magnetic effect on people. I see it with all the people you work with, whether it's doctors, nurses, or patients and their families. You exude this incredible, natural warmth that embraces everyone you focus your attention on." Erica blushed as Adrianna touched her chin. "Your Mother Teresa image is rather nauseating, my friend. Please try and be human like the rest of us once in a while, would you?"

Erica burst into laughter.

They were suspended in time, locked into each other's intense eyes. Erica gently broke the silence. "Your relationship with Shannon ended five years ago. Who is the lucky woman that is sharing your life with you now?"

"There isn't anyone in my life right now and hasn't been for two years."

Erica watched Adrianna as she caught a glimpse of anguish flutter across those sapphire depths before she quickly turned away. Erica allowed her a moment to collect her thoughts. "Who was the special woman you shared your life with after Shannon?"

Adrianna entwined her hands on the table. "Her name was Hailey. We met four years ago at a law conference where I did a symposium on laws protecting battered women. She was also a lawyer and did some pro bono work at a shelter for battered women. She stood up and added her comments to my lecture and instantly won my heart."

Erica saw the depth of anguish in Adrianna's eyes and watched her smile quickly fade.

"We'd been together for two years when Hailey started having a lot of abdominal pain. I had taken her to our doctor several times, and he never did any tests yet came up with a different diagnosis each time. They ranged from the stomach flu, lactose intolerance, food allergies, gastric reflux disease, hiatus hernia, and he even went so far as to insinuate that it was in her head." Adrianna shook her head as Erica watched anger cloud her eyes. "Hailey never complained about anything before, Erica, so I knew that this was serious." Adrianna looked down at her hands. "This went on for a year, and Hailey kept trying to convince me to let it be and it would just go away. Well, it never went away and only intensified with time. I tried to respect her wishes, but I told Hailey we had let this go on long enough. I had enough of this quack doctor, so we started shopping around for someone who would listen to us and investigate this pain more thoroughly." Adrianna wrung her hands together, swallowing hard as she did.

Erica reached across the table and took her hands.

Adrianna looked up into her warm eyes and saw a compassion that made her feel safe to share her story. She felt Erica encompass her hands in her own and felt a surge of warmth fill her soul. "Then one night after we made love she started to bleed vaginally, and I was terrified. We didn't understand what would have caused her to start bleeding like that. As the bleeding got worse, so did her abdominal pain. I rushed her to the hospital and a female gynecologist did an abdominal CAT scan. Within two hours, that gynecologist shattered my world. She told us that Hailey had uterine cancer that had spread to her ovaries, bowels, and liver. We sadly found the source of her abdominal pain."

The tears began to fall from Adrianna's eyes. She reached for her napkin. Erica handed her tissues from her pocket.

Adrianna wiped her eyes and took a deep breath. "Hailey died six months later. She was only thirty-six when she died of cancer that should have been detected much sooner. She might have had a chance if our pathetic doctor had not blown us off like we were neurotic women. It was his apathy and refusal to perform diagnostic tests that made me livid and led me to practice personal injury law."

Erica watched as Adrianna dried her eyes. "Did you sue him?"

Adrianna looked into Erica's eyes. "Yes, I did."

Erica sensed Adrianna's hesitation as she gently touched her chin and guided her eyes back to her. "What happened?"

"He was grossly negligent, Erica. I didn't have a hard time proving that. With the help of a group of investors and all the money from the lawsuit, we built a cancer treatment center downtown. It's called the Hailey Center for Women. It has served thousands of women in the past year."

Erica caressed Adrianna's soft hands. "Wow! I'm impressed. I've heard of the wonderful work being done at the Hailey Center, and now I've met the woman behind it. Hey, isn't tomorrow night the big gala fundraiser for the Hailey Center?"

"Yes, it is. How did you know about that?"

"One of my friends is an oncologist there, and she has invited all the physicians from here to attend tomorrow night's fundraiser. She feels we should all get a closer look at the Hailey Center so we can appreciate the work that is being done there."

"Were you planning on going, Erica?"

"Yes, I was. I was planning on going with my friends Trina and Abby. As the mastermind behind this wonderful establishment, will you also be there?"

"The timing is awful because I would rather be here with my mom, but as the guest of honor I guess I can't just back out. Besides, my mother wants me to be there, for her and for Hailey."

Erica squeezed her hands and held them close. "I'm so sorry about Hailey, Adrianna. You've suffered a terrible loss. You and I have experienced a deep loss that few people can understand. Not only have you had to deal with losing Hailey, you have also had to deal with Carolyn's breast cancer, your own breast cysts, and now Carolyn's brain tumor. How have you managed to keep going? I would've been a mess."

"It's been a rough couple of years. I still have times when I'm home alone and I can't stop crying, but somehow my spirit won't let me give up and keeps forcing me to put one foot in front of the other. The Hailey Center always makes me feel like there was a greater purpose to Hailey's life, and I know that she would be pleased that women have a place to go to receive proper treatment that was not an option for her."

Erica felt the strength and determination in Adrianna's spirit that glowed in her personality. "Building the Hailey Center was the greatest gift you could have given her. I'm so proud of you, Adrianna, and now I understand why you jumped all over me when you thought I was not acting on your mother's seizures."

"Yes, Erica, that's why I went ballistic on you. I'm so tired of pathetic doctors that don't act." Adrianna looked into their entwined hands and hesitated briefly. "But I was ignorant about the treatment of seizures, as you clearly pointed out to me and everyone else in my mother's room that day."

A mischievous gleam danced across Adrianna's eyes. "You've been excellent with my mother, Erica. I appreciate everything you've done for her."

Adrianna ran her thumbs across the backs of Erica's hands. "I don't want you to think that I focus my career on suing doctors. I have only accepted twelve cases of negligence by doctors and won them all because they were so blatant. Six of the cases involved negligence against lesbians, and those cases were very rewarding for me." Adrianna carefully watched Erica's expression and felt the warmth of her hands. "I'm very particular about the cases I handle, and I don't enjoy flushing a physician's career down the toilet, but these men were dangerous.

"What I've also learned over the past two years is that there are some lawyers out there that prey on the vulnerability of doctors and the difficult decisions they make every minute of every day. It's a very gray area, and I don't like what I have been seeing. In the beginning, my father was not particularly proud of my work in this area and had always been my biggest critic. He feels that doctors' jobs are very stressful and that they deserve room for error. I disagreed with him and challenged him to help me investigate some of those cases to prove the doctors' innocence and to prove me wrong."

Adrianna smiled at her memories of working with her father. "He had the spare time on his hands, and he can never turn down a good challenge. It turned out to be a great working partnership. We both learned a lot through those cases about the lives of physicians and about each other. I will always cherish the work I was able to do with my father and the time we spent together on those difficult cases."

"I can see that David loves you very much. He mentioned that he's upset that you never joined his law firm."

"Erica, I love him very much, but our strained relationship started when I came out to my parents and told them I was gay. He has never accepted my sexual orientation and always treated the women in my life like they were just friends rather than my girlfriends. I tried to talk to him about this several times, and he told me that he feels responsible for the fact that I hate men. I have tried in vain to explain to him that I don't hate men. I just love women, and my preference is no reflection on my relationship with him. He went so far as to say he feels I go after these doctors because I hate men and feel the deep need to protect the gay community."

Erica was shocked as she felt the deep conflict between Adrianna and her father. "Wow. That's painful stuff."

"It sure is. To him my life has all been about my lesbianism. He has no idea that my dream was to gain as much law experience as I could to eventually come and work with him someday and make him proud to add me to his firm. I have come to realize that I will never gain his approval in my personal life, so I have long abandoned that dream. I do feel a deep commitment to the gay community and enjoy the work that I can do to protect the rights of gays and lesbians. David will never understand that need in me, so I have had to choose between pleasing my father and pleasing myself. I won and in the interim I feel like there will always be this distance between my father and me. David is seventy years old, Erica, and still works part-time at his firm. His mind is as sharp as a tack, and I learned so much from him when he talked to me about the different cases he was working on. He's a brilliant man and tries to be a good father, but I have never been the daughter that he wants me to be. To make matters worse, Leah is the perfect daughter, wife, mother, sister, and Grant is the perfect husband. And they both make me sick."

Erica burst into laughter.

"Don't get me wrong. I love them to death, and Leah and I have always been close. They both have given me a beautiful niece, Amanda, but their lives are a continuous example of what my father feels should be my life.

"Carolyn has always been my biggest supporter, and I think she goes the extra mile for me because of David's disappointment in me."

Adrianna looked down at her hands and blushed slightly. "Now that you know my entire life story, do you have any questions, comments, concerns?"

Erica smiled as she looked down at their entwined hands. "I think that David is like every other father of a gay daughter. He worries about you because he wants someone to take care of you like Grant takes care of Leah. He underestimates your willpower, independence, and self-confidence and refuses to believe that a woman is what you really want. I have seen the way he looks at you, Adrianna. I think he's extremely proud of the woman you are, regardless of his personal feelings. He's of a different generation that's still trying to deal with homosexuality. You've thrust it right into his family and expect him to be as incredibly wonderful as Carolyn is about your life."

"Are you defending my father, Dr. Beaumont?"

"I would never defend David for not trying to understand the incredible woman that you are, but I think we have to cut him some slack and remember that he was raised to believe in the institution of husband and wife. Little does he know how happy and committed gay couples can be. I also don't think you see his incredible love for you because you want him to accept you as his gay daughter and not just his daughter."

"How is it possible that you can be so incredibly beautiful and so annoyingly wise?"

Erica laughed. Adrianna looked over Erica's shoulder and watched a woman dressed in a lab coat approach their table. Her petite five-foot-four-inch frame easily navigated the lush courtyard. Her straight, light brown hair was pulled back in a tidy ponytail, giving her a youthful exuberance. Her light brown eyes glowed with a mischievous smile as she scanned Adrianna's face.

Erica followed the path of Adrianna's gaze. She rose to her feet and enveloped Dr. Abby Cooper in her arms. "Hello, darling."

Abby reached on her tiptoes and kissed Erica softly. "Hello, beautiful. Speaking of beautiful, who is this gorgeous woman?"

"This beautiful woman is someone I would like you to meet." Adrianna rose from her chair. "Dr. Abby Cooper, this is Adrianna Taylor. Adrianna, this is Abby. Abby is a cardiologist and has been my best friend for the past thirty years. We were roommates in medical school." Erica stepped away and grabbed Abby a chair.

Adrianna reached out and shook Abby's hand. "It's nice to meet you, Abby."

"It's a pleasure meeting you, Adrianna. I've been looking for Erica for the past hour. Sarah tipped me off as to where I might find her. I certainly didn't think I would be going on a jungle trek and find her with a beautiful woman in the garden."

"We were seeking some privacy, Abby, but I guess I'm going to have to try harder to hide Erica from you and Sarah."

Abby turned and looked up at Erica. "This one doesn't hold a thing back, does she?"

Erica placed a chair in behind Abby. "No, she doesn't hold back any punches at all, Abby. Be forewarned."

Everyone took a seat as Abby looked down at the checkered tablecloth. "It looks like you guys had a picnic."

"We did have a picnic. Adrianna made me spinach salad, chicken salad sandwiches, and bought lemon poppy seed muffins from a bakery. It was delicious."

Abby looked from Adrianna to Erica. "You did all that for her? Gosh, you must be nuts about her. And who the heck are you? How did you slip into Erica's life without me knowing about you till now?"

Adrianna turned to Abby and recounted the story of Carolyn's brain tumor and the emotionally charged way that she met Erica.

Abby sat back in her chair and folded her arms across her chest. "Wow! What a story. You two just about throttle each other twenty-four hours ago, and now you're sharing a romantic dinner. Sometimes women are totally incomprehensible to me." Erica and Adrianna laughed. "How is your mother doing, Adrianna?"

"Beautifully. Erica has done a great job with her, and she's not had another seizure in twenty-four hours. You'll have to come meet her, Abby. She would get a kick out of you. Don't you think, Erica?"

Erica was engrossed in watching Adrianna share her story with her dearest friend. "Carolyn will certainly find Abby quite entertaining. But I don't know if she's ready for this much stimulation."

Abby scowled at Erica and turned to Adrianna. "I would love to meet your mom some day, and I'm really happy to hear that she's doing so well. Something as devastating as this is so difficult to get through, and I bet your mother has enjoyed having you at her side even though it disrupts your whole life."

"Adrianna has been wonderful with her mom, but she's a lawyer, Abby. It's her job to disrupt everyone else's lives."

Adrianna balled up her napkin and threw it directly at Erica's chest.

Abby laughed. "What kind of law do you practice, Adrianna?"

"Personal injury, among other specialties."

Abby threw her head back and covered her eyes with her hands. "Oh my God! An ambulance chaser." Abby looked directly at Erica. "What are you doing sharing a meal with an ambulance chaser?"

Adrianna leaned close to Abby. "I'm not an ambulance chaser, Abby, and I resent that label. I go after doctors that deserve to be punished, and I would appreciate it if you would keep that in mind for future reference. Also, remember that cardiologists are particularly delicious to devour."

Abby looked from Adrianna to Erica. "She's a force to reckon with."

"You're not kidding, Abby. I've already experienced hurricane Adrianna at its worst."

Adrianna leaned back in her chair and folded her arms across her chest. She glared at Erica. "I thought I'd been forgiven for that, Dr. Beaumont."

"You have been forgiven, counselor. I now understand why you reacted the way you did the first time we met. It doesn't mean that I'm still not cautious of flying debris."

"Ouch! You've been told, Adrianna. I hope you're repenting for your sins."

"Actually, Abby, Erica has decided that I have to cook her dinner when my mother is better to repent for my sins, so I thought I'd give her a little sample with this picnic tonight."

Abby looked at Erica in admiration. "You sly dog! That's a punishment that I'm sure you're both dreading. Speaking of dates, the reason I've been looking for you, Erica, is to remind you about the gala fundraiser for the Hailey Center tomorrow night."

Erica gestured grandly toward Adrianna. "Abby, I would like you to meet the woman who envisioned the Hailey Center and made it a reality."

Abby looked at Adrianna in sheer disbelief. "What do you mean, made it a reality?

Adrianna explained her story to Abby as she had to Erica. "I'm really touched that you both are going to be at the fundraiser."

144

"Geez, Adrianna, I'm moved to be able to meet the woman who put that center into action. It was a badly needed institution in this city, and you created that from your grief. What a story. My Trina would love to meet you."

"Who's Trina?"

"Trina is the love of my life. I know that Trina would love to meet you even though she will be devastated to know that there is another woman in Erica's life."

Adrianna laid her hand on Abby's arm and leaned closer. "How long have you and Trina been together?"

"Ten years. I can't believe it but we have been together for ten beautiful years."

"That's incredible, Abby. You and Trina must have a beautiful relationship." Abby blushed. "How did you and Trina meet?"

"It all began when Erica wanted to have a sun room built onto her house. Our friend Dr. Michael Thomas knew of a female architect and passed her business card on to Erica. That architect was my Trina. Erica and Trina met a few times to discuss the plans, and Trina needed to arrange a day to go into Erica's house to take measurements and make some sketches. Well, that week Erica was going to a medical conference in Dallas, so Erica set a date and time with me to let Trina into her house and let her do her work." Abby stopped. "And I didn't show up, Adrianna."

Adrianna burst into laughter. "Oh, no, Abby."

"Oh, yes. I was out to dinner with another woman I had just met when my pager went off. I called back this unfamiliar number, and Trina was livid. She had waited in Erica's driveway for half an hour in the dark of night before she thought she should page me to make sure I was all right. We had never met before or even spoken, and this was our first encounter. Trina gave me proper shit for wasting her precious time. I tried to get Trina to pick another time for me to let her into Erica's house, but she wouldn't hear of it. She demanded that I kiss my date good night and get my sorry ass over to Erica's place. She was so angry that I didn't dare argue with her. Come to think of it, I still don't dare argue with her."

They all laughed together as Abby told more about that fateful night. "I said good night to one very angry woman and drove to Erica's to be confronted by another beautiful, angry woman. I was batting a thousand that night. I have never been yelled at so much in my life as I was in that one night."

Adrianna listened intently to Abby's story.

"Once I calmed Trina down and apologized profusely, we headed to the front door. I slipped my key in, and it wouldn't turn very easily, so I really turned it and broke the key in the lock."

Adrianna burst into laughter. "This story can't get any worse."

Erica raised her bottle of water to her lips. "Oh, yes it can."

"I'm so glad you both find this humorous. My ass was really over the flames at the sound of that key breaking in that door. Trina was beyond livid at that point. You have to remember that she has now been outside of Erica's house for an hour. Erica lives in a very tight knit suburb in town, so whenever Erica goes away, she has her neighbors watch her house for her, and they spotted Trina and me milling about the front door. Before we knew it, there were two police cruisers pulling into Erica's driveway and flashing this high beam spotlight on us, practically blinding us."

Adrianna and Erica could not contain their laughter at this comedy of errors, so Abby had to laugh with them. "These female Rambo cops came bouncing out of their cruisers with their hands ready on their guns and demanding to know who we were. You can imagine at this point that Trina would have liked to take one of their guns and shoot me herself."

Everyone burst into laughter. "Trina had had it. She walked down the front steps and sat on the bottom step and buried her face in her hands. I spent twenty minutes trying to explain to these G.I. Janes who we were. They went through all our identification and even called in our driver's licenses to check on our records. It was ridiculous, and to add insult to injury the cops left their flashing lights on, so all of Erica's neighbors gathered on her front lawn to watch this escapade. You'd think we were fleeing fugitives showcased on *America's Most Wanted.*

"I thought the best way to resolve this whole nightmare would be to call Erica in Dallas and have her verify that we were indeed supposed to be there. Well, Erica thought this whole thing was hilarious and decided to prolong our agony by having the cops describe us to her to make sure we indeed were not a pair of cat burglars. I got back on the phone with her and just screamed at her, and she quickly realized that I was not finding the humor in this situation.

"An hour later, the cops felt satisfied that we were not about to break into Erica's house and finally left us to our own devices. I watched them pull away and bravely sat down on the step beside Trina. We sat in silence for the longest time because I didn't dare speak. Trina finally burst into uncontrollable laughter, and I put my head on my knees and wished I'd never gotten out of bed that morning.

"We finally started talking, and I asked Trina to come with me into Erica's back patio because I finally remembered where she hid her spare key back there. We walked around the side of the house, and I punched in Erica's security code to open the side gate. I let Trina into the backyard and watched her walk around the pool. She stood at the edge of the deep end and stared into the water as I went and stood beside her. After a few seconds, she looked over at me and said, "You're such a twit," and tried to push me in the pool. She knocked me off balance, and I felt like I was falling in slow motion. I reached for her and grabbed her arm, and we fell into the water together.

"We spent hours in that pool, floating around in our bras and undies and talking about anything and everything. I fell head over heels in love with that woman that night, and that love continues to burn passionately even after ten years."

Adrianna enjoyed the look of pure happiness in Abby's eyes.

Erica leaned forward. "Several days later, I returned a day early from Dallas to find my architect and my best friend floating around in my pool, totally naked and wrapped around each other. I tiptoed to the edge of the pool and said to them, 'I can see that things have really been building around here while I've been gone.' They both looked at me in shock and pulled each other down beneath the water." Erica smiled at Abby. "They've been together ever since, and Dr. Michael Thomas always reminds Abby that he's the source of her pure happiness for giving me Trina's business card."

"Michael is such a character," Abby said.

"Yes, he is, but we love him anyway," Erica added.

Erica thought she caught a flicker of unease in Adrianna's eyes as she quickly looked away. "That's such a beautiful story, Abby. I really look forward to meeting Trina tomorrow. I would also be honored if you and Trina and Erica would join me at my table for dinner."

Erica and Abby shared a warm smile. "We would be honored, Adrianna. Consider it a date. Now, speaking of the love of my life, I'd better get home."

They stood together. Abby stepped toward Adrianna and took her hands. "It has been a pleasure meeting you, Adrianna. I'm so glad I came into the garden looking for Erica because you certainly have been a pleasant surprise. I look forward to seeing you tomorrow and having you meet my girl. Most importantly, I hope your mom continues to improve and is able to go home soon."

"Thanks, Abby. I think that my mom is going to get better and stronger every day. I also look forward to seeing you tomorrow and meeting your Trina."

Abby leaned toward Adrianna and hugged her. Abby stepped toward Erica and hugged her close before kissing her.

"Good night, ladies. I'm going to go home and tell Trina all about you, Adrianna. I'll do my best to paint a bald, short, fat, ugly, toothless, no-personality picture so she won't be jealous of the fact that you're in her beloved Erica's life."

"Thanks, Abby. Thanks a lot."

Abby waved good-bye as Erica and Adrianna watched her walk back toward the hospital.

Adrianna turned to Erica. "She's incredible."

"Yes, she is. Abby rode her bike into my life when we were five years old, and she has been my dearest friend ever since. We even went to Harvard together, and she decided she would rather get into people's hearts, while I, of course, chose to get inside people's heads."

Erica held Adrianna's chair out for her as they both took a seat. "Abby and Trina are very special to me. They were there with me every step of the way as I grieved for Laura. They would catch me every time I would fall. I don't know what I would have done without them. I give them all the credit for getting me back on my feet and helping me to get on with my life."

"I can see that she loves you very much." Adrianna reached across the table and placed her hands over Erica's. She traced her thumbs across her knuckles and watched as their hands entwined. "I wish that I could have been there for you when Laura died."

Erica smiled at the warmth in Adrianna's eyes. "As I wish I could have been there for you when Hailey died." Erica watched Adrianna, as a need so great burned in her belly, a need she had not experienced in two years. She was consumed by the intensity and awe of the woman before her. She felt engulfed by the energy and passion that flowed from this alluring lady. The sexual tension danced around them like a ring of fire as Erica cautiously touched Adrianna's chin. "We are here together now, and I'm very grateful that you exploded into my life."

Erica saw the unease skirt across Adrianna's eyes as she quickly looked down at their entwined hands.

Adrianna skimmed her thumb over the simple braided, gold bracelet at Erica's wrist. "Are you okay with being seen out here with me like this?"

Erica was touched by Adrianna's concern and noted the quick change in subject. "My lesbianism is a well-known fact throughout this hospital since the day I met Laura. We never hid our life together and were pleasantly surprised at the overwhelming support we received from those closest to us at work. When Laura died, everyone was very loving and compassionate, and I was truly touched by the outpouring of sympathy from everyone from the medical staff to the housekeeping staff."

"I'm glad to hear that you were easily accepted and it did not cause you any problems professionally. However, the fact that you are a lesbian must have tarnished your Mother Teresa imagine a tiny bit?"

Erica tilted her head and vowed to find the cause of Adrianna's discomfort. "Never. I'm too wonderful to be seen in less than a perfect light."

Adrianna burst into laughter. "I love your sense of humor, Dr. Beaumont. I think my goal in your life is to disrobe you of this 'holier than thou' garb that you hide beneath."

Erica raised her eyebrows and grinned. "Now you're talking." Erica watched a warm smile ignite Adrianna's exquisite eyes. "May I be so bold as to ask if you have a date for tomorrow night?"

151

"As a matter of fact, I do."

Erica felt panic gripping at her belly. "May I ask if this person is someone I can have removed from the face of the earth prior to the gala event?"

Adrianna burst into laughter. "Why, Dr. Beaumont, I think that Leah and Grant would be terribly hurt if they knew you felt that way about them."

A smile creased the corners of Erica's full lips. "You were going with your family?"

Adrianna leaned in closer and glowed with mischief. "Yes, Dr. Beaumont. I had originally planned to go with my whole family. Because of what has happened to my mother, my dad is going to spend the evening here with her while Leah, Grant, and I attend the fundraiser. That's the way my mother wants it. She wants us to be there for her. So we're going to do this for her. My plan is to meet Leah and Grant at the Arizona Biltmore. So I was wondering if you would be my date for tomorrow night, and if you would give me the pleasure of picking you up."

Erica leaned in closer. "As Abby said, consider it a date."

Erica's pager vibrated at her waist. She took her pager off her belt and looked at the display. "The emergency department has monopolized my time all day today. Unfortunately, I should go see what they need."

They rose together, Adrianna grabbing the cooler bag.

Erica slid the tablecloth off the table and folded it. "Did you get a chance to stop by your office to collect your work?"

Adrianna looked at Erica as she zipped the cooler bag closed. "Yes, I did."

Erica was aware of Adrianna's hesitation and watched a cloud darken her eyes. "Adrianna, please tell me if I'm out of line, but I sense you're not comfortable sharing your work with me, so I get the feeling that your recent case involves another doctor."

Adrianna carefully put the cooler bag back down, leaning against the table. "It's not because I don't want to share my work with you, Erica. I really do. There isn't anything that I don't want to share with you. It's just that there's so much that I can't tell you at this time."

Adrianna looked into Erica's eyes. She felt her heart constrict as she took the tablecloth from Erica and placed it on the table. Adrianna stepped closer to Erica and took her hands. "I've been working on this case for two years now. This case does involve doctors but for different reasons than the obvious." Adrianna watched the concern tumble across Erica's eyes.

"It's a very complicated case that involves many people." Adrianna reached up to the silky smoothness of Erica's warm cheek. "I wish I could tell you so much more, but for confidentiality reasons I can't. I just hope that in the end you will understand my actions in this case."

Erica watched the distress deepen Adrianna's frown as she reached up and touched her cheek. "I believe in you, Adrianna. You're a very compassionate and conscientious woman. You care too much about people to destroy someone's life for the sole purpose of advancing your own career."

"Please remember those words when this case hits the newspapers. Please know that I would never be malicious for the heck of it. I would never prosecute a doctor without a clear-cut case of negligence. I have a deeper agenda in this case, and I have to believe that everything will work out in the end."

Erica glided her thumb across Adrianna's cheek as Adrianna leaned her face into Erica's strong hand. "Your faith means a lot to me, Erica. I would never want to do anything to destroy that. Please trust me and remember that I do care about the difference between right and wrong. This case takes place in New York City and I'm starting to resent all the time I spend away from my family and friends. After this case, I know that I want to make some changes in my life."

Erica enjoyed Adrianna's determined smile as she held her face in her hands. "Do what you have to do, Adrianna. Just remember that I'll always be here for you."

Adrianna's smile illuminated her eyes as she stepped into Erica's strong arms. She buried her face in that sea of cascading ringlets as she was enveloped by the scent of fresh apples. She slid her hands across Erica's lower back and up along the firm contours of her spine. The heat soaring between them caressed her belly and blazed between her thighs.

Erica held her tight as she marveled at how perfectly Adrianna fit in her arms. She rubbed her cheek against the smooth softness of her forehead as she inhaled the subtle scent of peaches. Her hands gently roamed across her petite, silk-covered back as she wished to ease all her sorrow. The tingling surge in her chest mushroomed throughout her entire being as she luxuriated in Adrianna's warmth.

Adrianna slowly touched her cheek to Erica's before leaning back. "Thank you for that incredible hug."

Erica's pager vibrated against her hip as she leaned her forehead against Adrianna's. "Thank you for your wonderful hug. Unfortunately, I should get going." Erica picked up the cooler bag and tablecloth and walked Adrianna to the doors of the ICU.

Erica handed Adrianna her things. "I almost forgot to ask you. Have you spoken to the Kirkland family today?"

Adrianna set the bag down beside her. "No, not yet. I was going to go see them this evening."

"The reason I ask is because I spoke to them earlier, and they were telling me that they would like to seek legal advice concerning their daughter's accident. They feel pretty lost, being from out of town. I asked their permission to speak to you about this. I thought maybe if you felt comfortable talking to them professionally, you could help them to seek the counsel they need."

"Of course, Erica. I would be happy to help them."

Erica reached out and touched her cheek with the soft pad of her thumb. "I knew you would. Thank you."

Adrianna reached up and touched her arm. "You're very welcome. Oh, I almost forgot. I want to show you something." She pulled a business card from the pocket of her slacks and handed it to Erica.

Erica looked at the card and read the date and time. "What's this?"

155

"It's my mammogram appointment. It's in eight weeks. You're welcome to come with me if it fits in with your schedule. If you would still like to do that."

Erica's smile deepened her eyes to a dark coral green. "Of course I still want to go with you. It has to be frightening to go to another mammogram appointment after what you've been through. I'll be there with you so you won't feel frightened or alone."

Adrianna was overwhelmed as she swallowed past the swell of emotion in her throat.

Erica gently brushed a stray strand of hair away from Adrianna's moist sapphire-blue eyes. "I'll come and check on you and Carolyn before I head home."

Adrianna nodded slowly as she watched Erica turn and head down the hallway toward the emergency department.

Erica rounded the corner and waved back at Adrianna through the glass wall. She thought to herself, "Maybe you're right, Michael. Maybe some rules are meant to be broken."

Adrianna was awestruck as she watched her walk away. She had spent the past two years pulling her life together after Hailey died. Those years of anguish and despair were slowly starting to loose their tenacious hold on her life. Now she was ready and strong enough to put her professional life in order. A step that would consume her entire being for the next several weeks. She had been preparing for this for a long time now. She was nowhere near prepared for what was happening. She was blindsided by her mother's diagnosis and completely enamored by her mother's neurosurgeon.

She hated being caught unaware and unprepared. She couldn't deal with everything that was happening. She needed to step back and put her energy where it was needed most. Something was going to suffer. She hoped and prayed it wasn't the woman that completely captured her heart.

Chapter 8

Two hours later, David stood in the doorway of Carolyn's room and hugged Adrianna tight. "I'll call you when I get home, Addie. Thanks for staying with your mom again."

"It's my pleasure, Dad. I wouldn't have it any other way. Please do call us when you get home, otherwise you know Mom will worry."

David leaned closer and kissed Adrianna's forehead. "I will, darling. Good night." David turned and blew Carolyn a kiss before heading out the door.

Adrianna returned to her chair at her mother's bedside. They talked about the surgery and their day's events. They turned as they heard a lot of commotion in the unit and looked up, seeing someone being wheeled in on a stretcher. The woman's face was covered in blood, and Adrianna saw the distress in Carolyn's face. She rose from her chair and pulled the curtain slowly across the glass wall and slid the glass door partially closed.

Carolyn took Adrianna's hand as she returned to her seat. "Thank you, Adrianna. That was awful."

They could hear Erica's calm, authoritative voice putting the nurses and residents into action.

Adrianna looked at her mother with concern. "It will be nice when you're ready to be transferred out of this ICU and into a regular room."

"I don't want to be transferred to another room, Adrianna. I want to be discharged home to my own bed."

Adrianna laughed at her mother's spirit. She lay in a hospital bed a day after brain surgery with her head wrapped tightly in a white bandage, exhausted eyes, a shade pale for her normal olive Italian skin and still that dynamic woman was ready to fight for what she wanted. "Take that up with Erica, Mom. I refuse to get in between the two of you."

"Chicken."

Adrianna glared at her mother as she held her hand close.

"Speaking of chicken, how did your picnic with Erica go?"

Adrianna shared the story with her mother. "She's a very special woman, Mom. I really care about her. We're going to the fundraiser together tomorrow night."

Carolyn's smile danced across her blue eyes. "How wonderful, Adrianna. I knew that she was special the moment I met her." Carolyn watched her daughter carefully. "Why do I get the feeling that there's a storm brewing in that beautiful head of yours, Adrianna?"

Adrianna ran her thumbnail along the seam of her armrest as she hesitated. "I'm not ready for this, Mom. I'm not ready to fall in love again. It's just bad timing right now, and I don't know if I can handle everything that's happening."

"I have to agree that the timing is terrible for you, Adrianna, with what is going on at work for you and my hospital stay. Before you know it, I'll be home and you can get on with your life and do the things you need to do."

"It's not that easy, Mom. I plan on dividing my time between you and work, so that leaves no room for anything or anyone else. You both are my priorities right now."

Carolyn brought Adrianna's hand to her lips and kissed it before holding it close to her heart. "What are you afraid of, Adrianna? What is it about Erica that has made you create excuses for keeping her at a safe distance?"

"Those are hardly excuses, Mom. You know my life better than anyone, and right now it's pretty hectic."

Carolyn squeezed Adrianna's hand. "That doesn't answer my question, Adrianna."

Adrianna leaned her head back against the headrest of her chair and closed her eyes. "It would never work, Mom. How can Erica accept my career choices? She's a doctor. I've sued doctors. That's quite a conflict of interest right there. How can she respect me as a person when I doubt she can respect what I do for a living?"

"Have you talked to Erica about those cases?"

"A little. We talked about Hailey's case."

"And how did she respond to Hailey's case?"

"She was pretty impressed by the fact that I used the winnings to build the Hailey Center. She didn't ask a lot of questions about the case itself."

"Then how do you know she disrespects your work?"

"Because she didn't ask a lot of questions, Mom. It's too close to home for her, and I don't think she wants to know all of the details. I think someone close to her has been through the experience, so she doesn't care to relive it."

"So because you sense that Erica has had a bad experience with a lawyer through this friend of hers, you feel she will clump you in with all lawyers."

"It's only natural, Mom. Most doctors avoid lawyers like the plague. Who can blame them with what I've uncovered over the past couple of years?"

"By any chance did you share any of your research and goals for the future with this doctor who hardly seems to feel you have the plague?"

Adrianna could not suppress a smile. She slipped her hand from Carolyn's and toyed with a button on her cuff. "No. What's the point, Mom? This would all be difficult for Erica to understand."

"You surprise me, Adrianna. You're the one who doesn't want to be judged only by the cases you take on, and you're doing the same thing to Erica. You're the one not giving her the benefit of the doubt here. I think you're grossly underestimating our Dr. Erica Beaumont. But you're right about one thing. She's only a brain surgeon. Your cases would be much too difficult for her to understand."

162

Adrianna shifted in her seat and stared at her mother. "You know what I mean, Mom. It's the emotional elements of the cases that I think will be difficult for Erica to understand."

"You don't know that lovely creature at all if that is how you see her, Adrianna. I think you're in for a wonderful surprise. The question is, are you willing to risk your heart at how she does respond to your world? I think the bottom line is that you're afraid to fall in love with Erica. You're afraid to open your heart to find the joy that could be there for the two of you. You have been through so much these past two years, Adrianna. Don't let the pain and grief of the past close your doors to future happiness. I want to see you in love again. Don't walk away from her before you even know what she thinks or feels about your world. That's the coward's way out, and you, my darling daughter, are far from a coward."

Adrianna leaned her head back in her chair. "I just can't handle Dr. Erica Beaumont right now, Mom. My feelings for her scare me. I haven't felt this way about another woman in a long time. I care about her so much that I don't want to hurt her or disappoint her. I need to sort out my life before I can make room for anyone else."

"All of your hard work over the past two years is going to pay off very soon, Adrianna. Everything in your life is going to finally fall into place because of all of your efforts. I know that you believe everything happens for a reason, so you have to believe that Erica has come into our lives for a reason."

"Yes, to remove your brain tumor."

"And to rock your world."

163

Adrianna turned in her chair and stared toward the curtained doorway. "That she has done already. That's for sure."

Carolyn ran her hand along Adrianna's hair. "Don't close any doors to possibilities, Addie. Regret is a terrible burden to carry. That is the last bit of advice your tired mom has to offer you today."

Carolyn snuggled deeper into her pillow as Adrianna stood to pull the covers up over her shoulders. She brushed her hand across her mother's head dressing and pressed her lips to her forehead. "I love you so much, Mom. Don't give up on me, okay?"

Carolyn turned her head and kissed Adrianna softly. "Why would I ever do that? I'm so proud of the woman you are. I just wish you believed in yourself half as much as I believe in you."

Adrianna kissed her mother's cheek. "Well, just keep believing for both of us, okay?"

Carolyn smiled as she touched Adrianna's face. "Always."

Adrianna stayed close as her mother drifted off to sleep, then quietly rose to turn out the light.

Adrianna slipped into her chair and leaned her head back as she thought of her mother's words.

The glass door slid open, and the curtain moved slightly.

Erica gave her a tired smile as she stepped into the room and knelt before her chair.

Adrianna leaned forward and touched Erica's arm. A swell of heat surged in her chest and tightened her throat. She longed to ease the concern in Erica's eyes and protect her from the emotions that battered her with each new patient. "Is your patient going to be okay? She looks badly injured."

"I'm sorry you had to see that. Is that why the curtain is pulled?"

"My mother was really upset by all the blood, so I closed the curtains."

Erica looked over at Carolyn sleeping peacefully. "Has David gone home?"

"Yes. He left a little while ago."

Erica turned to Adrianna. "My patient and her lover were broad sided by a drunk driver tonight. Her girlfriend is in the surgical intensive care unit and has multiple fractures of her legs. She should be okay, but my patient has a very serious head injury, and I fear the outcome."

"That's horrible, Erica. What happened to the drunk driver?"

"He died at the scene, just like the guy who killed Laura."

Adrianna was deeply moved by Erica's passion for her patients and her work. "Carolyn was so right when she said you're truly an angel sent from heaven. I look forward to tomorrow night and having the opportunity to take you away from all this for a night."

Erica leaned back slightly and touched Adrianna's soft cheek. "I'm really looking forward to tomorrow night. I respect and admire the way you've been here for Carolyn. I wish all my patients' families were as wonderful as your family. Your love for your mother is absolutely incredible, and I firmly believe it is one of the reasons why she has done so well. You're a special woman, Adrianna."

"We did get some help from Santa's replacement. I wanted the real thing to come into Carolyn's room and stop her seizures but it looks like his fill in has done a pretty remarkable job. Even though she can't find her red suit and reindeer."

Adrianna reached up and tucked back a loose ringlet falling across Erica's forehead. "I spoke to the Kirkland family after you left. I got them in touch with an excellent lawyer who lives in their area. They made an appointment to meet with her in two days. They seemed really pleased to have someone to talk to. My heart goes out to them. I can't imagine going through what they're dealing with."

"I know. It's one of the worst situations for any parent. Thank you for helping them. That means a lot to me that you went out of your way like that."

"It was my pleasure to be able to help."

Carolyn's sudden hacking cough interrupted their thoughts as Erica rose to her feet and stood over Carolyn. She laid her hand on her shoulder till her coughing subsided. "Are you all right, Carolyn? When did you start coughing like that?"

"That was the first time I coughed, Erica. Don't you dare start jumping to conclusions with that big, bright medical brain of yours."

Erica couldn't help but smile as she eased her stethoscope out of her lab coat pocket. "If you don't mind sitting up for me, Carolyn, I'd like to listen to your lungs."

Carolyn glared at Erica with those familiar menacing sapphire-blue eyes. She grudgingly obeyed her request as she muttered something in Italian.

Erica held her stethoscope in mid air. "What was that?"

"I said, don't you go looking for trouble, Dr. Beaumont. You took care of my brain tumor, and that's the end of it."

Erica slipped the stethoscope into her ears and leaned closer. "Humor my big, bright medical brain, would you, Carolyn?"

"Humph." Carolyn leaned forward and obediently began taking deep breaths.

Erica looked over Carolyn's head and loved the look of pure impish delight on Adrianna's face. "I can see that my Idiot's Guide to Learning Italian is going to be dog eared by the time the Taylor family leaves this fine establishment."

Carolyn picked up the end of Erica's stethoscope and spoke into the bell. "Hang on to that book, Erica. We are far from done with you."

Adrianna buried her laughter behind her hand as she winked at her mother.

Erica finished her assessment and folded her stethoscope into her pocket. She guided Carolyn to rest back into her pillows. "Your lungs sound excellent, Carolyn, but I'm going to order a chest x-ray for you in the morning. The last thing I want is for you to develop pneumonia while you're here."

Carolyn raised the head of her bed up higher. She tugged the sheet tightly to her waist before she folded her hands in her lap. "I won't develop pneumonia if you send me home."

Erica loved the defiant shrug of her shoulders. It left no doubt in her mind who fostered Adrianna's feisty spirit. She sat on the edge of Carolyn's bed.

167

"Nothing against your wonderful care and superb company, Erica, but I'm getting a little tired of being here. I don't want to be transferred to another room, I want to be transferred to my bedroom at home."

Erica folded her arms across her chest and watched Carolyn intently. "Are you quite finished, Mrs. Taylor?"

"No! When can I go home, Dr. Beaumont?"

Erica smiled. "You can put that pout away, Carolyn, because it's not going to help you here. We talked about this before your surgery. I told you I would like to keep you in the ICU for several days after your surgery to watch you closely for any complications, then when I feel you're ready, I will transfer you to the neurosurgical ward for several more days just to make sure everything goes well."

"But Erica, I feel great, and I've not had another seizure thanks to your wonderful care. My headaches are completely gone, and oh please, can I go home sooner than that?"

Erica listened to Carolyn's plea as she turned to Adrianna. "Now I know where you get your stubborn, argumentative streak."

Mother and daughter smiled at each other.

Erica folded her hands in her lap. "Let's make a deal here." Carolyn's face lit up. "I'm scheduled in the operating room tomorrow morning. After I am done, which will be around one o'clock, I'll come and look at your chest x-ray. If everything looks good and you have had another good night, then I will transfer you to the neurosurgical ward tomorrow afternoon. Then you will promise me that you will spend two days there without argument, and then on the third day we'll discuss whether you are ready to go home with David or not. Is that a deal?"

"Oh, Erica, that would be wonderful," Carolyn said as she leaned forward and gave her a big hug and kissed her cheek.

Erica blushed as Carolyn touched her crimson cheek. "Thank you, Erica. You're truly my angel."

Adrianna rolled her eyes and shook her head. "Here we go with the Mother Teresa image again."

Erica squeezed Carolyn's hand. "I should get home. I'll see you tomorrow morning before I head into the operating room." Erica hugged Carolyn before rising to her feet.

Adrianna rose from her chair. "I'll walk you out, Erica, so you can give me directions to your home for tomorrow night."

"That would be wonderful. We'll be in the garden if you're looking for Adrianna, Carolyn." Erica left with Adrianna and waved good-bye.

Erica held the glass door open to the garden for Adrianna and watched her slender figure as she followed her through. Erica guided Adrianna to their secluded table among the dwarf palm trees. She held a chair out for her as she watched her take her seat.

"You handled my mother beautifully, Erica. Not many people can go toe to toe with Carolyn."

Erica leaned back in her chair and folded her hands in her lap. "It seems that both Taylor women are determined to test my patience and perseverance while they're here."

Adrianna gave Erica a coy look. "Who are you kidding, Dr. Beaumont? You love a good challenge, and that's why Carolyn and I have walked into your life."

Erica leaned forward and placed her hands on the wrought iron table. "I know why Carolyn has walked into my life, but you, Adrianna, I don't think I've quite figured out yet."

Adrianna stared into those coral-green eyes and felt drawn to their depth of sensuality and tenderness. Her heart beat an erratic pace as she reminded herself to breathe. The fluttering sensation in her belly flourished into a smoldering heat that spread deep to her thighs. She had to break the contact with those spellbinding eyes and shift in her seat to dissipate that burning sensation. "I guess you're just going to have to take some time to figure me out."

Erica reached into the pocket of her lab coat and pulled out a folded piece of pink paper. She unfolded it before Adrianna and laid it on the table before her. "Okay. Let's start with tomorrow night." Erica tapped the pink paper. "I wrote out the directions to my house for you." Erica went over the map carefully, and they decided to meet at five o'clock.

Adrianna folded the directions and slipped them into the pocket of her slacks. "Thank you for these directions. I'll be here tomorrow after lunch to make sure Carolyn gets settled into her new room, so I'll see you then."

Erica leaned back slightly. "That doesn't allow you a lot of time to sleep."

"Sleep has not been a big priority this week. My mother has. My Dad has been here all day and he said he'd be back early in the morning so I can go home and get some sleep. I'm hoping that life will fall back into a more sane pattern once my mother gets home."

"Somehow I think your life is no more sane than mine." Erica slowly rose from her chair and extended her hand to Adrianna. "Come on. Let me walk you back inside."

Adrianna slid her hand into Erica's and slowly rose from her chair. Her hand felt immersed in the warm strength of Erica's as she tried to focus on standing and not the jolting arousal flowing from their joined hands. Adrianna cautiously removed her hand and started walking ahead of Erica, craving the tenderness and sensuality she felt in that simple touch.

They walked through the glass double doors and stood together in the hallway. Erica guided Adrianna around the corner to allow room for the cart full of IV pumps to pass through.

They leaned back against the wall as Erica touched a strand of Adrianna's thick, dark brown hair and brushed it over her shoulder. She watched it slip from between her fingers and wished she could bury her hand in that mass of flowing hair and hold her close in her arms. "Good night, Adrianna."

Adrianna swallowed past the lump in her throat as she toyed with the lapel on Erica's lab coat. "Good night, Erica. Sleep well."

"I will. I hope you can get some rest tonight. I'll feel better when Carolyn is out of the unit and I know you're getting more sleep. I worry about you."

"You worry about my sleep, and I worry about your tummy. We make a great pair, don't we?"

Erica touched Adrianna's chin with her fingertips. "I should go. I'll see you tomorrow." Erica stared at

Adrianna's moist, full, pouty lower lip and gently touched it with the soft pad of her thumb. The burning ache in her chest threatened to consume her as she abruptly took a step back. She jammed her hands in the pockets of her slacks as she tried to calm the raging need gripping her lower belly. "Good night, Adrianna." She turned quickly and headed down the hall and out of sight.

Adrianna leaned back heavily against the wall and buried her face in her hands. "Oh, God, Erica how am I ever going to make you understand?"

Chapter 9

The musical tune of her pager awakened Erica from a deep sleep. She looked at her alarm clock and groaned, four-thirty in the morning. Erica grabbed her pager and read the number. She reached for her bedside phone and hit autodial for the NICU.

One of the residents answered the phone. "I'm sorry for waking you so early, Dr. Beaumont. It's our female patient that was broadsided by the drunk driver. She's blown a pupil, and we're going to take her down for a repeat CAT scan."

"I'll be there shortly." Erica hung up the phone and jumped out of bed, hurrying to take a quick shower.

The cardiac arrest announcement shrilled throughout the hospital for the second time. "Code Blue, NICU, room ten. Code Blue, NICU, room ten." In an adrenaline rush, Erica barged into the unit and into the room of the patient who'd been broadsided by the drunk driver. The room was filled to capacity with four nurses, two respiratory therapists, three residents, and the cardiac arrest cart. Making her way to the foot

173

of the bed, Erica looked at the cardiac monitor and saw that her patient's heart rhythm was ominous. The nurses slapped the defibrillator pads on her chest and charged the defibrillator to two hundred joules as Erica ordered, "Shock her!"

Adrianna stood against the wall in her mother's darkened room and watched the drama unfolding on the other side of the unit. She watched in amazement as Erica calmly directed everyone's activities around her patient.

Adrianna gasped as she watched the patient's arm's lurch off her bed and drop down like a rag doll's. She watched it happen two more times and felt anguish for the patient and her partner.

It was forty-five minutes before Adrianna saw Erica run her fingers through her own hair in frustration and then tell everyone to stop. A few minutes later, Adrianna watched Erica and her residents leave the patient's room and step into the nurses' station.

Erica dropped the patient's chart onto the counter and ran her hands through her thick hair. She looked around and saw the defeated look on the faces of the residents and nurses. "You guys did a good job. We were fighting a losing battle here, and there is nothing that we could have done for her with her massive head injury." Erica sighed and leaned back against the counter. "This is really a blessing for her. I don't cherish telling her partner that she has lost her." Erica looked at her residents' distraught faces and felt their sense of failure. "You guys did a terrific job here. You did everything you could do. There's nothing more that any of us could have done. I know the outcome sucks, but we could not have prevented the inevitable."

Her residents smiled weakly at her compliment amidst the sadness that they felt for another young life lost.

Erica sighed and rubbed her weary eyes. "I'd better go tell her partner. Waiting isn't making this any easier." Erica looked at the wall clock behind the nurses' station and saw that it was six thirty. "Please let Peter and Sarah know we'll start rounds as soon as I get back." Erica handed one of the residents the patient's chart and headed toward Carolyn's room. Erica walked into the darkened room and allowed her eyes to adjust. Carolyn was sleeping peacefully; Adrianna stood against the far wall. Erica pulled the curtain across the glass wall.

"I'm so sorry, Erica."

She stood before Adrianna. "Yeah, me too. I wish it didn't have to be this way. I saw you standing in here. I just wanted to come in and make sure you were both okay."

"I'm okay. Carolyn was exhausted and has been asleep for the past several hours. I know I shouldn't have been watching. I'm sorry."

Erica reached up and touched her slender shoulder. "Don't apologize. It's hard not to watch something as dramatic as that. I should go and talk to her partner."

Adrianna reached out and placed her hands on Erica's elbows. "Go do what you have to do and know that I'm here for you."

Erica smiled before she eased away and walked out the door.

****

An hour later, Adrianna overheard Sarah ask Peter if he had seen Erica. "She just finished talking to the patient's partner and her family. She said she was going to go and collect her thoughts before we start rounds."

Adrianna felt deeply concerned for Erica. She checked that Carolyn was still sleeping comfortably and slipped out of her mother's room and into the garden. The early morning sun felt warm against her face as she looked around and headed toward their favorite table.

Adrianna saw Erica sitting forward in the wrought iron chair, with her elbows resting on her knees and her head in her hands. Adrianna dropped to her knees before her. Erica lifted her face, and Adrianna was moved by her tears. She slid her hands onto Erica's elbows and guided her to her feet. Her tears constricted the air in her chest and tore at her heart as she yearned to comfort her. She guided Erica into her arms and held her tight, allowing her to release her tears.

Adrianna leaned against her damp cheek and nuzzled against her face. "You're such a teddy bear. How did such an emotionally sensitive woman get into such a heart-wrenching profession?"

Erica laughed softly as she wiped her tears. "A moment of temporary insanity."

Adrianna laughed, then touched Erica's moist cheek. "A moment! You must have spent seven years specializing to be a neurosurgeon, and you call that a moment of temporary insanity? How in the world do you stand your job in situations like that?"

"The devastating cases make me appreciate the successful ones all the more. Besides, being Santa's replacement has its perks, you know. Who else gets a parking spot marked for Santa's sleigh only?"

They laughed together as Erica caressed Adrianna's cheek. She looked into Adrianna's eyes. "I'm so glad you're here."

Adrianna enveloped her in her arms and held her close as she ached to help Erica shed her pain.

Erica hugged Adrianna close, then guided her to sit on the chair beside her.

Adrianna laid her hand on Erica's thigh. "This was too close to home, wasn't it? This patient must have brought back your horrible memories of Laura's death, and that must be so difficult to deal with all over again."

Erica made an attempt to smile, then shook her head. "Same mechanism of injury, same age, similar injuries, and one partner left behind to carry the grief and heartache. Once again, there was nothing I could do but watch this woman slip away. The patient died of a massive intracerebral hemorrhage. They were even both in their thirties."

"I heard you say it was inevitable and a blessing for her, so you have to start listening to your own pep talks. If you did everything you could do, then you know in your heart that this was meant to be."

Erica smiled at Adrianna's words. "Hey, I'm supposed to be the one boosting the morale around here."

They both laughed as Adrianna leaned closer to Erica. "You once told me that you thought I had a tough time letting someone else take care of me and relinquishing a tiny bit of self-control. Well, my dear, I do believe we are cut from the same cloth."

Adrianna took Erica's hand and held it on her thigh. "How did her lover handle the news?"

"I think she handled it better than I did. She told me that she feels there is a meaning to her lover's death because just before the drunk driver hit them, a song came on the radio that they had dedicated to each other at their commitment ceremony. They played that song as they vowed till death do us part, and that's when they were hit. She actually felt her partner's spirit leave her in the car before the firemen arrived to pull them out. She told me that she felt that her partner had died in the car, so this was not a big shock to her."

Erica leaned back in the chair. "I sure as hell hope there is a meaning to her death and the death of Laura and Hailey because none of this makes sense to my mind."

Adrianna brushed away a stray ringlet from her damp eyes. "Maybe you and I need to step into that church and help each other find the deeper meaning of death."

Erica looked into Adrianna's eyes. "I feel so grateful to have you in my life and to have you as a friend." Erica gently squeezed Adrianna's hand. "I should get back in there and start my rounds before they think I was kidnapped by a beautiful blue-eyed maiden."

Adrianna laughed and stared into Erica's moist emerald eyes. "I would just love to kidnap you right now and take you away from all this emotional stress."

Erica leaned forward in her chair and took both of Adrianna's hands in hers. "Thank you, Adrianna, for your kindness and for being here for me."

"You're very welcome. You've certainly been there for me these past several days. I've appreciated all the support you gave me even though I didn't always show it." Adrianna stood before Erica and guided her to her feet. "Come with me, Dr. Beaumont. Let's get you inside to your other patients. There are so many people that need you." Erica took her hand and followed her back inside.

****

Adrianna spent the next hour helping Carolyn bathe and change her nightgown. Sarah changed the linen on her bed as David assisted Carolyn into her floral robe. They walked with her around the ICU several times before guiding her into the high-back chair.

Adrianna pulled up a chair beside her while Sarah reattached Carolyn to her cardiac monitor and checked her vital signs. "Everything looks great, Carolyn. I'm so happy to see how well you did walking around the unit. Adrianna and David didn't even need to help you very much."

David pulled his chair in closer and kissed Carolyn's cheek. "I'm so proud of you."

Ana Corman

Carolyn smiled and straightened her robe over her legs. "It felt wonderful to get up and walk around again."

Sarah smiled as she folded back her blanket and straightened her bedside table. She picked up the framed picture of a beautiful blonde, blue-eyed little girl. "Is this your granddaughter?"

"Yes, it is. That's Leah's daughter, Amanda. She just turned four. I miss her so much. I can't wait to see her again."

Sarah returned the photo to Carolyn's beside table. "You keep going at this pace, Carolyn, and it won't be long at all before Amanda can come and visit you. Now, you look great sitting up. Can I do anything else for you?"

"Not at all, Sarah. Thank you for all of your help."

"You're very welcome. Call if you need anything."

"We will, thank you."

Sarah checked Carolyn's vital signs and head dressing one final time before she stepped out of the room.

Adrianna reached inside her mother's overnight bag and pulled out a tube of her favorite vanilla hand cream. She popped the top and poured a generous amount into the palm of her mother's hand.

"Thank you so much, darling. This place is disastrous to my youthful skin."

Adrianna laughed as she spread some on her own hands and placed the tube on the over-bed table.

David nodded toward the doorway. "It looks like they've come for Nicole Kirkland."

180

They all looked through the glass wall and watched for several minutes as the O.R. crew came and gathered all of Nicole's equipment. She watched as Mr. and Mrs. Kirkland bent down to her and kissed her for the last time. They wept and held each other tight as they watched their daughter being wheeled out of her room and through the large automatic double doors.

As the crowd left with Nicole, Adrianna saw Erica walk toward James and Madeleine Kirkland and touch them both. She guided them into nearby chairs and stayed to share their grief.

David leaned forward in his chair. "God, that must be awful."

Carolyn brushed away her own tears. "That would be my worst nightmare."

Adrianna reached into her mother's bag and pulled out a new box of tissues and pulled one out for both of them. "I can't begin to imagine what they're going through."

They saw Erica help the Kirklands gather their things and walk them to the door. Adrianna stood and squeezed her mother's shoulder. "I'm going to say good-bye."

"Please do, Adrianna. Tell them we'll pray for them."

"I will, Mom. I'll be right back."

Adrianna slowly approached the Kirklands. She watched Erica hug Madeleine. She stood at a respectful distance until their eyes met. Madeleine stepped toward Adrianna.

"I just wanted to say how sorry my family and I are for your loss. You're both so brave for what you've done. We'll pray for you and the people that are blessed to receive these gifts from Nicole."

Madeleine stepped into Adrianna's arms and hugged her tight. "Thank you. We could use your prayers right now. I'll also pray for your mother's speedy recovery."

"Thank you. That would mean a lot to my mother."

They held each other's hands as Madeleine tried her best to smile through her tears. She squeezed Adrianna's hands one final time and stepped toward her husband. She linked her hand in his and secured her purse over her shoulder. She looked into his eyes. "I'm ready to go now."

They both waved good-bye and headed out through the doors of the NICU for the last time.

Erica stepped in beside Adrianna and slipped her arm across her shoulders and pulled her in close. Adrianna slid her arm around Erica's slender waist and leaned into her side. She looked up into Erica's moist, vibrant green eyes and wiped at her own tears. "That's so awful."

"It sure is. One family is mourning while several others are rejoicing for the organs they are about to receive. It's such extremes in emotions."

Adrianna shook her head and reached in her pocket for more tissues. "I don't know how you deal with all this, Erica, and still have so much more to give to the rest of your patients."

Erica turned and faced Adrianna. "Some days are better than others, but this situation makes being kidnapped by a blue-eyed maiden seem really appealing at this very moment."

Adrianna could not help but smile through her tears.

Ana Corman

Chapter 10

Carolyn pulled a tissue from the pocket of her floral robe and leaned her head back against the high-back chair. She laughed as Adrianna cursed softly in Italian. It was the fourth time in an hour they had been interrupted by Adrianna's cell phone. She watched her read the message displayed on her cell phone and snap the cover closed.

"It's the office again, Mom. I'll just call and see what Molly needs." Adrianna picked up the receiver on Carolyn's bedside phone and dialed her office. "Hi, Molly. It's me. What's up?" Adrianna listened for several minutes.

Carolyn watched her massage her temple as her foot started swinging faster. She knew it was difficult for Adrianna to spend so much time away from work but knew she could not convince her to go to the office. She could be very stubborn, and this time Carolyn loved her for it.

"That's fine, Molly. Reschedule those appointments for next week and overnight those briefs

and the paperwork you want me to sign to my house.
I'll take care of it and get it back to you in the next
couple of days."

Adrianna reached for the pad of paper and pen on
Carolyn's over-bed table and wrote down several
names and phone numbers. "I'll return these clients'
phone calls this afternoon, Molly. Thanks for covering
for me and rearranging my schedule on such short
notice. You're the best secretary a girl could ask for."

Adrianna laughed as she slipped the pen and paper
into her purse. "I owe you more than lunch, Molly. I
owe you a vacation. I will give Carolyn your love.
Thanks again, Molly. I'll talk to you tomorrow.
Good-bye."

Adrianna replaced the receiver in its cradle.
"Molly said to give you a hug and all of her love."
Adrianna looked at Carolyn and followed her gaze to
the woman standing in the doorway. "Dr. Abby
Cooper." Adrianna walked toward Abby and hugged
her close.

Carolyn watched this beautiful stranger with her
daughter and read the stitching on her crisp, white lab
coat. "Dr. Abigail Cooper. Cardiologist. Why in the
world is there a cardiologist in my room? I don't need
a cardiologist. There's nothing wrong with my heart.
Erica never said anything about my heart, did she,
Adrianna?"

Adrianna laughed and guided Abby into the room.
"Relax, Mom. Abby is a cardiologist, but she's not
here to see you professionally. Erica introduced me to
Abby yesterday. Abby has been a friend of Erica's for
thirty years."

Carolyn looked up at Abby. "What, did you meet in the womb?"

Abby and Adrianna burst into laughter. "You're right, Adrianna. She's a character."

Adrianna guided Abby to take her chair as she sat on the edge of her mother's bed. "You just missed my dad, Abby. He stepped out to get us some lunch. He should be back shortly."

Abby slipped into Adrianna's chair and faced Carolyn. "I'd love to meet him. I had some spare time before lunch, so I just stopped by to meet you and say hello to Adrianna. Purely personal reasons, I promise."

Carolyn reached out and laid her hand on Abby's arm. "All right then, Dr. Abigail Cooper. It's a pleasure to meet you if you promise you have only come to visit with Adrianna and me."

Abby placed her hand over her heart. "Scout's honor. I have come to visit with both of you. I promise not to use my stethoscope on either one of you. But if you don't stop looking at me like I'm the Wicked Witch of the West, then I'll be forced to put you through my most rigorous stress test."

"Don't you dare. My Erica will be very cross with you if you do anything to increase my intracranial pressure."

Abby turned to Adrianna. "'My Erica'? What's that? 'My Erica'?"

"Nauseating, isn't it? They're wrapped around each other's baby fingers."

Abby and Adrianna rolled their eyes as Carolyn smiled. They sat close together, talking about Carolyn's surgery and her steady recovery.

187

"The other reason I came to visit besides scaring you to death, Carolyn, is to ask Adrianna if it's okay if Trina and I meet you at Erica's tonight before heading to the Biltmore? We thought we would follow each other from there."

"That would be terrific, Abby. Why don't we drive down together in one vehicle?"

"I'm on call tonight, so we thought we would take separate cars in case I had to leave."

"That makes sense."

Abby reached into her lab coat pocket and pulled out a business card. She handed it to Adrianna. "That's my card, and on the back I wrote my pager number and our home number. In case you should ever need it or just want to give us a call. I wanted you to have that."

Adrianna looked up from the card and smiled at Abby. "Thanks, Abby. I really appreciate having your numbers." Adrianna slipped off her mother's bed and reached inside her purse. She pulled out a business card and a pen and wrote her home and cottage phone number on the back. She turned and handed it to Abby. "And that's for you and Trina. I want you both to have my numbers."

Abby took the card and slipped it into the breast pocket of her lab coat. "We'll have these numbers programmed into autodial mode before you know it." Abby slid forward in her chair and faced Carolyn. "It was a pleasure meeting you, Mrs. Taylor. I hope we meet again soon in much better surroundings than this."

Carolyn squeezed her hand. "It was a pleasure meeting Erica's womb mate. You must come and visit with us when we are out of this fine institution. I'd much rather visit with women who do not wear their specialties embroidered across their chests."

Abby laughed and stood before Carolyn's cardiac monitor. She stared at her cardiac rhythm and tapped the screen with her fingernail. "I don't like the looks of this, Carolyn. This is quite worrisome."

Abby turned just as Carolyn whacked her across the bottom with the pillow off her bed. "I'll give you something to worry about, Dr. Abigail Cooper, if you spend so much as another second staring at my perfect heart rhythm. I'll have Erica paged in here so fast and I'll tell her you're the cause of my chest pain. You'll be so sorry you messed with my Erica and me."

Abby stepped toward the door. "Oh, I'm so scared." She winked. "See you tonight, Adrianna."

"Bye, Abby. See you tonight."

Abby turned to leave as David walked in the room with a bag of food in each hand. Abby was impressed by his thick wavy, silver hair, and warmed by his deep tan and bright, natural smile. "You must be Mr. Taylor."

David handed Adrianna the bags of food and extended his hand to Abby. "Yes, I am. Please call me David." David leaned closer and read the stitching on Abby's lab coat. "And you are Dr. Abigail Cooper, Cardiologist." David turned and looked at Carolyn. "Are you all right, sweetheart?"

Abby was touched by his genuine concern. "I'm starting to feel very unwelcomed by this family."

Adrianna laughed and stood next to her father. "Everything's fine, Dad. Abby is a friend of Erica's.

Abby and her partner, Trina, will be joining Erica and me at the fundraiser tonight."

David placed his hand over his heart. "Thank God. I thought something had happened with your mother's heart while I was gone." David turned and smiled at Abby. "I'm glad to hear you're not here on official business, Abby."

"I hope to see this family only on a personal level, David. Especially since your wife already smacked me on the bottom with a pillow when I commented on her heart rhythm."

David smiled at Carolyn. "That sounds like my girl."

Adrianna opened the bag of sandwiches. "Abby, it looks like my dad brought enough sandwiches to feed the entire unit. Why don't you take one with you? Do you prefer tuna or chicken salad?"

Carolyn watched David slip into the seat beside her and reached for his hand. "Make sure you leave a chicken salad sandwich for Erica. It's her favorite."

Abby and Adrianna rolled their eyes. Abby reached for the chicken salad sandwich in Adrianna's hand. "In that case I'll take the whole bag of chicken salad sandwiches."

"Not if you don't want to feel that pillow meet your bottom again, Dr. Abigail Cooper."

Abby laughed as Adrianna walked her to the door. "Thank you for the sandwich, David. I'll go find Erica and tell her I took the last one."

They all laughed as Abby heard Carolyn say something she did not understand. She stared at her before turning to Adrianna. "What did she just say?"

"When you find Erica and tell her you ate her lunch, you might want to ask her if you can borrow her Complete Idiot's Guide to Learning Italian."

They all burst into laughter as Abby waved and headed out the door.

❋❋❋❋

Erica completed the operative note on the spinal cord tumor she removed from her patient, closed the chart, and handed it to the recovery room nurse.

She checked her watch and saw that it was already one thirty in the afternoon. She checked the patient one final time and headed out of the recovery room.

Erica turned the corner toward the NICU. She saw Grant and Leah standing outside the doors of the unit. Wrapped around one of Grant's legs was a beautiful, blonde, blue-eyed little girl. Erica greeted Grant and Leah before squatting down before the girl. "You must be Amanda. Your Aunt Adrianna told me how much she loves you."

Amanda gave Erica a smile, then buried her face against Grant's thigh and hung on to his leg.

Leah knelt down beside Erica. "Amanda, this is Dr. Erica Beaumont. She is the doctor that made Grandma all better."

Amanda turned her wide-eyed face to Erica. "Thank you for making my grandma better, Dr. Erica."

"You're welcome, Amanda." Erica noticed the strip of stickers held firmly in Amanda's tiny hand. "Are those stickers you have there? I love stickers."

Amanda slipped from her father's security and stepped tentatively toward Erica to show her the strip of red, glimmering heart stickers. "Would you like one, Dr. Erica?"

"I would love one of your stickers, Amanda. I would even wear it on my hospital identification badge, if you would be so kind as to put it on for me." Erica unclipped her badge and held it for Amanda as they all watched her peel a sticker and apply it to Erica's badge. Erica clipped her badge back on her lab coat and held it out for everyone to admire. "Thank you, Amanda. Now I have the prettiest badge in the whole hospital. I think you deserve a hug for your kindness."

Grant and Leah stood together and smiled as they watched their daughter bounce into Erica's arms. Amanda squeezed Erica's neck tight and gave her a wet kiss on the cheek.

Erica held the child close. "I bet if you give your grandma a hug and kiss like that every day, then she can't help but get better and better."

Erica watched Amanda's huge blue eyes sadden and a familiar Taylor family pout form on her lower lip. "I can't give Grandma a hug right now because I'm only four years old, and Mommy and Daddy said I'm too little to go into Grandma's room. I have to wait here till Grandma is moved to her new room, then I can visit with her."

Erica smiled at Amanda's expressive face. "We do have rules about children in the intensive care unit, but since your grandma is itching to see you, I think we can make an exception in your case." Erica leaned close to Amanda's ear and whispered, "Here's my plan."

****

Carolyn had just returned from her walk around the unit with David and Adrianna and was repositioning herself in the reclining chair. Sarah had finished reconnecting her to the cardiac monitor and left the room. David pulled a chair up for Adrianna and one for himself and sat on the other side of his wife. He leaned in close and kissed her rosy cheek. "I'm so proud of you. It's so great to see you up walking. We'll let you rest for a while, and I'll see if Sarah will let me take you outside for some fresh air."

Carolyn reached up and touched her husband's face. "I would just love that, sweetheart. And maybe you can park the car near a convenient exit and I can just slip inside and we can drive home and go for a walk down our own street. What do you think?"

David and Adrianna burst into laughter.

"She's been pushing to have Erica send her home since last night. It'll be a fascinating battle to see who will be victorious in the end."

David took Carolyn's hand and brushed a kiss across her wrist. "We'll go home when Erica says you're ready to go home. Okay?"

Carolyn frowned at her husband and leaned back in her chair. "I can see I'm not going to get any support from the people who profess to love me the most."

David smiled and kissed the back of Carolyn's hand. "Those of us who profess to love you the most want the best for you, and that's why we are going to listen to Erica."

Carolyn huffed at her husband. "What does that young pup know anyway?"

Adrianna narrowed her eyes at her mother. "Oh, yeah, now you're starting to come around to my way of thinking. Where were you when I was butting heads with that beautiful young pup?"

David and Carolyn laughed. They looked toward the doorway and watched Leah and Grant slip into the room, looking all around the doorway.

Carolyn looked at David in bewilderment. "What in the world are you two doing, and where's my grandbaby if you two are in here?"

Grant held his finger to his lips for everyone to be very quiet, and he signaled outside the room.

Erica tiptoed into the room behind him with Amanda snuggled in her arms. Carolyn squealed with delight as Erica placed Amanda in her lap. She stepped back and watched Amanda hug her grandma tight.

Erica crouched down beside Adrianna's chair and smiled with the glee of a mischievous child. She admired her thick dark brown hair bouncing at her shoulders and the way her black, short-sleeved dress flowed against her body and accentuated her slender, feminine curves. "You look absolutely radiant."

"Thank you for the compliment and for smuggling Amanda in here. Carolyn has been dying to see her."

"It was my pleasure, but if it tarnishes my Mother Teresa image, there will be hell to pay."

Adrianna looked over Erica's shoulder to the doorway. "Oh, oh. I think the guardian of the gate has arrived."

Erica slowly turned around and watched Sarah step into the room. "Oh, oh is right. I think I'm about to get a dent in my halo."

194

Sarah dramatically cleared her throat, and everyone looked at her.

Carolyn sat Amanda in her lap. "Amanda, this is my wonderful nurse, Sarah."

Sarah knelt beside Carolyn's chair. "You're such a beautiful little girl, Amanda. We know that your grandma is so happy to see you. She even has a picture of you on her bedside table."

Amanda smiled brightly at her grandma.

"Tell me, Amanda, how did you manage to get in here without us seeing you? Did you float in like a beautiful butterfly, or did you magically appear like a fairy princess?"

Amanda giggled and looked directly at Erica. "Dr. Erica hid me in her lab coat and snuck me into Grandma's room. She said if the nurses caught me, to give you one of my heart stickers and you would let me stay."

Sarah turned and scowled at Erica as she dropped her eyes and grinned sheepishly.

Erica raised her hand and pretended to look shocked. "I've never seen this child before in my life."

Amanda looked confused as she looked up at Erica. "That's not true, Dr. Erica. We met outside in the hallway."

Everyone laughed at Amanda's honesty. Erica buried her head in guilt and luxuriated in the sound of Adrianna's giggles.

"I even put a heart sticker on Dr. Erica's picture card. Show them, Dr. Erica."

Erica unclipped her hospital identification badge and showed everyone her new heart sticker.

Sarah turned to Amanda and smiled. "I would love one of your stickers, Amanda, and as long as you promise to be good you can stay here with your grandma."

Amanda clapped her hands together with glee, then peeled off a sticker for Sarah. Sarah helped her place it on her identification badge and thanked her for the sticker.

Sarah rose and stood before Erica. She loved the warm, playful look in Erica's eyes as she tugged on her badge and pulled her even closer. "Queens have been beheaded for lesser crimes than this, so I would watch how many precious children you smuggle into this unit, Dr. Beaumont." Sarah let the badge drop against Erica's chest and walked out of the room with a royal wave.

Adrianna laughed at Sarah's regal exit.

Erica looked down at her and narrowed her eyes. "I'm threatened with a beheading and you laugh." Erica took one step toward Amanda and picked her up in her strong arms. "You squealed on me, you little tattletale." She placed Amanda on Carolyn's bed and proceeded to tickle her into a fit of laughter.

Erica let Amanda catch her breath and calm down. Carolyn took the moment to tug once on her lab coat. "Dr. Beaumont, when can I get transferred out of here? I walked around this unit half a dozen times and I'm ready to walk home if you don't get me out."

Amanda stood on the bed behind Erica and wrapped her arms around her neck as Erica held her arms securely. "Your chest x-ray is here in the unit. I'll go and look at it now."

Carolyn looked at Erica indignantly. "You mean you haven't seen it yet? As your favorite patient, I expect to be your number one priority." Carolyn folded her arms across her chest. "What have you been doing all morning, Dr. Beaumont?"

Erica pulled Amanda into her lap and gave Carolyn a menacing look. "I have been up since four thirty this morning. One of my patients died, and I have operated on two other patients. That's a synopsis of my morning, Mrs. Carolyn Taylor. Don't push my buttons, or I'll keep you here in this unit for another day."

"Please don't torture me like that, Erica."

Erica eased Amanda off the bed and took her hand. "Come on, Amanda. Let's go look at your grandma's chest x-ray before I send her to the time-out corner."

Amanda looked up at Erica with a shocked expression. "Do you have a time-out corner here too, Dr. Erica?"

"We sure do, Amanda. Your Aunt Adrianna knows it well."

Everyone burst into laughter as Erica winked at Adrianna.

"If you would hurry up and look at my chest x-ray, Dr. Beaumont, we might be able to find you a chicken salad sandwich in this bag of food David brought."

Erica looked down at Amanda waiting patiently at her side. "Let's hurry then, Amanda."

Amanda gripped Erica's hand and waved at everyone. "Good-bye, everybody. I'm going with Dr. Erica to look at Grandma's chestray."

Erica stopped in the doorway. "Chest x-ray, Amanda. Repeat it after me. Chest x-ray." Erica walked out of the room with Amanda as they all heard her voice repeating, "Chest x-ray. Chest x-ray."

Erica and Amanda returned fifteen minutes later. Amanda had on an O.R. cap and O.R. shoe covers. Erica had found her an extra small O.R. shirt and draped her stethoscope around the little girl's neck to make it official.

Amanda twirled slowly for everyone to see her ensemble as Erica stood by her. Amanda stopped and held Erica's hand. "Now I'm a doctor like Dr. Erica."

Adrianna stepped in beside Erica. "Hey, I thought you wanted to be a lawyer like me."

Amanda reached her other hand toward Adrianna. "I do, Aunt Addie. Can I be a doctor and a lawyer?"

"You have to choose one or the other, Amanda, because only nice people can be doctors," Erica interjected quickly.

Adrianna poked Erica's ribs as she giggled and quickly moved away. Adrianna took Amanda into her arms and scowled at Erica. "You can be whatever you want to be, sweetheart. Don't listen to Dr. Erica."

Erica leaned in close and readjusted Amanda's O.R. cap, "Amanda, I love the way you say 'Aunt Addie.'"

Adrianna looked at Amanda lovingly and kissed her forehead. "When Amanda started to talk, she could never say Adrianna and adopted Addie instead. That has always stuck."

Erica watched Adrianna hug her niece close.

Carolyn cleared her throat and interrupted them. "Well, my dear, Dr. Beaumont. What's the good word on my chest x-ray?"

"After conferring with my colleague, Dr. Amanda, we decided that your chest x-ray looks excellent, and therefore I will write your transfer orders to the floor." Erica stepped toward a gleeful Carolyn, helped her out of her chair, and bent to give her a big hug.

Adrianna watched their warmth as she sat on the edge of Carolyn's bed and held Amanda in her lap.

Carolyn touched Erica's cheek. "Thank you for everything, Erica. You will remain in my heart and in my life forever."

Erica was overwhelmed by Carolyn's love as she smiled shyly. "You're very welcome, Carolyn."

Carolyn reached into the pocket of her robe, pulling out a small gift-wrapped box and handed it to Erica.

"What's this?"

"Open it and you'll see. It's a gift from me to you."

Erica looked over at Adrianna.

"Go ahead and open it, Erica," Adrianna said.

Erica opened the gift and pulled out a sparkling crystal angel pin. Carolyn took it from her and pinned it to the lapel of her lab coat. "It's a fitting gift for you, Erica, because you're truly my angel."

Erica took Carolyn into her arms and hugged her close.

✻✻✻✻

Sarah pushed Carolyn in a wheelchair as David, Grant and Leah carried her belongings. They headed down the hall to the neurosurgical ward and Carolyn's new room.

199

Amanda was walking between Erica and Adrianna, firmly hanging on to each of their hands and skipping. Erica looked across at Adrianna and smiled. "You look great for someone who couldn't have had much sleep today."

Sarah turned slightly to look at them both. "What are you talking about? Adrianna has only been gone one hour this morning since she arrived here last evening. Isn't that true, Carolyn?"

"Sure is. She only left long enough this morning to go home and shower and change. She was back in no time. I told her to stay home and sleep because David was coming in this morning, but you all know what it's like trying to get a daughter to take her mother's advice."

Erica looked at Adrianna in shock. "You haven't been home to sleep since yesterday?"

Adrianna looked at her sheepishly and turned to her mother and Sarah. "Tattletales."

Sarah stopped and checked a door number before wheeling Carolyn in. "Here's your new room, Carolyn."

Adrianna looked up at Erica's shocked expression and dodged in the doorway. "Saved by the bell."

Erica made sure Carolyn was comfortable before promising to see her before she went home. She said good-bye to everyone before stepping into the hallway with Adrianna.

Adrianna handed Erica the container with her chicken salad sandwich. She stepped closer and brushed her fingertip across the crystal angel pin on Erica's lapel. "Please don't be angry with me. I promise that I'm going to make sure Carolyn has everything she needs, then I'm going home to sleep."

Erica ran the soft pad of her thumb across Adrianna's cheek. "Please get some sleep this afternoon. If you're really tired, please call me, and I would be more than happy to come and pick you up. I don't want you driving around when you're tired. Okay, Adrianna?"

Adrianna saw the concern and fear in Erica's eyes. "I'm exhausted, so I can promise you that I'll get some sleep this afternoon. Speaking of being tired, you're the one that's been up since four thirty this morning."

"Yeah, but I'm used to these insane hours. You're not. Besides, I plan on getting out of here at a reasonable hour so I can catch a nap before you arrive to pick me up. I'd hate to be falling asleep on our first date and have you think I'm boring company."

Adrianna touched the heart sticker on Erica's badge. "Not a chance of that happening. You're probably a fascinating woman in your sleep, Dr. Beaumont."

Erica smiled and squeezed Adrianna's shoulders. "Go say good-bye to your wonderful family. I should get back to work if I want to get out of here early."

Adrianna stepped toward her mother's room. "See you tonight, Dr. Beaumont, and make sure you eat that sandwich. You're lucky Abby even left you one"

"I'll have something to say to Abby about that tonight. Thanks for saving me one. I'll certainly enjoy it." Erica waved good-bye and headed toward the nurses' station.

Chapter 11

Adrianna followed Erica's directions and checked the house number on the brick pillar before easing her sporty, cobalt blue BMW Z8 Roadster into the driveway. She pulled to a stop before the two-car garage and admired the magnificent pristine white home. Lights shone from the two levels of the house, giving it a warm welcoming ambiance. Huge windows showcased the home elegantly with California shutters slightly tilted to shade the evening sun. She stepped out of her BMW and was awestruck by the well-manicured lawn and endless bushes of pink oleander bordering the property. Along the entire driveway were blooming rose bushes of every color. Adrianna stepped before a blooming tricolor rose of peach, pink, and red and held it delicately in her hand. She bent down and closed her eyes as she inhaled the sweetest perfume she had ever smelled from a single flower.

Erica looked into her floor-length mirror that reflected back her beautiful, slender figure elegantly dressed in a form-fitting, sleeveless, black-sequined dress that glittered each time she moved. She checked the zipper at the back one final time before slipping into her black evening sandals. She nervously ran her fingers through her ringlets and stopped when she heard a vehicle pull into her driveway. She looked down at her slim gold Movado watch and saw that is was already five o'clock.

An uncomfortable constriction gripped her chest as she walked down the staircase to open the ornate oak double doors. She stepped out onto the front terrace and watched Adrianna. She looked radiant standing there in a powder-blue opalescent sequined slip dress. The square neckline and slim shoulder straps accentuated her flawless olive skin and petite figure. Each time she moved, the material slid along her feminine curves and spun the desire tighter in Erica's belly.

Erica walked down the wide front steps and watched Adrianna touch her fingertips to another blooming rose. "Snazzy car and don't you look just beautiful this evening, counselor."

Adrianna stood tall and stared at Erica. Her dark brown cascading ringlets floated over her naked shoulders and blended into her exquisite black shimmering dress. The heat surged in her chest and fluttered in her belly as she laid her hand over the unsettling sensation.

Erica looked so vibrant and elegant as she stood before Adrianna and took her hands. "Welcome to my home. Would you like to come inside?"

"That sounds wonderful. Let me just get my things from the car."

Erica watched Adrianna reach into the passenger seat and pull out her purse and a large gift bag. She handed the gift bag to Erica and turned back to lock her car.

"I love your car, Adrianna. This sporty little thing fits you perfectly, and the color matches your eyes."

"Thank you. I really love my little roadster. You'll have to drive it sometime to see how well it handles."

"I'd really like that."

Erica guided Adrianna toward the front steps.

"Your roses are beautiful, Erica. I've never seen so many in so many different colors and shades."

Erica looked back at her garden. "I love these roses. I have someone take care of them for me because I don't have a lot of spare time to be in my garden, but I do enjoy the time I spend playing in the dirt. Gardening allows me to empty my mind and nurture something to life."

"Well, you've done a beautiful job nurturing them to life."

Erica guided Adrianna through the front door and followed her in as she locked the door behind them. Adrianna stepped into the foyer and was mesmerized by Erica's spectacular house.

Adrianna slowly turned to Erica and swallowed hard past her dry throat as she stared into those astonishing coral green eyes. "Your home is so beautiful, Erica." Adrianna took one small step back from Erica's magnetic pull and slowly looked her up and down. "And speaking of beautiful, you look rather ravishing yourself, Dr. Beaumont."

Erica blushed. "Thank you. This is just something I threw on at the last minute."

Adrianna laughed and moved closer to Erica, placing her hands on her slim waist. "Sure you did."

Erica ran her fingertips along the slim powder-blue shoulder strap. "This is a beautiful dress on you, Adrianna. You look absolutely gorgeous and elegant."

"Thank you," Adrianna whispered as she stepped into Erica's arms and hugged her tight. She buried her face into that mass of ringlets and breathed in her faint smell of fresh apples and a subtle perfume. She slid her hands across her strong, naked shoulders and down the slim contours of her back as she melted into her loving embrace.

Erica felt the warm softness of Adrianna's cheek against her own as her gentle sighs ignited a raging surge of heat that bolted in her chest and flowed to her tingling thighs. Erica's heart beat an erratic pace as she forced herself to breathe evenly. Her hands glided along Adrianna's lower back and moved up to find the opening of her dress. Her fingers tentatively skirted over the loose material and surrendered to the silky softness of her naked back. Erica felt Adrianna inhale sharply as her fingertips found their way along the subtle recess of her spine and up to her slender neck. She felt her quiver against her as she watched Adrianna take a tentative step back. Erica fought the undeniable urge to cover those full, moist sensuous lips with her own as she took her face in her hands. "Are you okay?"

Adrianna had to take a moment to catch her breath. "I'm fine."

Erica saw the uncertainty and vulnerability in those shimmering sapphire blue eyes and wanted to ease her tension and chase away that look of panic. She carefully took her hand. "Come in and I'll show you around."

Adrianna calmed her breathing and squeezed her hand. "I'd like that."

Erica guided her down three steps and into the sunken living room.

Adrianna looked around at the spacious room with rich white couches that gently divided the area into a living room and dining room. Thick soft pink carpeting warmed the room and extended out to meet glossy, hardwood floors.

A huge marble tiled fireplace divided two rooms and drew Adrianna's eyes to the floor-to-ceiling windows encased in the corner of the room. Near the crystal clear windows was a black Yamaha baby grand piano. The view through the massive windows was of the majestic Camelback Mountain in the distance and the city of Phoenix below. Adorning the faux finished walls were astonishing framed photos. One depicted rays of sunlight filtering through the leaves of a massive willow tree, showering brilliant light onto a well-manicured lawn. Another picture portrayed a cluster of three pink roses with dewdrops glistening on their delicate petals. The third photo was a dusty rose water lily floating effortlessly in a pond filled with orange speckled koi.

Adrianna stepped forward and touched the frame surrounding the photo of the delicate roses. "Did you take these photos, Erica?"

"Yes, I did. I love taking pictures. Its just another peaceful pleasure of mine."

"They're so beautiful. Where did you take them?"

"A very close friend of mine and her partner run a resort for spinal cord-injured adults in northern Ontario, Canada. I took the photos of the willow tree and roses at Bradley Bay when I went to visit Kaitlin and Sierra last month. The water lily among all those fat koi was taken at the home of dear friends of mine, Megan and Rebecca. They live in Austin, Texas. Come into the next room and I'll show you pictures of my friends and family."

Adrianna admired the richly detailed leaf pattern in the moldings as she walked into the next room. She looked around at a u-shaped floral print sectional couch that filled the center of the room. Adorning one entire wall were inlaid bookshelves filled with hardcover and paperback books. Adrianna slid her hand along the back of the couch and walked toward a wall lined with photos of smiling faces. She stopped before a black-and-white picture of Erica holding a woman in her arms. The wind was gently blowing through their hair, and they both looked so happy. She touched the picture gently and turned to face Erica. "Laura."

Erica stared into the picture. "Yes."

Adrianna was mesmerized by the love and joy in their eyes. "She's beautiful."

Erica smiled fondly. "Yes. She was. She would have really liked you."

Adrianna smiled and slipped her hand into Erica's.

Erica pointed to the next photo. "Those are my parents, Mackenzie and Grace."

Adrianna was moved by the way Mackenzie enveloped Grace so completely in his arms as they smiled at the camera. The depth of their love glowed in their genuine smiles.

"The next picture is of my entire family. Quite a brood, aren't they?" Erica moved Adrianna a step closer. "My sisters, Jenna, Brianna, and Ashley. My brothers, Braden and Dylan."

"Your family is beautiful, Erica. You've all been blessed with your parents' incredible DNA."

"Thanks. These next pictures are ones I took of my friends. Here's one of Kaitlin and Sierra, Megan and Rebecca, and the last one is of Abby and Trina."

"Your friends are beautiful, Erica." Adrianna stood before the picture of Abby and Trina. "Trina looks as I had imagined. Gorgeous and impish all in one."

Erica laughed. "You hit that little Hispanic nail on the head. I can't wait for you to meet her. I hope you can meet all of my friends in the near future."

Erica missed the fleeting look of sadness in Adrianna's eyes as she stared back at all the photos displayed elegantly along the wall.

Adrianna slipped her hand from Erica's and touched her elbow. "Your home is incredible, Erica. It's truly beautiful."

"Thank you, but I can't take all the credit. When Laura died, Trina made me start redecorating one room to keep my mind busy. Before I knew it, I had redecorated several rooms. It was a constructive use of desperate energy, and in the end I think it was very therapeutic. It forced me to take care of her things and to change some things that brought back constant memories of us." Erica reached out and touched

Adrianna's cheek. "I'm sure you know all about that. Especially on a night like tonight." Erica lifted up the large gift bag in her hand. "What do you say we go into the kitchen and investigate what you have in this bag? Whatever is in here weighs a ton."

Adrianna smiled and appreciated the change in subject. She gladly followed Erica into her sun-filled kitchen. Erica carefully lifted the bag onto her marble countertop of swirled caramel.

Adrianna stood in the middle of the cozy kitchen and admired the rich oak cabinets and gleaming white appliances. She set her hand on the cool marble top of the kitchen island and loved the way two chairs nestled into one end of the island. In the alcove, a crystal bowl filled with candy-red apples sat royally atop the round oak table.

"Can I pour you a glass of wine, Adrianna?"

"I'd like that. Just half a glass, please, since I'm driving."

"Okay. Red or white?"

"Red, please."

Erica poured them each a glass of red wine and handed Adrianna a crystal goblet.

"Thank you. I love this kitchen, Erica. It's really beautiful."

"Thank you. I enjoy the little time that I do have to cook when I'm home."

Erica stood before Adrianna and gently tapped their wine glasses. "To a successful night for the Hailey Center and to our first date."

Adrianna smiled over her wine glass as they both took a sip. "This is wonderful wine. What kind is it?"

"J.P. Tinto. It's a Portuguese wine and happens to be one of my favorites." Erica handed Adrianna the wine bottle.

Erica set her goblet down on the counter and peeked into the gift bag. "Now, tell me what's in this bag, Adrianna. The suspense is killing me."

Adrianna stepped in beside Erica and set the bottle of wine and her wine glass down beside hers. "I brought you something." Adrianna reached into the bag and pulled out two separate bags. She moved one closer to Erica and pulled out two bottles of wine, a red and a white. I brought you some of my favorite wines and I brought two bottles for Trina and Abby as well."

Erica picked up the bottle of red wine and read the label. "Petit Mouton. This is really nice, Adrianna. I didn't expect you to bring anything."

Adrianna smiled into Erica's glistening emerald eyes. "I know you didn't. It's just my way of saying thank you for being there for me and the Hailey Center."

Erica reached up and swept a stray strand of hair over Adrianna's slender shoulder. "It's my pleasure."

Adrianna hesitantly stepped away from Erica's searing touch and pulled the gift bag closer.

Erica picked up the bottle of German white wine and read the label. "Reichsgraf Von Kesselstatt. Abby and Trina will love this. They love white wine, so that's a gift that will be greatly appreciated." Erica set the bottles down on the counter as she watched Adrianna reach down deep into the bag.

"I also brought a gift for your teddy bear. It's just someone to keep him company on those long lonely nights when you're practicing your fine art of neurosurgery."

Erica watched Adrianna pull out a white teddy bear dressed in a red sundress. Erica laughed with delight. She reached for the bear and hugged it close and inhaled the gentle scent of Adrianna's peach scent. "She's beautiful, Adrianna, and she smells just like you."

Adrianna smiled and touched the cuddly bear. "This is little Addie. I bought her to keep your teddy bear company."

Erica gently took little Addie and set her down beside the wine bottles. She stepped toward Adrianna and touched her cheek with the soft pad of her thumb. "Thank you for the wine and little Addie. They're beautiful gifts."

Adrianna stepped into Erica's arms and melted into her embrace.

Erica rested her cheek against Adrianna's forehead. "Would you like to be the one to introduce little Addie to my teddy bear?"

"Yes, I'd like that." Adrianna reached for little Addie and slipped her hand into Erica's.

Erica took her hand and gave her a guided tour of her elegant home. They walked through her dining room, living room, sunroom, and three spare bedrooms before stepping into her master bedroom. Adrianna was in awe of this beautiful, feminine room painted in soft pink with coral-colored, plush carpeting and two cozy white couches before a magnificent marble fireplace. Adrianna looked around the room and marveled at Erica's beautiful mahogany four-poster bed elevated on a slight platform. It was nestled in an oval alcove, surrounded by picture windows. A floral-print duvet with lots of inviting pillows covered the bed.

Erica was enthralled watching Adrianna as she guided her beside her bed. There sitting alone in the center of the king-size bed was a beautiful brown bear with a black bow tie. Erica reached for the bear and handed him to Adrianna. "This is Teddy."

Adrianna cautiously sat on the edge of Erica's elegant bed and introduced Teddy to little Addie. She held them close in her lap as she watched Erica settle into a Victorian chair facing the bed.

Erica tried to settle the tightening coil of longing in her belly at the sight of Adrianna sitting in her bedroom. "It looks like Teddy and little Addie are going to be friends."

"I hope they will be." Adrianna sat them side-by-side against Erica's plush pillows and folded her hands in her lap. Her stomach was in knots, and her heart beat a volatile pace as she battled the overwhelming emotions raging throughout her entire being. "This is a beautiful bedroom, Erica."

"Thank you. I wish I had more time to sleep in it, but that's what happens when I choose to muck around in people's brains instead."

They turned their heads as a voice called out to them.

Erica smiled. "We're in my bedroom."

Erica and Adrianna stood as they watched Abby walk toward them holding the hand of a slender Hispanic woman with long dark brown flowing hair and shining mischievous brown eyes. Her gentle beauty and loving eyes struck Adrianna as they looked directly at each other and Trina tried to playfully hide her smile.

"When will you two ever learn to knock or use the doorbell?"

"We didn't see the need, considering we were invited over and we just happen to have been given a key to this house since the day you bought it. Why waste the energy using the doorbell."

Adrianna smiled at them both and watched Trina melt into Erica's arms. Abby turned to Adrianna and kissed her and pulled her into her arms. Adrianna felt the warmth from Abby as she held her close. "If we had known you guys were going to find your way to the bedroom before we even left for the gala affair, then we might have considered knocking. Next time, send up a smoke signal."

Adrianna laughed. "We were just introducing Teddy to his new friend, Addie."

Abby smiled at the bears on the bed. "She's adorable."

"I felt Teddy needed someone to keep him company on those nights Erica's at work."

Abby hugged Adrianna close to her side. "You're too sweet."

Adrianna leaned into Abby as they watched Trina bury her face against Erica's shoulder.

Erica held her close and kissed the top of her head. "Trina, there is someone I would like you to meet."

Trina stepped before Adrianna. "When Abby started describing you as ugly, toothless, bald, short, fat, and with absolutely no personality, I knew that meant you must be incredibly beautiful. You are even more beautiful than I imagined. That upsets me even more since Erica did not give me the opportunity to thoroughly check you out before inviting you into our lives."

Adrianna took Trina's hands in her own. "Trina, I know that you and Abby are Erica's dearest friends, and I don't ever plan on affecting that special friendship. Erica loves you both very much, and I would just love to be part of that friendship."

Trina gave Adrianna a beautiful smile that lit up her elegant face. "Let's see how tonight goes, and we'll see if I'll let you into our very tight circle." Trina squeezed Adrianna's hands.

Abby laughed and stepped closer to Trina and Adrianna. "Trina, you promised to play nice."

Trina gave her partner a mischievous grin. "I am playing nice."

"Adrianna is the only woman that Erica has brought to meet us in two years, so let's not put her through the shredder already."

Trina smiled as she admired Adrianna's beautiful dress. "For an ugly, toothless, bald, short, fat girl, you certainly look beautiful tonight." Trina looked from Adrianna to Erica. "You both look beautiful this evening."

Adrianna squeezed Trina's hands. "You both look gorgeous in your dresses."

Erica cupped Trina's chin in her hand. "Let's go into the kitchen, ladies, and I'll show you the gift Adrianna brought for those who can learn to play nice."

Trina stuck her tongue out at Erica. Erica guided them out of the bedroom and placed her hand on Abby's back. "Speaking of playing nice, I'd like to know what you were doing in my favorite patient's room today terrorizing her about her heart rhythm and stealing my chicken salad sandwiches, Dr. Abigail Cooper."

Abby smiled at Adrianna over her shoulder. "Carolyn Taylor is such a wonderful character. I can't wait for Trina to meet her some day. She'd keep anyone in line with that quick wit and sharp tongue."

Erica smiled at Adrianna. "Seems to run in the family."

Erica guided everyone into the kitchen, and Adrianna presented Trina and Abby with their bottles of wine. "I just wanted to thank you both for being a part of the fundraiser tonight."

Abby took one of the bottles and read the label. "This is really nice, Adrianna. Thank you."

"You're both very welcome." Adrianna looked down at her slim gold Rolex watch and saw that it was already six o'clock. "Speaking of the fund-raiser, we should probably get going. The festivities are supposed to start at seven."

✳✳✳✳

They walked into the Arizona Biltmore together, four beautiful women walking close and turning heads. The guests swarmed Adrianna as she greeted everyone warmly and introduced them to Erica, Trina, and Abby.

Grant and Leah made their way through the throng of tuxedos and evening gowns and found themselves being introduced to Trina and Abby. The four of them became engrossed in a conversation. Adrianna and

Erica made their rounds around the huge room and chatted with people one of them was bound to know. Adrianna loved watching Erica interact with strangers, friends, and colleagues. Her charm, emotional strength, and unshakable self-confidence were awe-inspiring.

An announcement up front asked everyone to take their seats. The waiters guided everyone to their assigned tables.

Adrianna settled in beside Erica and leaned in close. She smiled as she saw that Abby and Trina were asking Grant and Leah about Amanda.

Adrianna turned to Erica and watched her stare around the room in awe. She reached up and touched a soft ringlet dancing around her ear. "Are you enjoying yourself, Erica?"

"Are you kidding? This is incredible. I never expected to see so many people here. They must really believe in what you're doing at the Hailey Center, Adrianna. You should be proud of what you're seeing tonight."

"I'm very proud of the Hailey Center. If it weren't for all the believers and supporters in this room, the Hailey Center would never be as successful as it is. It's all about what we all put into it. Its success is a huge group effort."

The waiters poured everyone a glass of wine. Erica proposed a toast. "To the Hailey Center, Carolyn's recovery, and to friendships." They all clinked glasses and took a sip. Abby and Trina asked about Carolyn. Adrianna shared with them how well she was doing and talked about Carolyn's struggles with breast cancer and now her brain tumor.

Erica watched her in absolute wonderment at the ease in which she shared her life with Abby and Trina and the love she exuded for Carolyn.

The squeaky noise of the microphone brought all of their attention to the front of the room and the chief financial officer of the Hailey Center dressed elegantly in a white taffeta gown.

"Ladies and gentlemen, on behalf of all of the administrators, staff, and patients of the Hailey Center, I would like to welcome you this evening to our first annual gala fundraiser."

The audience applauded.

"I was told to make my greeting brief and get off the stage, and that suits me just fine. The person I am about to introduce is the one who issued those orders. Ladies and gentlemen, it is with great pride and pleasure that I introduce to you the founder and chief executive officer of the Hailey Center, the distinguished Ms. Adrianna Taylor."

The applause was thunderous as Erica took Adrianna's hand and guided her from her chair. Adrianna's smile bolted into Erica's chest and surrounded her heart with incredible warmth.

Adrianna touched Erica's cheek with her fingertips. "I'll be right back."

Erica pulled Adrianna's chair back and watched her walk to the front of the stage. Adrianna settled in behind the podium and thanked her colleague.

Abby leaned into Erica. "She's an incredible woman."

"I noticed that the moment I saw her, Abby."

Erica settled back into her chair and watched Adrianna take a breath. She reached for the microphone and lowered it to her height with the slightest shake in her hand. She looked out to the audience and caught Erica's eye.

"Good evening, ladies and gentlemen. I'd like to thank you for being here this evening and helping to support the work done at the Hailey Center. It's not often you can bring together a room full of doctors and lawyers and not see a bunch of scalpels and gavels flying. I envisioned a scene out of the movie *Braveheart* when I knew this group was going to get together under one roof."

Everyone burst into laughter as Adrianna looked over at Erica and saw her gentle wink.

"I ask that you take a look around you at the people at your table and the next table. Regardless of your profession, race, color, creed, religion, or beliefs, someone at your table will inevitably be touched by cancer. Cancer does not discriminate. It has no preference or bias. This is a fight we need to fight together.

"Many of us in this room have already been down that road and gone to battle. My partner, Hailey, lost her battle. She deserved a better fight. She deserved the best fighting chance and access to the best medical care and technology available to us today. We weren't given that opportunity, and we ran out of time.

"Hailey asked one thing of me before she died. She asked me to make sure I fought to make things easier for other women, their partners, and their families. The Hailey Center has been the answer to our prayers. My mother has been blessed to be treated at the center for her breast cancer, and if she could be here tonight, she would sing its praise. She unfortunately had been diagnosed with a brain tumor."

The hum of voices in the room was startling.

"My mother has undergone surgery, and she's doing very well. Those of you who know my mother know she is going to overcome this as she has her breast cancer. She has been blessed to be under the care of Dr. Erica Beaumont, and that alone gave her the best chance she could have."

Adrianna gave Erica a smile before she continued. "The Hailey Center has been blessed with the most dedicated physicians. Women from around the country have come to our center because of its reputation, success, and drive to be the best in its field. They know that when they walk in our doors, we will give them the best professional care from our doctors, nurses, and all our ancillary staff. We pledge to give them the best treatment we can offer them; thus, we give them hope.

"I know that Hailey is proud of the work we have done here. I know she is smiling down on us. Whenever Hailey would see something that would make her proud, she would clap her hands together and shout, "Bravo!" To all of you tonight, I say, "Bravo!" I hope you all enjoy this evening and God bless you for your support."

Adrianna had barely stepped away from the podium when everyone stood to their feet and filled the room with uproarious applause. She shook hands with people on her way back to their table, and when she reached Erica, she melted into her arms. The applause only stopped when Erica helped Adrianna back into her chair.

The evening flew by as musicians entertained them throughout their meal of grilled mahi mahi, filet mignon, or pasta primavera. Waiters cleared the plates, then served dessert and coffee and tea.

Abby asked Adrianna about Hailey. Adrianna told her story of losing Hailey and building the Hailey Center for Women. Abby and Trina were astounded. Adrianna promised to take them all on a guided tour of the Hailey Center in the next couple of weeks.

Erica was touched by the bond formed between Adrianna and her two dearest friends in such a short time. They all marveled at Adrianna's stories and easily warmed to her loving personality. Adrianna was interested in learning all about Abby and Trina as she encouraged them to share their lives with her. They all thoroughly enjoyed Trina's version of the night she met Abby outside of Erica's home. They laughed so hard that their sides hurt, calling for extra napkins to dry their eyes.

Leah leaned in next to Trina. "Trina, I'm proud of you for not wrestling one of those guns away from the officers and shooting Abby yourself." Leah looked over at her handsome husband. "I would have shot Grant if he had forgotten an appointment with me."

Trina set her hand on Leah's arm. "It wouldn't have been worth it. Erica would have made me clean up the mess on her front steps."

Grant leaned across the table. "Abby, you and I need to talk life insurance."

Everyone laughed as Leah kissed her husband's cheek.

Comediennes entertained the guests after dinner as the night wound down much too quickly. It was eleven o'clock when Adrianna thanked the last few guests and they all decided it was time to go home.

They all stood around their vehicles and hugged each other good-bye.

Trina hugged Grant and Leah before turning to Erica. "Are you sure you guys don't want to come over for a drink?"

"We would love to, Trina, but we're both beat. Adrianna has not had a lot of sleep in the past four days, so I'd like to get her home."

Trina stepped toward Adrianna and took her into her arms. "Your speech was beautiful tonight. I really wanted to dislike you, but you made that virtually impossible. I hate you for not allowing me to hate you."

Abby said sternly, "Trina!" But the others were laughing.

Trina gave Abby a mischievous look and turned back to Adrianna. "You are very special, Adrianna. We are blessed to have you in our lives." Adrianna leaned into Trina and hugged her close.

They all said good-bye as Trina slipped into their Toyota Sequoia. Abby waved good-bye and slid into the driver's side.

Adrianna walked with Erica over to her BMW and automatically unlocked the doors.

"Would you like to drive home, Erica?" She loved the beautiful smile that lit up Erica's face.

"I'd love to. I promise to be careful."

"I know you will. We both hardly finished our glasses of wine, so I'm not concerned about you being careful. I just want you to enjoy the drive and see what you think of my car." Adrianna handed her the keys and made her way to the passenger's side as she opened the door. Erica slipped into the driver's seat and brought the engine to life. "Oh, yeah, baby, hang on tight."

Adrianna clicked her seatbelt into place and slanted her eyes at Erica. "Don't you dare."

Erica laughed as she slowly eased the vehicle into drive and maneuvered out of the parking lot.

The drive ended much too soon as Erica pulled into her driveway and put the car into park. She reluctantly handed Adrianna the keys. "Thank you for that incredible driving experience, Madame. I'm going to have to get myself one of these toys someday."

Adrianna smiled as she accepted the keys and held them in the palm of her hand. "You're very welcome."

Erica leaned back against the plush leather seat and watched the uncertainty play across Adrianna's eyes. "I had a wonderful time tonight, Adrianna. Your speech was beautiful. Carolyn and Hailey would be so proud of you. I was proud of you."

Adrianna stared into those coral green eyes. "Thank you. That means a lot to me that you feel that way. I really enjoyed myself tonight. You were a wonderful date."

Erica watched Adrianna wind the strap of her purse through her fingers. She placed her hand over Adrianna's, calming her anxious movements. "Would you like to come in and have a cup of tea with me? It's one of my little nightly rituals."

"I would like that. It seems to share a similar nightly ritual."

They both slipped out of the car as Adrianna hit the automatic door lock on her key chain.

Erica guided Adrianna up the flagstone steps and into the foyer. She turned off the house alarm and locked the door behind them.

Adrianna followed Erica into her kitchen and settled into a seat at the kitchen island. "I really enjoyed Trina and Abby. They're both very special women."

Erica filled the teakettle with distilled water from her water cooler and set it on the stove. "They certainly enjoyed you too, Adrianna. It was really nice to see how much Abby and Trina enjoyed you and Leah and Grant. You'd think we had known each other forever."

Adrianna watched Erica reach into her ornate French walnut armoire and pull out a Royal Doulton floral teapot and two matching china cups.

She stepped around the kitchen counter and set it all out on a serving tray. "Would you like herbal or black tea?

"Black tea, please."

"And how would you like your black tea?"

"Just one teaspoon of sugar, please."

"Ah, a woman after my own heart."

Erica joined Adrianna at the island while she waited for the water to boil.

Adrianna still hummed with disquieted tension as Erica vowed to find the cause and put her at ease. "I had a fabulous time tonight, Adrianna. I haven't enjoyed myself like that in a long time. Thank you."

Adrianna had a hard time making eye contact as she stared down at her hands. "I had a wonderful time, Erica. You made it really special for me."

Erica watched Adrianna struggle with her emotions, then leaned forward and touched her chin, tipping her face up to her. "For a lady that just told me she had a wonderful time, you certainly don't look very happy. What's wrong, Adrianna?"

Adrianna eased her face from Erica's hand and leaned back in her chair.

Erica leaned closer. "Talk to me, Adrianna. Tell me what's upsetting you."

"I did have a wonderful time this evening, Erica. I meant that from the bottom of my heart."

"Okay. So why do you look so miserable?"

Adrianna took a deep breath and folded her hands in her lap. "I really enjoyed your company. I haven't enjoyed another woman like this since Hailey died. It seems like it hasn't been that long since Hailey died, and on the other hand it has been an eternity. Over this past week, I've been having a hard time coming to terms with my feelings for you.

"Tonight we celebrated Hailey and what has come from her death, and I was at that celebration with another woman. I think that just kind of felt strange for me."

Erica reached for Adrianna's hand. "I understand how you feel."

Adrianna quickly moved away from Erica and walked to the picture window. She hugged her arms across her waist and stared out onto the well-lit back deck.

The teakettle whistled. Erica went to the stove. She turned off the burner and set the kettle on a ceramic cooling rack. She slowly walked to the picture window and stood behind Adrianna.

225

Adrianna saw her reflection in the window and turned to face her. "I know you do, Erica. And I really appreciate your understanding.

"It's been a real whirlwind of emotions tonight. But regardless of what I was feeling inside, I could not help but enjoy myself with you. You were so thoughtful, courteous, engaging, entertaining, and fascinating to talk to. You have a wonderful personality, Erica, and a great sense of humor. I could barely tear people away from you once they met you. I even felt annoyed when people kept taking you away from me. That was time that I wanted to spend with you."

Adrianna stepped closer and fought her desire to touch her. "You're a wonderful woman, Erica. You really are."

Erica stared into her emotional sapphire eyes. "Why do I get the sinking feeling you're saying good-bye, Adrianna?"

Adrianna moved to the kitchen island. She clutched the edge of the marble countertop and tried to steady herself and her emotions. "Because it has to be good-bye, Erica. I can easily see myself getting totally wrapped up in you. But I'm trying to look ahead at the obstacles that would be in our way. You could never respect or understand the cases I have represented. How could you begin to respect me? Our professional worlds are so diabolically different. How could we ever get past that?"

Erica's heart beat wildly in her chest, and she slowly moved to stand on the other side of the island. "Thanks for giving me the benefit of the doubt, Adrianna. Thank you for assuming what I can and cannot respect about you. So what was tonight all about? Was I on trial, Adrianna? Were you testing the waters to find some sort of flaw to make yourself feel better about walking away? Or were you going to take what you could get and walk away anyway?"

Adrianna blinked back the tears threatening to spill as she struggled to contain her emotions. "I'm not like that, Erica. I have to believe you know that about me. I don't use people for my own selfish needs and throw them aside. I don't blame you for being angry with me. I'm having a hard time understanding my own emotions as well. I just feel like this is the best decision for both of us right now. I'm just trying to save you a lot of grief. My life is so chaotic and full of turmoil. Especially now. I need to put all my efforts into my mother and this current case. There are things I need to complete, loose ends I need to tie up. I don't want you to get to know me through this stressful time. It's not fair to either one of us."

Erica gripped the back of her chair and shook her head. "Adrianna, getting to know someone during a stressful time is when you get to see the real, raw unedited soul. What I saw of you during Carolyn's illness was very impressive. You're a very loving, devoted, sensitive, caring, thoughtful person. You put your family above all else. You're very conscientious and extremely bright. You went out of your way to help the Kirklands emotionally and professionally when you barely knew them. That's the kind of woman that I would like to spend time getting to know better. The kind of woman I have not met since Laura died. But you don't have to worry, Adrianna. You've made your position quite clear. You're not interested.

I choose to spend my time with people who want me around. Time is precious, Adrianna. I promise I won't waste anymore of yours."

Adrianna gathered her purse and hugged it tight to her belly. "I'm sorry for hurting you, Erica. It's the last thing I ever intended to do. Please believe that. You're the most incredible woman I've ever met. Saying good-bye to you is one of the hardest things I've ever had to do. But I have to believe it's for the best."

Adrianna walked around the island and stood before Erica. Adrianna reached up to wipe away the tear on her cheek as Erica jerked her face out of her reach. Adrianna slowly moved her hand away and covered her mouth. "Good-bye, Erica. I know this is hard to understand, but I love you. That's why I'm doing this."

Erica watched the tears spill from those sapphire-blue eyes and stood stone still. She watched her turn, walk out the front door, and close it softly behind her.

She leaned her back against the island and slid to the floor. Erica buried her face in her hands and cried as she had not cried in years.

Adrianna dropped her car keys twice before she was able to steady her hand enough to slip the key into the ignition. She managed to start the engine as she stared out the windshield, barely able to see past her tears. "If only you knew the whole story, Erica. Then you might begin to understand why I'm doing this." Adrianna grabbed a tissue from the console and wiped her eyes. She slowly backed out of Erica's driveway and onto the street. She managed one last look back. "Good-bye, Erica. I really do love you."

Chapter 12

Erica finished showering and stepped out of her bathroom dressed in a thick pink terry-cloth robe. She finger-combed her hair and walked to the bedside table to grab her watch. She stopped in midmotion as she saw the light blinking on her answering machine. She sat on the edge of her bed and contemplated whether she wanted to know who had called.

She had spent hours tossing and turning in her bed last night and barely got four hours of sleep. The last thing she wanted to hear right now was Adrianna's voice. Her curiosity got the best of her, and she hit the new messages button.

"Good morning, Dr. Beaumont. You must be in the shower because you could not possibly still be in bed. Trina and I want to thank you for a lovely evening. We really enjoyed your company and the company of that woman you brought along. What was her name? Oh yeah, Adrianna Taylor."

Erica dropped back on her bed and covered her face with her pillow. "Oh, Abby, if you only knew what happened last night."

The message played on. "Erica, we have not seen you this happy in a long time. A light in your heart went out the day Laura died, and we never thought we would see that glow in you again. Last night you were lit up brighter than a Christmas tree. Trina and I want you to know that we are very happy for you. Trina can't stop saying nice things about her, then every once in a while she'll catch herself and say, 'She's so perfect for Erica. I hate that woman.' Anyway, I'll try and catch up with you at work today, but if not, Trina wants to know if you guys want to have dinner together on Tuesday. She said it's your turn to cook. Think about it and let us know. We love you, Erica. I'll talk to you later. Good-bye for now."

Erica quickly sat up and reached to erase the message. "Looks like I'll only be cooking for three, Abby. I hate to disappoint you." Erica ran her fingers through her hair in frustration and headed into her walk-in closet to get dressed for work.

❋❋❋❋

Leah stood in the doorway of Carolyn's room as she handed the tray of baked goods to Adrianna. "Be careful, they're still warm."

Adrianna balanced it carefully in her hands. "Are you sure you won't take these into the NICU for me?"

Leah stared at Adrianna for a few seconds. "Regardless of what happened between you and Erica last night, I think it would be nice for you to give these

230

treats to the NICU staff for us. Besides, she may not even be there. You can just drop them off and make a clean getaway."

Adrianna shifted the package of napkins on top of the container. "Not the way my luck has been lately."

"I know you have your reasons for creating this distance between you and Erica, Adrianna, but I told you: I think you're nuts. You could have handled this all differently and you wouldn't be so upset about seeing Erica."

"It's the only way this situation can be handled right now, Leah. I'm doing the best I can under these circumstances. Regardless of what the people around me think." Adrianna saw the instant hurt in Leah's eyes. She closed her eyes and dropped her head. Adrianna sighed heavily before looking up at Leah. "I'm sorry, Leah. I didn't sleep very well last night, and I'm feeling really irritable. I didn't mean to take it out on you."

"I know. I'm sorry things turned out so badly between you and Erica. Hopefully you two can talk when things settle down. I really like her, Adrianna. I really like her because of the person she is and because of how she makes you feel. I've prayed for a special woman to come into your life, but I never expected it to happen this way.

"Go drop off these treats, and I'll wait for you here in Mom's room. Hopefully you'll come back unscathed."

"If Erica's there, you can be guaranteed I'll come back scorched. Mind you, things couldn't get much worse than last night." Adrianna stood tall and took a deep breath. "Okay, I can do this." She turned and headed down the hall. "Come looking for me if I'm not back in fifteen minutes. Better yet, send security."

Leah laughed as she watched Adrianna head down the hall. "Better, yet, I'll send Dad."

Adrianna stopped and turned back to her sister. "Don't bother. He's your protector, not mine. Remember?"

"That would change if you would find yourself a man."

"Well, it looks like nothing's going to change."

Leah laughed as Adrianna turned and headed for the NICU.

****

At four o'clock in the afternoon Erica was dressed in her O.R. greens. She was standing at the counter in the nurses' station in the neurosurgical intensive care unit, surrounded by her residents. Erica was discussing the postoperative complications of her last patient when she saw Peter look over her shoulder toward the ICU doors. Erica heard him say, "Here, Adrianna, let me help you."

Everyone's eyes turned to follow Peter as Adrianna walked in carrying two large containers of baked goods. All four of Erica's residents stepped toward Adrianna to help her with her burden. Erica was glued to her spot, mesmerized by the sight of Adrianna.

Adrianna handed her packages over and did her best to avoid Erica's eyes.

Erica admired Adrianna's petite frame dressed in a lilac crepe suit. The long jacket flowed to just above the hem of the slim mid-thigh skirt, drawing attention to Adrianna's shapely, slender legs. Erica busied herself placing a chart back on the chart rack. Anger and desire raged within her and battled for supremacy. Adrianna had a lot of nerve walking into this unit after what happened the night before. Erica was not going to let her know how badly affected she was by her.

The residents and the nurses surrounded Adrianna to ask about Carolyn.

"Carolyn is doing really well. She's hoping to go home in the next couple of days if she can sweet-talk her neurosurgeon into it." Adrianna made eye contact with Erica for the first time and gave her a forced smile.

"Leah and my niece, Amanda, made you guys a bunch of brownies and chocolate chip cookies. It's just our way of saying thank you for everything you all did for my mom while she was here." Adrianna uncovered the baked goods and handed over a bunch of napkins. "Enjoy, you guys."

Adrianna hesitantly moved away from the crowd delving into the brownies and cookies to stand before Erica. "I hope you will be able to have a brownie or cookie, Dr. Beaumont."

Erica capped her pen and clipped it onto her breast pocket. "I haven't been very hungry today, Ms. Taylor. But please do tell Leah and Amanda that it was really kind of them to bake us those treats."

Adrianna hesitated, clasping her hands tightly before her. "I will."

"If you'll excuse me, Ms. Taylor, I need to finish my rounds."

Adrianna stared for several seconds. "Of course. I didn't mean to interrupt your work."

Adrianna turned her back on Erica and quickly made her way out of the unit.

Erica ran her hand through her hair and had to struggle to control the anger and bitterness tainting her behavior. She had no right to talk to Adrianna like that with other people around and could have kicked herself for behaving like such an idiot. She hated what Adrianna was doing to her and knew she needed to get herself together before she started to really lose it. She needed to keep a safe distance from that woman till she could learn to get over her. That might take a while, but she promised herself she was not going to let Adrianna Taylor keep her down. She had been down that road before, and she promised herself she was not going to lose any more sleep over what Adrianna decided was the best for both of them. She would show her that she was a stronger person than that. Unfortunately, the moment she set eyes on her, she became enveloped by her desire and want for that woman. Well, she was just going to have to get used to the fact that what she wanted and what Adrianna Taylor wanted were two totally different things. She was just going to have to learn to let her go. Regardless of how deeply she felt for her.

Peter walked toward Erica with a mouthful of chocolate chip cookie. "These are delicious. You should try one, Dr. Beaumont."

Erica rubbed her burning belly that continually reminded her that she had not eaten anything all day. "No, thanks, Peter. I'm not very hungry."

Peter wiped his fingers on a napkin and tried to understand the sudden change in Erica's mood. "Can I share something with you about our top ten list?"

Erica looked at him suspiciously and crossed her arms. "What top ten list?"

Peter tossed his napkin perfectly into the nearest trashcan. "Since Mrs. Taylor arrived in this unit, all the residents here, including myself, had a little bet going to see who would be the first one to have the balls to ask Adrianna out on a date."

Erica dropped her face into her hands. "Oh, no."

"Exactly. One night when I was leaving late I saw the two of you walking in the garden. I never realized that you had a much better chance at asking her out than we did." They laughed together as Peter shook his head. "I had to break the bad news to the guys and told them to erase Adrianna's name from the top ten list of women we want to date. They all thought I had snatched her up. I told them it was you that had won her heart, and they all wished they were lesbians."

Peter laughed. "You have to give us a fighting chance here, Erica. Every male resident that comes through here asks me about your personal life, and I have to break many hearts by telling them that you prefer to chase a skirt rather than a tie. Then the women we want to date would rather date you than us. Give us a break, would you? At least throw us a few crumbs."

Erica shook her head and laughed. "Sorry for making it so difficult for you guys, Peter. That's not my intention, trust me. And just for the record, there's nothing going on between Adrianna and me. So you can squelch the rumor mill, okay?"

Peter looked into Erica's tired eyes and knew not to take it any further. "Okay."

Erica grabbed a chart off the rack. "Let's get everyone together and finish rounds so we can all go home."

Peter knew not to question that stern look. He turned to gather the rest of the residents.

****

The noise level in the neurosurgical ICU rose dramatically as the night shift arrived. Erica sat alone at the far end of the counter as she signed her progress note on the sixteen-year-old boy with meningitis and closed the chart. She slipped the chart into the chart rack and checked her watch. It was already seven fifteen in the evening.

Sarah stepped around the counter in the nurses' station and placed her hand on Erica's shoulder. "Are you finally going to get out of here tonight?"

"I'm done, Sarah. I'm happy to be heading home. I'll see you in the morning."

Sarah gently squeezed Erica's shoulder and frowned. "Are you sure you're okay, Erica?"

Erica squeezed her tired, aching neck. "I'm fine, Sarah. I have made a major decision though. I've decided to give up women."

Sarah burst into laughter. "The male population will be ecstatic. Don't tell Michael Thomas. He'll be down on a bent knee with a bouquet of roses in one hand and a ring in the other."

Erica laughed and rolled her shoulders. "Michael knows not to waste his efforts on me. I just wish that Adrianna didn't feel her efforts were wasted."

Sarah leaned closer. "She's scared, Erica. She feels very strongly for you. She's just not sure how to handle those feelings. Give her some time and then talk to her."

"She doesn't want my time, Sarah. She made that perfectly clear."

"I know you better than that, Erica. You're angry and you're hurt. Don't let those emotions cloud your true feelings for Adrianna."

Erica rose from her chair and tucked it under the counter. "I will definitely let Adrianna stew for a while. Let's see which one of us cracks first." Erica squeezed Sarah's hand. "Good night, Sarah. I'll see you in the morning."

Sarah watched Erica walk through the automatic double doors and out of the NICU with a final wave. Sarah hugged her clipboard to her chest and smiled. "This will truly be a war of wills."

****

Erica was about to walk by the garden when she stopped and looked through the glass wall. She turned and walked through the double glass doors.

She saw him sitting on a wooden bench beneath a towering Palo Verde tree, staring off into the distance.

He must have sensed Erica's presence. He quickly turned and smiled brightly.

Erica quietly slipped onto the bench beside him.

"You're still here, Dr. Beaumont. This is just another long day for you."

"Yes, it is David. And will you do me a favor and call me Erica?"

237

David smiled and turned in the bench. "Okay, Erica."

"I saw you sitting here alone and wanted to make sure you were all right."

"That was very sweet of you. I'm doing just fine. They have come and taken Carolyn down for that repeat CAT scan of her head that you wanted done after her surgery to make sure everything was all right. They were pretty backed up with traumas all day, so they finally were able to fit Carolyn in. I thought I'd take a few minutes to come out here and get some fresh air."

"I'm so pleased to see how well she has done, David."

David placed his hand on Erica's upper back. "And we have you to thank for that. I don't know how I can thank you for everything you have done for us, Erica. You truly were the answer to our prayers."

"You're very sweet, David, but as I said, Carolyn's strength and your family's love and support were just as important to her success."

David looked up into the vast branches of the lime green Palo Verde tree. "This is such a beautiful spot. Adrianna and I brought Carolyn out here earlier. She just loves this spot." David looked into Erica's weary eyes. "Adrianna was pretty exhausted today. I was worried about her. She spent her day at the office and the evening here with us. I managed to talk her into going home tonight and getting a good night's sleep. She said she felt more comfortable doing that now that her mother is out of the ICU."

David watched Erica lean back into the bench and stare straight ahead. "She told us about last night, Erica. I'm sorry it turned out that way."

Erica leaned forward on the bench. "Me, too. I was pretty shocked by Adrianna's reasons for shutting me out of her life."

David crossed his legs and stretched his arm across the back of the wooden bench. "You have come to mean a lot to Adrianna and our entire family, Erica. I have watched you and Adrianna together, and it's very heartwarming to see the bond form between you. Adrianna will tell you that I have never been supportive of her choice to be with a woman. I don't understand it, and I always felt it was a phase that Adrianna would pass through. I feel responsible for the fact that Adrianna has no interest in men or getting married and having babies. She loves children and would be such a wonderful mother."

Erica leaned back in the bench and turned to David. "I can only tell you from my own personal experience, David, that it is not a choice but a way of life. We are gay, and fighting it will only destroy who we are. We can't live a lie, so we live our lives to the fullest of our ability and try to find true happiness. We also need to try to help the people we care most about to understand. Adrianna can still be a wife and mother, David. She would just be sharing that with another woman."

"I know. It's just not what I had envisioned for Adrianna. I knew Shannon and Hailey were important to Adrianna, but that's all I wanted to see. Then I saw the absolute heartache Adrianna went through when Hailey died. Through her pain I saw her love and devotion to Hailey. By then it was too late. Hailey had died. Adrianna has led a very solitary life these past two years. She has been a shell of the woman she once was when she had Hailey. Now you have walked into her life and we are starting to see glimpses of our happy, vivacious Adrianna again. That's what I want for Adrianna. I want her happy again. If it takes falling in love with a woman, then I'll do my best to understand and be more supportive. If it is you that Adrianna has chosen, then we feel blessed."

Erica smiled and blinked back her tears. "She didn't choose me, David. She dumped me."

David placed his hand on Erica's shoulder. "As you said before, Erica, neither you or Adrianna can live a lie. You're just going to have to fight for the true happiness you both seek."

Erica looked away. "I'm exhausted, David. I don't know how much fight I have left."

David smiled and squeezed her shoulder. "She's Italian, Erica. I can tell you from my own experience that Italian women are well worth the fight."

David rose from the bench and extended his hand. "Let me walk you inside so you can get home. Carolyn should be back from her CAT scan." David held the glass door open for Erica and followed her inside. They stood together in the hallway.

"David, did you tell Adrianna what you told me about her happiness?"

David slipped his hands into his pleated navy blue slacks. "No. I thought I'd let her stew a little longer."

Erica laughed. "I just said the same thing to Sarah."

"Don't let her stew too long, Erica. Italian women need to be simmered at just the right temperature, or they are liable to blow up in your face."

Erica laughed. "I've already seen the boiling point, David. I hope never to get there again." Erica smiled and squeezed David's hand. "I know it would mean a lot to Adrianna to hear what you told me. Please share your feelings with her when you're ready."

"I will."

"Good night. I'll see you and Carolyn on morning rounds. In a few more days you will both be home, and this experience will be behind you."

"I can't wait to take my wife home, Erica. Good night and get some sleep. We'll see you in the morning."

"See you then, David."

David watched Erica walk down the hall and disappear around the corner. He ran his hand through his silver hair and laughed. "I think there is still so much ahead for you and Adrianna, Dr. Erica Beaumont. I hope you are ready."

Chapter 13

It had been a week since Carolyn had been discharged from the hospital. Adrianna was thrilled to watch her regain her strength and health. She helped her mother into her cabled sweater coat and watched her secure a brightly colored scarf over her head to protect her incision. They slipped on their sunglasses, linked arms, and stepped out into the late afternoon sun.

They both loved this part of the day when they would walk together to the park while David took his nap. This was their time together. A time they cherished.

They crossed the street together and stepped up on the sidewalk of the palm tree-lined street that David and Carolyn had lived on for fifty years.

"I'm going to miss you when you go home tonight, Adrianna. It's been wonderful having you here this past week. Just like old times."

Adrianna squeezed her mother's arm and pulled her in close. "I've enjoyed being with you and Dad.

243

It's been great watching you get stronger every day. We could have lost you, Mom, and I'm nowhere near ready to let that happen. You mean so much to me, and this and what we went through with your breast cancer just brought that all home again. I value our relationship, and I cherish what we share. I don't ever want to lose sight of that. Life is too short, and I want to take advantage of every opportunity I can to be with you and Dad and the people I care about."

Carolyn slipped her hand into Adrianna's. "You mean a lot to me too, sweetheart. You're very special to us. You know that I would never let some old benign brain tumor take me down. I'm made of much tougher Italian stock than that."

They laughed as they entered the lush park. They chose a bench facing the mammoth three-tiered water fountain. They sat and watched a two-year-old plead with his mother to let him get in the fountain. Carolyn leaned forward, removed her sweater, and laid it across her lap. "That child reminds me of you, Adrianna. Persistent and determined. The only difference between you and that child is that you would have known that water is pretty darn cold. You were always a very smart girl."

"Speaking of little girls, I'm glad that Leah and Grant are going to spend the weekend with you. I need to go home and take care of a few things. I'll feel a lot better knowing they are here with you. Amanda can keep you entertained and remind you of what it's like to have a persistent, determined little girl around."

Carolyn laughed. "That little girl will keep me entertained this weekend."

Carolyn watched Adrianna pick up a fuchsia bougainvillea blossom and hold it gently in her hand. She slowly turned to her on the bench. "That was really nice of Erica to call twice this week to check up on me."

Adrianna quickly looked up at her mother. "Yes, it was."

"I thought it was nice of her to ask about you each time."

Adrianna ran her thumb across the petals, thin as tissue paper. "She was just being polite, Mom. After the way we left things a week ago, I'm surprised she even cared to ask about me."

"She cares, Adrianna. More than you want her to." Carolyn touched a loose strand of hair at Adrianna's temple and tucked it behind her ear as she had when she was a child. "Why don't you give her a call this weekend and see how she's doing?"

"Because right now I think I'm the last person on the face of this earth she wants to talk to."

"What if it's you that needs to do the talking, Adrianna? Regardless of all the reasons you've created for not seeing Erica, you've been miserable this week. I've watched you when you didn't think anyone was looking. You've been so upset and so lost. I've never seen you like that. There have always been people around when I wanted to ask you what you were thinking. Then when we would come to the park, I wanted you to be the one to discuss your feelings. Instead, you have been that persistent, determined, stubborn two-year-old and refused to share what is deepest and most painful in your heart."

Adrianna looked away from her mother and took a deep breath. "I'm not exactly proud of the way I handled things with Erica, Mom. I feel like such a failure where she's concerned. I can't stop thinking about her. My mind has been filled with the last times we spoke, what was said, how it was said, and Erica's tears. All of that keeps replaying in my mind like an old movie. I never meant to hurt her, Mom. I never wanted to hurt her." Adrianna brushed away a tear and leaned forward to rest her elbows on her thighs. "But what's done is done. I have to stand firm in my beliefs. I need to do this for Erica right now. I need to protect her from all this chaos."

Carolyn ran her hand across the back of Adrianna's thick hair and laid it on her back. "I know you want to protect Erica, but are you also using that as an excuse to protect yourself from your feelings for her?"

Adrianna looked up at her mother. "Those feelings are irrelevant right now, Mom. Erica probably hates me right now."

"She hardly sounded like she hated you on the phone, sweetheart. She's worried about you. I'm worried about both of you." Carolyn caressed Adrianna's back and let her gather her thoughts. "You're an extremely intelligent woman, Adrianna, but this time I think your heart is much brighter than your head. For a young lady who said she cherishes the time she can spend with the people she cares about, you have a funny way of showing that to Erica. You said it yourself, sweetheart, life is too short. You're doing yourself and Erica a huge disservice by creating this chasm between you. The two of you can work through all your issues if you will only talk openly with her. She's brilliant, Adrianna, but she's not a mind reader. You'll never know how she feels about what's troubling you unless you let her in. By keeping her locked out, you only insult her feelings and her intelligence. You'll never know what could possibly be if you don't allow that opportunity to walk through your door."

Adrianna leaned back in the bench and took a deep breath. "I don't think that opportunity would dare come anywhere near my door after the way I hurt her."

Carolyn rose from the bench and slipped into her sweater. She bent forward and extended her hand to her daughter. "Now, you'll never know, will you, Adrianna? It's up to you to make amends. Whether you do it or not is up to you and your desire to set things straight. The ball is in your court. Bounce it or put it in your closet. The choice is yours. Mind you, you've never been one to live in the closet."

Adrianna laughed as she took her mother's hand and stood before her. "My ball feels pretty deflated right now, Mom."

"Maybe you just need to borrow someone's air pump."

Adrianna laughed as she linked arms with her mother and continued their walk through the park. "Oh sure, and I wonder whose air pump you have in mind."

Carolyn gave Adrianna her most mischievous grin. "Well, there is a beautiful young pup that comes to mind."

"I'm not in a position to fix this mess right now, Mom. I have to shelve it for now and hope that Erica will be receptive to talking when all the planets are finally properly aligned."

"Oh, good. Erica should be close to retirement by then. She should have some extra time on her hands to talk to you."

Adrianna glared at her mother and nudged against her shoulder. "Smart-ass."

✳✳✳✳

Two hours later, David helped Adrianna ease her suitcase into her trunk and slammed the trunk closed for her. He took her in his arms and hugged her tight. "Drive carefully going home, sweetheart, and thanks again for everything."

"You're welcome, Dad. I enjoyed my week with you and Mom. It should only take me about twenty minutes to get home. I'll call you once I get unpacked."

"Please do that. We're supposed to get a thunderstorm tonight, so it would be nice to know you're home safe." David kissed her one more time.

Adrianna shielded her eyes from the early evening sun and looked up at her mother standing on the front porch. She gave her a smile and blew her a kiss before slipping into her BMW.

Carolyn leaned against the redwood railing and waved good-bye. She watched Adrianna back out of the driveway and slowly head down the street. "Maybe you need to be put in a position to deal with this mess, sweetheart."

David made his way up the porch steps and looped his arm around Carolyn's waist. "What do you say we catch the evening news before Leah and Grant get here?"

"Sounds wonderful, darling. I have a few things to do in the kitchen, and then I'll meet you there."

David guided Carolyn into the house and kissed her forehead. "Sounds great."

Carolyn watched David head into their family room and turn on the TV before settling into his favorite spot on the couch. Carolyn walked into the kitchen and picked up the phone. She dialed and listened to the recording before leaving a short message and setting the cordless phone back in its cradle.

Minutes later, the phone rang. Carolyn snatched the cordless phone and put it to her ear. "Erica, thank you for calling back so quickly. Did I catch you at a bad time?"

"No, not at all, Carolyn. Are you all right?"

"I'm fine. It's Adrianna. She's at home alone, and she hit her head on a low-hanging light fixture. I always told her to be careful of that light. Anyway, she said she has a terrible headache, and she just doesn't sound like herself. I'm really worried about her, Erica, and I can't get over there to see her myself. I told her to call 911, and she told me I was being ridiculous. I'm just so worried about her."

"Carolyn, I'm just checking on a few patients in the ICU and then I was heading home. Why don't you give me directions to Adrianna's, and I'll stop by her house to check on her if you think it's necessary."

"Oh, Erica, would you please? I absolutely think it's necessary." Carolyn gave Erica directions to Adrianna's home, thanked her, and said good-bye.

Carolyn set the phone back in its cradle. She turned around and found Leah standing in the doorway with her arms folded across her chest.

"Would you care to explain what that was about, Mother?"

"What what was about?"

Leah moved away from the doorframe and stood before Carolyn. "Don't play dumb with me, Mom. It doesn't suit you. What were you telling Erica about Adrianna hitting her head?"

"I don't know what you're talking about, sweetheart. It must be a bout of amnesia after my surgery."

Carolyn was saved from further interrogation as Amanda bounced into the room and threw herself into her grandmother's arms.

✳✳✳✳

Erica followed Carolyn's directions and found herself pulling into Adrianna's circular driveway. She drove beneath two towering gothic pillars and pulled to a stop before her three-car garage. A strange fluttery sensation gripped at her belly and filled her chest. She put her midnight black Lincoln Navigator into park and pulled out the keys. She placed her hand over her chest to ease the humming vibration heating her skin. She was not going to go through this again. She was not going to let herself be vulnerable to this pain again. She needed to keep her feelings for Adrianna well hidden. She was just going to make sure that Adrianna was okay and get the heck out. That was exactly what she was going to do.

She eased out of her Navigator, hit the automatic lock, and closed the door. She looked up at the gorgeous two story, white-walled estate with red tile roof, huge windows, and mature trees. She felt unsure of herself and thought she had done so well this week burying her feelings for Adrianna. Now, standing on her driveway and looking at her home, it all slammed into her like a tidal wave. Well, she could keep it under control. She had been practicing all week. Miserably, but she was practicing. She was only here because Carolyn had called. It wasn't her idea or her intention to be standing on Adrianna's driveway struggling to catch her breath and get her heart to stop pounding against her ribs. Never mind that she'd jumped at the opportunity to see her. Erica only hoped that when Adrianna hit her thick skull, it knocked some sense into her.

Erica slipped her keys into the pocket of her tailored black leather jacket. She climbed several steps to the ornate double oak doors. Above the door was a half-moon window with two mermaids etched in the glass swimming together. The same etched glass of individual mermaids framed the double doors on either side. Through the glass Erica could see a crystal chandelier hanging in the foyer reflecting dancing prisms of multicolored light as the sun caught each teardrop crystal. Erica hit the doorbell twice, listening to its wind chime sound echo in the foyer of this gorgeous home. She paced across the landing and felt the tension building in her chest. She checked her watch and hit the doorbell twice again. "Where are you, Adrianna? Answer the door."

Erica saw the ornate mermaid doorknocker and slammed it harder than she intended. She stepped back from the door and looked through the etched glass when she saw her. She was standing at the base of the spiral staircase looking at Erica like she had just seen a ghost. She looked so sexy dressed in a sky-blue sleeveless tunic and matching leggings. Her hand was resting over her heart as she gripped the banister. Everything Erica tried so hard to tell herself she could not feel for Adrianna bounced through her chest and danced on every last raw nerve ending. She stood only a few feet away through a glass window, and Erica could feel her, hear her, and smell her. She awakened every tingling sense that Erica tried valiantly to numb since Adrianna had turned her back and walked out her door. Standing there alone, she looked so small and so scared. Well, Erica was scared too, and she wasn't going to feel like all she wanted to do was take her in her arms and hold her forever.

"Open the damn door, Adrianna!"

Adrianna cautiously walked across her marble foyer as she tried to recover from the shock of seeing Erica standing at her front door. Erica was the last person she expected to see impatiently trying to get in. She was the one person she dreamed of seeing here. Erica was obviously angry. Adrianna took a deep breath and steeled herself against what was to come. She unlocked the door and swung it open.

Erica marched right in before Adrianna could even speak and grabbed her by the elbow. She guided her inside and slammed the door harder than necessary. "What took you so damn long? I was worried sick about you. I was about to call the police and have them break down your door so I could get in here to find you."

Adrianna was speechless, mesmerized by those blazing coral-green eyes.

Erica took Adrianna's face in her hands, looked at her pupils, and checked her over for any obvious signs of injury. She ran her hands into her thick hair and attempted to gentle her urgency. "Now, where did you hit your head? Was there any bleeding? Did you lose consciousness? How bad is your headache?"

Adrianna gripped Erica's wrists and looked at her in shock. "Erica, what are you talking about? I never hit my head."

Erica stopped the gentle movement of her fingertips across Adrianna's scalp and stared into those sapphire-blue eyes. She fought against the undeniable urge to crush her lips against her full mouth as she swallowed hard. "Carolyn called me and told me you hit your head on a low-hanging light fixture. She said you had a terrible headache and asked me to check on you. I was worried, so I came straight from the hospital."

Adrianna closed her eyes and whispered, "Oh, no," as she dropped her face against Erica's shoulder.

Erica caressed her beautiful, thick flowing hair as she had dreamed of doing a thousand times. Her subtle scent of peaches filled her senses and burned a passion so hot it startled her. "Adrianna, what's going on?"

Adrianna lifted her face from the warmth of Erica's hands. "Look around you, Erica. I don't have any low-hanging light fixtures, and I never hit my head. I just left my parents' place, and I've been home for about an hour. I was upstairs putting my clothes away when I heard the doorbell."

Erica looked shocked and bewildered. She moved two steps back from Adrianna. "Carolyn."

"Yes, Carolyn. Who else would set us up like this?"

Erica's cheeks flamed with embarrassment as she ran her hand through her ringlets. "She had no right to do this to us. I'm sorry, Adrianna. I believed her when she called me, otherwise I would never have barged into your home like that. I'm so sorry."

Consumed with embarrassment and anger, Erica crossed the foyer to the front door and grabbed the door handle.

Adrianna stood frozen in her spot as her heart burst for this woman. Everything about her that moved Adrianna's soul stood raw before her. She took one step forward and reached out to her. "Erica."

Erica was partially through the door when she stopped. She turned and faced Adrianna.

"I've missed you so much."

Erica slowly closed the door. She cleared the foyer in seconds and took her into her arms. They held each other like they never wanted to let go.

Erica laid one hand on Adrianna's lower back and pulled her in tight. Her other hand slid up into her thick dark hair and tucked her head in to her face. She moaned ever so softly as she felt Adrianna sigh against her.

Adrianna wallowed in her heat and her need as she burrowed into Erica's flowing ringlets and leaned her cheek against her face. Her hands bunched the silky soft leather as she craved to strip her of all barriers.

Her lips moved to within inches of her ear as she nestled against her face and inhaled her subtle perfume. "I've been such a fool."

Erica moaned softly as she gently took her face in her hands and leaned against her forehead. "A big fool."

Adrianna leaned back and looked into those sea-green eyes that burned into her soul. "I've been so miserable since the day I walked out of your house. I can't stand my life without you in it. I'm going through so many changes personally and professionally. I pray that you will give me the opportunity to show you the new me."

Erica ran the soft pad of her thumbs beneath Adrianna's eyes. "I just wanted the opportunity to get to know you, Adrianna. Change is constant and a part of everyday life. You pushed me away when I was really enjoying the woman that you are. Give me the opportunity to get to know you, before we decide where we want to go from here. That's all I ask from you right now."

Tears brimmed in Adrianna's sparkling blue eyes as she nodded her head. "Can you ever forgive me for hurting you like that?"

Erica wiped away Adrianna's tear. "I should make you give free legal counseling to the entire hospital for the next year after what you put me through this week."

Adrianna smiled weakly as she leaned her face into the palm of Erica's hand. "Boy, you are upset with me."

"Damn right I am. You're just going to have to work really hard to earn my forgiveness."

"I'll just be honored if you would give me the opportunity to make this up to you, Erica. We have some things to talk about, and there are some things that I won't be able to fully explain to you till after my current trial is completed in New York. I just pray that you will be patient with me and let me explain things when the timing is right."

"I'm a pretty patient person, Adrianna. Just don't push me away without giving me the opportunity to understand what's going on. I really care about you, and I can't stand the thought of my life without you."

Adrianna slipped into Erica's arms and slid her hands beneath her leather jacket. She slid her hands over her silk-covered back and loved the way her shiny silver blouse fit her strong, feminine curves. Her hands gently caressed the contours of Erica's back in light gentle strokes. Erica's tailored black slacks fit her graceful athletic frame to perfection as Adrianna moved slightly against her hips. She leaned her face against Erica's cheek and inhaled her subtle perfume. "Thank you for giving us the chance to start again."

Erica leaned her forehead against Adrianna's, loving the way that Adrianna fit perfectly in her arms. "I was a fool for letting you go so easily. Then I was so angry I just wanted you to stew for a while. I'd hoped you were feeling as miserable as I was."

"I hadn't felt this kind of deep pain and despair in a long time, Erica. I haven't suffered like this in a long time."

Erica grazed her fingertips across Adrianna's soft cheek and along her jaw. "Good."

Adrianna laughed. "I'm glad you're pleased with my suffering."

"It didn't have to be like this, Adrianna. You just needed to talk to me and share your feelings with me. Pushing me away was not the answer."

Adrianna looked down from those intense green eyes. "I know that now. I just need you to promise me you will give me the opportunity to explain anything to you that you don't understand about my career. Anything that troubles you or doesn't make sense, I want you to give me the chance to explain it to you before you jump to any conclusions. Please make me that one promise, Erica, and I can promise you that after this trial in New York, there will be nothing that I can't explain to you."

Erica held her face in her hands and stared into those intense oval-shaped eyes. "I promise to give you the opportunity to explain. And I ask that you promise to give me the opportunity to understand."

Adrianna gave her a smile. "Promise granted."

Adrianna leaned her forehead against Erica's as she let her hands roam freely across Erica's lower back. "Can I ask you one more question, Erica?"

"You can ask me anything anytime, Adrianna."

Adrianna looked down as she leaned back slightly. "If Carolyn hadn't done this to us, would you have tried to contact me? I wouldn't have blamed you for completely turning your back on me after the way I treated you."

Erica touched her chin with her fingertips and raised Adrianna's face to meet her eyes. "You're not that easy to walk away from, Adrianna. You've found a very special place in my heart. But to answer your question, I'm off this weekend, and I was going to wait till really late on Saturday night when I was tossing and turning and wide awake in my bed like I have been all week. Then I was going to call you and make sure you were wide awake and confused too. See how mean I can be?"

Adrianna leaned back and unsuccessfully tried to stifle her laugh. "Oh, Mother Teresa would be so ashamed of you. That would have definitely put a dent in your halo."

"Just don't you forget about how bad I can be."

Adrianna laughed as she traced her fingers along the collar of Erica's silky blouse. She toyed with the top button before she traced the gold triangle framing the beautiful amethyst pendant. "I'd really appreciate it, Erica, if we could move slowly with our relationship. I want us to take the time to get to know each other better before we move any further. I couldn't stand hurting you again, so I want us to be able to spend some time together before we decide together where we want to take this. Does that seem reasonable to you?"

Erica swayed gently against Adrianna and held her close. "Perfectly reasonable. I'm not one to rush into a relationship, so I would appreciate the time to get to know you better. That's all I asked of you from the beginning, Adrianna. Nothing more and nothing less."

Adrianna set Erica's amethyst pendant down against her tanned chest as she slid her hands into her mane of cascading ringlets. "Does that mean you'll be okay tossing and turning restlessly for a little while longer?"

Erica leaned her forehead against Adrianna's. "I'll sleep better knowing we're okay, but I can't promise I won't toss and turn thinking about you as I have every night. I'll just have to keep asking Teddy and little Addie to keep sharing my bed with me."

Adrianna's smile lit up her entire being as she moved her fingertips across Erica's smooth cheeks. She outlined her jaw and held her face gently in her hands. "I will ask Teddy and little Addie to keep the other half of your bed warm for me until you're ready to invite me into your bed." Adrianna loved the sensual look in those sea-green eyes as she moved her hips slowly against her. She ran her thumb beneath her full, moist lower lip and had to hold herself back from consuming those lips with her entire being. "Dr. Beaumont, if you don't have any plans for dinner this evening, I'd love to have you join me. Carolyn and I made a whole bunch of homemade pasta this week, and I was just going to put together some spaghettini Bolognese and a salad if that interests you."

Erica gripped Adrianna's waist and pulled her in tight against her to slow the movement of those swaying hips that were making her lose her promise to take things slow. "I would love to join you for dinner. I don't think I'll kill Carolyn after all, but I will give her a piece of my mind for what she did."

Adrianna smiled as she slid her hands slowly along Erica's defined shoulders and eased her jacket down her arms.

Erica slowly held her arms out as she allowed Adrianna to step behind her and sensuously remove her jacket. She turned her head and watched Adrianna smile as she headed for the hall closet. Erica dropped her chin to her chest and knew that holding out for Adrianna could be the greatest test of her patience and self-control.

Adrianna returned and slipped her hand into Erica's. She guided her through her sprawling living room. Erica brought them to a halt. The room was breathtaking: vaulted ceilings and lavish cream couches surrounded a black and pink tiled fireplace. The view through the floor-to-ceiling windows showcased her lush green backyard. Several sculptures and statues of women in different poses accentuated the room and added the flair of an art gallery. The early evening sun cast long shadows across the cream plush carpeting and illuminated the large oval glass coffee table with the sculptured mermaid pedestal.

Erica turned to Adrianna in awe. "Your home is absolutely beautiful, Adrianna, and you're a fan of mermaids."

Adrianna laughed as she looked toward her coffee table. "I'm glad you like my home, and yes, I'm a big fan of mermaids. I just love their mythical grace and beauty."

"That coffee table is a work of art, and the crafted glass around your front door is amazing."

"I really love the mermaids that were etched in that glass. An artist in Sedona did that for me."

"Amazing, Adrianna. Truly amazing."

Adrianna squeezed Erica's hand and led her into the kitchen. The late evening sun streamed through the large picture windows and illuminated the elegant light pine cupboards. A gray and white speckled countertop framed the kitchen in a large L shape. An antique jam cupboard and hutch stood tall against one wall, and a rich mahogany table for ten filled the adjacent dining room. Adrianna guided Erica to a seat at the huge kitchen island covered in an exquisite pattern of blue and white Italian tile. Erica pulled out a bar stool and admired the natural sandstone tile floor.

"This is an incredible kitchen, Adrianna."

"Thank you. I really love it. Especially when I have the time to cook." Adrianna gave Erica a smile as she pulled a bottle of red wine from the fridge and presented it to Erica with a corkscrew. She reached into a cupboard and pulled out two crystal wine glasses and set them before her. "Would you do us the honors, Dr. Beaumont?"

"I'd love to." Erica read the label on the wine bottle and smiled. "This bottle of wine looks very familiar."

"Did you try the bottle of Petit Mouton I gave you?"

Erica looked over the bottle and gave Adrianna a menacing look. "No. I haven't exactly been in the mood."

Adrianna looked away. "I see. Well, this will be your opportunity to taste my favorite red wine and see if you will enjoy your gift or not. If you don't like it, just return the gift to the giver. She would be more than happy to make sure you have a wine you enjoy."

Erica inserted the corkscrew and deftly popped the cork. "Don't be too quick to renege on my gift. I'll let you know what I think of it, don't you worry."

Erica poured them both a glass and set the cork on the kitchen island. She handed Adrianna a glass and held her glass before her. "To the beginning of something beautiful." Adrianna's smile ignited a slow simmering swell of desire in Erica's chest as she moved one step closer.

Adrianna gently tapped her glass against Erica's. "To the beginning of something beautiful and long lasting."

They both tipped their glasses and took a slow sip of wine.

Erica beamed over the rim of her glass. "This Petit Mouton is exquisite. It is really smooth and not too sweet."

"My feelings exactly. I guess that means I'm not going to get my gift back."

"I hate to disappoint you, but it looks like you're just going to have to join me for dinner at my place to enjoy it with me."

Adrianna laid her hand on Erica's shoulder and leaned in close. "That I think I can handle." Adrianna set her glass down on the tiled island and stepped toward her kitchen counter.

Erica loved the soft sound of Adrianna's tiny bare feet against the sandstone-tiled floor. She watched her as Adrianna carried a cordless phone and set it on the counter in front of her. "Aren't your feet cold, Adrianna? You have nothing on your bare feet."

Adrianna looked down at her feet and wiggled her tiny toes painted with soft pink nail polish. "Not at all. I love walking around in bare feet whenever I can. I love the feeling of the tile and carpeting beneath my feet. I really love the feeling of grass and beach sand. It makes me feel so alive to be able to experience my environment with my feet."

Erica smiled at this delightful creature. "You're really something else, you know that?"

Adrianna smiled as she picked up the phone. "I haven't had a chance to call my parents and tell them I got home safely. I thought you might like to be the one to inform Carolyn that I have recovered from my head injury while I get the pasta ready." Adrianna hit the first preset button and handed Erica the phone.

Erica watched across the counter as Adrianna dug into the freezer and pulled out sheets of homemade pasta. She watched her stretch on her tiptoes into the high cupboard for a pot as the muscles bunched in her calves and the sky-blue tunic slid higher over her tiny, tight bottom. Erica almost forgot what she was doing when she heard Carolyn's voice in the receiver.

"Good evening, Mrs. Taylor. I just wanted to report to you that I have done a thorough assessment of your daughter's supposed knock on the head, and she seems to have made a miraculous recovery." Erica smiled at the girlish charm in Carolyn's laughter.

"Are you staying for dinner, Erica?"

"Yes, I'm staying for dinner, Carolyn, and what does that have to do with the line of garbage you fed me to get me over here?"

Adrianna laughed as she unfolded the pasta and set it on the counter. She had never felt so angry at and so touched by her mother as she was at this very moment.

"Please don't be angry with me, Erica. You both needed to sit down and talk, and I thought this evening would be a great opportunity. I hated to see you both so upset with each other. I knew you would straighten everything out when you two stubborn, strong-willed women had a chance to spend some time together. Is Adrianna making you her spaghettini Bolognese?"

"Yes, Adrianna is making me spaghettini Bolognese."

"Oh, good. It's one of her most delicious dishes."

263

Adrianna laughed at her mother's endearing manipulation from what she heard from Erica's end of the conversation. She pulled the Bolognese sauce from the fridge as she watched Erica drop her face into her hand and sigh with resignation.

"Carolyn, you can't do this. You have to promise me from now on that you will not try and manipulate Adrianna and me like this again. I know that you care about us, but you have to let us work this out together in our own time, okay?"

"Well, let me tell you something, the woman with the big, bright medical brain. If we waited till Adrianna was ready, you were going to wait till all the planets were aligned. And you obviously were moving at the speed of chilled molasses. I'd like to see all my ducks in a row in this lifetime, Dr. Beaumont, and for that to happen you two needed a good swift kick in the bottom. You're having dinner together, and that is a much better start then where you both left things off last week. You have restored a small measure of faith that I have in both of you. Keep up the good work, Dr. Beaumont, and you just might get that apple pie that I promised you."

"Carolyn, regardless of when the planets are in perfect alignment or the speed of chilled molasses, promise me that you will not pull a stunt like you did today. I don't care how many ducks are missing from your chorus line, but you will make me that promise. Adrianna and I are big girls, and we do not need to be put in a situation like we were this evening. It has worked out wonderfully, but it was also humiliating to know that we had been set up. And furthermore, you and your daughter owe me a lifetime supply of freshly baked homemade apple pies and home-cooked meals for the grief you have put me through this week. Now, promise me once and for all you will not do this to us again."

Erica looked across the island at Adrianna and had to stifle her laughter at the stunned look on Adrianna's face.

"I promise not to interfere, Erica. Just promise me you won't give up on Adrianna."

"Promise granted, Carolyn. Now, let's call it a truce. I'm going to say good night so I can help Adrianna make a salad."

"Wait one minute, Erica. I want to know every last detail of what happened when you arrived at Adrianna's."

Erica burst into laughter. "Oh, no you don't. Thanks for not interfering, Carolyn. Good night."

Adrianna could hear the distant tones of her mother's voice as Erica hung up the phone on her. She walked around the counter and stood beside Erica. She stared down at the phone in disbelief. "What was that all about?"

"Your mother is under the impression that you need to have all the planets aligned and that I'm as slow as chilled molasses, so she believes her meddling was called for to get all her ducks line-dancing in this lifetime."

They both burst into laughter as Erica handed her a glass of wine. Erica tapped her glass against Adrianna's. "To Carolyn and her meddling. God love her."

They both took a sip of wine before Erica set down her glass. "If you would be so kind as to show me around your kitchen, I would love to make the salad for us while you do the pasta."

Erica grabbed her glass of wine while Adrianna took her other hand and guided her around the counter. She pulled out a fresh head of iceberg lettuce and guided Erica to the cutting board. She reached for a large porcelain salad bowl and dug into the utensil drawer for a sharp knife. She set this all down beside the cutting board as she watched Erica roll up her sleeves and wash her hands.

Erica began washing the lettuce as Adrianna pulled out some fresh mushrooms, plump tomatoes, a shiny green pepper, mild cheddar cheese, and a bottle of raspberry vinaigrette dressing.

They worked side by side. Erica watched Adrianna pour her homemade Bolognese sauce into a covered dish and slip it into the microwave. Within seconds, the smell of tangy sauce filled the kitchen. "Here I thought Carolyn was resting at home this week, and I come to find out you were both cooking up a storm in her kitchen."

Adrianna leaned her hip against the counter and sipped on her wine. "That's her form of rest and relaxation. That and plotting seems to be where she spent her energy this week."

Erica smiled as she gathered the diced tomatoes and tossed them into the salad.

Adrianna slipped a loaf of French bread into the oven just as the timer on the microwave went off. She removed the dish and stirred the zesty sauce.

Erica leaned over Adrianna's shoulder and inhaled deeply. "That smells absolutely delicious."

"I hope you like it." Adrianna took a teaspoonful of sauce and brought it carefully to Erica's mouth. She watched the spoon disappear between those sensuous lips and had to force herself to look away.

"That's incredible sauce, Adrianna. You can cook for me any time."

Adrianna returned the sauce to the microwave for another two minutes. "I'd like that."

Erica sprinkled the salad dressing over the salad as Adrianna set two places at the island. Adrianna carried their half-full glasses of wine to the island. "Do you want me to fill your wine glass, Erica?"

Erica filled their plates with salad and set the bowl aside. "No, thank you. One glass of wine is usually my limit. After that, I usually start to get really tired or I lose total inhibition."

Adrianna set their glasses down by their plates. "We'll have to test that loss of inhibition theory some day. May I offer you a glass of water then?"

"I'd love that, thank you."

Adrianna returned with two glasses of water and slipped into the seat that Erica held out for her. They devoured their salads and dove into the spaghettini Bolognese and chunks of warm French bread. Their conversation was nonstop, as they talked about everything that had happened in the past week.

After they were pleasantly stuffed, they cleared the dishes and cleaned up the kitchen. Adrianna hung up the damp dishtowels as Erica rolled down her sleeves. Adrianna stepped toward her and gently took her arm to button her cuffs.

Erica held out her hands and smiled as Adrianna slid her hands into hers.

"Thank you."

Adrianna smiled, loving the silky softness of the palms of Erica's hands. "Thank you for helping me clean up. That was great."

"It's the least I can do after you made me such a delicious meal. I really did enjoy dinner, Adrianna. Thank you. And the company was equally wonderful. You just earned a point of penance with that meal."

"It was my pleasure, Erica. I'm just grateful to have had this time with you." Adrianna brushed her thumbs gently across Erica's wrists, feeling her strong bounding pulse. "Is this a good time for our nightly ritual?"

Erica smiled, basking in the warm sensation of Adrianna's caressing touch. "I would love a cup of tea."

Adrianna stepped away to reach into her cupboard and pull down an animated teapot and two china cups.

Erica laughed and pointed at the teapot. "What kind of teapot is that?"

Adrianna turned the teapot around so Erica could get a better look. "It's Cinderella. I love all the Disney classics, and I love collecting Disney teapots." Adrianna took Erica's hand and guided her to the glassed-in antique hutch. She ceremoniously opened the glass doors. "Dr. Erica Beaumont, I would like to introduce you to Belle from *Beauty and the Beast;* Snow White; Cruella De Vil; Tinker Bell; Jasmine, the bride of Aladdin; and Pocahontas."

Erica laughed as she admired the Disney teapots. She loved the look of pure delight in Adrianna's eyes as she admired her collection. "You mean you don't have a Little Mermaid teapot?"

Adrianna pouted. Erica forced herself to look away from that gorgeous mouth. "No, I don't, but that has not been from a lack of trying. I've been looking for Ariel for years with no success."

Erica touched her thumb lightly to Adrianna's chin. "Fear not, my little mermaid. Someday we will find you just that teapot if I have to contact the Disney family myself."

Adrianna smiled with delight and she stepped into Erica's arms and hugged her tight. She closed the doors to the antique hutch and guided Erica back into the kitchen.

Erica watched Adrianna set about making their tea as she leaned back against the speckled counter. "I bet you have all the Disney classics on video."

Adrianna carefully poured the boiling water into Cinderella. "Every last one and whatever has come out on DVD."

Erica shook her head and smiled at this delightful character. She took the tray of tea from Adrianna and followed her into the living room. They settled into a lush cream couch as Adrianna poured the tea and handed Erica a cup.

Erica tipped her cup toward the teapot. "Thanks for the tea, Cinderella."

Adrianna laughed as she blew into her teacup.

They sat back and enjoyed the tea. Through the huge panoramic window, they could see a cloud-covered half moon.

Erica set her teacup down as she watched Adrianna curl her tiny bare feet under her. She gathered Adrianna's foot in her hand and luxuriated in its warm softness. "Your feet are warm, Adrianna. That's amazing for a woman who's been walking around in bare feet all evening."

"I told you. You don't have to worry about my feet. They're quite happy in all their naked glory. However, if you keep massaging my foot like that, I will be yours forever."

Erica smiled as a sudden brilliant flash of light filled the room and knocked out the power. Adrianna jumped when another bolt of streak lightning exploded from the sky and momentarily lit up the room before plunging them into darkness.

Adrianna nestled into Erica's arms and looked out the window as the next bolt of lightning danced across the sky. "Well, isn't this romantic. Do you think my mother planned this as well?"

They both burst into laughter as Adrianna eased back. "I'll go start a fire and light some candles. Don't go anywhere."

"Where would I go in the pitch dark? I'm afraid I'll trip over a mermaid or one of the seven dwarves."

Erica could hear Adrianna's gentle laughter across the room as she brought the gas fireplace to life. She saw her kneeling before the fire as the lapping flames reflected off her smooth olive skin. She lit large vanilla candles on either side of the fireplace and carefully carried one to the glass coffee table. A soft yellow glow of light filtered around them as Erica held her hand out to Adrianna and guided her back onto the couch.

Adrianna nestled into Erica's side and laid her head on her shoulder as she swung her feet up on the couch.

Erica gathered Adrianna in close and leaned her face against the top of her head as they both stared into the mesmerizing fire. "Remind me to have Carolyn plot our evenings more often."

They both laughed softly. Adrianna laid her hand on Erica's thigh and never wanted to move from this heavenly place. "Thunder and lightning storms usually scare me, but right now sitting here with you, it seems so beautiful and powerful."

Erica smiled into Adrianna's hair and held her tight. They sat entwined like that and sipped their tea as the thunderstorm played out in front of them. The sky finally settled down and lay to rest for the night as the power surged back into Adrianna's home.

They both looked around the room at the sudden blaze of lights. Adrianna rose from the couch and turned out all the lights in the room and returned to her cozy haven.

Erica nestled into the top of her head and pulled her in tight. "Thank you. This is so much nicer." Erica felt Adrianna sigh against her chest as she felt surrounded by the gentle scent of vanilla and the peacefulness of her presence. She slowly ran her fingers through her thick, dark hair and rested her lips against her forehead. "My parents have a horse ranch about twenty minutes from here. I was going to have breakfast with them and go horseback riding tomorrow morning. Would you like to join me?"

Adrianna quickly sat up as her eyes danced with excitement. "I haven't been horseback riding in years. I would love to join you, and I would like to meet your parents. After all, you have certainly put up with my family for the past two weeks."

Ana Corman

Erica let her hair fall through her fingers. "Your family is wonderful, Adrianna. Consider tomorrow a date. How about I pick you up at eight?"

"That sounds wonderful." Adrianna looked down at her watch. "Erica, it's already after midnight."

"Unfortunately, that's true. I should probably get going so we can both get some sleep."

Adrianna looked so disappointed that Erica wanted to lean her back in that plush couch and show her what she would rather do than sleep. Instead, she gathered up their tray and followed Adrianna into the kitchen.

Adrianna held Erica's leather jacket out for her while she slipped into the sleeves. She tugged the lapels of the jacket close and hated to see this evening come to an end.

Erica slipped her hands onto Adrianna's slender waist and pulled her in close. "Thank you for a wonderful evening, Adrianna. I'll always remember this time with you."

Adrianna traced her fingertips along the seam of Erica's lapels. "Thank you for a wonderful evening. I think the planets are in perfect alignment."

Erica laughed softly as she pulled Adrianna into her arms and hugged her close. She slowly ran her hands along her petite back and felt the desire burn in her soul. "And I don't think I'm as slow as chilled molasses."

Adrianna burst into laughter. "Sweet as molasses but hardly slow as molasses." Adrianna stared into those vibrant green eyes and felt herself being embraced by a blanket of hunger and desire. She wanted to wrap Erica in that blanket with her and devour her endlessly. The intensity of her need jolted

Adrianna as she made herself step back and pull Erica's coat closed. "Be careful driving home, and please call me when you get there. I think you have my number since you were going to wait till tomorrow to call me as you were tossing and turning late at night."

Erica glided her fingertips down Adrianna's arm and loved the sudden intake of her breath. "The beauty of having access to family phone numbers in my patients' charts." Erica slid her hand into Adrianna's. She was moved by her vulnerability as she slowly brought her hand to her mouth and gently brushed her moist lips against her knuckles. "I'll call you when I get home and I'll see you in the morning." Erica released her hand and brushed her fingertips across her cheek before heading for the door.

Adrianna forced herself to move and followed behind her to the front steps. Erica headed toward her vehicle with a final wave and slipped inside.

Adrianna watched her taillights disappear down her street and barely managed to wave. She hugged her arm tight across her belly as she brought her hand to her mouth. "Good night, sweetheart. I love you."

Chapter 14

They pulled up to the huge black wrought iron gates with "The Beaumont Ranch" blazed across in elegant script. Adrianna was in awe as they sat and watched the gates move smoothly to let them in. Erica eased her Navigator through the stone pillars onto the lane, lined in towering aspen, pine, and sycamore trees. The center lane was an explosion of vibrant color of alternating bushes of hibiscus, oleander, and bougainvillea. Adrianna was drawn to the immaculately manicured pastures on either side of the lane. Magnificent horses of all colors grazed peacefully in their glorious surroundings. Only a few turned their heads to see the intruders. A few flared their nostrils and flicked their tails. Two golden-brown foals stood at their mother's sides as their curiosity piqued their interest.

"This place is gorgeous, Erica. I've never seen anything like it."

"It is beautiful. My parents have owned this ranch for forty years. I've been blessed to have spent my entire life calling this place home. I have so many beautiful memories of this place with my brothers and sisters."

Adrianna leaned forward and looked around as she tried to take in all the sights. "Do your parents breed horses for a living?"

Erica smiled and watched Adrianna strain to look out her window. "Not quite. It's more like a passionate hobby of theirs. They have a team of experienced staff that care for the horses. My father chose the same professional path as you did. He's a business lawyer and runs his own company. My mother was an incredible trauma surgeon. She retired about five years ago."

Adrianna looked at Erica in amazement. "I see that some of your intelligence might have been genetic."

"Please don't tell them that. I'll never hear the end of it. They're the greatest parents I could ever have wished for. It was tough for my mom to be such a successful surgeon and raise a family at the same time, especially back then. It just proves how strong she is."

"You are your mother's daughter, Erica. Without a doubt."

Erica smiled as she parked her Navigator beneath a huge rectangular arbor veiled in a thick passion vine filled with blossoming pale lavender flowers. She slipped out the driver door and walked around to the passenger side. She locked the vehicle behind Adrianna and smiled as Adrianna slipped her hand in hers. She squeezed gently as she looked into those beautiful sapphire eyes. "Are you ready?"

Adrianna took a deep breath and held her shoulders high. "As ready as I'll ever be."

Erica guided Adrianna past the stables and toward a beautiful, sprawling two-story Southern-style estate. Tall white columns framed the many rectangular windows and supported the endless porches. They headed toward a raised cedar deck that overlooked a huge section of the lush green pastures.

Adrianna saw a very fit, distinguished man with salt and pepper curly hair in his mid sixties sitting at an umbrella table with a newspaper held loosely in his hands. He watched a woman who could easily be Erica's sister lean against the cedar railing and feed pieces of apples to two gorgeous horses.

Erica guided Adrianna up the steps. "Looks like Samson and Delilah are getting breakfast before we are."

Erica's parent's smiles lit up their faces. Adrianna watched Erica embrace and kiss her parents.

Erica stood beside her parents and guided Adrianna closer. "Mom and Dad, I'd like you to meet Adrianna Taylor. Adrianna, meet Mackenzie and Grace."

Mackenzie shook Adrianna's hand and greeted her before Grace moved closer and took Adrianna's hands in her own. "Welcome to our home, Adrianna. You'll have to excuse my sticky hands. It seems that Samson and Delilah lost their manners and had to have their breakfast before you two got here."

"Please don't apologize, Dr. Beaumont. I don't blame Samson and Delilah for starting without us."

Samson swung his massive head over the cedar railing and unceremoniously started sniffing at Adrianna's back.

"Please call me Grace, and you'd better introduce yourself or Samson might just mistake you for something else to nibble on for breakfast."

Adrianna turned and faced the honey-brown horse. She placed her hands on either side of his massive head and started rubbing in firm gentle strokes. She caressed his strong jaw and was careful around his huge brown eyes. "You're a very handsome boy, Samson. But I would appreciate it if you would stick to nibbling on apples this morning." Adrianna stroked along his face and up to his ears as Samson leaned in further and rubbed his face against Adrianna's jeans-clad thigh.

Erica leaned back against the cedar railing and patted Samson's muscular neck. "Looks like you've made a friend, Adrianna. But you'd better say hello to Delilah as well. Otherwise you'll get her nose out of joint."

Delilah reached her neck over the railing and stayed coyly out of Adrianna's reach. She watched as Adrianna slowly made her way toward her. Adrianna carefully reached out and brushed her fingertips along the white marking on Delilah's nose. Delilah sniffed her hand and moved forward. She finally allowed Adrianna access to her entire head. Delilah nudged her nose gently against Adrianna's belly as Adrianna scratched behind her ears. "You're a cautious one, beautiful Delilah. I know how you feel. You have to be careful who you allow to scratch your ears these days."

Adrianna turned to Grace and Mackenzie. "I haven't been around horses in years. Samson and

Delilah are beautiful. All of your horses are gorgeous."

Grace and Mackenzie stepped in beside Adrianna as Grace touched Delilah's golden mane. "Thank you. These two are very special to us. Mackenzie and I bought them ten years ago from a man who was going to put them to sleep because they were just not winning for him at the track. We named them Samson and Delilah because I would have liked to have shaved that man bald and taken all his strength and power away from him."

Adrianna smiled at this exceptional woman. She knew she had just met two extraordinary people. Adrianna turned suddenly as she heard Erica shout, "Rosa!"

Adrianna watched Erica dash toward the sliding glass doors and dive into the arms of a robust Hispanic woman dressed in an apron. Rosa smothered Erica in a motherly hug before grabbing her by her shoulders and holding her back to have a good long look. "We only see you on weekends at your Mama and Poppa's house, Erica. You stay away too long."

"I know, Rosa. Work's been crazy."

"No excuses, Erica. You need to visit with us more often. We are your family." Rosa turned Erica around and pointed toward Adrianna. "Now, you introduce me to this Italian girl you have brought to your Mama's house."

Erica reached for Adrianna's hand and guided her closer. "Adrianna Taylor, I would like you to meet the woman that changed my diapers and has never let me forget it. This is Rosa, the woman who has kept my parents' house in order for forty years."

Adrianna extended her hand and shook Rosa's. "It's a pleasure to meet you, Rosa."

Rosa held Adrianna's hand and eyed her from head to toe. She reached out and held Adrianna's chin in the palm of her hand. "You are a beautiful Italian girl. You have a strong spirit and beautiful tired blue eyes."

"Rosa, Adrianna came here to join us for breakfast, not to have her fortune read."

Grace touched Adrianna's arm. "Erica told us about your mother's surgery, Adrianna. How's she doing now that she's home?"

Rosa squeezed Adrianna's chin and gave her a warm smile before letting her free. "You sit and talk with the family while I finish getting breakfast ready." Erica guided Adrianna to a seat at the table while Mackenzie poured them both a glass of orange juice.

"Thank you, Mackenzie. My mother's doing really well. It really has been miraculous how well she has done in such a short period of time." Adrianna smiled at Erica. "But I think we're going to have to keep her busy because she certainly has become more mischievous than she was prior to her surgery."

"When Erica called us this morning, she told us a little about what happened last night. Now that you're both here, I want to hear every last detail, and don't leave anything out."

Adrianna shared their story with Grace and Mackenzie and had them both laughing by the time she was done.

Rosa served a delicious breakfast of crispy French toast sprinkled with cinnamon sugar and garnished with fresh juicy strawberries. Mackenzie talked to Adrianna about their law careers and his business.

Adrianna asked Grace about her career and was moved when she shared her most touching patients with her. The conversation twisted and wound its way through many topics, finally settling on Carolyn's surgery and her recovery.

Rosa cleared the dishes and flatly refused any help as she served dishes of fresh strawberries and bananas.

After two delightful hours, Mackenzie patted his trim stomach and pulled back his chair. "You'd better get me moving, darling, or we may never get our errands done this afternoon."

Grace folded her napkin on her placemat and sighed. "You're right, sweetheart. We should get going and leave these lovely ladies to their horseback ride. Joe should have Samson and Delilah saddled and ready to go."

Everyone pulled back from the table and tucked in their chairs. Mackenzie stood next to Adrianna and touched her arm. "Thank you for sharing breakfast with us, Adrianna. You're going to have to come and spend some time with us when we can really talk and get to know you."

Mackenzie leaned forward and kissed her cheek. He moved past Adrianna and took Erica in his strong arms and hugged her tight. "As Rosa would say, don't be such a stranger at your Mama and Poppa's house."

Erica smiled and kissed her father. "Okay, Poppa."

Grace turned to Adrianna and took her hands. "Thank you for sharing your morning with us, Adrianna. You're the first woman Erica has brought home since Laura passed away."

Adrianna smiled and squeezed Grace's hands. "Abby and Trina said the same thing. I'm not sure whether to be flattered or frightened."

"Don't be frightened. Just enjoy each other. Time is a precious gift. Speaking of time, if you don't have plans tomorrow afternoon, we're having our entire family over for a barbecue. We'd be honored if you could join us."

Adrianna smiled and turned back to Grace. "I would love that, Grace. Thank you for inviting me."

Erica stood before her mother and hugged her close. They leaned back and stared at each other warmly. "We'll see you tomorrow, Mom."

Grace smiled and kissed her daughter. "Sounds wonderful, darling."

After saying good-bye, Erica and Adrianna headed down the steps, and Grace and Mackenzie headed indoors.

Adrianna slipped her hand into Erica's and walked with her through the corral gates. "Your parents are wonderful, Erica."

"They seem to feel the same way about you."

"I just loved Rosa. She must have been a lot of fun to have around when you were growing up."

"I love Rosa very much. She was always like a second mother to me. She taught us all to speak Spanish, and that was one of the greatest gifts she gave me."

Erica guided Adrianna toward the entrance of the stables. They heard the loud whinnying of nearby horses.

Erica and Adrianna turned as the stable manager led Samson and Delilah toward them. Erica reached out and took their reins. "Thanks for saddling the horses for us, Joe. I really appreciate that."

Erica stepped aside and introduced the stable manager to Adrianna.

"I put plenty of water in the saddlebags, Erica. You should be all set."

"Thanks, Joe. That's great. We'll be out for a couple of hours."

"Take your time. These two are itching for a good ride." Joe patted Samson's hindquarters before heading back into the stable.

Erica handed Delilah's reins to Adrianna. "Let me give you a hand up." Erica cupped her hands and provided a step for her well-worn cowboy boot and eased her into the saddle.

Erica gracefully swung into Samson's saddle and went over some basics with Adrianna about horseback riding.

"Am I going to have a sore bottom by the time you and Delilah are done with me?"

"Guaranteed. Nothing a warm bath won't cure."

Adrianna turned Delilah around to face the same direction as Samson. "Is that the only treatment you're going to prescribe, Dr. Beaumont?"

"Actually this is part of your penance, and that's what you get for sentencing me to all these nights of tossing and turning." Erica clicked for Samson and gently tapped his ribs with her legs to get him to move forward.

Adrianna was right at her side. "Poor sport."

Erica had to laugh as they headed onto a cleared trail leading into the wooded area. They rode side by side across rolling hills and through shaded trails.

They carefully maneuvered around boulders and across trickling streams. Erica kept asking Adrianna if she wanted to stop and head back, but she was in total bliss riding with Erica through this gorgeous land and refused to let her turn back.

Two hours later, Erica circled them back to a shallow river within sight of the ranch. A riot of orange, red, and white trumpet vine cascaded over the rocky hillside attracting a collection of vibrantly colored butterflies. A thick growth of bird of paradise lined the river's edge with clusters of red sage and fairy duster leaning toward the water as if in search of a drink.

They reached a large clearing. Erica dismounted and helped Adrianna out of her saddle. She guided the horses to the river's edge and secured their reins to a nearby apple tree.

Adrianna moved closer to the clearing and saw a huge cedar deck with umbrella tables and cushioned chairs. Several benches faced the river along with a very long picnic table and a stone bonfire pit. "This place is so beautiful."

Erica touched Adrianna's lower back and guided her toward the picnic table. "It is, isn't it." She unscrewed the top from a bottle of ice-cold water and handed it to her.

"Thank you. I'm parched."

They both took a healthy drink of water before setting their bottles down on the picnic table. Adrianna turned to face the river as Erica leaned back against the edge of the table.

Erica watched the gentle breeze ripple across the river's surface and bend the bright yellow goldenrod blooming along its sandy edge. Yellow-gold California poppies smiled brightly in the breeze amidst tall blue lupines. Desert bluebells swayed delicately as dark scarlet flax blanketed the sloping hillside. The gentle breeze stirred lightly around them and played with Adrianna's thick hair, brushing it back from her beautiful face. Her golden olive complexion glowed in the sun's rays as she hugged her arms across her belly and absorbed the beauty around her. Her loose white dress shirt flapped against her slender frame and opened wider to expose her fitted white tank top. Erica admired the form fit of her sexy jeans right down to the tips of her well-worn cowboy boots.

Adrianna absorbed the shrill sound of the mockingbirds and great-tailed grackles as she watched the mallard ducks and Canada geese float effortlessly on the water. "This place is so beautiful. It fills me with peace."

"I know what you mean. I love this place. My parents or Rosa would bring us down here all the time when we were little, and we would picnic and swim in the river. When I was a kid, this river seemed as big as an ocean. We'd have barbecues and bonfires, and when we got older we would pitch tents and camp out down here. There was just no place like it on earth for me. I'd bring a book and come down here to read for some peace and quiet. In high school, I would come down here and do my homework whenever daylight would permit. I spent so much time here that my parents started calling this Erica's room. When I would come home from med school, this is the first place I would stop. I just needed to stand here and take a deep breath, and then I knew I was home."

Adrianna watched her close her eyes and drink in the memories. Erica's dark, flowing ringlets framed her face as her dark, thick eyelashes sat peacefully against her high cheekbones. Her small nose tilted to the afternoon sun as her full, moist lips parted slightly. Adrianna loved the lines of her jaw and the slender column of her neck as she tilted her head forward. Her loose denim shirt did little to hide the allure of her feminine softness while her faded Levi's hugged her like a second skin. A tingling heat spread throughout Adrianna's belly and streamed to her thighs. She felt her pulse quicken.

Erica opened her eyes and saw Adrianna watching her. Her sapphire eyes swam with profound emotions. She looked so beautiful standing in her favorite place. She had spent so much time here alone over the past two years. There had been something missing, and now she stood before her.

Adrianna turned away and jammed her hands into her jeans. "When you walked into the quiet room after Carolyn's seizure and proceeded to explain to us what happened, I was in awe of your intelligence, strength, and self-confidence. Then you gave me the verbal whipping of my life for my behavior during that nightmare, Erica, and you instantly won my heart. It doesn't matter how hard I've tried to ignore what my heart has been telling me. I just have to look at you, and I feel so defenseless. You completely consume me. Everything I feel for you rushes to the surface when I'm near you. I've tried so hard to fight this and have failed miserably. Every time I'm near you, I want to touch you, feel you, hold you, and taste you. I have such a burning desire to spend every minute of every day with you.

"I never intended to fall in love with you, Erica. The timing is so poor right now, and you just slipped through my defenses and stole my heart anyway. That should be a federal offense, you know. I should just sue you."

Adrianna loved the sensitive, warm look in Erica's eyes as she moved to stand before her.

"I never wanted to need another woman like I needed Hailey. I didn't think I was going to survive when she was taken from me. Then I needed you to help my mother. I came to trust you and count on you, and you were the answer to our prayers. Now I need you for me."

Erica rested her hands on Adrianna's jeans-clad hips and pulled her in close. She glided her hands over Adrianna's slender hips and onto her lower back, pulling her in tight between her thighs. "The first time I saw you sitting at Carolyn's bedside, holding her hand after that first seizure, you looked so scared, yet so strong and brave and very angry. I just wanted to reach out and take all your worries away. At the time, you would have just bit off my hand, and that made you all the more alluring.

"Then I found myself just aching to see you, talk to you, and comfort you. I haven't wanted a woman like this since Laura. Then I would think about her, and I would miss her so much. I wasn't ready to let her go when she died, Adrianna, but I thought I was managing pretty well. Instead, what I was doing was cocooning in my grief and hoping never to feel the things I felt for Laura. Then I saw you there beside Carolyn, and you took my breath away. Your eyes, your face, your grief, your anger. I wanted to explore it all and understand everything about you.

"I have an unwritten rule never to date my patients or their family members. You must have missed that sign in the ICU, because in one foul swoop you stole my heart. I have fallen so madly in love with you that I can't do anything without thinking about you."

Adrianna slid her hands along Erica's defined arms and up over her strong shoulders. She moved gently over her slender neck and slid her thumbs under her intense eyes and across her cheekbones. She moved intimately close as she stared at her entrancing, slightly parted lips and felt a desire so poignant it flowed hot to her thighs. She slid her thumb across her full lower lip and looked up into those compelling coral-green eyes. "I love you so much, Erica."

Erica slowly lowered her mouth and barely touched her lips to Adrianna's. Her soft, throaty moan ignited a fire so hot it flowed like erupting lava through Erica's entire being. Erica leaned back slightly and stared into those heavy-lidded, torrid eyes. "I love you, Adrianna." Erica laid a soft, moist kiss on her pouty lower lip before taking her lips with the fervor that had consumed her every moment since she'd met this incredible woman.

Adrianna held Erica's face in her hands and immersed herself in this kiss that sent her to places she had never been before. She took her lower lip into her mouth and traced it with the tip of her tongue as she felt Erica's sharp indrawn breath and heard her bewitching moan. She gently touched her tongue to Erica's upper lip and felt her open her mouth in total surrender. She crushed her lips to Erica's and gasped in delirious pleasure as she timidly probed her with the tip of her tongue, instantly consumed in a passionate dance of discovery.

Erica leaned her forehead against Adrianna's and struggled to catch her breath. She held her close in her arms and gently skimmed the open palm of her hands over the subtle contours of her back. She tilted her head up and brushed her lips against her forehead. "Well, that should help me sleep at night."

Adrianna laughed softly as she glided her hands across Erica's shoulders. She playfully tugged on the collar of her faded denim shirt and traced her fingertip along the outline of her amethyst pendant against her chest. "I'm glad I could be of service to you, Dr. Beaumont."

Erica sighed impatiently and slid her hands onto Adrianna's slender hips and across her lower back. She tucked her thumbs into the back of her slim, southwestern-style leather belt and held her tight against her. "Now I may never be able to fall asleep at night thinking about that incredible kiss."

Adrianna slid her hands along the sides of Erica's neck and immersed them in her thick, flowing ringlets. She held the back of her head firmly in her hands and tilted her slowly forward. "I plan on filling your mind with our kisses till we are both ready to fill our nights with our passion."

Erica pressed her lips to Adrianna's and slipped her tongue between her slightly parted lips. Adrianna opened her mouth to her and immersed her in a kiss that sent them both soaring on a cresting wave of unbridled lust and need.

Adrianna nestled her face against her flushed neck and skimmed her hands over the well-defined muscles of her back. She rubbed her nose along her slender neck and kissed the sensitive spot behind her ear. A gasping moan escaped from her lips as Adrianna touched the tip of her tongue to her earlobe and skimmed her hands across the back pockets of her form-fitting, faded Levi's. "I'm so grateful you brought me out here, Erica. This was the most wonderful place to share our first kiss."

Erica brushed a kiss against her temple and rubbed her cheek against hers. "I'd like to share more than just our first kiss with you right now, Adrianna. You set me on fire. I'd better get us back on our horses before I strip you of your sexy jeans and make love to you right here in my room."

Adrianna leaned back slightly and looked into her moist, flaming green eyes. She touched her fingertip to the top button of her denim shirt and across her tanned chest. "When the time is right, will you bring me back here and fulfill that fantasy with me?"

Erica touched her chin with her fingertip and raised her eyes up to her. "That is one promise I look forward to keeping." Erica leaned closer and pressed her lips to the corner of Adrianna's mouth. She nibbled on her pouty lower lip and gently sucked it into her mouth. Adrianna's raspy moan sent waves of longing soaring through Erica's chest and crashing into a tidal wave of tingling heat between her thighs. She slanted her mouth across hers and consumed her lips with a scorching hunger that left them both ravenous for more.

Adrianna struggled to even her breathing as she luxuriated in the comfort and heat of Erica's arms. She brushed her lips lightly across Erica's cheek and leaned her forehead against her face. "Wow." Adrianna could feel Erica's smile against her cheek.

Samson and Delilah were whinnying loudly.

They looked over at the horses staring at them. Erica leaned back slightly and kissed Adrianna's forehead. "Looks like Samson and Delilah are getting tired of waiting for us."

Adrianna smiled and brushed a stray ringlet from Erica's eyes. "Good thing you tied them to that apple tree, or they would be back at the ranch by now."

Erica took Adrianna's hand and grabbed both bottles of water. She handed one to Adrianna and guided her back to Samson and Delilah.

Erica reached up into the apple tree and plucked a large golden yellow Anna's apple. "Maybe we should give them a treat for being so patient." Erica handed the apple to Adrianna and pulled a Swiss army knife from one of the saddlebags. She watched Adrianna step to the water's edge and rinse the apple thoroughly. She walked back to Erica and handed her the apple.

"Thank you, Madame." Erica crouched by a flat rock and proceeded to slice the apple into sections and handed them to Adrianna. "Keep your hands open flat, or they'll mistake your fingers for an apple wedge." Erica loved the way Adrianna crinkled her tiny nose as she watched her step before each horse and feed each a section of apple. In no time, the apple was gone, and Adrianna looked at Erica like a child with a flat tire on her bike. "Can they have more, Erica? One was not nearly enough for both of them."

291

Erica loved her childlike innocence as she touched her thumb to her cheek. "Just don't tell Joe. He's very particular about what the horses eat."

Adrianna rubbed both horses' noses. "None of us will tell, Erica. Our secrets are safe here."

Erica reached up into the tree and pulled down another apple. She cleaned it and sliced it into sections. She handed them to Adrianna, then sat back and luxuriated in the sight of this woman feeding her beloved horses.

Erica cleaned the knife and slipped it back into the saddlebag. She helped Adrianna back onto Delilah before swinging her leg easily over Samson. She took her the scenic route back along the rivers edge and around the back of the stables.

Erica and Adrianna guided Samson and Delilah to a halt before the stable doors, and Joe helped Adrianna down. She gushed with excitement as she told Joe all about their ride.

Joe took the reins from both horses and looked at Samson and Delilah. "And how many apples did these two finagle from you on this ride?"

Adrianna looked at Joe in shock. "How did you know?"

Joe laughed and rubbed the top of Delilah's head. "Because they both smell of sweat and apple juice."

Adrianna looked like a child who was caught with her hand in the cookie jar. "Just one each, Joe. I hope that's okay."

Joe smiled. "Not a problem, Adrianna. I can see they've learned to manipulate someone already." Joe waved at them both and guided Samson and Delilah into the stables.

****

They spent the next two weeks holding true to their promise to take things slowly, as painful as that was for them to part at the end of each time they were together. Adrianna thoroughly enjoyed the Sunday barbecue she shared with the Beaumont family and getting to know each of Erica's brothers and sisters. Adrianna and Erica took each other to their favorite restaurants and made their favorite meals, enjoying the time they shared between their busy work schedules. David and Carolyn invited Erica to dinner, and she basked in the delicious tastes of Carolyn's home cooking.

Their most treasured time was when they escaped on horseback to their favorite place to sit by the riverside, hold each other close, and talk endlessly.

****

The vanilla candle flickered with the gentle breeze as Erica and Adrianna sat at the glass table on Erica's back deck.

Adrianna savored the last bite of lemon meringue pie before wiping her mouth on her red linen napkin. "Dinner was excellent, Erica. Thank you. I loved the way you baked the pork chops on a bed of apples."

Erica rose and collected their dessert plates and cutlery. "You're very welcome, darling. And here you thought I was just another pretty face trying to wine and dine you."

Adrianna smiled. "Oh, you're much more than just another pretty face."

Erica leaned down and kissed her lightly. "Stay here while I put these dishes in the dishwasher."

"Are you sure you don't want any help?"

"Not at all. Relax and I'll be right back."

Erica returned and found Adrianna sitting on the steps of the back deck. She sat behind her and pulled her in tight between her thighs. She wrapped her arms around her and kissed her cheek. "What're you doing sitting down here?"

"I just had to stop and look at the stars one more time before I went home. They're just so beautiful tonight."

Erica looked up at the ebony canvas blanketed with bright stars. "They certainly are bright tonight."

Adrianna leaned her head back against Erica's shoulder and indulged in this moment. She entwined her fingers in Erica's hands and laid them on her belly. She briefly glanced at Erica and then looked down at their hands. "Do you remember when I told you about my cottage up in Flagstaff that's only two and a half hours from here?"

Erica was surprised by her sudden shyness as she leaned in close and held her tight. "Yes, I remember about this beautiful place you told me about."

"Well, I was wondering, since you're off this weekend, if you would like to spend our weekend there? I know that Friday is a busy day for you, so I thought we could leave when you get home from work. I would drive us up there, and you could rest in the car. If you'd be interested in doing that." Adrianna cautiously turned and looked at Erica.

Erica took her face in her hands and brushed her thumbs across her cheeks. She kissed the tip of her nose and gave her a beautiful smile. "How many bedrooms did you say this place had?"

Adrianna reached up and took Erica's hands and held them close to her chest. "It doesn't matter if I was inviting you to Buckingham Palace, I want you to share my bedroom. I want you to share my bed. I don't want to say good-bye to you anymore, Erica. I want to kiss you good night and cuddle into your arms, not see you off at the door. I want to kiss you hello and find you sharing my pillow. I want to wrestle you for the covers and race you for the bathroom. I want your toothbrush and your towel beside mine. I want to make love to you all night long and feel your naked skin next to mine. I want you, Erica. I want you in every part of my day and night without exception."

Erica leaned her forehead against Adrianna's. "I thought you'd never ask."

Adrianna looked up with moist eyes. "Does that mean you'd like to go?"

Erica laughed as she leaned back from Adrianna. "Are you nuts? I've been waiting four long weeks since the day I met you for you to invite me into your bed, and you want to know if I'd like to spend a weekend at your secluded cottage in all of nature's glory?" Erica spread her arms out wide and tilted her face up to the stars. "Yes, yes, yes! I would love to spend the weekend with you in Flagstaff. I don't care if you have as many bedrooms as Buckingham Palace because I'm going to be with you in your bed. I ache to make love to you all night long, Adrianna. How could you even question if I was ready to commit intimately to this relationship?"

Adrianna looked down and toyed with a button on Erica's purple blouse. "You've been so good about not pressuring me, and I just wanted to make sure you still wanted what I want."

Erica took Adrianna's face in her hands and looked deeply into her sensitive eyes. "I want you, Adrianna. I want you in every part of my day and night without exception. I don't want to miss a second of the sound of your tiny bare feet on these hardwood floors. I want to share our tea from Cinderella, Pocahontas, Belle, Snow White, Cruella, Jasmine, and Tinker Bell. I want to hear the sound of your little BMW roadster pulling into the driveway and know you have come home to me. I want you to curl up on the couch and share your work with me while I tell you about my patients. I want to eat your pasta and do our dishes. I want us to tangle in our sheets and never find a way out."

Adrianna burst into laughter and leaned her face into the palm of Erica's hand.

Erica brushed her cheek with her thumbs. "I love you so much, Adrianna. I want you completely. I want to make love to you and to love you for the rest of my life."

Adrianna leaned into Erica and kissed her softly. "I love you so much, Erica." Their lips met slowly and moved against each other in gentle caressing waves, in a kiss so different from the others.

Erica leaned her face against Adrianna's and sighed deeply. "Tomorrow night is a whole twenty-four hours away. Why put off until tomorrow what you can accomplish today?"

Adrianna laughed softly and kissed Erica's full lower lip. "I want our first time to be so special, Erica. This is so hard for me as well, but I really would like us to wait till tomorrow."

Erica groaned and dropped her chin onto her chest. "You've made me wait four weeks, I guess another night is not going to kill me. However, I'm getting really tired of taking tepid showers."

Adrianna laughed and gave her a seductive look. "I'll make it worth your wait, sweetheart. There's also this really neat place on the way to my cottage called The Rose where I would like to take you for dinner tomorrow night. It's one of my favorite little places, and it's owned and operated by two lesbians. It's quite the chic lesbian hangout. They have a lovely outdoor patio and great food. They created a dance floor among the trees and play really great music. Do you think you'd like to stop there on the way up?"

"It sounds fantastic, darling. Consider it a date."

Chapter 15

Erica and Adrianna had been driving for two hours along the scenic highway that wove through the Verde Valley and climbed over the Mogollon Rim. Adrianna pulled off the highway and guided her BMW into the parking lot of The Rose. Deep in conversation when they arrived, they hesitantly unhooked their seat belts and slipped out of the vehicle.

Adrianna secured her purse over her shoulder and walked around to Erica's side. Erica looked so elegant in her vibrant teal and purple print, long v-neck vest that flowed gently from a three-button front closure. The deep side slits swayed over her matching purple silk t-shirt and slacks with the help of a gentle breeze. She reminded Adrianna of the willowy models that graced the catwalks.

Adrianna took her hand as she guided her up the wooden front porch and into a beautiful barn that had been restored into a spacious, festive restaurant.

Adrianna asked to be seated outside. Erica was fascinated by the warm, inviting ambiance created by this place full of beautiful women. Adrianna guided Erica through the restaurant and out onto a huge cedar patio that ran the length of the barn and overlooked a calm, glistening lake. Adrianna smiled up at Erica's delighted expression as she guided her to sit at a cozy table for two.

Erica pulled out Adrianna's chair for her. Erica tucked in her chair, admiring Adrianna's sleeveless top of layers of coral silk that fell to soft tiers at her waist. A subtle peach scent seemed to surround her. Her sleeveless top accentuated her smooth olive complexion, and Erica bent down and kissed her delicate shoulder. The wraparound skirt flowed from her slender hips, and the side slit teased Erica with a brief glimpse of a smooth, bewitching thigh.

Cher's song, 'Body to Body, Heart to Heart,' began to fill the air as Erica looked over the edge of the deck. She could see a dance floor nestled among the trees with women dancing intimately to the rhythm of the music. Erica looked over at Adrianna's beaming face as she took her seat.

"What do you think, sweetheart?"

"This place is incredible! How did you find it?"

"My stomach led me here one night."

Erica watched Adrianna look around at the surroundings and saw the emotions cascading through Adrianna's eyes. "Tell me about your cottage."

"I bought the cottage shortly after Hailey died because I needed some place where I could run and hide from my memories and my pain. I've had it for a year now, and I've always come here alone. My family has used my cottage but always when I was in New York." Adrianna reached for Erica's hands and held them close. "Erica, you're the only person I've ever brought here. You're the first woman I've ever wanted to share this part of my life with."

Erica squeezed Adrianna's hands and brought them to her mouth, gently kissing each hand.

"I've always brought work with me when I come to the cottage. When I get tired of my own company, I would pack up my work and come here and sit on this patio. I always enjoy noise around me when I work, so this place was great for my professional creativity. It always gives me a sense of a world out there beyond my own sense of emotional isolation."

The depth of Adrianna's emotions mesmerized Erica. She smiled and squeezed Adrianna's hands tight.

"You're one of the few, rare people that I've ever talked to about Hailey. That alone has helped me to better understand my pain and frustration. Every time you and I talk, I learn about myself and about you, and that alone is a beautiful gift in any friendship. You're the greatest gift I've ever received, Erica, and I look forward to spending the rest of my life with you."

Erica leaned toward Adrianna and kissed her softly. They both noticed their waitress standing at the edge of their table smiling at them. Her bright pink, spiky hair impressed Erica. She had a round, pretty face and had to be in her late twenties and no taller than five feet five inches tall. A black pen dangled from behind one ear and looked dangerously close to tangling in her huge silver loop earrings. Her tight white tank top scooped low to her breasts and displayed a brilliant blue butterfly tattoo for all to see. Her skintight jeans left little to the imagination as her waist apron was filled to capacity with straws, pens and a receipt book. At least a dozen silver bracelets dangled together on one wrist while the other wrist was adorned with a huge watch on a wide leather watchband.

Adrianna smiled. "Hello, Tammy."

Tammy gave Adrianna a smile. "Hi there, beautiful. And speaking of beautiful, who is this gorgeous creature that you were just lip locked with?"

"Tammy, this is Erica. A very special woman in my life."

Erica stood and extended her hand to Tammy. "Hi, Tammy. Its a pleasure to meet you."

Tammy shook Erica's hand firmly and looked into her eyes. "You are one of the most beautiful lesbians I've ever met."

Erica took her seat and blushed as she looked toward Adrianna.

Tammy gently touched Adrianna's shoulder. "Adrianna, where have you been hiding her?"

"Erica and I met a month ago, and the only place I would like to hide her is in my bed."

"That would be very wise. This place is full of hungry lesbians who didn't fail to notice you two when you walked through the doors. Now, do you know what you would like to have this evening?"

"Erica, you've not had a chance to look at the menu, but I would love for you to try the chicken potpie."

"That sounds wonderful."

Adrianna ordered them both salads, bowls of chicken potpie, and glasses of white wine.

Tammy wrote down their order, then slipped her pen in behind her ear. "I'll let Sally know you're here. She'll be thrilled to see you."

"That would be great. I'd really like Sally to meet Erica."

Tammy laughed as she tucked her pad into her apron. "And I'm sure there are a hundred other women in this place who would love to meet Erica. You girls sit tight, and I'll have your salads and some bread right out."

Erica turned to Adrianna and held her hand. "Thank you for suggesting something from the menu. That made it really easy."

"You're welcome, sweetheart. It's a delicious dish, and I know you'll enjoy it."

Erica heard a squeal of delight as a woman called Adrianna's name.

Adrianna turned and quickly rose from her chair. Erica watched a plump woman in her fifties wrap her in a loving embrace. They leaned back and kissed each other. Erica was mesmerized by the maternal love this woman exuded toward Adrianna.

Adrianna and the woman excitedly said hello. "Grab a chair, Sally, and join us."

Sally slid her chair directly across from Erica and Adrianna. She gave Erica a smile.

"Sally, I'd like you to meet someone very special in my life. This is Erica Beaumont." Adrianna gently touched Erica's arm. "Erica, this is Sally Sinclair, the owner of this fine establishment."

Erica extended her hand. "It's a pleasure to meet you, Sally. You have an incredible place here."

Sally was mesmerized by Erica's eyes and continued to hold her hand. "Tammy told me you had incredible eyes, but that's an understatement."

Erica blushed and looked over at Adrianna as Adrianna laughed. "She certainly does have amazing eyes."

Sally hesitantly let go of Erica's hand. "I'm glad you like our little lesbian hideaway, Erica. I want you to know that you're the first woman I've ever seen here with Adrianna."

"Adrianna was just telling me that, and I'm truly touched that she invited me here. I can't believe that she was not swept off her feet by any one of these beautiful women before me."

"Let me tell you, Erica. Adrianna would always come in here by herself with her arms full of books and her laptop computer. Women would trip over her table just to meet her, but Adrianna was so lost in her own little world that she would pick them up and dust them off and send them on their merry way."

Erica smiled at this vision of Adrianna.

"Then one day, I served her some tea and noticed that she was reading a law book. I told her I hated lawyers. Instead of telling me to get lost, she invited me to join her. Before I knew it, I spilled my life story to her and told her how we were in financial trouble because we had not managed our books well, and the IRS was breathing down our necks. Adrianna set up an appointment for me with an accountant and tax lawyer from her firm, and within six months everything in our books was set straight, and the tax lawyer had managed to fight off the IRS for us. When all was said and done, I asked why we had not received a bill for legal services, and we were told that Adrianna had taken care of it. Adrianna did not know us from Eve, yet she took it upon herself to find us the help we needed and even footed the bill. Adrianna has flatly refused to let us pay her back, and even when I try to pick up her dinner tab she raises a big stink." Sally looked at Adrianna fondly and reached for her hand. "I have learned the hard way to let this little, stubborn woman do it her way. Since then, business has been booming, and we are much better organized financially."

Erica was mesmerized by Adrianna's loving generosity. Adrianna squeezed Sally's hand. "Sally, I've told you before, this place brings me such peace and entertainment that I could not bear to see you in trouble, so I was glad to help. Now I have the pure pleasure of sharing this place with the new love of my life."

Sally turned to Erica. "Are you a lawyer as well, Erica?"

"No, actually, Sally, I'm not particularly fond of lawyers myself. I'm a neurosurgeon."

Adrianna threw Erica a deadly look as Sally burst into laughter.

Sally was thoroughly impressed as she looked at Adrianna. "Adrianna, you fell in love with a brain surgeon."

Adrianna smiled deeply and took Erica's hand in her own. "Actually, Sally, I fell in love with Erica. The fact that she's brilliant is just one part of the incredible person that she is. Erica diagnosed my mother with a brain tumor four weeks ago and operated on her. My mother is now home and has more energy than all of us put together."

"Oh, my God! That's horrible, Adrianna, but I'm so glad to hear that your mother's okay. Please say hello to her for us, and tell her I will pray for her."

"I will, Sally, thank you."

"I would love to sit here and chat some more, ladies, but I must get back to the kitchen."

"Thanks, Sally."

Sally rose from the table. "Are you girls going to be at the cottage all weekend?"

"All weekend long. It's our official honeymoon."

"I was going to say I look forward to seeing you both again this weekend and chatting some more when it's a little quieter around here, but you two might not make it out of bed."

"That wouldn't bother me in the least, Sally."

"If you girls need a breath of fresh air, know that we're here and we would love to see you both again." Sally hugged them both and waved good-bye.

Erica helped Adrianna into her chair and seated herself. They both laid their napkins across their laps. Adrianna leaned closer and placed her elbows on the table. "I really like that way you tuck my chair in for me. It's so gallant."

Erica smiled and reached for her hands. "It gives me an opportunity to stand close to you and smell your peach scent."

Erica loved her seductive smile and was about to taste it with her own lips just as their wine, bread, and salads arrived. She moaned with frustration as they both sat back and dug into their food together.

Erica pierced a cucumber slice with her fork and offered it to Adrianna. "I'm so proud of you for what you did for Sally. You went out of your way for her and never expected anything in return, and that's what human kindness is all about. You're an exceptional woman, Adrianna, and the depth of your spirit amazes me."

"Sally is a wonderful woman, and I was just glad to be able to help."

As they finished the last of their salads, Tammy arrived at their table and removed their salad bowls. They talked about the swift business the restaurant had been doing with the population growth in the area.

Tammy returned with two steaming bowls of chicken potpie and placed them down gently. "Be careful, girls, they're hot." She set another basket of freshly baked bread between them.

Erica and Adrianna finished their potpies right down to the last spoonful. Erica wiped her mouth on her napkin. "That was delicious. My tummy thanks you. You can order for me anytime, my love."

Tammy approached their table. "Did you save some room for dessert?"

"I would love Erica to try the blackberry crumble, Tammy."

"Good choice. One blackberry crumble coming up."

"Do you want more wine, sweetheart?"

Erica smiled and looked at her empty glass. "I have reached my quota. If you feed me any more wine, I will be ready for a nap."

Adrianna gently brushed her lips against the rim of her own wine glass. "Naps are about all you're going to get this weekend, my lover."

Tammy returned with their blackberry crumble and two spoons. She set these down between them and leaned toward Adrianna. "You've always been special to us around here, Adrianna, and we're tickled to see you so happy."

Adrianna touched Tammy's chin and kissed her cheek.

Erica watched Tammy blush. "Tammy, your cheeks are now as pink as your hair."

Tammy smiled softly and swatted Erica with her dishtowel. "You're just jealous, Erica, because you don't have the lesbian look like I do." They all laughed together as Tammy made a hasty exit.

Adrianna picked up a fresh blackberry from their dessert and gently placed it in Erica's mouth. She slowly removed her finger from her moist lips and stared into Erica's seductive eyes. She oozed sensuality and passion as she slowly consumed the luscious fruit.

Erica took the spoon from Adrianna's still hand and dug into the dessert. She brought the spoon to Adrianna's lips and watched it disappear into that enticing mouth. "I think we might have to take this dessert home with us."

Adrianna smiled and took the spoon from Erica. She fed her a spoonful of berries and used her thumb to brush a crumb from her full lower lip. "Once we get home, the last thing we will be sharing is this dessert, so I highly recommend that we finish this here."

Erica picked up a plump berry and held it out to Adrianna. "I think we should finish this dessert really quickly. I don't know how much more of this I can take."

Adrianna slowly leaned toward Erica's hand and took the berry into her mouth. She seductively sucked on the tip of Erica's finger just before letting her go.

Erica closed her eyes and moaned softly. She slowly opened her heavy-lidded eyes to find Adrianna a breath away. She kissed her softly, slowly, gently, tasting the sweet nectar of blackberry on her tongue.

The beginning of Tina Turner's song "You're the Best," filtered up to them as Adrianna leaned her face against Erica's. She touched her moist lips to Erica's cheek and her temple. "Please come dance with me, my love. I would like one dance with you before I take you home and slip you between my sheets."

Erica rose from her seat and took Adrianna's hand.

The sun had set, and soft outdoor lamps and citronella candles beautifully lit the dance floor. Towering pines, aspens, and cottonwood trees bordered the dance floor. Rainbow lights dangled between the trees, embracing the dance floor in their festive glow.

Adrianna guided her down the patio steps and onto the dance floor. They stood facing each other as Erica gently glided her hands onto Adrianna's slender waist and pulled her close.

Adrianna entwined her fingers behind Erica's neck, and they rhythmically swayed to their own intimate beat. They fit together like two pieces of a puzzle as the heat emanated from their joined bodies. Women stopped to watch their dance of pure passion.

Their hips moved together in perfect union as they seductively swayed and rocked to the beat, never wavering from each other's eyes.

Erica slipped her hands along Adrianna's lower back and lost them in a layer of coral silk that fell to soft tiers. She slid the open palm of her hands across her lower back and traced the subtle recess along her spine.

Adrianna moaned softly and swayed her hips against Erica's. She loved watching her close her alluring eyes as she ran her hands over her well-defined shoulders. The vibrant purples in her outfit illuminated her beauty and her grace. She was absolutely radiant in the shadows of the soft lighting.

Adrianna gently slid her hands deep into Erica's hair. She watched her slowly open her misty eyes as she kissed her with the intense passion that burned between them. Adrianna leaned her face against Erica's and brushed her lips over her closed eyelids. She lightly touched her lips to her slender neck and loved her throaty gasp.

When the music ended, Adrianna leaned her cheek against Erica's. "God, I want you."

Erica leaned back slightly and held Adrianna close. "Lady, I've wanted you since the moment we met."

Adrianna's smile lit up the night sky as she took Erica by the hand and led her back to their table. Adrianna paid their bill and tipped Tammy generously. Within minutes, they were headed toward Adrianna's cottage.

Fifteen minutes later, Adrianna pulled into a paved driveway and parked in front of a gorgeous two-story log house. They grabbed their bags and groceries as

Erica followed Adrianna through the front door and set down their things.

Adrianna walked around and turned on several lights as Erica stood in awe. The vast openness was like a breath of fresh air. Erica faced a living room with two large chocolate couches facing each other on a cream floral Persian rug. The rich warmth of the hardwood floors shone brightly even in the subtle lighting. A light pine staircase angled upward elegantly to a second-story walkway. The swirling designs engraved in the open doorways added an element of antiquity to the modern home. A large vase with glass lilies presided in one corner while a statue of a single mermaid graced the angle of the staircase. A huge stone fireplace took up one wall.

Adrianna smiled and placed a bag of groceries in Erica's arms. "Let's put these groceries away, and I'll show you around."

Erica followed Adrianna through an elegant living room and dining room. Entering a large mint green and white kitchen, they set down their grocery bags. Adrianna began putting the food away as Erica walked to the sliding glass doors leading to the back deck. Erica stared dumbfounded through the glass doors out onto the lake.

Adrianna finished putting everything away and stood beside Erica. She gently took her hands. "Do you like your getaway, my love?"

Erica was awestruck as she turned to Adrianna. "It's absolutely beautiful, sweetheart. How can you call this oasis a cottage when it's as big as my house?"

Adrianna smiled sweetly as she looked around her cottage. "It's not quite as big as your house,

311

sweetheart, but it is deceiving to call it a cottage. It's my home away from home, so I have always called it my cottage. It's more than what I needed, but when I saw this place I instantly fell in love with it. The price was right, so I bought it."

"This place is a piece of heaven on earth."

Adrianna was moved by Erica's reaction. She leaned toward her and kissed her with the passion and desire that had consumed her since the day they met.

Adrianna hugged Erica tight and kissed her cheek. "Come on, I'll give you a little tour." Adrianna showed Erica through the two spare bedrooms, living room, dining room, den, library, and sunroom. She slid the patio doors open and watched Erica walk out onto the deck.

Erica stared up at the full moon and star-filled sky as Adrianna stood beside her. Erica wrapped her arm around her and pulled her in tight. She leaned down and kissed her forehead. "It's absolutely beautiful here, sweetheart." She leaned her head against Adrianna's and admired the silhouette of the tall trees and the moonbeam bobbing on the lake's surface.

Adrianna laid her hand on Erica's belly and looked up into her bright coral-green eyes. "There's one room I haven't shown you yet." She took Erica by the hand and stopped to allow them to grab their bags. Adrianna guided Erica through the kitchen and up the stairs. She led her down the hall and opened the door to the master bedroom.

Erica set her bag down and looked around. The soft mint-green hues warmed Erica's soul. She smiled at the sight of the king-sized oak sleigh bed that adorned the center of the room. A flowing mint-green

312

floral duvet covered the bed. Lots of overstuffed floral pillows lay against the headboard invitingly.

One wall contained a huge bay window overlooking the lake, accentuated by a cushioned window seat. A mahogany desk and computer filled a small alcove, accompanied by a white love seat and couch. Two white couches faced each other before a pristine stone fireplace that completed the room.

Adrianna turned on the Tiffany lamp at the bedside and removed several pillows as she stepped beside Erica. "What do you think, sweetheart? Do you like our bedroom?"

Erica laughed softly and took Adrianna into her arms. "I love it, and I would like to spend the rest of my life here in this room with you. It's absolutely beautiful, darling." Erica took Adrianna in her arms and hugged her close. "You have a very special place here, Adrianna, and I'm thrilled you asked me to be here with you."

Adrianna reached up and brushed a stray ringlet away from Erica's eyes. "I've been waiting a long time to share this with you, Erica."

Erica leaned down and touched her lips to Adrianna's. She kissed her softly, leisurely before their longing inflamed their desperate need and swept them up into a fiery kiss of unbridled passion.

Erica brushed her lips against Adrianna's forehead as she attempted to catch her breath. She touched her lips to her cheek and across her jaw before finding her moist, slightly parted lips. "I bought you a present," she whispered against Adrianna's sensuous lips.

"You did?"

Erica kissed the corner of her mouth and touched her tongue to her pouty lower lip. "Yes, I did." She momentarily stepped away from Adrianna's warm embrace and dug into her bag. She pulled out a small gift bag from Victoria's Secret and handed it to Adrianna.

"I like the looks of this already." Adrianna dug into the bag and pulled out two bottles of peach hand and body cream.

"I kind of like the smell of peach on you."

Adrianna smiled and set the cream down on her dresser. She looked back down into the bag and pulled out the most beautiful, short sapphire-blue negligee she had ever seen. Adrianna held it up before her.

"I thought it would look beautiful with your blue eyes."

Adrianna looked up at Erica with moist eyes and stepped toward her. "Thank you so much, Erica. It's beautiful. I'll put the hand cream to good use, and I would love to model this for you."

Erica reached out to touch the lacy negligee. "I was hoping you would say that."

Adrianna kissed her deeply. She hesitantly stepped back and touched Erica's mouth with her fingertips. "I'm going to change in the bedroom next door. Feel free to slip into something more comfortable. The bathroom is right behind you. You should find everything in there that you might need."

Erica watched Adrianna step away. "Adrianna."

Adrianna turned around. "Yes, sweetheart?"

"I love you."

Adrianna smiled deeply. "I love you with all my heart, Erica."

Adrianna gave her a gentle wink and blew her a kiss as she walked out the door.

Fifteen minutes later, Adrianna stepped back into the bedroom and saw that Erica had turned out all the lights except the bedside Tiffany lamp. She adjusted her eyes to the soft glow and saw Erica sitting on the window seat staring out at the lake. She was absolutely stunning. Her thigh-length jade-green silk robe emphasized her tan complexion and displayed her long, sexy legs to perfection.

Erica saw Adrianna's reflection in the window. She slowly swung her legs down from the window seat to see the most incredible vision before her. The sapphire-blue negligee flowed over her slender body and displayed her subtle feminine curves to alluring madness. The thin straps accentuated her fine bones, and the v-neck gently dipped, exposing the soft curves of her perky breasts. The silk swayed against her with each step, igniting a warm, tingling sensation in Erica's belly. "You are so beautiful, Adrianna."

Adrianna stepped in front of Erica and self-consciously looked down at herself. "Do you like it, sweetheart?"

Erica rose from her seat and stepped toward Adrianna. "You look absolutely radiant, my darling." Erica took her into her arms and held her close, feeling the cool silk beneath her hands. "You look radiant and ravishingly sexy. I hope you don't mind if that doesn't stay on you for very long."

Adrianna laughed softly as she leaned back and took in the sight of Erica's silk robe. "This robe is exquisite on you. I finally get a glimpse of your sexy legs."

Erica blushed. "I'm so happy to be here with you, Adrianna."

"I'm so happy to be a part of your life, Erica."

Adrianna leaned toward her and teased her lips with soft kisses. The sound of Erica's moan against her lips fueled her aching need as she kissed her with uninhibited passion.

Adrianna leaned her face against Erica's and struggled to steady her breathing. Her heart beat an erratic pace as she ran her hands over her silk-covered arms and under the collar of her robe. She leaned back slightly and skimmed her hands along the front and gently tugged at the tie at Erica's waist. She easily loosened the knot and slipped it from her waist, tossing the silk belt onto the settee. She held the robe closed as she looked into Erica's sensitive eyes. "I want you so much, Erica."

Erica held Adrianna's face in her hands and kissed her with gentle passion and unrestrained yearning. A wave of desire surged into her chest and crested over her break wall of self-control. Nothing else existed but the feel of Adrianna's face in her hands, the subtle pressure of her hips moving against her and the hot, sweet taste of her playful tongue.

Adrianna leaned back and watched the silk robe slowly part. A hunger so intense burned in her chest and set her pulse racing as she caught a glimpse of smooth, tanned skin. She slowly ran her fingers along the seam of the elegant silk robe and timidly touched the few freckles on Erica's chest. She traced the outline of her amethyst pendant and placed a soft kiss along the slender column of her neck.

Erica's moan echoed deep in her throat as she tilted her head to allow Adrianna better access. She threaded her fingers deep in Adrianna's thick hair and held her head close. A tingling heat raged in her chest and gripped the muscles of her belly as she luxuriated in the caress of her moist lips.

Adrianna gripped the front of Erica's robe in clenched fists as she kissed the hollow at the base of her throat. She touched her tongue to Erica's upturned jaw and luxuriated in her tense gasp. She left a trail of soft brushing kisses along her chest and pressed her face between her breasts. She slowly parted Erica's robe and watched the silky material glide across her firm breasts and pool at their feet. She stared at Erica's gorgeous breasts and let her eyes roam freely over her entire body. She hesitantly ran the palms of her hands along the soft underside of her breasts and looked up into Erica's smoky green eyes. "You're so beautiful, Erica." She tentatively ran her thumbs across her erect nipples as Erica's rasping moans ignited a seething passion like Adrianna had never felt before.

Erica held Adrianna's face in her hands and kissed her softly, slowly, and tenderly. She touched her lips to her pouty lower lip and gently sucked it into her mouth. She touched her lips to the corner of her full mouth and delighted in Adrianna's throaty moan. She tempted her with teasing kisses as she glided her hands along her smooth neck and felt her bounding, erratic pulse. Her subtle peach scent filled Erica's senses as she hungered to taste every part of her.

Adrianna leaned her forehead against Erica's and struggled to catch her breath. She gently swayed her hips against her and slid her hands across Erica's shoulders and down her smooth back. She brushed her fingertips across the shallow indentation of Erica's lower back and over her tight bottom as she explored her naked skin for the first time.

Erica arched her neck and groaned with impatient need. She gripped Adrianna's face firmly in her hands and kissed her with fierce hunger. She tried valiantly to control her desperation only to have Adrianna provoke her unrestrained desire with her thrusting tongue. Her control snapped as she gave Adrianna as much as she demanded.

Erica leaned her forehead against Adrianna's as they both gasped for their next breath. Erica slid her hands over Adrianna's slender shoulders and traced the thin strap of her negligee with her thumbs. She brushed her fingertips across the lacy bodice and over the contours of her heaving breasts. She felt Adrianna tense against her fingertips as she traced the outline of her straining nipples.

Adrianna moaned with burning anticipation as she pressed her breasts into Erica's hands. She gripped her shoulders tightly and arched against her in complete surrender.

Erica left a trail of warm, moist kisses down Adrianna's arched neck and across her exposed chest. Her smooth, olive skin was hot beneath her lips as she eagerly tasted her skin. Erica crouched lower and brushed her face across her heaving breasts before touching her tongue to a straining, silk-covered nipple.

Adrianna cried out and balled her hands into Erica's hair, guiding her face closer. She threw her head back and groaned as she felt Erica take her deeply in her mouth.

Erica released Adrianna's peaked nipple and saw it strain against the wet material. She looked up into her blazing eyes as she slipped her hands over her smooth, shapely thighs and under the hem of the negligee. She eased the satiny material over her hips and up over her head. She carelessly tossed it on the settee as she knelt before her. She placed the open palm of her hands on Adrianna's heated thighs and slowly slid them up to her slender belly, exploring the contours of her beautiful body as if Adrianna were a priceless work of art. She traced her thumbs around her belly button before skimming her fingertips through her dark mound of hair. Adrianna's cries inflamed her scorching desire as Erica pressed her open mouth to her slender belly.

Adrianna's knees buckled as she gripped Erica's face to her belly. "Please, sweetheart, I can't take this any longer. I need to lie down."

Erica stood before her and swept her into her arms and gently laid her across the soft, mint-green sheets. Erica eased herself over Adrianna and nestled her hips between her parted thighs as their naked skin touched in an intimate, sensuous connection.

Adrianna gripped Erica's hips and pulled her in tight against her. She moaned in pure ecstasy, closing her eyes and floating on the blissful sensation of Erica's gentle weight against her.

Erica buried her face in Adrianna's hair fanned out on the pillow and inhaled her peach scent. She touched her lips to her earlobe and her jaw as Adrianna groaned deliriously. Erica kissed her smooth neck and touched her tongue to her erratic, bounding pulse. She left a trail of moist kisses across her chest and down between her straining breasts. She struggled between wanting this moment to last and the raging need to consume this woman in one bite.

Adrianna wove her fingers into Erica's thick ringlets and pressed her firmly against her chest. She arched her parted thighs against her and wallowed in the tingling sensation of Erica's breasts and belly so intimately against her.

Erica gently rocked her hips against Adrianna's warm thighs and was inflamed by her throaty moans. She felt Adrianna wrap her legs around her waist and rock her hips to their own intimate rhythm. Erica brushed her lips beneath Adrianna's nipple and along the outside of her breast. Adrianna's pleas for more and her writhing body filled Erica with a scalding need as she took her nipple in her mouth and bathed it with her warm, wet tongue. She sucked on it gently and scraped it through her teeth before granting some attention to her other breast. She slipped the rigid nipple in her mouth and caressed it with her tongue as Adrianna arched her neck and pressed her breast firmly in Erica's mouth.

"Oh God, sweetheart, that feels so wonderful."

Erica slowly allowed the rigid nipple to slip from between her wet lips as she kissed a hot path to Adrianna's moist, sensuous mouth. She looked deeply into her smoky, sapphire-blue eyes and kissed her softly. "I love you." A single tear escaped from Adrianna's thick dark lashes and slid down her cheek. Erica brushed it away with her thumb as she kissed her cheek, her upturned jaw, and her closed eyelids. She trailed a path of moist kisses down her throat and across her chest till her lips found a taut nipple and drew circles around it with her tongue.

Adrianna's eyes flew open as she watched Erica tease her breast. "God, sweetheart, you're making me crazy." Adrianna gripped the back of Erica's head with one hand and guided her nipple deeply into Erica's mouth. She dropped her head back onto the pillow and groaned with pure sexual bliss.

Erica smiled as she sucked on her nipple and taunted it with her teeth. She supported herself on one hand as the other skimmed the soft underside of Adrianna's breast. She skimmed her fingers along her side and delved in the feminine curve of her hip. She grazed her fingertips across Adrianna's hip and along the inside of her thigh and loved her erotic, impatient moans. She made light feathery circles along the inside of her thigh and felt her part her thighs wider in urgent need. She skimmed her fingertips over her hip and across her slender belly. She traced a circle around her belly button before tauntingly gliding back to the inside of her thighs.

Adrianna groaned impatiently. She tilted her hips to encourage Erica to explore her. Her scintillating touch drove her to the brink as her body teetered on the edge of ecstasy.

Erica grazed her hand over Adrianna's hip and belly button. She opened her palm flat and laid it over Adrianna's belly. She filled her with a loving heat before combing her fingertips through her dark mound of hair and delving into her incredible wetness.

Adrianna arched her neck and groaned with pure uninhibited ecstasy, "Oh, God, yes!" She gently rocked her hips to the rhythm of Erica's light touch. She slipped her hands down Erica's smooth back and over her tight bottom. She gripped her hips firmly and rhythmically thrust against her scintillating caress.

Erica kissed Adrianna's exposed neck and touched her tongue to her earlobe. "God, darling, you feel so incredible."

Adrianna turned her face and touched her lips to Erica's. "I love you so much."

Erica smiled and kissed her deeply as she explored her velvety folds. She felt a gentle shudder at her fingertip as Adrianna hardened with each feathery stroke.

Adrianna held her breath and leaned her face against Erica's. She dug her fingertips into her shoulders as her entire body quivered beneath Erica's. She felt herself teetering on the jagged edge of utter bliss as she struggled to hold on to this moment.

Erica luxuriated in her womanly scent as she kissed her face. She watched Adrianna struggle to open her heavy-lidded eyes, loving the look of passionate surrender burning within her. She saw her pearly white teeth bite into her lower lip in an attempt to restrain her release.

Erica touched her tongue to Adrianna's lower lip and watched it escape from its tight hold. She traced the slight indent and kissed her softly. "Don't hold back, sweetheart. I want to hear you scream for me."

Adrianna stared into Erica's eyes and ran her fingers deep into her ringlets. She held her head firmly in her hands and kissed her with unbridled desire.

Erica heard Adrianna's gasp and felt her entire body quiver. She slid her fingertip slowly across her wet, rigid essence in repetitive tight circles as Adrianna's body suddenly stilled.

Adrianna pressed her face against Erica's and felt the tightly coiled tension in every muscle of her body. A tingling heat burned at Erica's touch and fanned into her belly and chest like a raging fire. She thrust her hips against Erica's feathery touch one final time before groaning, "Oh, God, baby, yes." She dug her fingers into Erica's shoulders and screamed her name with explosive ecstasy as her body felt like molten lava erupting from a dormant volcano. Adrianna dropped her head onto the pillow as vibrant hues of blue and green flashed before her eyes like fireworks exploding behind a stained glass window.

Erica laid her face next to Adrianna's and slid her finger over her pulsating essence and plunged deep inside her. She was instantly pulled into a tight, hot, wet cavern and felt so emotionally connected to her.

They lay side by side, cocooned in each other's arms, as Erica watched Adrianna's gentle rhythmic breathing. Her hair fanned out around her beautiful face, and her long, dark eyelashes lay softly against her flushed cheeks. Her full lips were slightly parted as her tongue reached out to moisten them. Minutes later, Erica slipped her fingers from deep within her and saw her wince with the heightened sensitivity. She glided her hand through her dark mound of hair and across her warm belly. She touched her fingertips along the outside of her soft breast and saw the thin, four-inch scar running from her right nipple toward her right shoulder.

Erica reached toward the scar and traced it gently with her fingertip. Adrianna watched the deeply concerned emotions tumble across Erica's eyes.

She placed her hand over Erica's. Erica looked into her warm, loving eyes. "I wish I could have been with you for your surgery."

Adrianna reached up and caressed her cheek. "I wish you could have been there too, sweetheart. I'm just glad you were there for Carolyn."

Erica gently entwined her fingers in Adrianna's and retraced the scar. "How does that feel?"

"It feels really nice. The surgeon said I might lose sensation in that breast because of the surgery, but that's not something that was important to me at the time." Adrianna gently traced Erica's lower lip. "Prior to this moment with you, I've not been touched since my surgery. I didn't really know what I would be able to feel." Adrianna touched her fingertips to Erica's eyebrows and down over her face. "You're an incredible lover, Erica. I never imagined feeling as much as I felt with you. You sent me to heights I've never experienced before."

"You were wonderful to love, Adrianna." Erica gently brushed her thumb across Adrianna's right nipple and luxuriated in its erectness. "I would be more than happy to work with this beautiful breast and slowly reintroduce it to a lifetime of very stimulating sensations." She slowly traced the soft pad of her thumb around the budding nipple and over its dimpled contour. "I think we should create our very own conditioning program. I feel it's my duty to help your breasts reach their highest level of pleasure."

Adrianna laughed and guided Erica's face closer. "I like the sounds of that." Adrianna kissed Erica softly and whispered against her lips, "Ti amo. That's 'I love you' in Italian."

Erica kissed Adrianna softly as she leaned back and looked deeply into her eyes. "That's by far the nicest thing you've said to me in Italian. I love you so much, sweetheart. I hope I didn't hurt your breast when I touched you."

Adrianna gently touched her face. "You would never hurt me, darling. Your loving was nothing but tender and exquisite. Let me see if I can return the pleasure." Adrianna merged their lips in a deep, probing kiss of explosive passion. She threaded her fingers deep into Erica's thick ringlets and held her head firmly in her hands. Adrianna's tongue dueled and caressed with Erica's as she ached to consume her. Adrianna gently rolled Erica onto her back as she floated herself to lie on top of her.

Erica groaned with unrestrained desire as she slid her hands down Adrianna's smooth back and over her slender hips. She skimmed her fingertips over her tight, gorgeous bottom and delved into her feminine curves.

Adrianna nuzzled into Erica's neck and basked in her sensuous moans of pleasure. She left a trail of moist, soft kisses from Erica's neck and across to her throat. She gently moved her amethyst pendant aside and touched her moist lips to her tanned chest and down to her breasts. Erica gasped as Adrianna slowly took her soft, warm nipple into her mouth and easily brought it to attention. She caressed it with smooth long strokes as it budded harder against her tongue.

Adrianna let her taut nipple slip from between her moist lips as she kissed the underside of her breast. She slowly, tauntingly lowered herself, brushing her breasts against Erica's dark mound of hair. She brushed her lips across her slender belly and touched her tongue to the sensitive skin beneath Erica's belly button.

Erica arched beneath her and released a deep guttural sound of sensuous pleasure. She swayed her hips against her and felt Adrianna make light teasing, circles against her belly with her tongue. Her erotic touch sent tidal waves of caressing heat across her belly and down between her thighs. Erica moved restlessly as she begged for fulfillment.

Erica leaned up and took Adrianna by the shoulders and guided her back up to her face. She stared into her passionate sapphire-blue eyes and crushed her mouth to hers. They both fell back onto the bed and consumed each other's lips with the hunger of insatiable lovers.

Adrianna immersed herself in Erica's desperate need as she kissed her with unbridled passion and desire. Adrianna probed her sweet mouth with her tongue as she molded her hand to Erica's warm breast and felt her rigid nipple burrow against the palm of her hand. She slid her nipple between her fingers and caressed it with long, even strokes. She heard Erica's deep cries of pleasure and need as she slid her hand over her breast and down over her slender hip. She trailed her fingertips over the subtle curve of Erica's hip and across her trim belly. She touched the soft pad of her thumb to her belly button and caressed it with slow, gentle circles.

Erica moaned with burning anticipation and leaned her face against Adrianna's. She glided her hands down her smooth back and over her hips, gripping her firmly and thrusting gently against her. The tingling heat raged between her thighs as it threatened to consume her.

Adrianna loved her lusty moans as she felt Erica separate her own legs and encouraged Adrianna to discover her. Adrianna's desire to intimately explore her was overwhelming. She gently slid her hand down Erica's belly and combed her fingertips through her mound of tight, dark curls and slowly, gently thrust within her. They both moaned together as Adrianna explored her hot, tight, wet center.

Erica buried her face into Adrianna's shoulder and released a raspy moan as she wallowed in Adrianna's incredible touch. Erica dropped her head back onto their pillow and closed her eyes as she moved her hips to Adrianna's erotic rhythm.

Adrianna gently kissed Erica's neck and throat as she luxuriated in her throaty moans. She slipped her fingers from within her and explored her warm, silky folds. She caressed her slowly in her own wetness, luxuriating in the feel of her firm arousal. Adrianna caressed her in small, light circles as Erica swayed against her.

Erica suddenly stopped moving her hips, gently arched her neck and screamed an erotic, passionate moan of pure ecstasy. She gripped Adrianna's shoulders tightly and thrust one final time against her as a thunderous spasmodic eruption ripped from Adrianna's touch and tore straight through her.

Adrianna gently slid inside her as her spasms pulled her in deeper. Adrianna lay beside Erica and rested her head up on her elbow and watched her lie in peaceful oblivion. Adrianna felt a deep sense of love and fulfillment as she gently played with a stray ringlet and kissed Erica's eyes. She loved the way her long dark eyelashes lay against her high cheekbones. A smile curled the corners of Erica's moist, sensuous lips as Adrianna leaned down and kissed her softly.

"Wow. That was incredible. You're an incredible lover, Adrianna."

"I've dreamed of being with you like this for weeks. I knew it was going to be beautiful, but this was really incredible."

Erica gently rolled to her side and eased herself over Adrianna. She parted Adrianna's thighs with her knee and lowered her body to connect with her intimately as she luxuriated in the sound of her gentle moan. "You're an incredible woman, Adrianna."

Adrianna reached up and touched Erica's face with her fingertips. She slowly traced her full lower lip and skimmed her fingers along her jaw. "I love you, Erica."

Erica kissed her softly and gently swayed against her. She kissed her face and brushed her lips across her tiny chin. She skimmed her tongue under her upturned jaw and down the slender column of her neck. She was thoroughly aroused by Adrianna's purring sounds as she touched her tongue to her scar and consumed her nipple with an insatiable hunger.

Adrianna arched with each scintillating stroke, guiding her breast deeper into Erica's mouth. She reached above her head and gripped the edges of her pillow as she floated on a euphoric cloud of sexual bliss.

Erica brushed her lips down Adrianna's belly as her hands explored the subtle curves of Adrianna's waist. She slid her hands over her hips and along the inside of her thighs, gently parting her legs wider. She slid her hands under Adrianna's sexy, firm bottom and inhaled her heady, feminine scent. She grazed her lips along the inside of Adrianna's thigh before delving into her wetness and tasting her for the first time. Her wondrous, sensual strokes drove Adrianna into a sexual frenzy as they continued to make love for hours.

****

A brilliant flash of lightning momentarily filled the bedroom with bright blinding light. Erica lay on her side facing Adrianna as she watched the lustrous light display illuminate the night sky outside the picturesque bay window. The rain began to fall in large drops against the window before coming down in sheets. Erica was mesmerized by the sound of the rain as she watched Adrianna sleep so peacefully in her arms. She brushed a stray strand of hair away from her eyes and tucked it behind her ear. She trailed her fingertips across Adrianna's naked shoulder and down her arm. She felt cool to her touch as Erica pulled the duvet up over her shoulder and tucked it under her chin.

Erica quietly slipped out from under the warm covers and knelt before her travel bag. She reached inside and pulled out her well-worn, oversized denim shirt and slipped her arms into the sleeves. She left the shirt unbuttoned as she stepped before the fireplace.

She moved aside the cast-iron fireplace screen, opened the flume, and placed some newspaper, kindling, and several logs into the hearth. She found a supply of long matches in a bronze holder beside the fireplace tools. She struck the match and held it to the newspaper until the small flame licked at the paper. The paper was quickly engulfed in flames as Erica watched it embrace the logs. She replaced the cast-iron screen and brushed off her hands.

She slipped into the bathroom and washed her hands before stepping back into the bedroom. She stopped before the fire and instantly felt its warmth.

"You're an incredibly beautiful woman just standing there in your denim shirt, Dr. Beaumont."

Erica turned and smiled as she saw Adrianna leaning up on her elbow. "I didn't mean to wake you. You felt cool, so I thought I would light a fire for us."

"That was really sweet. It feels so warm and cozy in here now." Adrianna pulled back the bed covers as she watched Erica slip out of her denim shirt. She laid it across the footboard before slipping in beside Adrianna. Adrianna pulled the covers over her and melted into her arms.

"You feel cold, baby. Let me warm you up." Erica pulled her in tight and cocooned Adrianna in her arms. She tucked her head in under her chin and kissed the top of her head. "That's one incredible thunderstorm happening out there. I was hoping to light the fire and slip back into bed before the storm woke you up."

Adrianna laid her face on Erica's chest and stared out the bay window as another clap of thunder rumbled across the lake. She slid her hand across Erica's cool belly and bent her leg across her thighs. "I reached out for you and realized you were gone when I heard the storm outside the window. I felt scared and confused and then I saw the fire in the fireplace and heard the water running in the bathroom. Then I knew you hadn't gone far."

Erica kissed her forehead and held her tight. "I'm sorry for scaring you, sweetheart. I'll never be far."

Adrianna leaned her face against Erica's and kissed her cheek. "When I was ten, we had a wonderful old oak tree in our backyard that I used to play in all the time. One night during a terrible thunderstorm, a bolt of lightning split my favorite oak tree in half, and it had to be cut down. I was devastated, and ever since then I have never been a big fan of thunderstorms. I saw the damage that lightning can do, and storms have always scared me since then."

Erica gently caressed Adrianna's hair. "I'm sorry about your favorite tree, babe. That must have been a terrible experience. Maybe over time we can change your feelings about thunderstorms. We can create a conditioning program kind of like the one we are going to have to pleasure your breasts. Every time there's a storm, we will be automatically conditioned to tear off each other's clothes and make love for hours before a roaring fire. What do you think of that plan?"

Adrianna gave Erica a seductive, passionate look as she eased herself over her. "That's one conditioning program that I would love to embark on with you, my darling. How about we start right now?" Adrianna leaned into Erica's neck and kissed her with moist, sucking kisses.

Erica reached for her pillow and tossed it to the foot of the bed as she arched her neck to allow

Adrianna to wander freely. She moaned with euphoric pleasure as she wove her fingers into Adrianna's thick hair. "But we don't have any clothes to tear off each other."

Adrianna touched her tongue to Erica's earlobe and nipped at it gently as Erica cried out with delight. "All the easier to devour you then, my love." Adrianna disappeared beneath the covers and engulfed Erica in a delirious adventure of pure sensual bliss.

Chapter 16

Erica leaned over Adrianna and kissed her face with warm, soft kisses. She watched her thick dark eyelashes flutter and slowly open.

Adrianna smiled at the beautiful, bright look in Erica's eyes and snuggled in closer to her. "Good morning, sweetheart. I can certainly handle being awakened like this every morning."

"Good morning, my incredible, insatiable lover."

Adrianna seductively slid her leg between Erica's thighs as Erica pulled her into her arms. Erica gently ran her finger along Adrianna's shoulder and down her arm to her thigh. "There is the most incredible sunrise happening out there, and I can even see a rainbow over the lake."

Adrianna leaned back and looked out the window, where the vibrant hues of red and orange illuminated the early morning sky. She turned back to Erica and touched her face. "Let's go sit on the window seat and watch it, darling."

Erica slipped out from under the covers and pulled them back for Adrianna. She helped her out of bed and reached for her denim shirt. "Here, slip into my shirt. It's big, but it will keep you warm." She held it out for Adrianna and watched her slip her arms into the sleeves. Adrianna twirled around and modeled Erica's shirt for her. It enveloped her as it seductively fell to her midthighs with the sleeves dangling well past her arms.

Erica stepped back and whistled softly. "I love the look of you in my denim shirt, sexy lady."

Adrianna pulled the collar up to her face and inhaled the subtle scent of Erica's perfume. "It feels so wonderful against my skin. You'll be lucky if you ever get to wear this shirt again, my love."

Erica stepped toward her and rolled the cuffs of the shirt up for her.

Adrianna took Erica's silk robe off the footboard and held it open for her. "I just love this robe on you, sweetheart." Adrianna stood back and watched Erica secure the silk tie around her waist. She took the end of the ties and guided her closer. "I need to pee."

Erica took Adrianna's face in her hands and kissed her forehead. "Let's go do that and then I'll go get us some orange juice." She took Adrianna by the hand and guided her into the bathroom.

✳✳✳✳

Adrianna leaned back into Erica's arms as they sat together on the window seat in silence. Together they watched the most amazing show before them as a blazing ball of orange sun rose to warm their souls.

They sipped their orange juice and marveled at the double rainbow. Erica set her glass down on the mahogany table beside her. She caressed Adrianna's slightly disheveled hair and kissed her temple. "Thank you for such a beautiful night last night."

Adrianna turned to face Erica and saw the loving look in her eyes. "Thank you, sweetheart. That's only the beginning of many wonderful nights together for us." Adrianna leaned forward and kissed her softly.

Erica combed her fingers through Adrianna's thick hair. "After last night, you deserve to have my world-famous strawberry banana pancakes. How does that sound?"

Adrianna leaned closer and kissed Erica softly. "Sounds wonderful. I'm starving. After breakfast, I'd love to show you around this lovely town."

Erica smiled and gently caressed Adrianna's soft skin. "That sounds wonderful." She helped Adrianna up off the window seat and gathered their glasses of orange juice.

Adrianna took her glass from her and slipped her hand into hers, guiding her down the stairs to the kitchen.

****

Adrianna left Erica to finish stacking their breakfast dishes in the dishwasher as she headed into the master bathroom. She brushed her teeth again and set out Erica's toothbrush for her before sliding open the large mirrored shower door. She reached in and turned on the dual cascading jets of water. She held out her hand and let the tepid water run over her palm and through her fingers. Once the water reached a comfortable warmth, Adrianna took one step back and slid the mirrored door closed.

Erica stepped behind her. She reached into the shower and turned off the jets of water. She stared into the mirror with eyes filled with sensitive passion. "I love to watch my denim shirt slide across your sexy bottom."

Adrianna was a captive of her bewitching stare. "Were you watching me, Dr. Beaumont?"

Erica slowly slid her hands from Adrianna's elbows up to her shoulders, feeling the soft denim beneath her hands. She brushed her lips against Adrianna's ear and kissed her temple. "I love watching you. I haven't stopped watching you since the day you scorched me with those incredible sapphire eyes."

Adrianna tilted her head and sighed. She leaned back into Erica and felt the warmth and strength emanating from her body.

Erica touched her lips to Adrianna's jaw and down her exposed neck, feeling her bounding pulse beneath her moist kisses. She slipped her fingers around the collar of the denim shirt and eased it over her smooth shoulders and down her arms. She carelessly tossed it across the back of an antique Victorian chair beside the double vanity.

Adrianna stared into the mirror, riveted to Erica's emerald-green eyes gazing at her reflection before them. She was awestruck by the glimpse of Erica's beautiful, naked body standing so close behind her. The gentle slope of her soft breast and the subtle curve of her slender hip were all that was reflected back to

Adrianna and all she needed to fuel the insatiable desire she had for this woman.

Erica molded her hands to Adrianna's shoulders and slid them down to her hands. "You're so incredibly beautiful, Adrianna." She entwined their hands and held them before the mirror, enamored by their perfect fit.

Adrianna hugged Erica's hands to her belly. She closed her eyes and turned her face slightly to kiss Erica's cheek. She nuzzled her face against Erica's and slowly released her hands. She reached back to grip Erica's hips and gyrated her bottom against her soft, dark mound of hair. Erica's erotic moans inflamed her desire as she arched back against her, loving the feeling of her breasts pressed firmly against her back.

Erica glided her hands over Adrianna's thighs and up to her belly, infusing her with her warmth. She pressed Adrianna's hips firmly against her as she slowly, teasingly rubbed herself against her shapely bottom.

Adrianna groaned deliriously as she begged for more. She gripped Erica's hips tighter and leaned her head back against her shoulder.

Erica stared into the mirror in wonder at Adrianna's passion. She slid one hand down Adrianna's belly and lightly combed her fingers through her dark, tight curls. She slipped her fingers between her parted thighs and delved between her velvety folds and through her lush wetness. Adrianna's moans burned hot between Erica's thighs and spread like wildfire into her belly and chest. She nuzzled her lips against Adrianna's ear and touched it with the tip of her tongue. "So incredibly beautiful and so incredibly wet."

Adrianna lifted her head from Erica's shoulder and turned her face to her. She brushed her lips against Erica's slowly, sensuously, and stared into her glistening sea-green eyes. "I love the way you love me, Erica."

Erica touched her lips to Adrianna's and lightly teased her with her tongue. "I'm going to show you exactly how I'm going to love you. Please look into the mirror."

Adrianna turned her head to face the mirror and moaned as Erica nuzzled into her neck with hot, wet, sucking kisses. Adrianna struggled to keep her eyes open as she surrendered herself to her lover.

Erica slowly swirled her fingertip over Adrianna's erect center, lightly moving in small circles. She slid one hand over Adrianna's belly and gently cupped her right breast in her hand. She slid the soft pad of her thumb across her breast and over her rock-hard nipple.

Adrianna was riveted watching the reflection of Erica's loving. She rocked her hips slowly against Erica's fingertips as the sensation of Erica's lap bumping against her bottom spun her into a tightly coiled ball of erotic tension screaming to be bounced free.

Erica slid the palm of her hand across Adrianna's turgid nipple and captured it between her fingers. She gripped it firmly and rubbed her thumb across its rigid peak as Adrianna dropped her head back against her shoulder and cried out in euphoric bliss.

Erica kissed her flushed cheek and brushed her lips down her neck to the feminine hollow at her shoulder.

"No, baby. Don't close your eyes. I want you to watch."

Adrianna laboriously lifted her head and stared into the mirror with smoky, heavy-lidded eyes. She watched Erica slide her hand down from her breast and over her belly. She floated her fingers through her tight, dark curls and deep within her. Adrianna gasped with exotic pleasure and dug her fingertips into Erica's hips.

Erica slid her wet finger from deep within her and brought it back to Adrianna's right breast. She luxuriated in her aching need and pleading moans as she stared into her eyes reflected so deeply blue in the mirror. She touched her wet fingers to Adrianna's erect nipple and watched her inhale sharply. She coated the nipple in Adrianna's own wetness and moved her fingers in the same light, small circles.

Adrianna's moans were frenzied as Erica took her to the edge of a euphoric abyss. She struggled to hold on with all her might as each feathery stroke of Erica's touch threatened to tumble her over the blissful edge. Adrianna finally had to close her eyes as a hypersensitive tingle vibrated at Erica's fingertips.

She leaned her face against Erica's and felt the building tension swirling tighter and tighter between her thighs. She thrust one final time against Erica's fingertips and felt Erica slip deep within her. That intimate connection immediately ignited her.

Erica held her tight against her as Adrianna screamed her name and crumbled in her arms. Erica guided her to the plush cream carpeted floor and guided her to lie on top of her. Erica held her tight in her arms and brushed her hair back from her face as she watched her come back down to earth.

Adrianna stirred after several minutes and softly kissed Erica's neck and sighed, "Wow." She raised her head slightly from her chest and looked into Erica's shining eyes. "That was incredible."

Erica touched Adrianna's flushed face and brushed a loose strand of hair away from her eyes. "I rather enjoyed that myself."

Adrianna leaned closer and kissed Erica deeply. She brushed her lips across her strong jaw and touched her tongue to her full lower lip. "I have more enjoyment planned for you, my incredible lover." Adrianna kissed Erica passionately and consumed her lips with astonishing hunger. She slowly raised herself over Erica and stared into her glimmering emerald eyes. She kissed her temple and lightly toyed with her ear. "Roll onto your tummy for me, baby."

Erica obediently rolled over and moaned deeply as Adrianna eased herself onto Erica's back. She luxuriated in the sensation of Adrianna's breasts brushing against her back and the way she rotated her hips against her bottom.

Adrianna brushed the mane of thick ringlets away from Erica's back and exposed the long slender column of her neck. She brushed her neck with soft moist kisses and moved to her shoulder. She fueled by Erica's throaty gasps as she kissed her way across her shoulders with moist, sucking kisses. Adrianna slipped her knees between Erica's thighs and smiled as she parted them wide for her. Adrianna was aroused by her open invitation as she kissed the base of her neck and trailed her fingers slowly down the subtle indent of Erica's spine. She slowly delved between the contours of her firm bottom and immersed herself in her incredible wetness.

Erica gripped the plush carpet in clenched fists and moaned wildly as she tilted her hips to allow Adrianna to explore her. The sizzling heat bubbling at Adrianna's touch threatened to consume her entire being without warning or recourse.

Adrianna moaned into Erica's ear and slipped her fingers deep inside her. She thrust slowly against her and moaned with the rhythm of her rocking hips. She moved from within her and found her wet, erect center. Erica's gasping moans completely spun Adrianna's desire out of control as she ached to satisfy her burning need. She slowly caressed her erect essence as Erica suddenly stopped moving. She arched as her thighs clamped tightly to Adrianna's. The sudden spasms gripped Adrianna's fingers as Erica arched her neck and screamed her exultant release.

Erica felt like flowing molten lava as she limply dropped her face into the carpeting. She felt Adrianna quiver and press her wetness against the back of her thigh. She felt her thrust once then twice before dropping her face against her back and groaning her own blissful orgasmic release. Erica smiled as she entwined her hand in Adrianna's and felt her melt into her back.

They lay immersed like that in each other for the longest time before Erica sighed. "That was amazing."

Adrianna kissed her shoulder and rubbed her cheek against the smooth skin of her back. "I couldn't agree with you more, my love. I think we should just stay like this forever."

Erica rested her face on her hands and smiled. "I'm all for that. I've never enjoyed a carpeted floor so much in my life."

Adrianna laughed and gingerly eased herself off Erica and knelt down beside her. She helped Erica sit up, and slowly they both rose to their feet. Adrianna stepped into Erica's arms and hugged her tight. "Should I start the shower again, my love, or do you have some other wonderful adventure in mind for us?"

Erica laughed and kissed Adrianna's forehead. "I think that now we are sufficiently ready for that shower. We weren't quite ready for it earlier."

"I can see that. Remind me to have you around every day when I start the shower."

Erica kissed her softly and guided her toward the double sinks.

Adrianna slid the mirrored door open and reached inside the shower. She turned on the jets of water once again and let the warm stream flow through her spread fingers and down her arm. She stepped inside and let the soothing spray cascade over her face.

Erica stepped in close behind her and entwined her hand in Adrianna's, letting the warm water bathe their joined hands. The steam swirled around them.

Adrianna turned to face her and guided her forward to submerge them both beneath the pulsating spray of steamy water. She just stood there and watched Erica tilt her face to the water, allowing it to stream over her delicate features. A fluttery sensation gripped her chest and tightened the muscles of her belly as she watched her finger-comb the water through her thick, cascading ringlets. She stood beneath the pulsating spray as if worshipping the water as her lush, dark eyelashes trapped large droplets of water. Adrianna was mesmerized watching her as a few errant drops of water threatened to spill over her pillowy lower lip.

The water trailed over her strong shoulders and down over her firm breasts, teasing her erect nipples with a few stray drops. Adrianna watched the rivulets flow down Erica's slender belly and try to find its way through her thick v-shaped mound.

Adrianna was in awe as she reached for the white mesh sponge and drizzled on her favorite peach liquid body soap. She stepped closer to Erica and ran the filmy sponge between her breasts and down her belly, leaving a trail of frothy white soap. She slowly circled her belly button and helped guide the water droplets and soap into her soft mound.

Erica released a deep throaty moan and reached for Adrianna's face. "I think that shower is going to have to wait a little while longer." She stared into Adrianna's blazing blue eyes and crushed her lips to hers in a hot, scorching kiss.

Adrianna forced her back up against the cold Italian tile and dove into that uninhibited kiss. She let the sponge fall from her grip and buried her fingers in its soapy trail.

✳✳✳✳

An hour later, Adrianna and Erica slipped into summer dresses. Erica carefully followed Adrianna's directions and parked her BMW in front of a café on Flagstaff's San Francisco Street. She eased herself out of the driver's seat and stared in awe at the Mount Humphrey's Peaks.

Adrianna grabbed her purse off the backseat and slipped the strap over her shoulder. She walked around the front of her car and watched Erica. She stood mesmerized by the sight before her as she leaned back against the car. Adrianna felt a stir of panic in her chest as she wondered how Erica would react to her current case. She shook herself mentally and knew she would do whatever she had to in order to make Erica understand her actions. She couldn't lose her. She loved her so much and couldn't stand that thought.

Adrianna stepped closer and laid her hand on Erica's arm. "Beautiful, isn't it? It's the tallest mountain in the state, 12,670 feet."

"All the time I've lived in Phoenix and I've never made the time to drive up here to Flagstaff. It's even more beautiful than people have described. When people say they come up here skiing, that's always hard for me to believe. But now I see that mountain."

"I've never skied at the Flagstaff Snow Bowl myself. Maybe that's something we can do together this winter."

Erica brushed her fingertips across Adrianna's cheek and tucked a loose strand of hair behind her ear. "I'd like that."

"Flagstaff is a huge contrast from living in Phoenix. The town itself is at 7000 feet, so it's always at least ten degrees cooler than the city." Adrianna tucked her hand behind Erica's elbow and guided her up onto the sidewalk. "Come on, I'd love to show you some of the shops, cafés, and my favorite bookstore."

They headed out and spent two hours walking through the picturesque town. Adrianna showed Erica through the quaint little shops and historic sites as they shared a piece of homemade fudge. They were blissfully happy in each other's company as they slipped back into Adrianna's BMW.

Adrianna drove them to the Flagstaff arboretum. They spent a few hours walking around the botanical garden, and Erica was in her element taking pictures of the blooming flowers and cactus. They found a bench on the edge of the wildflower meadow and stared in awe at the San Francisco Peaks.

Adrianna ended their afternoon at the Lowell Observatory. Erica focused her camera on Adrianna and took several pictures as she leaned back against the observation deck. She stepped in beside her and gazed at the sea of pine trees before them. "This place is incredible. My friend Kaitlin Bradley would love it here. She's such an astronomy nut. She even has a fancy telescope on her front deck at Bradley Bay. You can see amazing things through her telescope. I can't even begin to imagine what they see here."

"This is a marvel of science. It always amazes me when I hear the tour guide say that Dr. Percival Lowell built this wooden observatory in 1894. He must have had such insight into the future of astronomy."

"He must have been an amazing man." Erica slipped the strap of her Canon over her shoulder and stared out onto the astonishing view.

Adrianna leaned closer and grazed her fingertip across Erica's amethyst pendant. "This is so beautiful. It must be special to you."

"It is. My mom had it made for me when I started med school. The amethyst stone represents the balance between the intellect, emotions, and physical body. She told me it was to give me the faith and strength I needed to take care of my patients on all three levels. The gold triangle framing the amethyst represents my sexuality. A part of who I am."

Adrianna smiled and outlined the triangle. "That's beautiful. Your mom is a special lady."

"She sure is."

Adrianna skimmed her hand down Erica's arm and squeezed her hand. "Ready to go home, sweetheart?"

Erica sighed and looked into Adrianna's eyes. "Only if you promise to bring me back here again. I'd love to take some pictures with my wide angle lens."

Adrianna smiled and touched Erica's arm. "I'd be happy to fulfill that promise for you." Adrianna guided Erica off the deck.

Erica eased Adrianna's BMW into her garage. They grabbed their parcels from their day and headed into the cottage. Adrianna set the bags on the kitchen table and looked out onto the lake. "Oh, Erica, look at the swans floating along the shore."

Erica reached for her hand and brought it to her mouth, gently brushing her lips across her knuckles. "Can we walk down there and watch them for a while?"

Adrianna guided her to the sliding glass doors. "Absolutely, sweetheart."

They walked down to the water's edge and sat together on a wooden bench. The late afternoon sun was just beginning its descent behind the pines, the lake's surface shimmered with reflected light. They sat close together watching the two elegant white swans glide effortlessly along the shore.

Erica tucked a stray strand of hair behind Adrianna's ear and let her fingertips skim down her smooth neck. "I love being with you. I hate the thought of this weekend coming to an end. I wish you didn't have to go to work on Monday and I didn't have that medical seminar to attend at the Pointe Hilton Resort."

"I know how you feel, sweetheart. I love being with you too. I always dreamed of finding the one person that I could share my life with completely again. I've always dreamed of the perfect love, Erica, and I feel I've found that with you."

Erica wrapped her arm around Adrianna's shoulders and hugged her close. She leaned her face against hers and kissed her temple. "I love you so much, darling."

Adrianna smiled and leaned back slightly from Erica. She looked out onto the lake and watched the swans glide gracefully side by side. She toyed with a button on her sundress and battled to contain the emotions she had struggled with for weeks.

Erica frowned as she sensed her despair. She gave her a minute as she watched a cloud of sadness appear in Adrianna's sapphire eyes. She touched the crease on her forehead, wishing to erase her emotional tension. "What's wrong, darling?"

Adrianna slipped out of her sandals and curled her leg under her on the bench, turning to completely face Erica. "I have to go to New York next weekend to finish preparing for my current case. The final hearing is that following Monday morning at ten o'clock, and I arranged months ago to use this coming weekend to get together with my colleagues, Mia and Darby, to put the final touches on this case. I'm determined to present the last of my evidence before the judge Monday and end this trial then and there."

Erica was impressed by Adrianna's passionate determination. She reached to touch her cheek. "This case sounds very intense. I'm supposed to be on call on Saturday. Why don't I get someone to cover for me, then I can come with you?"

Adrianna took Erica's hand and held it on her thigh. She gently caressed the back of her hand and sighed heavily. "No, Erica, you can't come with me."

Erica leaned back and studied Adrianna.

Adrianna looked into her questioning eyes. She leaned forward and took Erica's face into her hands. "Please don't feel hurt, Erica. That look of abandonment in your eyes is so hard for me to see. I would never intentionally hurt you, and I need you to believe that. There's so much I wish I could tell you about this case to help you understand. Instead, I have to wear a shroud of secrecy and just pray that you will be patient with me and wait till Monday till I can finally talk to you about this case."

Adrianna gripped Erica's hand fiercely and wished she could tell her more. "I'm sorry, Erica. This case is so emotionally exhausting, and I really wish I could talk to you about it. Unfortunately, I can't. Next weekend, I will be spending all my time with Mia and Darby, and we will be working long hours putting the final points together. I never want you to feel neglected by me, and if you came to New York, you would barely see me all weekend. This is purely a work weekend, and I promise you that this is the last time we will ever have to be apart like this because of my work. This case will mark the end of my work in

New York. After the hearing on Monday, I will finally be able to tell you about this case and the reasons for all the secrecy.

"I'm sorry I can't explain more to you, Erica. I would love to have you with me, but it wouldn't be fair to you, and I promise I will make it up to you."

Erica pulled Adrianna into her arms and hugged her tight. She caressed her hair and kissed the top of her head, willing the emotional turmoil to release its tight hold. "I'll hold you to that promise, and you don't owe me an apology. I respect your oath of confidentiality, Adrianna. I remember what it used to be like when my father tried cases before he established his own business. I just wish I could make this easier for you somehow."

Adrianna leaned back and wiped away her tears. "Just being with you and feeling your support and understanding makes this a lot easier for me."

Erica kissed the tip of her nose and leaned her face against hers. "When do you have to leave for New York?"

"I'll have to double check, but I think my flight leaves Friday afternoon at three, and I have a return flight booked to arrive home Monday at six o'clock in the evening. Again that depends on what happens with this hearing on Monday morning."

Erica hugged her close in her arms. "I'm going to be lost without you."

"I'm going to miss you so much. I'll be counting the minutes till I arrive back home and can jump into your arms."

Erica held her tight in her arms and felt the tension ebb from her soul. "Adrianna," she whispered.

Adrianna leaned back and looked into Erica's loving eyes. "Yes, sweetheart?"

"I'm starving."

Adrianna tilted her head back and laughed as she looked at her watch. "We should be starving. I can't believe it's already seven o'clock. What are you hungry for, sweetheart?"

Erica gave her a seductive look from head to toe. "Besides you, I crave your homemade pasta."

Adrianna leaned up and kissed Erica softly, slowly, and whispered against her lips, "I brought some of my homemade spaghetti sauce and fresh spinach tortellini from the deli. How does that sound with a spinach salad and Carolyn's homemade apple pie that she insisted I bring here for you?"

"My stomach says lead the way."

They changed into comfortable jeans and pastel T-shirts and descended upon the kitchen.

Erica was busy whipping together their spinach salad while Adrianna placed the tortellini in a pot of boiling water. Adrianna told her about the history of the cottage and the surrounding area while Erica finished their salad and cleaned up the countertop. She dried her hands on a hand towel, listening intently to Adrianna's story and watching her slip a dish of her homemade spaghetti sauce into the microwave. Erica could smell the fresh garlic bread in the oven. She smiled at the sight of Adrianna floating around in her sexy fitted Levi's and bare feet. Erica watched in wonder as Adrianna checked everything one final time and went to the sink to wash her hands. Erica handed her the hand towel and watched Adrianna hang the towel back on the rack and step toward Erica.

Erica guided Adrianna to set her petite frame on the counter and seductively slipped in tight between her jean-clad thighs.

Adrianna entwined her fingers through Erica's thick ringlets and laid her hands on her shoulders. "You're a gifted surgeon, an incredible woman, and an amazing lover. On top of all that, you can cook. You can't possibly be from this earth plane. You must be an angel that Mother Teresa has sent to me to make you more like the rest of us humans. Your sparkling halo needs a few dents if you're going to pass as one of us humanoids."

Erica burst into laughter and leaned her forehead against Adrianna's. "I'm just grateful that Mother Teresa has sent me to you."

Adrianna wrapped her legs securely around Erica's slender waist and pulled her in tight. She released a passionate sigh as she held Erica's face in her hands and guided her slowly forward, claiming the lips that now belonged to her.

Erica reached around and held Adrianna's bare feet as she felt her happily wiggle her little toes. Erica watched Adrianna close her eyes and rest her forehead peacefully against hers.

Adrianna kept her eyes closed and luxuriated in their warmth. "I love the touch of your hands on my feet."

Erica squeezed her wiggling toes. "You are truly incredible, Adrianna Taylor. I love all these things about you."

Adrianna guided Erica's face toward her and kissed her with arousing passion. She arched against her and consumed her lips with a voracious need.

Erica slid her hands over Adrianna's ankles and along her calves. She skimmed her hands over her thighs and gripped her hips, pulling her tight in against her. Adrianna's lusty moan echoed in her throat as Erica kindled a ravenous hunger that only Adrianna could feed. Erica took as much as Adrianna gave, both aching to nourish each other's insatiable need.

Adrianna slipped her hand beneath Erica's T-shirt as the timer on the microwave chimed. She lightly grazed her hand over her erect nipple and whispered against her wet lips, "I'd better take care of our dinner."

Erica stood in shock as Adrianna slipped off the counter and headed to the microwave. Erica threw herself down on the counter and groaned painfully.

Adrianna could not suppress a giggle as she pulled open the microwave door. "Could you please pass me the oven mitts, my love?"

Erica leaned on the counter and gave Adrianna a look that could kill. "You're such a tease, Adrianna Taylor." She picked up the oven mitts in the shape of the Little Mermaid and threw them right at Adrianna.

Adrianna quickly ducked around the counter and watched the oven mitts hit the floor and slide under the table. "Ah, ha. You can be human like the rest of us plebeians, Dr. Beaumont. Hooray!"

Erica pushed off the counter and headed for Adrianna. "I'll show you just how human I can be." Erica took off after her and chased her through the kitchen and into the family room before she tackled her onto the beige cotton twill couch.

Adrianna burst into laughter as Erica tickled her into a frenzy. She lifted her soft yellow T-shirt and began placing moist kisses on her slender belly.

Adrianna immediately stopped fighting and cooed softly. She lay flat on her back to allow Erica's lips to roam freely. Adrianna laid her hand on the back of Erica's head and held her close.

Erica circled her belly button with her tongue and slowly undid the fly buttons on her Levi's. She basked in Adrianna's hot-blooded gasp, touching her tongue above the waistband of her white lace panties.

Adrianna writhed beneath her and begged for more as she felt Erica rise above her. She slowly opened her heavy eyes and looked into Erica's radiant face.

"I'd better go check on the garlic bread."

Adrianna was stunned as Erica rose from the couch and sauntered into the kitchen with a deliberate swing of her slim hips. Adrianna brought a pillow to her face to muffle her screams. She flopped over on the couch and pummeled the pillow with her fists.

Minutes later, Erica quietly tiptoed back into the living room and knelt down beside the couch. Adrianna slowly raised her face from among the pillows and gave Erica an evil stare. "The garlic bread looks great. Ready to eat?"

Adrianna dove off the couch and tumbled with Erica on the carpet. She lay on top of her and pinned her arms above her head. "To hell with the garlic bread, it's you I want to devour." Adrianna fused her lips with Erica's and obliterated any thoughts of dinner. The garlic bread would just have to be reheated.

After dinner, Adrianna and Erica snuggled together on a lounge chair on the back deck listening to the sounds of the night. They watched the moon cast a shimmering beam across the still lake as a gentle, warm breeze caressed their souls.

Erica held Adrianna in her arms and kissed her forehead. "Dinner was amazing, and Carolyn's pie was delicious. You're an excellent cook, Adrianna. You make me and my tummy very happy."

Adrianna looked up into Erica's emerald eyes and gently caressed her face. "I love to make you happy." Adrianna guided her face closer; teasing her with soft, gentle kisses.

They shared a glass of Petit Mouton as Adrianna laid her head against Erica's shoulder and curled her legs in her lap. Adrianna kissed Erica's cheek and nuzzled her face into her warm neck. "I have never felt so loved as I do with you, Erica."

Erica glided her hand over Adrianna's shiny hair. "I love you very deeply, Adrianna. You infuse me with an incredible surge of love and light. You are truly my love light."

Adrianna leaned toward Erica and held her face in her hands. "That was such a beautiful thing to say." Adrianna kissed her with depth and passion.

Adrianna leaned back slightly and entwined their hands. "I want to spend every moment we can together, Erica. How do you feel about living out of two homes while we take some time to decide what we would like to do?"

Erica rubbed her thumb along Adrianna's fingers. "I don't have a problem with that as long as I can be with you. I'm committed to you and our relationship, sweetheart. I just want us together, always."

Adrianna leaned forward and kissed Erica softly. "All I want is you, Erica. I want us both to be happy with whatever decision we make as far as living arrangements. All I know is that I want to spend every waking and sleeping moment I can with you."

Erica caressed her soft cheek as Adrianna leaned into the palm of her hand. Erica tilted Adrianna's chin up to her and kissed her with passion.

Adrianna glided her hand along Erica's slender abdomen and over her breast, immediately feeling Erica's arousal.

Erica leaned back and released a sensuous moan. "Let's go to bed, sweetheart."

"I love to hear you say that. Do you mind if I give Carolyn a quick call just to check and see how she's doing?"

"That's a wonderful idea. Let's go find out what kind of mischief my favorite patient has gotten herself into." Erica grabbed their glass of wine. Adrianna helped her to her feet, and they headed into the living room together.

Erica kissed the top of Adrianna's head and left her on the phone with Carolyn. She laughed to herself as she locked up the cottage, hearing Adrianna answering Carolyn's million and one questions about their activities since they arrived at the cottage.

Thirty minutes later, Adrianna hung up the phone with her mother and headed for the stairs. Something red and shiny on the first step caught her eye. She knelt down and picked up a ceramic reindeer Christmas tree ornament. She shook it lightly and smiled as the shiny red bell on its collar chimed. "Oh, you're precious." Adrianna looked up the steps and saw identical reindeer on every other step. She collected six reindeer before she reached Rudolph on the top landing. His beaming red nose shone brightly as Adrianna sat down on the landing beside him. She set the other reindeer down and picked up Rudolph and the neatly folded piece of floral pink paper under him. Adrianna balanced him gently in her hand as she unfolded the note: *Follow us and we'll take you to Santa.*

Adrianna held the note to her chest and smiled. She collected all the reindeer and stepped into the bedroom.

The light scent of vanilla filtered throughout the room from the several candles flickering on the mantel. Erica was sitting before a roaring fire, nestled among a sea of pillows. She was dressed in a white tank top and white drawstring pants. Adrianna had never seen a woman look so sexy.

Erica loved the enchanted look in Adrianna's shining eyes. "Welcome to the North Pole."

Adrianna set the reindeer and note atop her dresser and stepped before Erica. She took her extended hand and eased over her. She kissed her softly, gently before looking into those eyes that took her breath away. "If I had only known that Santa was this sexy under that big red suit, I would have volunteered to be one of his elves a long time ago."

Erica laughed as Adrianna touched her cheek with her fingers. "Thank you for sending the reindeer for me, even though someone told me that Santa doesn't exist."

Erica closed her eyes, enjoying Adrianna's light, feathery touch. "Santa may not exist, but my love for you certainly does."

Adrianna watched Erica slowly open her dreamy emerald eyes. "It's that love that I feel deep in my soul."

Erica immersed her fingers in Adrianna's thick dark hair and pulled her in close. She stared at her moist, slightly parted lips and guided her even closer before enfolding her in a scorching, consuming kiss.

Adrianna brushed her lips across Erica's jaw and up to her ear, tantalizing her lobe lightly with her tongue. "Does that mean I shouldn't expect any gifts from Santa under our Christmas tree?"

Erica smiled against Adrianna and kissed the tip of her nose. "I'd hate to take away Carolyn's pleasure since she still buys you gifts from Santa, so I'll let her continue playing the jolly old fellow. Speaking of the little imp, how is my favorite patient?"

Adrianna traced her finger across Erica's eyebrow. "She told me to rock your world."

Erica slid her hands over Adrianna's jeans-clad bottom and under her soft T-shirt. "I've been riding one wave after another since the day we met."

They were both lost in a kiss of fiery passion when the phone rang.

Adrianna leaned up on her arms and groaned. "Now, who do you think that would be?"

"Don't answer it." Erica reached for her face and kissed her deeply.

Adrianna melted into her kiss as the shrill of the phone shattered the ambiance. She finally got up with a frustrated sigh. Adrianna straddled Erica's hips and reached for the cordless phone on the coffee table. "This had better be good."

"Is that any way to greet your friends?"

Adrianna sat comfortably on Erica's hips and enjoyed the feeling of her hands running along her thighs as she softened her tone. "Hello, Dr. Abby Cooper. How lovely to hear your sweet voice at this very moment."

Adrianna loved Abby's robust laughter. "Are we interrupting anything, Adrianna?"

"Let me just say that you're quickly becoming my favorite pest."

"I'm touched to be held in such high esteem so early in our friendship."

Adrianna smiled at Abby's charm.

"Trina and I were just talking about you guys, so we thought we might call and see if you're bored with each other's company yet and might need us to drive up there and entertain you both for a while."

Adrianna laughed as Erica sat up and held Adrianna securely in her lap. Erica reached onto the coffee table and refilled both of their glasses of wine.

"Abby, I could never be bored with Erica's company. We seem to have no trouble entertaining each other, so thank you for the offer of your traveling road show, but I think we'll take a rain check for another weekend with you and Trina, if that's okay?"

"All right, but don't say I wasn't there when you needed me."

"I don't doubt that you would be there when I needed you, Abby. However, this weekend is not one of those moments. Let me hand the phone to Erica so she can say hello. Hang on."

Erica took the phone from Adrianna. "Hello, Abby."

"Are you floating on an orgasmic cloud, my dear friend?"

"Like I've never floated before."

"Good. That's all we needed to hear. Trina and I just wanted to make sure you guys were okay and to tell you that we're thinking about you both."

"Thanks for thinking about us, Abby. How are you guys doing?"

"We're great. My wife is in the mood for a late night movie, so we're off to the theater. We would invite you both to come and share some popcorn, but you seem otherwise occupied."

"Sounds like a lot of fun, Abby. How about we exchange rain checks for a cottage weekend and an evening at the movies?"

"Sounds wonderful. Enjoy the rest of your weekend and give us a call when you guys get home tomorrow."

"We will. Thanks for calling. Let me let Adrianna say good-bye. I love you both, Abby."

"I love you too, Erica. That goes without saying for Trina."

Erica smiled as she handed Adrianna the phone. "Thanks for calling us, Abby. It really was nice to hear your sweet voice."

"Love her completely, Adrianna, and know that we love you both."

"We love you and Trina too, Abby. We'll call you when we get home tomorrow, I promise." Adrianna and Abby said good-bye. Adrianna reached across

Erica and replaced the phone in its cradle and turned off the ringer.

Adrianna rose to her knees and set her hands on Erica's shoulders. "No more interruptions. I promise." She skimmed her hands down Erica's arms and slid her fingers beneath the bottom of her tank top. She eased it slowly over her head and tossed it carelessly aside. She grazed her fingertips along her sides and across the soft underside of her breasts. "You're so beautiful, sweetheart." She leaned into Erica and touched her lips to her arched neck with moist, subtle kisses. She reached down and tugged the ties at her waist loose and slid her pants over her hips and down her legs.

Erica reached for Adrianna and freed her of her T-shirt and bra. She looked up into her luminous eyes and slowly slid the palms of her hands across the front of her jeans. She skimmed her hands over her belly and felt her quick indrawn breath. She molded her hands to Adrianna's exquisite breasts and felt her nipples budding hard against her palms. She leaned closer and took a straining nipple into her mouth as Adrianna moaned ecstatically.

Erica bathed the turgid nipple with smooth long strokes as she gripped Adrianna's jeans and impatiently undid each button of her button-fly jeans. She slipped her fingers into her waistband and tugged the jeans down over her bottom, aching to strip her of this final barrier.

Adrianna stood above her and allowed her to guide her Levi's and white lace panties to her feet. She stepped out of her clothes and kicked her jeans aside before straddling Erica's lap. She shifted forward and rested intimately against her as she basked in their sensuous contact.

Erica felt totally aroused by this lovely naked vision of Adrianna straddling her lap. She moaned as she gently glided her hands along Adrianna's smooth thighs and onto her hips. She slipped her hands over the contours of her shapely bottom and pulled her in tight against her. She yearned to completely consume this woman as she struggled to make this moment last. She loved the way Adrianna arched toward her as she leaned forward and slipped a straining nipple into her mouth, bathing it with slow, gentle strokes.

Adrianna ran her fingers through Erica's ringlets and laid her hands on the back of her head. She gently guided her closer and burrowed her nipple deeper in her masterful mouth. She rocked in Erica's lap and tossed her head back, groaning as a swell of blistering lust enveloped her in its urgency.

Erica skimmed her fingers up Adrianna's back and tauntingly back down as she basked in her moans of pleasure. She released the straining, wet nipple and leaned back to look into Adrianna's smoky, heavy-lidded eyes. She traced her fingers along the inside of Adrianna's thighs and skimmed her thumbs across her tight dark curls.

Adrianna's eyes were brimming with passion and seduction as she rose up on her knees. She leaned toward Erica and brushed her lips across her cheeks and eyelids. "Please touch me, baby. I don't think I can stand this much longer."

"That would be my pleasure." Erica slid her hands along the back of Adrianna's thighs and up over her tight bottom. She skimmed her hands around to her belly and over her dark, curly mound. She brushed her fingertips through her mound and felt the moisture of her arousal as she slid her fingers between her wet, velvety folds and plunged deep within her. She loved watching her tilt her head back and cry out with pleasure as she entered her rhythmically.

Adrianna rocked her hips against Erica's touch and battled to stay afloat on their sea of cresting ecstasy. She swayed and thrust till a swell of tingling heat surged at Erica's touch and threatened to scorch them both. She slowed her rhythm and gripped Erica's shoulders tighter as she felt the coiled tension straining to spring free. She thrust one final time as her blissful release tore from her.

Erica held her tight and eased her down among the pillows beside her, keeping her cocooned within her arms.

Minutes later, Adrianna stirred against her and brushed her lips against her cheek. "That was amazing."

Erica rolled onto her back and guided Adrianna over her. "That was earth shattering, my darling."

Adrianna loved the sensual look in her eyes as she gently teased her neck with her tongue. "Now it's my turn to rock your world." She loved Erica's writhing gasps as she nibbled seductively on her ear. "God, I want you." Adrianna glided her hands across Erica's breasts and enjoyed the feeling of her smooth skin. Her nipples peaked against the palm of her hands as Adrianna teased them with slow, light circles. She longed to devour her as she leaned toward a straining nipple and resumed the same pattern with her tongue.

Erica moaned with pleasure and arched her hips against Adrianna's. "That feels so wonderful."

Adrianna moved to her other nipple and sucked it into her mouth. She held her erect nipple between her fingers as her tongue bathed it with long, smooth strokes. She released her nipple and slid her hand across the soft underside of Erica's breasts and slowly, tauntingly, down her abdomen. She dipped her thumb into her belly button before trailing along the inside of her thigh.

Erica gasped and arched her hips in urgent anticipation. She ached for fulfillment as she writhed beneath Adrianna and parted her thighs wider.

Adrianna kissed her softly and watched her struggle to keep her eyes open. She touched her tongue to her full lower lip and luxuriated in her wondrous cries for more. She lightly scraped her nails through her thick, dark mound and plunged deeply into her pool of wetness.

Erica arched her neck and cried out, "Oh, Adrianna!" She slid her hands over her bottom and gripped her tight as she rocked her hips against Adrianna's rhythm.

Adrianna smiled deeply as she watched Erica float with the sensations consuming her body. She slid her fingers from deep within her and found her erect center. She caressed her lightly in her own wetness as they rocked and swayed together.

Erica moaned with erotic pleasure and gasped, "Oh, Adrianna, yes!" She was tossed wildly within the cyclone of spiraling ecstasy as she waited breathlessly for the moment she would soar free. She gripped

Ana Corman

Adrianna's hips tighter as she struggled to hang on seconds longer.

Adrianna could feel the tightly coiled tension in her entire body aching to spring free as she awaited Erica's exultant release. She skimmed her finger ever so lightly across her budding essence and felt it spasm against her fingertip.

Erica suddenly arched her back and stopped moving her hips. A wave of spasms rippled through her entire being as she threw her head back and screamed Adrianna's name.

Adrianna carefully lay down beside her, resting her leg across her thighs and basking in her gasps of pure pleasure. Erica's hand rested across her own abdomen as Adrianna gently traced each finger and interlaced their hands.

They held each other tight in peaceful silence as the blue flames danced across the logs and cast a soft, yellow light across their entwined bodies. Erica slowly opened her eyes and wove her fingers through Adrianna's hair. "You're incredible." She gently caressed Adrianna's head as she felt her lover's smile against her face.

Erica slowly opened her eyes and watched the flickering flames of the fire cast a golden hue across Adrianna's olive skin, accentuating its smooth richness. She eased away and watched Adrianna lie on her tummy, nestled among the sea of pillows.

Erica slipped herself over her and lay gently on her back, luxuriating in the feeling of her warm skin. A beautiful smile curled the corners of Adrianna's lips. "You have such a sexy ass, my little mermaid."

"I'm so glad you think so, Dr. Beaumont, because I certainly can't keep my eyes off your shapely ass."

Erica smiled deeply and slowly brushed Adrianna's hair off her back and over her shoulder, planting soft, wet kisses down Adrianna's spine. She gently placed her hands on Adrianna's hips and rolled her onto her back. She eased herself between Adrianna's legs as she reached for her face and kissed her passionately.

Erica devoured Adrianna's lips as she rolled Adrianna's erect nipples between her fingers and delighted in her responsiveness.

Adrianna moaned heavenly. "This is quite a conditioning program, Dr. Beaumont. I'm going to have to see if we can extend this program for a very long time."

"You'll have to speak to your program coordinator about that, and right now she's rather busy." Erica pressed moist kisses beneath Adrianna's ear as she gently brushed her fingers along her side and hip, trailing down her thigh. She brushed her fingers along the inside of Adrianna's thigh as she eased her fingers within her.

Adrianna closed her eyes and arched her hips, easing Erica in deeper. Adrianna wove her fingers into Erica's thick ringlets and gasped her next breath. A tingling vibration swelled with each stroke, as Adrianna struggled to stay afloat in the sea of blissful sensations.

Erica nibbled on Adrianna's ear, whispering, "You feel so wonderful." She slipped her fingers toward Adrianna's erect, wet center and slowly caressed her into a frenzied rhythm.

Ana Corman

Adrianna turned her face and met Erica's lips. She moved with Erica's rousing touch and emitted raspy, throaty moans of pure ecstasy.

Adrianna suddenly stopped moving, and her thighs tensed around Erica's hand. She pressed her face against Erica's and shouted, "Oh, yes, Erica!" An undulation of spasms swept over and through her like a crashing wave as she gripped Erica's shoulders, arched her neck, and screamed her euphoric release.

Erica gently guided her fingers from within her and luxuriated in her explosive ecstasy. She lay beside her and tenderly brushed her hand across Adrianna's slender abdomen and watched her return to earth.

Adrianna slowly opened her eyes and looked into Erica's emerald eyes. "Wow," she said, her voice cracking. "That was beautiful."

Erica leaned down and kissed Adrianna softly. "That was absolutely incredible. Let me help you into the bathroom, my love." They made their way into the bathroom together, then slipped under their cool sheets.

Adrianna nestled into Erica's arms and laid her sleepy head on her shoulder. "That's one incredible conditioning program, my darling."

Erica pulled their duvet snuggly around Adrianna's slender shoulders. "I'm glad to hear the program is meeting your needs."

Adrianna laughed softly. "The program and you are meeting my needs like I've never had my needs met before, my love." Adrianna sighed contently and laid her hand on Erica's breast. "Good night, my green-eyed captive. I don't think I'll toss you off that pirate ship after all."

"I'm so glad to hear that. Sweet dreams, my blue-eyed maiden." Erica listened to the peaceful breathing that had become so soothing to her as she held her close. "Good night, my love light."

Adrianna slid her hand beneath Erica's breast and molded it to the palm of her hand. She slid her fingertips along the soft outer side and gently outlined the dimpled skin around her soft nipple. It immediately sprang firm as Adrianna teased it with the soft pad of her thumb.

Erica looked down into Adrianna's seductively playful eyes. "And I thought you were falling asleep." Erica succumbed to her arousing touch as she leaned back into the pillow and enjoyed the incredible effect this woman had on her body.

Chapter 17

Erica awakened at five o'clock in the morning and saw the first rays of morning sun trying to peek in between the partially closed blinds. She gently kissed Adrianna's warm cheek and watched her slowly open her groggy eyes. "Wake up, sleepy head. There's the most spectacular sunrise outside the window."

Adrianna slowly leaned her face up from Erica's shoulder and squinted at the window. She looked over at the bedside clock and groaned as she buried her face in Erica's chest.

Erica laughed as she easily rolled her onto her back. "Oh, come on, baby. I know it's only five o'clock in the morning, but there's a gorgeous morning out there, and I want to share it with you."

Adrianna reached for Erica's face and held her close. "I see that we're going to lose a lot of sleep in this relationship."

"I hope that's the only thing we lose. Come on, babe. Let's go play."

Erica slipped off the bed and hauled Adrianna to her feet.

Adrianna yawned and leaned her face against Erica's neck. "We'd better put on some warm clothes, sweetheart. It's going to be much too cold to be out there half dressed. And promise me you wouldn't expect me to carry on an intelligent conversation till I've had a least a half cup of tea."

Erica smiled and held Adrianna's face in her hands. "Warm clothes and a hot cup of tea it is."

The sun eased itself high into the sky as they cuddled in a lounge chair on the back deck. They had both slipped into a pair of jeans. Adrianna wore a white tank top under Erica's denim shirt while Erica had on a red turtleneck. Adrianna sipped on a hot cup of green tea as Erica drank orange juice.

Erica heard Adrianna's stomach growl and guided them both into the kitchen. She made cheese and mushroom omelets that they ate on the back deck while watching the squirrels and chipmunks forage for nuts.

Adrianna cleared their breakfast dishes and returned with a bag of peanuts, two flannel blankets, a pillow, and both of their sandals.

"Where are you taking me, my blue-eyed maiden?"

Adrianna guided her into her sandals. "I'm taking my green-eyed captive into an enchanted forest." Adrianna handed her the blankets and took her by the hand toward the lake. They walked through aspen and pine trees and stopped every few feet to leave a pile of peanuts for their furry little friends. They had walked about fifty feet and come to the cedar dock at the edge of the lake. Adrianna bent down and emptied the rest of the peanuts on the ground. She looked up and saw Erica smile at the hammock swinging between two majestic cottonwood trees.

Adrianna slipped her hand into Erica's and guided her toward the hammock. She pulled back the mosquito netting and took one blanket from Erica and laid it down on the cushioned hammock. She guided Erica to get in as she took the other blanket and pillow from her hands. Adrianna held the hammock still and slipped in beside Erica and unfolded the other blanket over their legs. She reached out and closed the mosquito netting around them before nestling into Erica's open arms.

Erica was smiling from ear to ear as she gently swung the hammock and held Adrianna snuggly in her arms. "This is wonderful."

Adrianna leaned up and kissed her soft cheek. "I figured the only way we were going to get any sleep this morning was to take my nature girl outdoors and let you sleep among the trees." Adrianna looked into Erica's brilliant emerald eyes. "I love you so much."

"I love you, my little mermaid."

Adrianna kissed her softly and nestled back into Erica's arms. She pulled the cozy flannel blanket up to their waists as she snuggled into Erica's denim shirt and easily drifted off into a peaceful sleep.

Erica held her in her arms and caressed her hair. She listened to Adrianna's gentle breathing and watched the mockingbirds and tiny sparrows bounce among the branches of the cottonwood tree. She felt completely connected with this incredible creature in her arms as she hesitantly gave in to her tired eyes and drifted off to sleep.

Ana Corman

Adrianna and Erica awoke several hours later and shared a long, hot shower.

They spent the afternoon picnicking at the edge of the lake and walking hand in hand among the beautiful trees, taking pictures and talking about their love, their lives, and their families. They hesitantly returned to the cottage and packed their things to return home.

Erica finished loading their vehicle and watched Adrianna lock the cottage door. "I had such a wonderful weekend with you, sweetheart."

"This is only the beginning of many beautiful weekends we will spend here together, sweetheart." Adrianna leaned up and kissed Erica softly.

Chapter 18

Adrianna stood at the edge of the circular mahogany worktable in the glassed-in conference room. She looked at two conflicting sheets of evidence in front of her. Her colleagues, Darby and Mia, waited patiently. They had learned to be patient when they saw that look on Adrianna's face from the very first case they worked on with her four years before.

Darby was tall and slender and always had a mischievous gleam in her eye. She liked to look at things from every different angle. Adrianna called her intellectually creative. She reminded Adrianna of a toddler who would find ten different uses for a single toy.

Mia was shorter and softer around the edges. She was much more serious and fanatical about doing everything by the book. Adrianna called her the bookworm and respected her intellectual intensity. Darby and Mia drove each other nuts, but their differences brought varying insights and depth to

Adrianna's cases. They made a great team, and Adrianna treasured their contributions.

Adrianna had recruited Darby and Mia herself fresh out of law school. They had attended one of her seminars on the rights of gays and lesbians and had immediately impressed Adrianna with their questions and intelligence. They had continued to impress Adrianna over the years and had been a pleasure to teach and work with. They had asked to work with Adrianna on her current case two years ago and had been her team of young lawyers ever since.

"This makes no sense. We need to find out why the child's vital signs recorded by the cardiac monitor are totally different than the ones recorded by the emergency room nurse." Adrianna dropped the sheets onto the table. "I don't like the looks of this, ladies. This looks eerily similar to the pattern we saw in Dr. Michael Thomas's case. There are still too many unanswered questions. This case is too important to everyone involved for us to leave any loose ends. Let's dig deeper into these problems and get a clearer picture of what really happened when that child arrived in the emergency department." Adrianna looked at the two bright young lawyers before her. "I want us to feel 100 percent sure about what we're presenting Monday morning, so let's hear what other conflicting evidence you guys have found."

Adrianna had the complete attention of her colleagues as they began to discuss other crucial evidence. Adrianna stepped toward the wet bar and grabbed the insulated pitcher of ice water. She returned to the conference table and refilled everyone's water glass as she looked out the glass wall enclosing the conference room. The huge bouquet of long-stemmed red roses ascending in the glass elevator caught her eye first before she saw the gorgeous delivery person dressed in a fitted black pinstriped suit. Adrianna set the pitcher on a tile trivet and silently raised her hand, immediately halting the conversation.

Darby and Mia's attention were riveted on Adrianna as she opened the conference room door. They leaned forward in their chairs and caught sight of the arrangement of flowers and the beautiful woman stepping off the elevator.

Adrianna squealed with delight and shouted Erica's name.

Erica barely had a chance to set the flowers down as Adrianna threw herself into her arms. Adrianna took Erica's face into her hands and kissed her softly.

Darby and Mia made their way to the open doorway and smiled. Mia cleared her throat. "Adrianna, are you going to introduce this gorgeous woman, or are you in the habit of greeting all flower delivery people this way?"

Adrianna blushed. She entwined her hand into Erica's and guided her into the conference room. "This is my soul mate, Dr. Erica Beaumont. Erica, these are my colleagues Darby and Mia. They're working on my current case with me."

Erica shook their hands. "It's a pleasure to meet you both."

The lawyers smiled at Erica. "So you're the mystery woman who's put that magnificent smile on Adrianna's face," Mia said.

Darby turned to Erica. "We couldn't believe it when Adrianna told us she was going to take someone

Love Light

my calls, and try to behave yourself." Adrianna guided Erica into her office and gently closed the door behind them. She stepped toward Erica, rested her forehead against hers, and held her tight. "You certainly know how to brighten up my Monday afternoon, sweetheart. This is such a wonderful surprise. How did you manage to find time to slip away from your conference?"

Erica reached up and caressed Adrianna's soft cheek. "I had an hour before the next lecture, so I thought I would sneak away and make an urgent delivery. Speaking of my urgent delivery." Erica turned and reached for the spectacular bouquet of roses and handed them to Adrianna. "These are for the woman who has captivated my heart and soul."

Adrianna's eyes were moist as she took the flowers and smelled their subtle fragrance. Adrianna set the roses down on the table and held Erica's face in her hands. "They're so beautiful. Thank you so much." Adrianna leaned slowly toward Erica and kissed her.

Erica looked into Adrianna's tender eyes. "I missed you so much, I just had to come and see you."

"I missed you too, sweetheart. Come sit with me and tell me about the lectures this morning." Adrianna took Erica's hand and guided her to her burgundy leather couch. Erica scanned Adrianna's spacious, sun-filled office and admired the antique furniture and elegant leather couches. An exquisite rosewood desk filled one end of the office with Queen Anne chairs facing the desk. Two burgundy couches sat facing each other on a floral Persian rug with a rosewood coffee table nestled in the middle. One wall was neatly lined with law books, and another held Adrianna's law certificates from Stanford.

Erica leaned closer and touched Adrianna's law degree. "What did you think of Stanford's law program?"

Adrianna stood in beside Erica. "I loved it. It's one of the best programs in the country. My dad also graduated from Stanford."

"I'll bet that made your dad proud."

Adrianna rolled her eyes. "At least something did."

Erica smiled and touched Adrianna's cheek. "Your office is beautiful, babe. It makes me want to curl up in here with you and a good book." Erica took Adrianna's outstretched hand and joined her on the couch.

"I'm glad you like my office, sweetheart. Now, tell me about your morning."

They settled in side by side and eagerly shared the events of their morning.

Thirty minutes had quickly passed when Erica glanced down at her watch and sighed. "I hate to say good-bye, babe, but I should make my way back to the Pointe Hilton. I promised Abby I would be back in time for our next lecture. Thank you for your time."

Adrianna smiled and kissed her softly. "Thank you for the beautiful roses and for the wonderful surprise visit. I look forward to seeing you at my house around five o'clock."

Erica held Adrianna's face in her hands. "I can't tell you how much it means to me to hear you say that."

They were engulfed in a passionate kiss as they heard the office door slowly creak open. Molly peeked in as Erica and Adrianna embraced.

Adrianna peeked at the door. "If that door does not close in two seconds, there will be a secretary looking for a new job." Adrianna leaned away from Erica and saw the door continue to slowly open. Adrianna slipped off her leather sandal and hurled it at the door, which quickly slammed shut.

Erica burst into laughter and looked at Adrianna in shock. "Nice throw. Remind me not to sneak up on you."

"I don't usually make a habit of throwing things, but my sandal certainly came in handy there."

"Well, I guess I should feel blessed that you rarely wear anything on your feet around the house."

They both burst into laughter and kissed each other once more before Adrianna entwined her hand into Erica's and guided her out of her office.

Adrianna watched Erica descend in the glass elevator and waved one final time. She took a deep breath and prepared herself before she headed down the hall into the conference room. She opened the glass door and found Darby and Mia sitting on the edge of the mahogany table, patiently waiting for her.

Mia slid off the table and stood before Adrianna. "You owe us an explanation, Adrianna."

Adrianna exhaled. "I was worried you guys would recognize Erica's name." Adrianna gently closed the glass door, knowing this was going to be a complicated story.

Michael walked past the registration counter of the Pointe Hilton Tapatio Cliffs Resort and headed for the Cascade Café. He stood before the hostess stand and scanned the restaurant. The pretty blond in the skintight black outfit scanned him from head to toe and gave him a winning smile. "May I help you, sir?"

Michael smiled. "Actually I see my lunch date. But thank you." Michael waked through the bustling restaurant and stepped out onto the patio.

Abby set her cup of coffee down and rose from her chair. "It's about time you got here. I thought I was going to be stood up by both you and Erica."

Michael hugged Abby close. "Sorry I'm late. My lecture went way over the scheduled time. What do you mean stood up by both of us? Where's Erica?"

Michael tucked the chair in under Abby before seating himself. "Erica decided to skip lunch and run a bouquet of beautiful red roses to her new lady love. She should be back shortly. She called me on her cell phone and said she was on her way back. Our next lecture doesn't begin for another twenty minutes so she should be here in time."

"A bouquet of red roses to her new lady love. That sounds serious. Is this new lady love Mrs. Taylor's daughter?"

"It sure is. They just got back from spending the weekend up in Flagstaff together."

Michael leaned back in his chair and steepled his fingers under his chin. "Wow! I haven't talked to Erica in a while, but the last time we talked she mentioned she was quite taken by Mrs. Taylor's daughter. She didn't seem sure of how she was going to handle things at the time. It sounds like the picture is much clearer now."

The waitress greeted Michael and handed him a menu. She took his order for a glass of lemonade and left him to scan the lunch menu.

Michael dropped the menu on the table. "What do you think of this new woman in Erica's life, Abby?"

"She's terrific. You would really like her, Michael. She's perfect for Erica. It's so exciting to see her so happy again. She's had a long two years since Laura died. I think she's found the woman who will make her life complete again."

Michael thanked the waitress for his lemonade and ordered a club sandwich. He took a long drink of the ice-cold lemonade before setting the glass down on the coaster. "When am I going to get a chance to meet this new lady love?"

"Hopefully soon. I can't wait to hear what you think of her." Abby looked past Michael's shoulder and glanced at her watch. "Looks like you're going to be eating alone, Michael. The blushing bride has arrived just in the nick of time for our next lecture."

Michael turned in his seat and watched Erica weave around the tables and make her way to the patio. "Wow, you're right, Abby. I haven't seen Erica glow like that in years."

Chapter 19

Erica was dressed comfortably in a white-ribbed, sleeveless turtleneck and pleated black twill pants. She worked the corkscrew into the bottle of wine and watched Adrianna thread burgundy linen napkins through ceramic napkin holders and set them at each place setting. She thought Adrianna looked absolutely sexy in her sleeveless slate blue tunic and matching skirt. The hem of the skirt sat just above her knees and exhibited her shapely tanned legs.

Erica popped the cork and set the corkscrew and cork on the island. She set the bottle of wine down beside them to allow it to warm to room temperature.

Adrianna stepped back from the table and assessed the place settings to make sure nothing was missing.

Erica touched her cheek. "It's beautiful, babe. Abby and Trina will be touched by all the trouble you went through for them."

Adrianna wrung her hands together and scanned the table one final time. "I just want everything to be nice for them, especially since this is the first time they will be joining us for dinner here at my place."

Erica took Adrianna into her arms and held her close. "Its perfect, babe. Abby and Trina will be thoroughly impressed."

Erica hugged Adrianna tight and kissed her forehead. "There's something I want to show you before those guys get here." Erica stepped away from Adrianna and walked toward the foyer. She picked up the letter she'd left on her antique cream, half-moon table and returned to Adrianna. She handed her the folded piece of floral paper. "I received this letter today in my office mail from the Kirklands. I wanted to share it with you."

Adrianna looked into Erica's eyes before unfolding the letter and reading it out loud.

Dear Dr. Beaumont:

We just wanted to take a minute to thank you for the care and kindness you showed our daughter and our family. You were a bright light in a very dark storm. We continue to grieve for our daughter, and we're still having a tough time dealing with the fact that she's truly gone. It still seems like a nightmare that we pray we could wake up from. But we know that's not so. Nicole is gone, but her spirit still lives strong in our hearts.

Donating her organs was a really difficult decision for us, but we feel good about what Nicole has given to others in her death. We received a lovely letter from the Organ Donor Network informing us that Nicole's heart went to a thirty-eight-year-old woman, her lungs to a twenty-year-old girl. One kidney went to a thirty-two-year-old man and the other to a nine-year-old girl, both suffering from kidney failure. Her liver went to a thirty-four-year-old nurse. Nicole has given each one of them the greatest gift, yet their paths have never crossed. I wish they could have met Nicole. But that was never meant to be.

We wanted to share this wonderful news with you, Dr. Beaumont, and to thank you for everything you did for us. Please thank all the nurses in the neurosurgical intensive care unit for their kindness. They are a special group of people and went out of their way to take care of all of us. You will all be in our thoughts and prayers. Thank you for taking care of our Nicole when she could not take care of herself. God Bless.
Madeleine and James Kirkland

Adrianna's tears filled her shining eyes. "What a beautiful letter, sweetheart. How wonderful for the Kirklands to learn of the people that Nicole was able to donate her organs to."

Erica took the letter from Adrianna and handed her several tissues. She set the letter on the kitchen counter and took Adrianna in her arms, kissing her damp cheek. "I was really moved by that letter. I hope that gives the Kirklands some comfort in this tragedy."

Adrianna dried her eyes and melted into Erica's arms. "What a beautiful ending to a family's tragic story. Will James and Madeleine ever get to meet the organ recipients?"

"That's up to the organ recipients. If they express the wish to meet the Kirklands and both parties have the desire to do so, then the Organ Donor Network will arrange for that to happen. I can't imagine how emotional that would be for both parties."

Adrianna leaned her cheek against Erica's. "I can't imagine either." Adrianna hugged Erica tight as they both heard the doorbell ring. They stepped out of the kitchen together and saw Abby and Trina standing on the front porch looking around in awe. Erica swung the front door open, and Adrianna squealed with delight, rushing forward to hug Abby and Trina. "Welcome to my home, ladies."

"This place is gorgeous, Adrianna. Absolutely gorgeous," Trina said.

Abby stepped into Erica's arms.

"It's nice to see that you guys are capable of using a doorbell for a change. Unlike at my house."

Abby smiled brightly. "We wanted to make a good impression on Adrianna for the first time. Next time we bypass the doorbell."

Trina held Adrianna's hands and looked around her entranceway. "Oh, this is beautiful, Adrianna. Let's just start here, and you can show us the rest of your lovely home."

Erica locked the door behind them. Abby gave her a triumphant grin and stepped into Adrianna's arms.

The tour ended in the kitchen. Abby sniffed the air and peeked in the oven. "Something smells delicious."

Erica stepped in behind her and shut the oven door. "Adrianna and I made vegetable lasagna, spinach salad, and garlic bread."

"That sounds wonderful. We're starving. When do we get to eat?"

"The food's ready, so let's take a seat at the table." Adrianna guided them all to the dining room where they spent the next two hours devouring their delicious meal and sharing the events of their lives since the Hailey Center gala event. They laughed and talked, forging a deeper bond in their friendship.

Adrianna wiped her mouth on her linen napkin and set it back down on her lap. "I have a favor to ask of you guys. I'll be away in New York this weekend completing my current case, and I was going to ask you both to please keep an eye on Erica for me and keep her safe."

"I would be delighted to keep Erica safe and make sure that all of her needs are met," Trina answered excitedly. She winked at Erica.

Adrianna leaned toward Trina and faced her nose to nose. "Just look out for her for me, Trina. I'll always make sure that all of Erica's needs are met. Got it?"

Trina backed away cautiously. "She can be a tenacious little woman. Did you guys notice that?"

Adrianna and Erica cleared off the table together and sent Abby and Trina into the living room with steaming mugs of coffee. Adrianna placed the leftover lasagna in a container and slid it into the fridge as Erica loaded the dishwasher and poured them both a mug of tea.

Erica carried the tray of tea as they headed into the living room. Erica looked over to Abby and Trina nestled in the cream couch before the roaring fire. Erica and Adrianna settled into the other cream couch facing Tina and Abby.

Abby blew into her coffee mug. "What are you going to do this weekend while Adrianna's in New York, Erica?"

"You mean besides sulking and moping around the house?"

"Yeah, besides behaving like a lost puppy."

Erica smiled and entwined her hand in Adrianna's. "I'm on call Saturday for Dr. Mark Worthy. His newest granddaughter is getting baptized. I'll be off Sunday and then hopefully Adrianna will be back Monday evening. That leaves me Sunday to sulk and mope. What have you guys planned for the weekend?"

"We're going to go horseback riding at your parents' place on Saturday. We were hoping to spend some time with your folks, but they said they're going to Santa Barbara for the weekend to check out some horses."

Erica set down her cup of tea. "That's right. They said they wouldn't be back till late Monday or even Tuesday."

Adrianna sipped slowly on her tea. "Mackenzie and Grace are wonderful."

Abby set her mug against her knee. "They sure are. Grace was our inspiration to go into medical school. We were always astounded by what she did and how she could make people better.

"Both Grace and Mackenzie are special people. When I was five years old, they took me in like I was one of their own. I was an only child and both my parents managed high-end restaurants in the big hotel chains here in town. They were never home. I spent more of my life at the ranch than I did in my own home. My parents had hired a nanny to stay with me, but Grace and Mackenzie convinced them to leave me at the ranch with them and Rosa after school. It would be so late by the time they closed the restaurants that I would spend the week at the ranch and every Monday and Tuesday with my parents. It was a great life. It worked for them, and it certainly worked for me. I was so grateful for the first day of school when I met Erica. Little did we know that we would be roommates from that point on."

Abby slipped her hand around Trina's shoulders and held her close. "That was till this lovely creature dove into my life."

Trina sipped her coffee. "Took you a little while to get used to my rambunctious Hispanic family didn't it, sweetheart?"

Abby shook her head and laughed. "Trina has five sisters, so it was quite the adjustment. I was surrounded by Erica's brothers and sisters my entire life but this group of women is something else. I can't wait for you to meet them, Adrianna."

Trina smiled and turned to Adrianna. "That would be a lot of fun. Two of my sisters are also lesbians, Adrianna, so be forewarned. There'll be a thousand questions as to where you've been hiding."

Erica laughed. "My bed, that's where she'll be hiding till you get those sisters of yours to stem the flow of their estrogen."

Trina smiled. "Let's pick a date when we can have a barbecue at our place and get everybody together."

Adrianna quickly looked away and stared into her cup of tea. "I'd really like that, but can we wait till after this trial is done, Trina? I'd like to get this behind us before we make any plans."

Trina didn't miss the look of trepidation in Adrianna's eyes. "No pressure, Adrianna. Are you worried about this case on Monday?"

Adrianna's foot started swinging as she gripped her cup with both hands. "There's so much resting on this case on Monday. I just look forward to closing this case and getting on with my life." Adrianna looked from Trina to Erica. "I'll be able to explain more when it's all over."

Adrianna looked off into the fire. Trina saw the uneasy look in Erica's eyes. Erica leaned in close and kissed Adrianna's temple. "Monday is but a heartbeat away."

Chapter 20

Adrianna took Carolyn into her arms and hugged her tight. She kissed her cheek before leaning back. "Thanks for dinner, Mom. It was great."

"You're very welcome, sweetheart. It was so nice to have you and Erica here with us."

Adrianna and Carolyn looked down the front hallway and watched Erica hug Leah, then bend down to scoop Amanda into her arms.

"She's one in a million, Adrianna. You make a wonderful couple."

"Erica is a rare gem, Mom. She's the partner I've always dreamed of and given me more than I thought was possible in a relationship. Once this trial is over next week, I'll be able to share myself completely with her rather than just giving her parts of my life. I can't wait for that to happen because that's what Erica truly deserves, complete honesty. I just continue to pray that when this case hits the media, Erica will give me the chance to explain my side."

Carolyn touched Adrianna's face and felt her emotional tension throughout her entire being. "Have faith in yourself and what you're doing, Adrianna. I do. I'm so proud of you. You've always been a champion of right and wrong. The little I know of this case is no different. Erica believes in you. Once everything is out in the open, she will understand. Believe in yourself and believe in her. That will help to carry you through this difficult week."

Adrianna hugged her mother tight. "I love you, Mom."

"I love you so much, sweetheart."

Erica stepped in behind Adrianna and touched her back as she watched her hug her mother.

Carolyn gave her a smile and stepped into her arms. "Good night, Erica. Thank you for joining us for dinner."

"Are you kidding, Carolyn? Dinner was fabulous. You know you just have to waft the scent of your apple pie our way, and we would both come running."

Carolyn kissed her cheek and looked into Erica's emerald eyes. "Take good care of my daughter for me, Erica. Continue to love her well."

Erica bent down and kissed Carolyn's forehead. "I plan on doing just that for the rest of our lives, Carolyn."

"Well, if that's true, then why haven't you two decided where you're going to live? I'm going to have to start keeping a schedule of which house you're at which day so I know how to reach you."

Erica laughed as Adrianna rolled her eyes. "Mom, I keep telling you to just call my cell phone, and that way you will always be able to reach us no matter what house we're currently staying at. And stop being so bossy. Erica and I will decide where we are going to hang our joint mailbox when the time is right."

Erica hugged Carolyn tight to her side. "When Adrianna gets back from New York, Carolyn, we're going to start looking at homes. We decided that we would like to sell both of our homes and start our life together in our own place."

Carolyn clapped her hands together in glee. "That's so exciting! It's about time you two came to your senses. They say that lesbians rent a U-Haul on the first date. Huh! They haven't met my lesbian daughters. You two move like a U-Haul on four flat tires."

Erica burst into laughter. "Carolyn, does this have something to do with having all your ducks floating downstream?"

"The phrase is all my ducks in a row, my big bright, medical brain. Now you two just go home. I don't know how you do it, juggling your time between both places."

Adrianna took her mother's face in her hands and kissed her loudly. "Good night, bossy boots. Thanks for the support on moving our relationship slowly and responsibly."

"Please, that's your father's way of thinking, not mine. You're so much like him, Adrianna."

"If I'm so much like him, then why can't he understand me?"

"He can't understand you because he refuses to accepts parts of your life. Give him time, Addie. He's starting to see things in a different light."

Adrianna rolled her eyes, then waved to her mother as she moved down the front porch steps.

Erica hugged and kissed Carolyn. "Thanks for dinner, Carolyn. It was great." Erica waved good-bye and followed Adrianna down the front steps. Grant and David finished placing the leftovers in the back of Erica's Navigator as they hugged the girls good night.

Erica held open the passenger door for Adrianna.

"I'll call you guys when I arrive in New York tomorrow night," Adrianna called out to her parents.

Grant moved past Carolyn into the house as David stood beside his wife.

Carolyn blew them one final kiss. "Please do, Adrianna. We'll be waiting for your call."

Adrianna waved good-bye and slipped into the passenger seat.

Erica closed the door and headed around the front of her vehicle. She waved one final time and slipped into the driver's seat. She eased away from the curb and headed for home.

Adrianna sat silently staring out the passenger window. Erica squeezed her knee. Adrianna entwined their hands and sighed.

"What's wrong, babe? Is it what Carolyn said about your Dad?"

"That didn't upset me. But I do wonder what she meant when she said he's starting to see things in a different light."

"After what he shared with me in the garden that day, I really believe he accepts our relationship on his own level. I think that's a good start. Give him time. Maybe when you get back from New York you can talk to him about it."

"I just think it's interesting that he felt comfortable enough with you to share his feelings about us, yet he has never said anything to me. My mother implied that he's been talking to her about us."

"Perhaps he's waiting for you to talk to him."

"I've tried in the past, Erica. It was an exercise in futility."

"I know you love David too much to give up on him like that. When you feel ready, talk to him about us, Adrianna. I would be more than happy to be there with you when you do want to talk to him. He knows we are very committed to each other. I know it would mean a lot to you to have his blessing, so when you're ready, we will talk to him. Okay?"

"Would you do that with me?"

Erica smiled. "Without hesitation. I know how much it means to me to have my parents' acceptance and understanding. Carolyn is very happy for us. Let's talk to David and see if we can help him understand that what we share is very special and here to stay."

Adrianna brought Erica's hand to her mouth and brushed her lips across her knuckles. "I love you. Let me think about it, okay?"

"Absolutely. Just let me know when you're ready."

Erica watched Adrianna for several minutes. She watched the frown crease her forehead. "If it's not your dad, then what's bothering you, babe? Was I wrong in asking for vanilla ice cream on my apple pie?"

Adrianna laughed. "Don't be silly, sweetheart. Carolyn just loves doting on you."

"Why the worried look on your face? Carolyn's been doing just great since her surgery. I'm thrilled at how well she's recovered."

"I'm thrilled too, sweetheart. I never knew what to expect after her surgery, but to see her doing so well and enjoying the things in life that she loves to do without her nagging headaches is such a joy for all of us." Adrianna picked up Erica's hand and pressed it to her cheek. "We have you to thank for that."

Erica smiled and negotiated the next turn. "Carolyn deserves a lot of the credit for her remarkable recovery. She's a very strong woman with a determined spirit. Somewhat like her precious daughter that I love so much."

Adrianna smiled at their entwined hands and brushed the soft pad of her thumb across Erica's fingers.

"If it's not Carolyn that's worrying you, is it your trip to New York?"

Adrianna stared out the window for a moment before turning back to Erica. "I'm not thrilled about leaving you for New York tomorrow."

Erica drove the rest of the way home in silence before she pulled her vehicle into her garage and eased it into park. She pulled the keys out and turned to Adrianna. "If it makes you feel any better, I'm a lot less thrilled than you are. However, that does not change the fact that you have a case to take care of. Unfortunately, that case takes you away from me, and that tears me up inside. Thank God that it's for a short period of time because I can tell you right now, Adrianna Taylor, I'm going to be waiting right here for you in this house with bated breath till you come through that front door and right into my arms."

Adrianna unclipped her seatbelt and flew into Erica's arms, kissing her with all the passion deep in her soul.

Erica unlocked the door adjoining the garage to the house and followed Adrianna inside. She watched her reset the house alarm before they carried their leftovers into the kitchen. Erica set the bag of Tupperware containers on the kitchen counter.

Adrianna reached for the fridge handle and swung the door open. "I'll make some room for those leftovers."

"That'd be great. I'll go make sure everything's locked up for the night."

Fifteen minutes later, Adrianna stood in the doorway of the master bedroom and saw Erica sitting on the beige couch, staring out the panoramic window facing the backyard.

Erica looked so beautiful and stoic, battling the emotions tearing at her heart. Adrianna wished she could ease her pain and spare her from any further heartache; knowing that the situation they would face was guaranteed to bring them more pain before this was all over.

Erica looked up and saw Adrianna standing in the doorway. "I'm going to miss you so much when you're gone."

Adrianna slipped onto the couch beside her and took her hand. "Oh, sweetheart. I wish I didn't have to make this trip, but hopefully before you know it, it will all be over, and we won't ever have to be apart like this again."

Erica reached for Adrianna and held her close in her arms. She caressed her hair and kissed her temple.

Adrianna leaned back slightly and kissed Erica. "I have something for you."

Erica watched Adrianna leave the bedroom and return with a floral gift bag. She settled in beside Erica and set the bag on her lap. "Happy one week anniversary, sweetheart."

Erica smiled brightly and peeked inside the bag. "This is a wonderful surprise!" She pulled out two gift boxes and handed the square one to Adrianna. She set the gift bag down on the coffee table and carefully examined the flat package in her hands, wrapped beautifully in red paper with tiny gold hearts. She carefully pulled off the gold shiny bow and ribbons before picking off the pieces of tape on the ends of the package. She loosened both ends before she meticulously unfolded the paper from around the gift.

Adrianna shook her head. "I can see that it's going to take us days to open our Christmas presents."

Erica nodded her head and handed Adrianna the neatly folded wrapping paper. She held a long, flat velvet box delicately in her hands. She ran her fingertips across the plush black velvet before easing the lid open. Tears welled in Erica's eyes as she removed a diamond bracelet of gold interlinking hearts. "This is the most beautiful bracelet I've ever seen."

Adrianna took the bracelet from her hand and linked it on her wrist. "I love the way the hearts all weave around each other. It reminded me of how our hearts have woven together so beautifully."

Erica twirled the bracelet around her wrist and admired the way the light reflected off each diamond. "Thank you, babe. I love it. It's truly a beautiful gift." Erica leaned toward Adrianna and united their lips in a kiss of tender passion.

Erica touched Adrianna's moist, full lower lip and kissed her softly. "I have something for you to commemorate our one week anniversary."

Adrianna watched Erica rise from the couch and walk toward her bedside table. She slid open the center drawer and removed a beautifully wrapped slender package. She then reached under the bed and pulled out a large square gift-wrapped box.

Erica returned to the couch and handed the gifts to Adrianna. "Happy one week anniversary, my love."

Adrianna kissed her softly. "Which one should I open first?"

Erica set the large gift on the coffee table and placed the smaller package in her hands. "That one."

Adrianna looked down at the slim package in her hands wrapped in pink rose-print paper. She ran her finger across the white ribbon and tore the large white bow off the package. She stuck the bow to Erica's thigh and swiftly tore the rest of the wrapping paper off and handed the shreds to Erica.

Erica looked at the mangled paper in the palm of her hand. "Good job, Edward Scissorhands."

Adrianna giggled. "I can't stand the anticipation, sweetheart. I have to get to the gift as quickly as I can before I burst."

"Well, you certainly were much more patient in waiting to unwrap me."

"Yes, but you were the greatest gift I've ever unwrapped."

Erica leaned toward Adrianna and kissed her softly. "Please open the gift, babe. The anticipation is killing me."

Adrianna smiled. "See, sweetheart, you know what I mean."

Erica watched Adrianna jerk open the lid on her gift box. The tears filled her sapphire-blue eyes as she removed the diamond heart pendant from its velvet box.

Erica removed it from her fingers and linked the gold necklace behind her neck. She straightened it from the collar of her powder-blue blouse and left it to rest against her smooth chest. "My heart belongs to you, Adrianna. Now and forever." Erica took her into her arms and hugged her tight.

Adrianna sniffled against Erica's neck and kissed her cheek. "Thank you so much, sweetheart. It's such a beautiful gift." Adrianna leaned back and kissed her softly.

Erica handed her a tissue and watched her dry her eyes. She reached to the floor beside her and picked up the larger gift, placing it in Adrianna's lap. "I'm sure you'll unwrap this gift in short order."

Adrianna beamed as she tore the bright yellow floral paper off in record time and handed the balled-up mess to Erica. She squealed when she saw the picture on the side of the box and tore the box open, pulling out a Disney Little Mermaid teapot. Adrianna hugged the teapot to her chest and screamed with delight. "Where did you find this teapot, sweetheart?"

Erica laughed at Adrianna's excitement and leaned in close. "The day after you showed me your Disney teapot collection, I called the Disney head office in California and ordered your teapot. I had it delivered to my office, and it just arrived this afternoon."

Adrianna gently set the teapot on the coffee table and admired it. She turned and hugged Erica tight. "Thank you so much, sweetheart. That is the most beautiful teapot in my collection. It means so much coming from you."

"You are so welcome. I was really excited to be able to find that for you. I look forward to having Ariel serve us endless cups of tea for many years to come."

Adrianna leaned up to Erica and kissed her softly. "That sounds so wonderful."

Adrianna reached to the coffee table and handed Erica her other gift. "We're not quite done yet, sweetheart."

"This is starting to feel like Christmas already." Erica held the square box up to her ear and shook it gently.

"Don't shake it, sweetheart. It's breakable."

Erica gingerly brought it back down to her lap and smiled. She examined it carefully to decide which corner she would begin to unwrap.

"Oh, for God's sake, will you open it already?"

Erica laughed as she painstakingly removed the tape and unfolded the wrapping paper from the edges. She handed the paper to Adrianna and carefully opened the lid. She peeled back the pink tissue paper and removed a delicate night light of a cherry-red stained-glass heart. Erica held up the nightlight to the lamp and watched the light filter through the stained glass.

"That is our love light, sweetheart. When I saw that in a store, the light shone so brightly through the heart that it reminded me of what you said about infusing you with love and light."

Erica leaned toward Adrianna and kissed her softly. She rose from the couch and stepped toward the panoramic window beyond the foot of the bed. She bent down, slipped the nightlight into the outlet, and flipped on the switch. The rich red heart shone brightly, and Erica smiled. She slowly rose to her feet and extended her hand to Adrianna.

Erica took her face in her hands and kissed her deeply. "Thank you for the diamond bracelet and the love light. They are both absolutely beautiful and mean so much to me."

"You mean so much to me, Erica." Adrianna took her face in her hands and kissed her softly, slowly, intensifying their desire and need as they wordlessly moved to their bed. They began by removing each other's jewelry, and their clothing soon followed. They slipped beneath the cool cotton sheets as their gifts of love lay on the bedside table and their sounds of love filled their hearts.

Chapter 21

Erica was dressed for work in her pleated black dress slacks and pale pink blouse. She held the front door open with her foot as she reluctantly went outside and loaded Adrianna's suitcase and carry-on bag into her BMW. She walked back into the house to find Adrianna slipping into her powder-blue leather sandals. Erica felt that familiar fluttering in her belly as she watched the shapely muscles of Adrianna's thighs strain as she slipped into each sandal. Her gorgeous legs disappeared beneath her fitted powder-blue dress. The square neck accentuated her sparkling diamond heart pendant and the healthy glow of her olive skin.

Adrianna stood tall and turned to Erica.

"You look absolutely beautiful, Adrianna." She handed her the car keys and leaned back against the floral print couch. "I finished packing your car."

Adrianna stepped between her parted legs and rested intimately against her, holding Erica's face. "I'm going to miss you so much. I wish I didn't have to do this to us. I promise this will be the last business trip I will take without you."

Erica slid her hands onto Adrianna's slender waist and pulled her in tight. "I'm going to miss you terribly, and I wish I could at least take you to the airport."

Adrianna smiled at Erica's distress as she touched her beautiful diamond bracelet. "Sweetheart, you know that Darby and Mia are coming with me, and the flight leaves at three o'clock. The firm has arranged for a limo to take us all to the airport straight from the office. I wish I could spend every possible minute with you as well, but that's probably the most organized way to handle this with both of our schedules today." Adrianna looked into Erica's worried eyes. "I promise to be in your office at noon so we can have lunch together. At least I will be able to spend that hour with you before I leave in the afternoon."

Erica linked her hands behind the small of Adrianna's back and sighed heavily. "That'll be great. If that's all the time I can have, I'll take it."

Adrianna held her close and kissed her softly. She was touched by Erica's valiant fight to hold back her tears.

Erica took a deep breath and asked for the third time, "Are you sure you have everything you'll need?"

Adrianna toyed with the beautiful hair band holding Erica's hair back in a ponytail. "Yes, sweetheart. I have money, credit cards, my identification, plane tickets, and clothes. All I'm missing is you."

Erica smiled and leaned her forehead against Adrianna's. "I packed my denim shirt for you."

Adrianna held Erica's face in her hands and stared into those expressive green eyes. "You're so precious."

"Please be careful with your carry-on bag because Teddy is hiding in there. Teddy and little Addie decided that if we have to be apart, so should they. Teddy volunteered to go with you to New York and look after you for me. I packed his identification and p.j.'s, and all that he asks is that he gets to sleep on the side of the bed closest to the bathroom because of his prostate problems."

Adrianna burst into laughter. "I will do my best to accommodate Teddy's prostate, but I really wish it was you I was sharing my bed with." Adrianna stroked Erica's cheeks and felt her heart swell for this woman. "I promise to call you every spare moment I have while I'm away."

Erica leaned her forehead against Adrianna's cheek and held her new heart pendant. "I love you."

Adrianna traced Erica's moist lower lip and watched it quiver. "I love you, sweetheart. I can't wait to feel your arms around me when I get home."

They held each other tight as Erica kissed Adrianna softly. "Do what you have to do in New York, Adrianna, and know that I love you."

Chapter 22

Erica pushed through the trauma room doors and found Michael standing in front of the view box scanning a series of x-rays. He turned and waved her over. Erica carefully walked around the portable x-ray machine. One nurse was hanging an IV bag and another inserting a Foley catheter. The patient was not appreciating the tube being passed through to his bladder one bit.

"What have you got, Michael?"

Michael looked around Erica. "Where's Peter?"

"He's checking on one of our patients on the floor with a sudden onset of confusion. You're stuck with me."

Michael smiled and tapped the CAT scan of the patient's head. "Eighteen year old was standing in the school parking lot this morning with his buddies when he made a snide comment about one guy's girlfriend. The guy went to his car, pulled a bat out of his trunk and proceeded to introduce the bat to our patient's skull. By the looks of this x-ray he made contact before his buddies pulled him off."

Erica frowned and leaned closer to the images. "Looks like a small acute subdural hematoma."

"The kid's lucky so far. He certainly complains of a headache, but other than that he has no neurological deficits."

"That's great. Hopefully the blood will reabsorb and he'll avoid a trip to the operating room."

"And they say you're just another pretty face."

Erica smiled and pulled the x-rays off the view box and slipped them into a large manila envelope. "Is there any family here, Michael?"

"His parents and girlfriend are in the E.R. waiting room."

"I'll assess the patient and go and talk to them."

Michael watched Erica reach for the phone on the wall. "Hi, Sarah, it's Erica. We need to admit this E.R. patient into the unit." Erica read the name on the manila envelope: "Patient's name is Joel Hanson, eighteen years old. Thank you." Erica returned the phone to its cradle.

Michael leaned back against the counter. "Before you run off, how are things with you and this mystery woman?"

Erica's smile removed the worried look in her eyes. "She fabulous, Michael." Erica looked down at her watch and saw that it was nine o'clock. "We're meeting in my office at noon for lunch. If you can get away, why don't you come up and meet my mystery woman?"

Michael folded his arms across his chest. "I think I'll just do that."

Erica set the manila envelope down on the counter behind Michael and squeezed his arm. "We'll see you then."

Erica grabbed a pair of gloves and a yellow gown and started putting them on as she walked toward Joel Hanson."

****

Erica gathered the wrappings from their chicken salad sandwiches and tossed them into the trashcan beside her office desk.

Adrianna stood beside her and touched her arm. "I'm just going to use your bathroom before I head back to the office."

"Of course, babe. You know where it is."

Erica watched Adrianna slip into the bathroom in the corner of her office as she leaned against her mahogany desk. She picked up the beautifully framed photo of the two of them among the trees at the cottage that Adrianna had enlarged for her office. She loved the look of unconditional love and carefree joy on both of their faces.

A loud knock on the door startled Erica back to reality. "Come in."

Dr. Michael Thomas leaned around the door with his usual charming smile. "Hello, beautiful. I didn't see your secretary at her desk, so I took a chance and knocked on your door."

"Diane's gone to lunch. Come in, Michael."

Erica stepped into his arms and felt engulfed by his bear hug. She leaned back and kissed his cheek, but she felt him tense rigid as a phone pole. She followed his gaze and saw him staring at the framed photo of Erica and Adrianna lying on her desk.

Michael stepped away from Erica and walked toward her desk. The muscles in his jaw tensed and twitched as he exhaled sharply. Erica watched with concern as he gripped the framed photo with white knuckles.

Erica was bewildered as she scanned his troubled eyes. "What is it, Michael? What's wrong?"

He jerked the photo at Erica. "Is this the new woman in your life, Erica? Is she that one that you've been telling me about?"

"Yes. That's Adrianna Taylor. What's wrong, Michael? Why are you so angry?"

Michael cautiously placed the picture face down on Erica's desk, not trusting his initial instinct to want to throw the picture across the room and see it smash into a thousand satisfying pieces. He turned away from Erica and ran his hands through his wavy chestnut hair. "When you told me about Mrs. Taylor's daughter, I would never have connected that patient to Adrianna Taylor. I thought she worked in New York and prayed that is where she would always stay. As far away from me and my life as possible. As far away from anyone I cared about, and now I hear you're sleeping with this damned woman."

Erica looked at Michael with deep concern and utter confusion. "You'd better start explaining yourself, Michael, because I'm not going to have you stand here and slam Adrianna when I don't have any idea what the hell you're talking about."

Michael couldn't believe that Erica was pretending to be oblivious to what this was all about. He stepped to within inches of her concerned face and lost the flimsy control he had on his anger. "Stop it, Erica. Don't try and tell me that you don't know what Adrianna has done. I bet I've been a hot topic of conversation during your many hours of pillow talk."

Erica felt anger burning at her stomach. "Stop shouting at me, Michael. If you need to talk to me, talk to me, but I promise you that I have no idea what this is about or what the hell you're accusing me of talking to Adrianna about. I had no idea that you and Adrianna even knew each other."

Michael recoiled as if he had been slapped. He scanned Erica's moist eyes. The many years they have known each other tumbled through his numb brain, and he suddenly believed that Erica was truly in the dark.

He stepped closer to her and softened his tone. "You really don't know what your lover has done to me, do you, Erica?"

"I have no idea what this is all about, Michael. What has Adrianna done to you that has upset you so much?"

Michael ran his hand through his hair. He stepped toward her picture window and leaned against the frame. He finally turned back to Erica and shook his head. "The infamous attorney, Adrianna Taylor, tried to destroy my career and my life."

Erica stepped toward Michael in utter shock. "What?"

Michael took a deep breath and leaned back against the window seat. "Remember two years ago, when my mentor and role model, Dr. MacGregor, was sued for malpractice and medical negligence in the case of a woman who died of uterine and liver cancer? The allegations against him were that he did nothing to investigate her complaints of abdominal pain. Subsequently another physician diagnosed the woman with cancer, and she died six months later."

"I remember the case. You were so upset by the allegations brought against Dr. MacGregor."

"Damn right I was. Dr. MacGregor was so distraught over the case that he shot and killed himself three months after the settlement was awarded. The attorney pushed him to that edge of desperation, and I'll give you one guess as to who that attorney was."

Adrianna walked out of the bathroom and cautiously stepped around Erica's desk and stood before them. She had run out of time and prayers. The one part of her life she had hoped to keep hidden from Erica for a little while longer just blew her protective walls down with one mighty breath.

"Hello, Dr. Thomas. Dr. MacGregor is the one who put that gun to his head. Not me. I was not responsible for his death. I do hold him responsible for Hailey's death."

Michael eased himself off the window seat and took two measured steps toward Adrianna. "God, how I've prayed never to see you again, lady. You alone decided he was responsible for your lover's death, and you stopped at nothing to bring him down. He was one of the finest doctors and professors in medicine. He was adored by his colleagues and revered by his patients. You destroyed him with your lawsuit. I hold you responsible for his death."

"Where were those adoring colleagues when he started popping three different pain killers for his disc pain, Dr. Thomas? Those same adoring colleagues were the ones who prescribed those pills that made him forgetful, irritable, argumentative, and absent-minded. His practice started slipping right along with his ability to provide reasonable and prudent medical care."

"You used his back pain to twist him into an unstable physician."

"I presented fifteen patients who testified to the fact that his personality, attentiveness, bedside manner, professionalism, thoroughness, critical thinking, and concentration span all changed in the last year. His own office staff even testified to the fact. They were the ones who disclosed his drug use. They even stated they witnessed him having a drink at lunch and at the end of his work day."

"So what, Ms Taylor?"

"If he's such an excellent doctor and mentor, Michael, he would know better than to mix alcohol and three different pain killers. Other doctors even stepped forward and documented their concerns about his lack of patient care, his volatile mood swings, absenteeism, and worst of all, their inability to contact him regarding his patients.

"Hailey's case was the worst example of his lack of patient care. He left a suicide note, Michael, taking full responsibility."

Michael took one step closer to Adrianna's fiery blue eyes and scanned them for a shred of truth. He despised the tentacle of unease that was threading through his mind. "I never heard of any suicide note, and I never heard of these complaints documented by colleagues."

"That was obvious the day you confronted me outside the courthouse. You told me yourself you had

413

not been in touch with Dr. MacGregor for three years. You would have had no idea of all the changes that were happening with him personally and professionally. After I was informed of his suicide, I knew you would be devastated. I sent you letters through Dr. MacGregor's lawyer trying to help you understand everything that went on at his trial."

"I never opened your damned letters. You were the last person in the world I wanted to have any contact with. And you didn't stop there, did you? You grabbed the first opportunity you could get your hands on and came after me exactly a year later. Did you hate me that much for telling you what I thought of how you handled Dr. MacGregor's case?"

"What?" Erica said.

Michael turned to her and saw the look of shock and bewilderment. "Remember just over two years ago when that two-year-old kid was rushed into our emergency department by his father after swallowing that piece of hot dog into his airway?"

"How could I forget. That was horrible. He was dead when he arrived."

"Well, it seems the family didn't agree and tried to sue me for the death of the child because they felt I could have done more to save his life."

"That's absurd, Michael. There was nothing more that any of us could have done."

Michael shoved his hands into the pockets of his gray tweed slacks and thought about the twenty years he had spent as an emergency room physician. "That was the first time anyone had tried to sue me, Erica, and I was scared to death."

Erica touched his arm and stood close as she allowed him to catch his breath. "You never told me the family had filed a lawsuit."

Michael looked back at Erica with moist eyes and took a deep breath. "I didn't tell anyone, Erica. That's how scared I was. I was first informed of the family's intentions to sue two months after the incident, but the hospital lawyers laughed and told me not to worry about it because they had no grounds on which to sue. I did my best to go on with my life while I held my breath every day waiting to hear what was going to happen to me." Michael shook his head as if to rid himself of those ghosts. "I reviewed that case a million times in my head wondering what else I could have done to save that child's life. Knowing that there was nothing else I could do."

Michael turned to Adrianna. "What happened, Adrianna? Was the group of lawyers from our hospital just too much for the hot shot attorney from New York to annihilate? My case never made it onto your turf. The lawyers kept telling me not to worry, and then I finally heard that the judge threw my case out even before you had a chance to get your vicious claws into me."

"Is that what you were told, Michael?"

"That was enough for me, Ms. Taylor."

"And obviously you never opened the transcripts I sent you of that preliminary hearing."

"It went right into the same pile of unopened mail with the rest of your worthless letters."

"I see. You wouldn't even give me the chance to explain."

"Why should I? As far as I was concerned, you were the one person doing everything in her power to destroy my life and my career. You don't deserve the air you breathe."

Erica was numb with shock as she stepped toward Adrianna. Their few conversations of Adrianna's recent case started filtering back into Erica's stunned brain as she recalled Adrianna's pleas for secrecy and understanding. Erica shook her head as she realized that her secrecy had been shattered along with her heart. All she could feel was anger and betrayal. "How could you, Adrianna? How could you do this to Michael?"

"Please don't judge me, Erica, before you give me the chance to explain the facts of what happened."

"I don't really care for any of your facts right now, Adrianna. Is everything Michael said true?"

Adrianna looked down at her hands and struggled with the ability to make Erica understand and not lose total faith in her.

"Answer me."

"Yes. Everything Michael has said is the truth. This is why I tried to keep us apart, Erica. I knew when you found out about my involvement in Michael's lawsuit you would hate me. I was hoping and praying that you wouldn't find out till after my recent trial, and then I could explain everything to everyone. Then you might begin to understand the whole story, not just fragments like what you're hearing now. You promised me you would give me the opportunity to explain without jumping to conclusions. You made me that one promise, Erica."

"That was before I knew you tried to sue one of my dearest friends for malpractice."

"I asked for that promise before I realized that you and Michael were friends."

"So what, Adrianna? It's your professional ethics that are in question here, not my relationship with Michael. How could you do this to him? How could you even have thought to sue Michael in the case of that child?"

"You need to give me the chance and the time to explain this to you, Erica. Unfortunately, we don't have the time. I have a plane to catch."

"You're not giving me the time, Adrianna. Why should I give you the chance?"

Adrianna grabbed her purse and stepped toward the door. She gripped the knob and opened the door. She stood in the doorway and turned back to Erica. "I love you, Erica. Please don't ever forget that." Tears welled in Adrianna's eyes as she turned and walked out the door.

Erica slumped back against the edge of her desk and dropped her face into her hands. How could this be happening? How could Adrianna have done this?

Michael felt Erica's despair as he touched her shoulder. "I'm sorry, Erica. I really thought you knew that Adrianna had tried to sue me for malpractice."

Erica looked down at her feet and took a deep breath, attempting to control her anger. The tears were brimming in her eyes as she looked back into Michael's eyes. "No, I had no idea that Adrianna had tried to sue you for malpractice in that case. She's been very tight-lipped about her malpractice cases and promised me she would explain things to me when this current case is over next week. Now I don't want to hear what she feels she could possibly explain." Erica shook her head in disbelief. "I feel like such a fool, Michael."

Michael pulled Erica into his arms and held her close. "I thought you were making a fool of me by knowing all this information and not talking to me about it when the truth of the matter is we have both been taken for a ride." Michael held Erica tight as he felt her sob against him. "You're not the fool, Erica. I hate to say it, but Adrianna is the fool for prosecuting a case like that."

Erica stepped toward her desk and grabbed a handful of tissues to dry her eyes. "I'm angry and I'm in shock, Michael. This just doesn't make sense. This just doesn't sound like anything that Adrianna fights for and believes in personally or professionally."

Michael stepped toward the picture window and looked out onto the South Mountain range, oblivious to the view before him. "Some of the things Adrianna said are really bothering me. I didn't know some of that information about Dr. MacGregor's case. I didn't know anything about a suicide letter or complaints from colleagues. I don't like the way she was shocked that my lawyers said my lawsuit was just dropped. The look in her eyes said there are volumes that I don't know about and should know about."

Michael stepped away from the window and sat on the arm of the couch. He dropped his face into his hands and rubbed his tired eyes. "These two cases have been haunting me for years, and I chose to deal with them by shoving them far away in a dark recess of my mind. That shocked look in Adrianna's eyes bothers me as much as all the unanswered questions." He moved restlessly from the couch and stood beside Erica's desk.

"If I'm going to put my demons to rest, I'm going to have to look into what really happened with Dr. MacGregor and my own case. I was just so devastated by his malpractice suit and his death at the time that nothing else mattered but the fact that he was gone." Michael stood beside Erica and touched her arm. "I'll look into what happened in both cases. I threw Adrianna's letters into a box in the bottom of my closet. Maybe I should sit down and read them to see if I can find the truth."

Michael's pager went off. He looked down at the numbers displayed on the tiny screen at his waist. "I have to go, Erica. The E.R. is paging me."

Erica slipped her hand into his and squeezed tight. "We need to know the truth behind Adrianna's actions, Michael. I refuse to believe that everything she has come to mean to me was a total lie."

Michael attempted a weak smile as he squeezed Erica's hand. "Okay. The least I can do after dropping this bombshell in your lap is to look into the events and see if anything Adrianna said is the truth. You deserve that, and I guess so does she. I'll be really pissed if I have to apologize to that woman." Michael gently touched her chin. "I'm sorry to have done this to you, Erica."

"Don't apologize, Michael. You were the first one to open my eyes to Adrianna's professional world. That's a lot more than what Adrianna trusted me with. She has heard me mention your name and knew that you were a friend of mine. I can't believe she wouldn't have told me about your case herself." Erica stepped around her desk and grabbed a piece of paper and a pen. She quickly scribbled down a name and number and handed it to Michael. "That's the phone number for David Taylor, Adrianna's father. He has helped her with a few of her malpractice cases. He might be able to shed some light on Dr. MacGregor's and your case for you."

Michael stared at the note. "You're asking me to go talk to Adrianna's father?"

"He's a wonderful man and a sharp lawyer. He's also been Adrianna's biggest critic. I think you'll get a fair assessment of Adrianna's work from him."

Michael kissed Erica softly and held her close. "Okay, I'll start with Mr. Taylor. Hang in there. I'll let you know what I find out."

"Thanks. Michael, as sick as I feel about what happened to you, I just can't believe that there isn't more to all this that we don't know. Adrianna is truly a wonderful person, and this just doesn't sound right from everything I have learned about her in the past several weeks. Let's not jump to any more conclusions about Adrianna than we already have. I have a gut feeling that this will not be the first time you and I will feel like fools."

"All right. There has to be something good about that woman if you've fallen in love with her. Let me look into these cases and I'll get right back to you. Are you on call this weekend?"

"Just Saturday."

"Okay. I'll call you when I find something out."

"That would be great."

Michael squeezed her shoulder and headed for the doorway. "Hang in there, Erica. I'll talk to you soon." He waved and gently closed the door.

Erica rubbed her forehead as the tears spilled from her eyes. Her anger burned at her stomach, and disappointment tore at her heart. She released an anguished cry as she grabbed her jacket and headed out the door. Fool or no fool, she didn't really care right now. There were a few things she had left to say.

Chapter 23

Adrianna bent over a box and double-checked that she had all of their documentation for the trip to New York.

Molly entered her office and watched Adrianna thumb through a file. Adrianna had been upset since returning from lunch and made it quite clear that she wanted everyone to stay out of her way if they knew what was good for them. She cautiously cleared her throat. "Adrianna, the limo will be here in one hour to pick you guys up."

Adrianna checked her watch. "Thank you, Molly."

Molly watched her reshuffle a few files. "Are you sure you're okay?"

"I'm fine, Molly. I have a few things to do before we have to leave, so please just let me get them done."

Molly silently stepped toward the door and passed Darby and Mia on their way in. "Be careful," Molly told them, "She's still not talking, and her mood's only getting darker."

"I heard that, Molly." Adrianna rose to her feet with several files in her hands. "I believe you are all paid to work around here, so let's try and spend less time irritating me and more time getting our work done. We are on a very tight schedule here." Adrianna stepped toward her desk to place the files in an open box.

The three women exchanged a stunned look. Darby and Mia stepped into Adrianna's office and wordlessly filed several documents in the evidence box. Moments later, Mia looked over Adrianna's shoulder and smiled. "Hello, Dr. Beaumont. What, no flowers this time?"

Adrianna spun around and froze in her spot. She saw the look of absolute despair and anger in Erica's teary eyes.

"No, I didn't bring flowers this time. If you ladies will kindly excuse us, I need to talk to Adrianna."

Darby and Mia gathered the boxes of files and gladly exited Adrianna's office.

Adrianna took a deep breath. She stepped toward Erica and tried to fight the fear in her heart. She reached to touch her arm, but Erica quickly backed away from her touch. Adrianna suddenly felt her heart drop and knew that everything she had attempted to protect Erica from in this case was about to explode in her face. Adrianna was terrified by Erica's reaction as she looked into her eyes. "Erica, please give me the chance to explain."

Erica shot daggers with her eyes as she stepped close to Adrianna. "Yes, Adrianna, I think it's about time you started talking."

Adrianna watched Erica's eyes. "How did Michael find out about us?"

"He knew there was someone in my life, but he didn't know your name. Not till he came by my office this afternoon and saw the photo of the two of us at the cottage. He asked me if I enjoyed our many hours of pillow talk about him and your attempt to sue him for malpractice."

Adrianna dropped her head and ran her hands through her hair. "Oh God, Erica. I can't believe this is happening."

Erica cupped Adrianna's chin in her hand and guided Adrianna's eyes up to her. "Would you care to explain what this is all about, Adrianna, or do you plan on playing me for a bigger fool?"

Adrianna took a deep breath as Erica removed her hand from her chin. Adrianna looked into Erica's eyes. "I never intended to make a fool of you, Erica. I was hoping and praying that you would not find out about this till this final case was over."

"What do you mean 'final case'? Does this case have anything to do with Michael's malpractice case?"

"Yes, it does."

Erica was shocked and attempted to control her voice. "You really believe you could have hid this from me when you were trying to destroy one of my dearest friends? You've heard me mention Michael's name. You knew he was a friend of mine, and you still hid this from me. What else are you hiding from me, Adrianna? Do I really even know who you are? How could you do this to Michael? How could you have taken his case on?"

Adrianna wrapped her arms around herself in an attempt to shield her heart from Erica's onslaught. Adrianna knew that she couldn't tell her what she needed to know to ease her pain and resigned herself to absorb Erica's anger. She ached to reach out and comfort her but only felt Erica slipping farther away.

Adrianna stood facing Erica, engulfed by her own despair and sick that she had caused Erica this pain.

Erica looked into her distraught eyes. "You can't even defend your own actions, can you, Adrianna? Well, let me say my peace, and I will let you go about your little charade." Erica watched the turmoil tumble across Adrianna's eyes. "I was there in the emergency department when that father rushed his child in in an absolute panic. That child was dead when he arrived, Adrianna. There was nothing more that Michael could have done to save his life."

Adrianna took a deep breath and moved one step closer. "That's not what the documentation showed, Erica. I have documented vital signs on that child."

Erica was stunned as she leaned toward Adrianna. "That's impossible. I watched them work on that child for twenty minutes, and there were no signs of life whatsoever. I could give you a statement as to what I witnessed."

Adrianna looked away from Erica's pleading eyes and rubbed her neck as she slowly looked back at her. "You can't do that, sweetheart. You're my lover, so you would have a conflict of interest in this case."

Erica was stunned as her anger raged. She stumbled back and felt like she had just been slapped. "Well, doesn't that conveniently eliminate me from the picture? Was that your plan all along, Adrianna, to seduce me into your bed and strengthen your case? Is that why you spent so much time at the hospital with Carolyn?"

Adrianna was shocked by Erica's accusations. She felt her heart stop and her head spin.

"Am I next on your hit list, Adrianna? Or even better, why don't you go after Abby and me and get yourself a two-for-one special?"

Adrianna was outraged by Erica's words, and she grabbed her by the lapels of her jacket and pulled her closer. "Stop it, Erica! Stop it right now. You're so angry with me that you're not listening to what you're saying."

Erica carefully grabbed Adrianna's wrists and removed her hands from her jacket. She bent her arms and held them in front of her. She watched the tears sting Adrianna's cheeks. "There was nothing Michael could have done to bring back that child. He's an exceptional physician. He did everything in his power to save Laura's life, and now I come to find out that the only woman that I have loved since Laura tried to destroy him and his career. What am I supposed to think or feel, Adrianna? Should I have sued him for Laura's death as well? You tell me where the law draws the line as to when a physician should be sued for not doing enough."

Adrianna tried to entwine her fingers in Erica's hands and felt her abruptly pull away. Adrianna wiped away her own tears and tried to will away the tightness in her throat. "Prudent and reasonable medical care, Erica. That's all the general public asks for. That's all Hailey and I asked for." Adrianna watched the anger and disbelief darken Erica's green eyes. "Let me ask

427

you a question, Erica. Let's say that child did have vital signs in the E.R. when he first arrived."

"I already told you he didn't."

Adrianna held her hand up. "When you saw that father running in with his child, were you right there when they first hooked him up to the cardiac monitor to know that there were no vital signs?"

Erica groaned in disgust. "No, I wasn't. I walked into his trauma room a few minutes after I saw him arrive to see if I could help."

"I knew that already from the E.R. documentation. Thank you for being honest with me. Now, let's say for argument's sake that he did have initial vital signs and you were the physician caring for that child that night. Would you have done anything else for him that Michael did not?"

Erica was stunned by Adrianna's question. "Why should I answer that question, Adrianna? Are you looking for more evidence to damage Michael with? This sounds like I'm the one on trial here."

Adrianna rubbed her aching neck and looked back into Erica's livid eyes. "Michael's not on trial, and neither are you, Erica. As Michael said, the judge dismissed his case. I just need to know if you would have handled things differently."

Erica walked away from Adrianna and stood next to her couch. She stood and thought for a minute before turning back to look intently into Adrianna's eyes. "I would have performed a tracheostomy, but Michael was adamant against it because the child was already dead. He did not want to further torture the parents with that unnecessary procedure."

"That is why the family sued, Erica. They felt that Michael could have done more. The evidence pointed to the fact that the child had vital signs while in the trauma room. Michael should have done everything in his power to save the child's life, and that included performing a tracheostomy. That initial evidence is what drove me to take the case."

Erica was stunned as she shook her head. "You should have done more research, Adrianna, because what you're telling me is not what I saw. You just had to look at Michael's documentation and see for yourself."

"You have no idea how much research I have done into that one incident, Erica. Michael's handwriting was pathetic and certainly did not help him one bit in that case. You doctors should have to take penmanship 101 in med school to protect your asses."

Erica stepped closer to Adrianna and seethed with anger. "Protect us from whom, Adrianna? Vicious lawyers like you?"

Adrianna recoiled from Erica's stinging words. She desperately tried to find the words to diffuse her anger. "Erica, please, remember the day we had dinner in the garden and I told you I have a deeper agenda in this case than the obvious?"

"What is that agenda, Adrianna? Do you hope to bag yourself a prominent doctor so you can make partner in this pathetic firm? Is that your selfish agenda, Adrianna?"

Adrianna's anger bubbled bile into her throat as she stepped back from Erica in horror. "You're right, Erica. You really don't know me if that's what you think I'm up to."

Erica looked into Adrianna's eyes. "You also told me that night that you could never be intentionally malicious and would only prosecute doctors in a case of clear-cut negligence. What kind of bullshit was all that, Adrianna? You also wanted me to believe that you were an advocate for justice and the simple difference between right and wrong. You have blown all that right out the window by prosecuting this case. God, I've been such a fool for believing in you."

Adrianna stepped back and covered her mouth with one hand to stifle a sob at Erica's words. Silence blanketed the room as they stood facing each other, Adrianna aching to help Erica understand and Erica aching to be awakened from this horrible nightmare. "There was nothing clear-cut about Michael's case, Erica. It was a rude awakening for me and led me on the road to this final case in New York."

Erica stormed before Adrianna's distraught face. "A case you won't tell me anything about."

"A case I can't tell you anything about until it's over. I thought you at least respected my oath of confidentiality."

"That's about all I respect about you right now, Adrianna."

Adrianna's secretary beeped into her office. "Adrianna, I'm sorry, but the limo is here, and Darby and Mia are downstairs waiting for you."

Adrianna stepped toward the speakerphone. "I'll be there in a few minutes, Molly."

Adrianna grabbed several tissues and dried her eyes. She stepped back toward Erica and saw her emotional grief exploding in her eyes. She hesitantly reached up to wipe away her tears.

Erica grabbed her wrist. "Don't! Don't touch me."

Adrianna felt her chest constrict as she absorbed the depth of Erica's anger and betrayal. She felt her slipping farther and farther away.

Erica watched Adrianna's grief-stricken tears course down her cheeks. She released Adrianna's wrist and headed toward the door. She grabbed the door handle and turned back to watch Adrianna stand in anguished isolation.

"You've always said to me, 'Adrianna, do what you have to do and know that I'll always love you.' I've carried those words in my heart throughout this past week and always believed that you truly meant that."

Erica covered her mouth to attempt to control her tears as she took a deep breath. "I'm so angry right now, Adrianna, that I don't know how I feel about you or our relationship."

Terror struck at Adrianna's heart as she watched Erica turn away and open the door. "Erica, I love you. Please don't leave like this." Erica's shoulders heaved with her tears.

Erica slowly turned around. "Adrianna, do me a favor when you're in New York? Try and find your conscience." Erica turned and walked out of Adrianna's office.

Adrianna hugged herself tight and held her heart pendant in her hand as she fought against the sob tearing at her chest.

Erica stepped off the elevator in the parking garage and slipped into her Navigator. She locked the doors as tears streamed down her cheeks. She screamed Adrianna's name and slammed her hands against the steering wheel. She dropped her head, sobbing uncontrollably. Erica cursed herself for letting her anger get so out of control.

Her pager chimed at her waist. She grabbed it off her belt and stared at the display reading: "I'm so sorry for causing you such pain. I love you. Now and always."

Erica dropped her head against the steering wheel. "I love you too, Adrianna."

✳✳✳✳

Adrianna slipped into the limo and looked into Darby and Mia's faces. "Erica knows about Michael's lawsuit."

They groaned with disbelief, and Mia took her hand. "Oh, Adrianna. We're so sorry. We were afraid this was going to happen when we realized who your new lover was."

As the limo pulled away from the curb, Adrianna stared out the window and wished that the women in this car were not the only ones who knew what her true agenda was. Mia squeezed Adrianna's hand as she watched her stare out the window and cry softly.

"What does Erica know, Adrianna?"

Adrianna took a deep breath and dried her eyes. "All Erica thinks is that I tried to destroy Michael Thomas's life. I refuse to tell her otherwise till everything is said and done in court. That's the way it has to be for now. I need to protect Erica in case the judge wants to review Michael's file and she gets called in as a witness. Erica is quickly losing her faith in me, so I need to end this Monday, or I may lose her completely."

Darby handed her more tissues. "Adrianna, you're always harping at us about not sleeping with our clients or witnesses. Now I understand why. Thanks for being a fine example of what not to do."

They laughed softly as Adrianna gave her a coy look and dried her eyes. Adrianna turned and stared out the window. The image of Erica's angry tears burned in her heart. "Erica captivated my entire being like no other woman has before. I had no control over falling in love with her. I just hope I have not completely dimmed her love light."

Darby leaned toward Adrianna and touched her knee. "You have to believe that everything will be all right, Adrianna, regardless of how angry she is right now."

Adrianna looked into Darby's eyes. "I have to believe that Erica's anger stems from her search for the truth, and seeking the truth is what this case is all about. We all have so much at stake in this case, but Erica is not one of the chips I had ever intended to gamble with."

They sat back in their seats as the city moved past them in a blur.

Chapter 24

Erica collected herself, shelved her anger, and drove back to the hospital. She was in a horrible mood and prayed that absorbing herself in her work would numb the pain. But as the hours passed, she knew it wasn't working. The staff was aware of her cantankerous mood. Erica was not very receptive to their concerns and made it very clear to everyone that she was not willing to talk about what was bothering her. They stayed out of her way.

Erica moved through her work without emotion and wallowed in her agony. She handled each patient and situation with cool, professional detachment. Her staff had never seen her like this, and as the day turned to night she became more irritable and less tolerable.

Erica and her residents had just admitted a nineteen-year-old male patient into the unit who had crashed head first into a wall after trying to do some stunt on his skateboard. Erica stood before the view box and impatiently scanned through his x-rays, sighing as her frustration grew. The residents and nurses were in the nurses' station as Erica grabbed the envelope of x-rays and walked stiffly toward them. "Where are the x-rays of his right arm?"

Everyone stopped and looked at Erica. Peter slowly swiveled in his chair. "I thought I brought all of his x-rays up from the E.R. with him."

Erica brimmed with an anger that she had never displayed at work before. "Well, you thought wrong, Peter. Now find me those x-rays." Erica moved one step closer to Peter and dropped the package of x-rays into his lap. The x-rays slid off Peter's legs and scattered all over the floor.

Sarah had seen enough. She carefully set her clipboard aside and rose from her chair. She stepped to within inches of Erica's distraught face. "That's enough, Erica. I've had enough of your irritable behavior. You would never tolerate behavior like this from me or any of the nurses or residents, so why should we tolerate it from you?"

Erica looked into Sarah's stern eyes and saw the emotional strain that she had caused all of them. Sarah scanned her eyes and gently touched her arm. "We all know you're hurting, Erica. That much is obvious. I also know you don't want to talk about it, and we respect that. But you have become so difficult to get along with tonight." Sarah squeezed her arm. "Go home, Erica. Peter's team is on call tonight and can take care of things here. Please go home before you destroy what remaining bit of sanity I have left."

Erica looked at their faces and felt enveloped in shame. "I'm sorry, you guys. I really am. You don't deserve to be treated like this." She choked back her tears and squeezed Sarah's hand before she walked out of the ICU and drove herself straight home.

Erica felt numb and emotionally exhausted as she entered her house at eight o'clock. She walked around each room aimlessly and turned on the lights as if in search of something. She headed into the kitchen and absentmindedly opened the fridge, but she didn't dare put anything in her stomach. She slammed the fridge door closed and was about to walk away when she looked back at the picture of Adrianna she had put on the fridge door. Erica reached for the picture and carefully removed it from beneath the angel magnet, instantly transported back to the moment she took it up at the cottage.

They had been out on their walk around the lake. Adrianna had poked her head out from behind a tree when Erica snapped the shot. The wind had gently ruffled her beautiful, flowing chestnut hair, and her cheeks were rosy from the afternoon sun. She looked so vibrant and so full of life and love that Erica's eyes filled with tears. She felt the burning, raw pain of Adrianna's betrayal all over again. Erica slid along the fridge to sit on the floor, crumpling the picture in her hand. She threw it across the kitchen and sobbed.

An hour passed before Erica could collect herself and control her tears. She forced herself to head into the bedroom and into a warm, soothing shower. She slipped into a soft pink nightshirt and climbed into bed. She looked at the flashing red light on the answering machine that she had been avoiding since she arrived home. Erica grabbed her pillow to prop herself up against the headboard when she found a card that Adrianna had left beneath her pillow. She sat up and pulled the duvet up to her waist, staring at the pink envelope and the beautiful flow of her name in Adrianna's handwriting.

Tears stung Erica's cheeks as she played with the envelope in her hands and looked back toward the answering machine. Adrianna had paged her several times throughout the evening, but Erica had not responded. Erica knew that Adrianna would have called her at home and struggled with needing to hear her voice and hoping that she would give up trying.

Erica slowly reached for the new messages button and listened to the first message: her mother telling her that they had arrived safely in Santa Barbara and inviting Erica and Adrianna over for dinner next week. She listened to the next message and had to laugh as Trina invited Erica over for dinner and said that if Erica felt lonely tonight, Trina would be more than happy to share her half of the bed with her. Just to keep Erica safe as Adrianna had asked them to do. Trina giggled and told Erica to call them. After Trina's message, Adrianna's soothing voice filled the bedroom.

Erica hugged her knees to her chest and pulled little Addie into her arms. She inhaled the subtle scent of Adrianna's peach hand cream. She listened to the next four messages of Adrianna asking her how she was and softly asking for Erica to be patient with her and to try and believe that there was so much more that she could not tell her right now. Each message ended with Adrianna apologizing for the pain she was causing Erica and a soft teary good-bye ending with "I love you."

The messages finally ended, and Erica held little Addie tight and cried as her heartache consumed her. Erica reached for the box of tissues on the bedside table and jumped as the phone rang. The taped message played before a beep sounded and Adrianna's voice sent Erica's emotions into another tailspin. Erica pulled her hand away from the phone and listened as she heard the exhaustion in Adrianna's voice.

"I hope I'm not waking you, Erica, but I just couldn't sleep, so I thought I would try you one more time and see if you got home safely from work. I'm really worried about you, sweetheart. I don't blame you for not wanting to talk to me. I appreciate you just listening. I understand how you feel, and I wish I could give you the answers you so desperately seek."

Erica sat back against her pillows and listened to Adrianna.

"I didn't call to try and make you understand my actions when I know that's impossible right now. I just called to see if you're okay. I know that your stomach is probably just as upset as you are. I hope that you can eat something to soothe your tortured stomach since I can't seem to be able to soothe your tortured heart just yet. I only pray that you will give me the opportunity to explain everything when this is all over."

Erica's tears streamed down her cheeks as she heard Adrianna cry.

"I want you to know that I love you, sweetheart. I miss you, and I wish that I'd never brought such pain and agony to your life. You probably wish you'd never met me. I can't imagine what it's like at the hospital for you right now, but please don't let this

Ana Corman

affect your work. Your patients need you as much as I do. I love you, Erica. Now and always. Good-bye, my love."

Erica heard her choke back tears and heard the gentle click of the phone. She leaned her head back against the headboard and cried till she had no more tears left.

Chapter 25

Startled awake by her pager, Erica looked around her bedroom in groggy confusion. She had fallen asleep on Adrianna's side of the bed with her unopened card in her hand and little Addie nestled against her chest. Erica rolled over and checked the alarm clock: five o'clock in the morning. She had probably been asleep for only four hours.

She reached for her pager and read the message to call the NICU. Erica sat up on the edge of the bed and hit the autodial button for the unit. Peter answered the phone.

"I'm sorry for waking you up so early on a Saturday morning, Erica."

"It's all right, Peter. What's up?"

"It's Joel Hanson, the eighteen-year-old patient who was hit with the baseball bat. He's become drowsy, agitated and confused. We've taken him down for a stat CAT scan of his head."

"I'll grab a quick shower, Peter, then I'll be on my way in."

"That would be great. I'll see you when you get here."

Erica hung up the phone, jumped out of bed and headed into the shower.

✳✳✳✳

Erica spent three hours operating on Joel Hanson to remove a blood clot from his brain. She walked beside his bed as they wheeled him from the recovery room back to the neurosurgical intensive care unit. Joel's parents and girlfriend were standing in the hallway outside of the ICU as they arrived. They stood stone still with fear and anxiety etched on their faces as they carefully leaned in close to catch a quick glimpse, yet terrified of what they would see.

Erica touched Joel's mother's arm. "Please follow me so we can talk." Erica guided them down the hall to the quiet room. She carefully opened the door and peeked inside to find the room empty. She held the door open and followed the family inside.

Joel's girlfriend, Lisa, stood before the floor-to-ceiling underwater mural. "I hate this room. I hate this painting. It makes me feel like I'm drowning in bad news."

Erica touched her arm. "Believe it or not, I know how you feel. Please have a seat so we can talk." Erica slipped into the nearest chair facing Joel's family. "I removed a large blood clot on his brain that was causing pressure and causing him to not respond to simple commands. In the recovery room he squeezed my hand and wiggled his toes for me. That's a wonderful sign, as you all know. Before his surgery

442

this morning he wasn't obeying simple commands. We'll be watching him in the ICU very carefully over the next forty-eight to seventy-two hours for any recurrence of bleeding or swelling. His situation is less critical than this morning, but we will watch him very carefully, and each day I hope to see improvement."

Erica spent another thirty minutes with Joel's family, answering all of their questions before walking them back into the ICU.

She mechanically completed her rounds on all of her patients in the hospital and saw several patients in the emergency department. She completed her work with numbed proficiency as she saw the concern in the eyes of the emergency room staff. She knew they wanted to reach out and comfort her, but she exuded an aura that screamed, "Don't mess with me!" The staff wisely did their best to stay clear of her.

Once Erica was done in the E.R. she returned to the NICU at five o'clock in the evening to check on Joel Hanson and carefully reviewed his vital signs in the nursing documentation.

Peter and Sarah watched Erica stand outside Joel's room and flip through his chart. Peter straightened and clipped his pen onto his breast pocket. "Looks like grumpy's almost done with Joel Hanson."

"I see. Well, I think we've all about had enough of grumpy for one weekend. She looks exhausted, and I don't think I've ever seen her look that pale. I'll make sure she heads home soon."

"Thanks, Sarah. You're a lifesaver. I've updated the team on call tonight on all of the patients. I think we're all just about ready to call it a day. I think I'll head home myself before I get singed by grumpy's wrath once more."

"I'll try and protect you till you get out of here, Peter. But just to be on the safe side, you'd better keep your fire retardant suit on till you get to your car."

Their laughter caused Erica to look their way.

She was pleased with Joel's progress and stepped toward the nurses' station to make a note on his chart. Suddenly, a wave of nausea sent her into a dizzying spin. Erica grabbed for the nearest chair and almost stumbled right over it.

Peter lurched forward. He caught her and gingerly eased her into a chair. He was deeply concerned as Erica winced and grabbed her stomach. She leaned forward and gently rocked herself to ease the storm churning in her stomach. The staff gathered around her and exchanged worried glances.

She leaned back in her chair as beads of sweat appeared on her face. Erica looked up at all their concerned faces. "I'm okay, you guys. I just haven't eaten."

Sarah asked for water and handed the cup to Erica. "I haven't seen you eat or drink anything all day. Now, drink this water, Erica, before you pass out on us."

Erica looked into her eyes and took a sip of the water.

"Drink it all, Erica. It should help to settle your stomach."

Erica obediently brought the cup to her lips. "Who taught you to be so bossy?"

Sarah smiled at her and shook her head. She grabbed a washcloth and ran it under cold water before taking a seat across from Erica. "Press this cloth to your face and see if it helps."

"Thank you." Erica looked up at everyone standing around her. "Will you guys please stop staring at me and go back to work? I'm okay. Really I am. I'll eat something, then I'll be fine. Now go away before I deviate from my normally sunny personality and start getting uncharacteristically cranky."

They laughed and went back to work. Sarah stayed sitting across from her, concerned by her pale, drawn features.

Erica wiped her face with the cool cloth and looked over at Sarah's troubled eyes. "Stop looking at me like that, Sarah. I'm fine, really."

Sarah leaned forward in her chair. "Who are you trying to convince, Erica? You or me?"

Erica looked away.

"Let me tell you what I see. You look emotionally and physically exhausted. You obviously have not eaten or slept much in the past twenty-four hours, and you scared the hell out of me by almost fainting a few minutes ago. And just to add insult to injury, you've deviated from your normally sunny personality all day and been extremely cranky and irritable."

Erica pressed the cool cloth to her face. "Please, Sarah, don't stop there. You sound like you're on a roll."

Sarah smacked Erica's knee and glared at her. "This is no joke, Erica. I'm worried about you, so don't feed me this rubbish that you're fine."

Erica took another drink of water to curb the buildup of bile assaulting her stomach.

Sarah laid her hand on her knee and felt her anger melt away at the sight of Erica's moist eyes. "You're not on call for the rest of the weekend, so go home and take better care of yourself. I hate to see you so upset, but whatever you're going through, I have to believe that everything will work out for you in the end. Life is a pain in the arse sometimes, and you probably couldn't feel any lower right now." Sarah watched Erica's tears tumble.

Erica pressed the cool cloth to her eyes. "I don't know if Adrianna and I are ever going to be able to fix this mess we've made." Erica dried her eyes and rose from her chair. "I do need to go home, Sarah. I feel pretty lousy."

Sarah rose from her chair and touched her arm. "Are you okay to drive home?"

"Yes, big sister. I'm okay to drive home. I probably look worse than I feel, so stop worrying about me, would you?"

Sarah smiled and squeezed her arm affectionately. "It's hard not to worry about someone you care about, Erica, and if it makes you feel any better, you're still beautiful, even when you look like shit."

Erica smiled and tossed her empty cup into the nearest trashcan. "Thanks, Sarah, I needed that." Erica bid everyone good night and headed out of the NICU.

Chapter 26

David set the double porch swing in motion with
one foot and smiled at the stunned look on Carolyn's
face. Her denim hat with the front bill turned up by a
huge felt daisy added to her youthful exuberance. In
the time she had been home from the hospital, she had
regained her vitality and effervescent spirit. Her short
denim dress flowed over her slender frame and
revealed the shapely legs that always made David sigh
with appreciation.

"That medical malpractice case that Adrianna was
embroiled in a year ago involved Dr. Michael Thomas.
The wonderful Dr. Michael Thomas who saw us in the
E.R. and referred Erica to us."

"The one and the same."

"Why didn't you and Adrianna tell me this
sooner?"

"You know that Adrianna never states the names of
the people involved in her cases. Besides you weren't
quite up to this type of discussion two weeks ago."

Carolyn frowned and tilted her head. "If I remember correctly, the case against him was thrown out."

"See, that big old brain tumor never affected my girl's memory."

Carolyn reached for David's hand. "Now Michael has called you and wants to discuss his case with you."

"Yes. His case and the case of his medical professor, Dr. MacGregor."

"Now this is getting really convoluted. Our darling Dr. Michael Thomas knows Dr. MacGregor, who cost Hailey her life. Adrianna successfully sued MacGregor and was also involved in Dr. Thomas's lawsuit. One year later he wants to come and talk to you about all this. Why didn't he just talk to Adrianna?"

"This is where it gets really twisted. Michael just found out yesterday that Erica and Adrianna are partners. Apparently he pitched a fit in Erica's office and confronted Adrianna about the lawsuits. Erica knew nothing about Adrianna's involvement till that big confrontation."

Carolyn leaned back in the swing. "Oh, my God."

"Yes. I guess it got pretty ugly with a lot of harsh words and tears. Adrianna stormed out and Michael and Erica were left to figure out what was really going on. Michael felt really uneasy about the things Adrianna said and felt it was about time he found out the truth of what happened around his lawsuit. Erica gave him my name and number and told him to give me a call."

Carolyn was temporarily speechless. "I have to give Adrianna and Erica a call to make sure they're all right."

"I think that would be a great idea, sweetheart. I'll see what I can do to answer Dr. Michael Thomas's questions."

Carolyn was about to slip off the swing when she turned back to David. She placed her hand on his knee. "Do you realize that is the first time that you have ever acknowledged the fact that Adrianna has a partner? Do you have any idea how much it would mean to her to hear you refer to Erica as something much more than just a friend?"

David shifted in his seat and stared off across the street. "I know. I saw right away how much Erica had come to mean to Adrianna. She's a wonderful woman, and she makes our daughter happy. If Adrianna is happy, what more could I ask for?"

Carolyn leaned in close and kissed David softly. "I knew you would come around. You're not such a pig head living in the Stone Age after all. Nothing would make Adrianna happier than to hear you say what you just told me. Think about that, Fred Flintstone."

David couldn't help but smile as he watched Carolyn walk to the front door. "Give Erica and Adrianna my love."

Carolyn came back to step before him, and she ran her fingers through his thick silver hair. "I'll give Erica your love. I'll let you give Adrianna your love yourself."

"I have always loved Adrianna."

"Now you can tell her that you love her completely." Carolyn turned and headed for the front door. She squealed as she felt David playfully smack her bottom.

David set the swing in motion once again as he watched a four-door gold Lexus pull up into his driveway. Dr. Michael Thomas stepped out of his vehicle and waved. David slipped off the porch swing as he watched him head up the front steps. He extended his hand. "Hello, Dr. Thomas."

"Hello, David. Please call me Michael. Thank you for seeing me. I hope I'm not interrupting your Saturday evening."

"No, you're not, and this sounded very important to you. Please come in." David held the front door open for him.

"Is Carolyn home?"

"She sure is. I told her what happened in Erica's office yesterday, and she has gone to call Adrianna and Erica. You're probably safer with me once she finds out how upset Erica and Adrianna are over all this."

"Maybe you should show me where the emergency exit is just in case Carolyn corners me."

David laughed and clapped Michael's shoulder. "You may be able to run from Carolyn, but you can't hide. Trust me, son, I learned that lesson the hard way."

David guided Michael into the library. "Can I get you something to drink, Michael?"

"Water would be fine."

David swept his hand toward the storage file box on the center of the round mahogany table. "With what I have to show you, you might want something stronger. I have Coors lite in the fridge, will that do?"

"That would be great."

"Two Coors lites it is. Please make yourself at home."

Michael watched as David left the richly furnished room. He brushed his hand across one of the six high back leather chairs gathered around the mahogany table. He walked past the floor-to-ceiling inlaid bookcases filled with law books, current fiction, murder mysteries, business, how-to books, history, gardening, and investment. He walked past the books and stood before a wall of family photos and David's law degree from Stanford. He straightened a beautiful photo of Adrianna in her graduation cap and gown. She was absolutely glowing. Michael noticed she hasn't changed a bit since her graduation from law school. "Lady, it looks like you and I are going to see this thing through, whether either one of us wants to or not."

David walked into the room with a tray holding two tall ice-cold glasses of beer, a bowl of pretzels and a plate of homemade chocolate chip cookies. He set the tray on the mahogany table. "Carolyn said to tell you she hopes your beer is flat and bitter. She's on the phone with Adrianna. I would hate to hear what she would have said if she saw I was feeding you her chocolate chip cookies." David handed Michael an icy glass of beer and tapped his glass lightly. "Ah, to the women we love."

They both took a healthy sip before David placed two sandstone coasters on the mahogany table, set his beer down, and pulled out a chair for Michael. "Have a seat so we can get started."

451

Michael took a seat and watched David slide the file box closer. "Is everything in that box from my case?"

David smiled as he took the seat next to Michael. "Yes. Your file and Dr. MacGregor's are in here. I have always taken a keen interest in Adrianna's cases and loved to watch her work. When she started taking on medical malpractice cases, I was pretty disgusted. Doctors have a tough job, and I found it really upsetting to see how some lawyers made a career out of pouncing on their every mistake. Adrianna tried to tell me her cases were different. She challenged me to help investigate her cases to see if I could prove the doctors innocent of the charges brought against them. Each time our investigation was done, I was standing on Adrianna's side of the fence and appalled at the mistakes some doctors thought they could get away with. Adrianna really opened my eyes to the world of medical negligence. Dr. MacGregor's case was the most frightening."

"What happened in Dr. MacGregor's case, David? Adrianna accused him of taking three different painkillers for back pain and abusing alcohol while on these meds. She accused Dr. MacGregor of poorly managing Hailey's case so that it was too late by the time Hailey was diagnosed with cancer. Is any of that true?"

"First of all, let me tell you that Adrianna never makes accusations. Even as a child she could never lie. Anything Adrianna tells you you can take at face value." David rose and pulled a white, three-inch ringed binder from the box. He sat back down in the chair and opened the binder in front of Michael. This

452

is the index of all the documents in Dr. MacGregor's
file that Adrianna presented at his trial. Sworn
statements of fifteen patients who attested to his
medical negligence, complaint letters from twenty-five
of his colleagues because of his lack of medical care
and attention to his patients, medical documentation of
his low back pain, copies of the prescriptions of the
three pain killers he obtained from three different
colleagues that he filled at three different pharmacies
on several occasions, sworn statements from his office
staff of his alcohol consumption during office hours,
statements from his closest friends that the alcohol
consumption never stopped at the office.

"Hailey's case was the biggest example of his
blatant disregard for his patients and his total inability
to deliver reasonable medical care. She should have
had some basic tests done that even a first-year
resident out of medical school would have known to
order. Those tests would have diagnosed her cancer.
Instead he ignored Hailey's complaints and made up
one bogus diagnosis after another. It was too late by
the time Adrianna took Hailey into the E.R because of
bleeding. The cancer had spread throughout her
abdomen.

"Hailey was very special to us. Carolyn and I
loved her. We were devastated when she died." David
looked away from Michael and stared at the framed
photo of Adrianna. "Hailey's case was Adrianna's
biggest personal and professional challenge. Ethically
she could represent Hailey's case as long as she was
able to behave professionally. You can imagine how
hard that would be for anyone in Adrianna's situation.
I offered to try the case for Adrianna, but she refused.

She wanted to do if for Hailey. She did ask for my help in investigating all these allegations against Dr. MacGregor. We uncovered so much against him that it didn't take much to convict him of medical malpractice and negligence in Hailey's death. As you already know, three months after the settlement was awarded, Dr. MacGregor sat at his office desk and shot himself in the head, killing himself instantly. He left a suicide note." David flipped to the last page in the binder.

"He took full responsibility for Hailey's death. He admitted to his addiction to painkillers and alcohol. He stated that he had hurt so many of his patients and before anyone else died, he felt he needed to end his own life. He even apologized to Adrianna for all the grief he had caused her."

Michael read the suicide note and flipped through several colleague complaints. "So Adrianna had every right to sue Dr. MacGregor. This must have been so difficult for Adrianna."

"More than any of us could imagine. I was so proud of her for the way she handled herself during that horrible ordeal and throughout the trial. She was so strong and brave. Hailey would have been proud of her. That case opened my eyes to Adrianna's world and the love she had for Hailey. I have never been very understanding or supportive of Adrianna's choice to be with a woman. I wanted her to find a husband who would take care of her. Through that trial I saw an incredible lawyer and an incredible woman. A woman who fought with each breath for the woman she loved. I just never understood their lives. Adrianna said she couldn't fight her desire to be with a woman. It wasn't a choice but a path. She couldn't fight it anymore than I could fight loving Carolyn."

David grabbed the glass of beer and ran his thumb along the icy lip. "I felt like Adrianna must hate men to want to be with a woman and perhaps that was a direct reflection of her feelings for our relationship. Carolyn told me that Adrianna's lifestyle had nothing to do with me. It's hard to believe that when you're a father trying to protect your daughter from a difficult path."

"I know how you feel. My closest female friends are lesbians, and that greatly diminishes a guy's chances to find himself a wife. If you can't change Adrianna's ways, David, maybe I could send you a few of my other friends to work on."

David laughed and sipped his beer. "I'm done fighting what just is, Michael. Adrianna has taught me that much. The love she shares with Erica is beautiful, and it's about time I told her that. Otherwise, my wife is going to be feeding us both flat, bitter beer."

Michael closed Dr. MacGregor's file and handed the binder back to David. David set his beer on the coaster and slid the binder on the table. "When you called, you said you had questions about your own case. Did the hospital lawyer not discuss what happened with you?"

Michael crossed his legs and ran his finger around the edge of the sandstone coaster. "I was terrified, David. The hospital lawyer told me my case was dropped, and I felt nothing but relief and anger. I was relived it was over and livid at Adrianna. I held her responsible for Dr. MacGregor's death and for all of my fear and sleepless nights. I didn't want to know anything else, just that that nightmare was behind me."

"So you never opened the letters and transcripts Adrianna sent you of Dr. MacGregor's trial and those from your pre-trial?"

Michael pushed the coaster forward. "They're unopened in a box in the bottom of my closet."

David leaned back in his chair. "No wonder women think we're thick. Do you really want to know what happened at your trial and what has brought Adrianna to her current case in New York City?"

"Yes, I do."

"When are you scheduled back at work?"

"Wednesday."

"Good." David pulled the cell phone off his belt and scrolled through his phone directory. He hit several buttons before bringing the phone to his ear. "Yes, I'd like to book a flight on your next plane leaving Phoenix Sky Harbor for New York City."

Michael watched as David waited patiently. "Nine o'clock would be fine. Thank you." David recited a credit card number and confirmed the flight information. He ended the call and clipped the phone to his belt. "I have you booked on an America West flight out of Sky Harbor at nine o'clock tonight for JFK. I'll book you a room at the Mayflower Hotel on Central Park. That's where Adrianna is staying. You need to sit in on Adrianna's trial Monday morning to fully understand everything that's going on." David stood and extended his hand to Michael. "Go home and pack a bag. Take the letters Adrianna sent you and use the time on the plane to read them. You might find yourself feeling enlightened." David wrapped two chocolate chip cookies in a napkin and handed them to Michael. "Take these with you. They're quite good." David walked Michael to the front door.

"Call me when you get to your hotel room. If you have any questions, we can talk about them then. It's up to you if you want to make contact with Adrianna in the hotel."

Michael extended his hand. "I'll pay you back for all this, David."

"Just find the answers to your questions. I think you'll see Adrianna in a different light by the time this is all over."

They both turned and looked down the hallway as they heard Carolyn calling out to David. David grabbed Michael's arm and shoved him out the door. "Run, son, while you have the chance. Otherwise you may not be alive to enjoy those cookies or sit in on that trial Monday morning."

Michael smiled and squeezed David's shoulder. "I'll call you once I get to New York."

"That would be great. Now get out of here while you still can."

Michael dashed down the front steps and slipped into his Lexus. He eased down the driveway and headed down the street as Carolyn came to stand beside David.

"How could you let that scoundrel get away before I gave him a piece of my mind?"

David slowly closed the door and put his arm around Carolyn's shoulder. "He's on his way to New York to sit in on Adrianna's case Monday morning. I'm going to book him a room at the Mayflower. What do you think the chances are of getting him a room next to Adrianna's?"

Carolyn grinned like the Grinch on Christmas Eve. "Oh, please let me make the reservation. At least one Taylor woman can wrap her knuckles against his thick skull."

David watched Carolyn head into the kitchen as he turned and peered out the front window. "Michael, you have no idea what trouble is till you tangle with an Italian woman." David laughed and headed into the kitchen.

Chapter 27

Abby and Trina stepped into Erica's house and set down their bags, letting their eyes adjust to the dim lighting. Abby slid her hand along the doorframe and flipped on the lights. She locked the door behind them and reset the house alarm. Trina called out to Erica, but there was no reply. They gave each other an uneasy look, and Trina slipped her hand into Abby's. They walked through the living room and dining room and headed toward the flickering candlelight in the kitchen.

Abby flipped the kitchen light switch, and they both started at the sight of Erica, dressed in jeans and a T-shirt, sitting on the kitchen floor with her back against the cupboards.

Erica quickly shielded her eyes from the bright light. "Turn that damned light off, Abby."

Abby and Trina were stunned. Erica was holding a full glass of white wine, and the empty bottle was on its side at her feet. A vanilla candle flickered its gentle scent into the air, and little Addie lay among several scattered pictures of Adrianna on the floor. At Abby and Trina's feet sat an empty wine glass holding Erica's diamond bracelet.

Abby and Trina ignored Erica's request and knelt before her. Abby touched Erica's dampened chin and lifted her tear-stained face up to her. "Jesus, Erica. You look like shit."

Erica slapped Abby's hand away and looked away. "Thank you, Dr. Cooper. Your supportive words have touched my heart." Erica carelessly lifted her wine glass and took a big sip.

Abby felt deeply concerned as she picked up the empty bottle of Reichsgraf Von Kesselstatt that Adrianna had bought them all. She held it up to the light and shook it lightly. "Erica, please tell me you didn't drink this all by yourself?"

Erica looked at Abby with a glazed look. "Of course I did. I'm a big girl. I can drink if I want to."

"Well, big girl, your stomach is going to make you pay for this, and I think you've had enough." Abby took the glass of wine from her and handed it to Trina.

Trina was about to get up and dispose of the wine when Erica grabbed for her. "Don't take my wine, Trina." Erica reached for the glass. She smacked the back of Trina's hand and sent the glass of wine careening against the cupboards.

Trina jumped back just as the glass shattered and wine splashed at her feet.

Abby quickly jumped up and pulled Trina back out of harm's way. "Are you okay, sweetheart?"

Trina nodded. Abby's anger burned. She reached down to Erica and grabbed her by her shirt, pulling her forward and shaking her. "Don't you ever do that to

Trina again, Erica. Do you understand me? Don't you ever do that again. We know that you're pissed at Adrianna, but don't you dare take it out on us."

Abby had shaken Erica into a sober state as tears of disbelief fell from her eyes. "God, Abby, I'm sorry." Erica reached up for Trina. Trina slipped in beside her and pulled her into her arms. Erica leaned her teary face against Trina's and sobbed. "I'm so sorry, Trina. I would never, ever mean to hurt you."

Trina held Erica close and talked to her soothingly. Abby shook her head and began cleaning up the mess.

Abby returned with pillows for all of them to sit on and a glass of water for Erica. Trina explained why they had come over. "Adrianna called us tonight and told us what happened."

Erica leaned her head back against the cupboards and dried her eyes. "I'm sorry Adrianna felt she had to get you guys involved in this mess."

Abby was stunned. "I hope that's the wine talking because I'm hurt that you didn't call us and tell us what was going on. Thank God Adrianna had the sense to call us, because you obviously had no intention of letting us help you through this. Let me remind you, Dr. Beaumont, that being there for each other is what friends are for."

Erica flinched at Abby's words.

Abby looked over at Trina and softened her tone. "Adrianna is worried sick about you. She said she has not been able to reach you for twenty-four hours now and asked us to come over here to make sure you were all right. It's a damned good thing we did."

"If Adrianna was really that worried about me, then she would be here explaining to me why she tried to destroy Michael's career."

"We don't fully understand what's going on, but what I can tell you is that we've only known Adrianna for two weeks now, and Trina and I both feel that she's a genuinely decent person. What she's doing definitely conflicts with what we know of her, but she asked us on the phone to please not lose faith in her and to try to understand that this case is a lot deeper than it appears. She promised us that she could answer all of our questions after the hearing on Monday and asked that we just do one thing for her: take care of you."

Erica dropped her head back against the cupboards and closed her eyes. Tears squeezed out from between her long, dark lashes. "None of this makes any sense. I've been racking my brain trying to understand it, but I just can't understand Adrianna's desire to take that case against Michael. It goes against everything I have learned about her true kindness and loving spirit."

Trina brushed Erica's hair away from her face. "Adrianna said it would be impossible for us to understand right now and asked that we be patient with her."

Erica shook her head. "My patience is quickly running out with Adrianna Taylor."

Abby and Trina watched Erica intently as she sipped on her water.

Abby collected all the pictures of Adrianna scattered at Erica's feet. Trina picked up the wine glass holding Erica's bracelet and held it up for everyone to see.

"Adrianna gave me that bracelet Thursday night. She felt it symbolized how our hearts are woven together. Our hearts are woven together, and our lives are quickly becoming unglued."

Trina handed Erica more tissues as Abby collected little Addie into her arms and held her close. She touched her damp head and smiled. "We're going to have to blow dry your head, little Addie. I think someone has been using you as an emotional substitute." Abby squeezed little Addie's paw. "She even smells like Adrianna."

Trina held Erica's hand. "Erica, all the answers to your questions are in your heart."

Erica dried her eyes and looked into Trina's eyes.

"You want to be totally pissed at Adrianna yet you have surrounded yourself with her essence. You're hurt and angry, yet you're trying hard to find the reasons for Adrianna's mission because you believe in her."

Tears flowed from Erica's eyes.

"We've all seen the good in her, and that's why this is all so baffling. She has asked a simple request of us, and that is for time. We all love her, so we should honor that request. We're not accustomed to judging people till we know all the facts, so let's give Adrianna the time she needs to prove to us that what she's doing makes sense. We want to be angry because she tried unsuccessfully to sue Michael, yet Adrianna keeps pleading with us to not pass judgment." Trina slowly caressed Erica's hair.

"There's obviously so much we don't know, but what we do know is that you and Adrianna share a precious love. Regardless of where Adrianna's career

is taking her, you are the most important thing to her."
Trina watched the tears flow from Erica's eyes. "I
know that you're hurting, Erica, but you fell in love
with an incredible woman, and regardless of what we
know or don't know, we have to give her the benefit of
the doubt and give her a chance to explain. I know you
love her enough to do that, otherwise we wouldn't be
sitting here in a puddle of tears."

Erica closed her eyes and cried in frustration.
Abby slid in beside her, and they both held her close.
Abby reached for more tissues and handed them to
Erica, who dried her eyes. Abby rubbed her back and
frowned. "A year ago, I heard some fleeting rumor at
work about one of the E.R. docs getting sued, but that
was all I heard. I had no idea what had happened with
Michael till Adrianna called us tonight and told us.
How did you find out about this mess?"

Erica looked at Abby with surprise. "Didn't
Adrianna tell you?"

"All Adrianna told us was a little bit about
Michael's case and her overwhelming worry for you
and your reaction to her involvement. She didn't want
to talk long because she wanted us to come and see
you. We tried to comfort her, but she made it clear
that you were the number one concern. We asked her
how you had reacted to all this, and she cried and said
she deserved everything you said to her."

Erica dropped her head in shame at the memory of
her nasty words. Abby gently rubbed her back.

"She said to be careful because you might be like a
bear with a thorn stuck in its paw."

Erica had to laugh through her tears.

"She also said to tell you she loves you."

Erica leaned her head back against the cupboards.

"Her love for you is true, Erica. She's made that very obvious since the day I saw her looking into your eyes in the garden."

Trina continued to hold Erica's hand. "Did Adrianna tell you about Michael's lawsuit?"

Erica dried her eyes and leaned back as she shook her head. "No, Adrianna was hoping I wouldn't find out till Monday, if you can believe that. Michael came into my office Friday afternoon, saw Adrianna's photo, and told me everything." She told them the whole story of her explosive Friday afternoon and did her best to recall the entire nasty conversation in Adrianna's office.

Abby and Trina were stunned. "You told her to find her conscience?" Abby said slowly.

Erica sadly shook her head.

Trina burst into laughter. "I can't believe you told her you thought she seduced you to eliminate you as a credible witness and to strengthen her case. Erica! I'm shocked. I never thought you had such nastiness in you. I'm so proud of you."

Erica played with the tissue in her hands. "Adrianna was pretty shocked as well. I'll never forget that look in her eyes of deep sadness and fear when I stormed out of her office, leaving her to feel my wrath. I could hear her call my name, and I felt my heart shatter. I wanted to run back to her and take her in my arms, but I was so blinded by my anger that I just took off and left her standing alone. I love her so much, and I hurt her so badly with all the terrible things that I said."

465

Abby and Trina sat in silence with Erica and let her drain her sorrow. Abby handed her more tissues. "Have you eaten anything today?"

"I had some toast when I got home from work tonight, but even that did not sit well. There are bags of food in the fridge from Chinese to deli sandwiches that Adrianna had delivered here. She knew I wouldn't be feeding myself very well. So help yourselves if you guys are hungry."

Trina touched Erica's cheek. "She really does know you, doesn't she? She asked us to make sure you had something to eat but said that your stomach is going to be as unhappy as you are."

Erica smiled and leaned back against the cupboards.

Abby squeezed her shoulder. "You look exhausted, Erica. Do you want to lie down for a while?"

Erica stared at the wine glass holding her bracelet and hugged her knees to her chest. "I don't want to get into that bed without Adrianna."

Abby leaned closer to Erica. "Well, since she's not here to fulfill that request, I'll go to bed with you."

Erica looked at Abby. "I've waited thirty years for you to offer, Abby, and now you do it out of pure pity. Forget it. I'm going to take an ad out in the local paper and see who responds."

"With the shape you're in, you'll be lucky to get them to walk in your front door."

Erica grabbed Abby and pulled her down into her lap. Abby shrieked as Erica pretended to pummel her.

Abby finally freed herself, then looked into Erica's face and saw her suddenly turn pale. "Erica, are you okay?"

Erica quickly bolted to her feet. "I'm going to be sick." She steadied herself on the counter then quickly headed toward her bedroom.

Abby helped Trina to her feet just as the phone rang. Trina hopped up on the counter and grabbed the kitchen phone. "Oh, Adrianna, we're so glad you called us."

Abby smiled as she tidied up the kitchen. She listened to Trina tell Adrianna a little about Erica's inebriated state of mind. Abby heard the shower go on in Erica's bathroom.

Twenty minutes later, Trina hung up the phone and rubbed her eyes. Abby placed the wine glass holding Erica's bracelet on the counter and stepped before Trina, slipping in between her legs and pulling her into her arms.

Trina hugged her tight. "I don't know which one of them is a bigger emotional mess." Trina sighed and leaned her forehead against Abby's. "What are we going to do with these two, babe?"

"Just be there for them, darling. Then when this is all over and we find some logical explanation for this craziness, let's kill them both."

Trina laughed. "That's a deal, sweetie pie." She guided Abby's face closer and kissed her tenderly.

Abby helped Trina slide off the counter, and they headed into Erica's bedroom hand in hand. They found her dressed in her cozy pink nightshirt, sitting on the edge of the bed, staring into the carpeting.

467

Abby looked at her sideways. "Erica, what are you doing?"

Erica never moved her fixed gaze from the carpet. "Trying to get the bed to stop spinning."

Abby and Trina burst into laughter. Erica looked up and said irritably, "I'm so glad you guys find this funny."

"What did you expect, my friend? You drank a whole bottle of wine. In thirty years, I've barely seen you finish one glass, let alone one bottle."

Erica looked away.

"Did you throw up?" Abby asked.

Erica shook her head and grimaced. "No. There's nothing left in my stomach. Just a lot of dry heaves."

Trina reached forward and touched Erica's damp curls. "Can we get you anything to ease your nausea, Erica?"

Erica made a weak attempt at a smile. "No, thanks, Trina. I just need to sleep this off. Hopefully tomorrow I can put something in my raw stomach." Erica shifted on the bed uncomfortably and looked up at Trina and Abby. "Who was on the phone?"

Trina hesitated.

"I asked you a question, Trina."

"It was Adrianna."

Erica looked down at her feet and slowly shook her head.

"We're not taking sides here, Erica. We're just as concerned about Adrianna as we are about you, and her biggest concern is you."

Erica looked back into Trina's eyes. "I didn't expect you guys would take sides, and I don't give a shit if you talk to Adrianna even though I choose not to. I really wish you guys would leave me alone and get the hell out of here."

Trina took one step back and reached for Abby's hand. She stared wide-eyed at Erica and blinked back her tears.

Erica swung her legs under the covers and turned her back on both of them.

Abby watched Trina and gently squeezed her hand. Abby's patience was quickly running out. She stepped toward the edge of Erica's bed and put one hand on either side of her and proceeded to shake the bed violently.

Erica whipped her eyes open and grabbed Abby's arm and hung on for dear life. "Abby! Stop it or I'm going to puke all over you."

Abby stopped shaking the bed. She leaned right down into Erica's face and looked her straight in the eye. "I will stop shaking this bed when you stop being such a bitch."

Erica's eyes filled with tears. She turned her head sharply away from Abby and buried it in her pillow.

"You owe Trina an apology, and I expect to hear it in the next ten seconds."

Abby stepped away from Erica, grabbed two Victorian chairs from her sitting area by the window, and placed them beside her bed. She set them side by side and guided Trina into a chair.

Trina leaned into Abby and kissed her softly. "Thank you."

Erica cautiously looked behind her and peeked at them. "There will be no kissing in this house while I feel like such a miserable bitch."

Abby and Trina smiled as Abby began the sound of a ticking clock. "Tick, tick, tick, tick, …"

Erica quickly got the hint and turned over to face them. "Sorry for being such a bitch, Trina."

Trina smiled. "You're forgiven. But I'd watch it if I were you. Abby is going to beat you senseless if you're mean to me one more time."

"Don't let her beat me, Trina. I'm in such a fragile state."

They all laughed together as Abby slipped her hand into Trina's. "I'm going to beat both you and Adrianna, if that makes you feel any better."

Erica rolled onto her back and laid her head on her pillow. She stared up at the ceiling and toyed with the seam on the duvet. "How was Adrianna, Trina?"

"She's an emotional mess like you. But unlike you, she's grateful that we're here for you."

Erica turned her head and looked at Trina and Abby. "I know I haven't quite shown it, but I am grateful that you're both here."

Abby grunted. "Then start showing it. And I'm sure Adrianna would be thrilled to know that the three of us are in your bedroom together."

"Actually, she'll be really mad to know she missed this pillow talk."

They sat together and talked for an hour as Erica began to fade. Abby and Trina stayed with her till she drifted off to sleep.

✳✳✳✳

Erica's full bladder awakened her in the middle of the night. She cautiously sat up on the edge of the bed and held her pounding head in her hands. She dropped her hands to grip the edge of the bed as a wave of nausea careened into her throat. She steadied herself, then looked toward the fireplace and saw the soft glow of dying embers. She stepped closer and saw Abby and Trina on the queen-size air mattress before the fire. They were sleeping in each other's arms and wearing the matching silk pajama tops that Erica bought them for Christmas. Their legs were entwined, and the cozy blanket was barely up to their waists as they held each other tight.

Erica quietly placed more wood on the fire and watched the flames caress the logs. She rubbed her pulsating temples in an attempt to ease the throbbing. She pulled the flannel blanket higher up on Abby and Trina and headed into her bathroom. She then headed to her kitchen for a glass of milk and two Advil.

Erica returned to the fire and sat beside Abby and Trina with her back against the couch. She watched their peaceful, rhythmic breathing. She loved the way Trina cocooned in Abby's arms. Erica looked up at the mantel clock and saw that it was four o'clock in the morning. She laid her head back against the couch and wondered what Adrianna was doing at this very moment. Was she sleeping, or was she also awake, tormented by the painful distance and lack of communication? Erica felt her eyes cloud with tears as she stared into the fire and remembered the thunderstorm at the cottage and the passion they had shared before a cozy fire. Her tears fell onto her nightshirt. She felt a hand on her leg. She looked toward Abby's concerned, sleepy eyes.

"What are you thinking about?"

471

Erica reached for several tissues and dried her eyes. "Adrianna."

Abby smiled and looked up at the clock. "Well, you're not alone. She's called here every two hours since you fell asleep, just to check on you. If I kissed you as often as she asked me to, I would have chapped lips."

Erica laughed softly. She balled the damp tissue in her hand. "How is she?"

"She's doing okay, I guess," said Abby. "She seems to be working nonstop, and she said that's the only thing that's helping to keep her sanity."

Erica attempted to control her tears as she looked toward the fire.

"Carolyn also called. She's worried about both of you. She said to tell you that you'd better get those ducks back line dancing before she hits both of you over the head with a low hanging light fixture. I had no idea what she was talking about. She said you would understand."

Erica smiled through her tears.

"She wants you to call her when you feel up to it." Abby watched her press a tissue to her trembling lips. "How are you feeling?"

Erica leaned her head back and closed her eyes. "My stomach is on fire, my guts are in an uproar, and my head is trying to mix classical and rap music."

Abby laughed softly as Trina lifted her sleepy face and looked from Abby to Erica to the clock. She groaned at the time and dropped her face back on Abby's chest.

"Why are you guys sleeping in here?"

"Because we wanted to be close by in case you needed us."

Erica looked into Abby's eyes. "Sorry for being such a bear, Abby."

Abby smiled as Trina lifted her sleepy face. "I told Adrianna she was right. You are a bear with a thorn in your paw," Trina added in a groggy voice.

Erica laughed softly and ruffled Trina's hair.

"Adrianna told us not to venture too close to the bear's cave till she could come home and try and remove the thorn herself. I told her it's too late. We've already felt the bite of the bear's jaws."

Erica grabbed a pillow from the couch and gently smacked Trina's back. "Thanks for squealing on me, Trina."

"You're welcome. That's only the beginning of our punishment for you for not calling us and telling us about your heartache."

Erica dropped her head back on the couch.

Trina shifted slightly in Abby's arms. "Adrianna said that she's probably no better company than you are. Her lawyers told her to quit being so bitchy and irritable or they were going to put her in a time capsule and ship her to the Russian space station Mir."

Erica tried to laugh but had to grab her head. "Oh, Adrianna. What a mess you've gotten us into." She leaned toward Abby and Trina and kissed them both. "I love you guys, but I can't hold my head up any longer."

Erica rose to her feet and headed back to bed. She pulled the covers up to her chin and tried to fight off another wave of nausea and chills. She felt her temples pulsating as Abby and Trina sang in unison, "We love you too, baby bear."

Erica grabbed for her head and grimaced. "Will you two please shut up and stop making me laugh? You're hurting my head."

Abby and Trina covered their heads with their blanket and continued to laugh as Erica smiled at her dear friends' playfulness.

✳✳✳✳

Erica awakened to the sound of clanking pots in her kitchen. She reached for Adrianna and suddenly remembered that she was not there. She rolled over and groaned with the heavy pain in her head. It was two o'clock in the afternoon. She held her head with both hands and sat up on the edge of the bed. Trina and Abby were no longer by the fireplace.

Erica climbed out of bed and made her way into the shower. She luxuriated in the soothing warmth of the cascading spray as she leaned her throbbing forehead against the cold tile. Overnight, the nausea had finally released its tight hold, leaving her abdominal muscles feeling like they had just done a thousand push-ups. She felt she had aged ten years and swore never to drink wine ever again. Well, at least not a whole bottle at one sitting.

Twenty minutes later, Erica made her way into the kitchen. Trina spotted her first. "Good afternoon, baby bear. Did we wake you?"

Erica walked slowly toward her and took her in her arms. "No, Trina, you didn't wake me. I'm used to awakening to the sound of a high school drum corps in my kitchen."

They laughed together as Erica hugged and kissed them both. "What smells so good in here?"

Trina smiled and pointed to the oven. "We made your favorite. Roasted chicken with roasted baby potatoes, asparagus, and green beans."

Erica inhaled the delicious aroma. "You guys are too good to me."

"I couldn't agree with you more," Abby said sternly. "How are you feeling?"

"My stomach feels a little more settled, but I can't get that freight train in my head to pull into a station. I certainly have a renewed appreciation for my patients who suffer from headaches. I guess I should thank Adrianna for that."

"Adrianna is still in shock that you drank that whole bottle of wine. She feels responsible for you feeling so sick."

"She didn't put the bottle in my hand. I'm responsible for the way I feel."

Abby looked into Erica's eyes. "I think it would mean a lot to Adrianna to hear you say that."

Erica looked away. Abby moved closer and touched her chin. Abby raised Erica's face to meet her eyes. "I think it's time you talked to her, Erica. This has gone on long enough. She's sick with guilt over what is happening to you, and she feels like she has lost you. We know how much you love each other, and I believe that love is still precious to both of you." Abby released Erica's chin. "If our roles were reversed, I know that you would never let me treat

Trina this way. Should I expect the same from you, Erica?"

Erica looked down at her hands. Abby placed her hand on her back. "Your mom called and left a message to tell you that they're having a fabulous time in Santa Barbara and to give her a call when you get a chance."

"She called me at work yesterday to let me know they had arrived. I only had a few minutes to talk to her between E.R. patients, so she has no idea what happened. I'll call her on Monday."

"Carolyn has called twice today. She's really worried about you, Erica."

"I'll call her on Monday as well."

Trina reached for both of their hands. "Come on, you guys, let's eat before the chicken decides it can't handle all these emotional women and tries to fly the coop." Trina slipped her hand into Erica's and guided her into the sunroom.

✳✳✳✳

It was eight o'clock when Erica walked Abby and Trina out and stood by as they loaded their things into the back of their Toyota Sequoia. Trina stepped toward Erica and hugged her tight. "Are you sure you're going to be okay, baby bear?"

Erica kissed her forehead. "Yes, I'll be fine, thanks to you guys."

Trina kissed her good-bye. "I love you, grumpy."

"I love you too, Trina."

Abby stepped into her arms and hugged her tight. "I love you," Abby whispered.

Erica leaned back and kissed her softly. "I love you too, Abby. I don't know how to thank you guys for everything you've done for me and for just being there regardless of my foul moods."

Abby touched her arm. "You would have done the same for us, Erica. All that we ask is that you be the one to call us next time when you're hurting. We're always here for you and Adrianna. Just think about how you would have felt if we shut you out."

"I would have killed you both."

"Exactly, my friend. Let's just pray that Adrianna's hearing goes well for her tomorrow and we get her back here to explain this thing to those of us in the dark."

"I can't wait for that to happen, Abby."

They hugged each other good-bye. Erica watched Abby guide Trina into the passenger seat before sliding in behind the wheel. Abby started the engine and glided the windows down.

Erica stuck her head into Abby's window. "Thank you both for everything. I mean that from the bottom of my heart."

Abby reached for Erica's face. "We know you really do appreciate us, regardless of how miserable and cranky you were." Abby caressed Erica's cheek. "Take care of yourself, Erica. I'll catch up with you at work tomorrow."

Erica stepped back as Abby put the vehicle in reverse. "Sounds great. I love you guys."

"We love you too, baby bear," Trina shouted.

Abby backed out of the driveway, and they all waved good-bye. Erica stood and watched their taillights disappear down the palm tree-lined street.

Erica returned to her empty house and finished tidying up the kitchen. She started the dishwasher and decided to get ready for bed. She slipped into her pink nightshirt, eased into bed, and propped herself up against the headboard, pulling little Addie into her lap. Erica held her tight, slid her bedside drawer open, and removed the unopened card that Adrianna had left under her pillow. Erica stared at it for the longest time and traced each letter of her name with her finger, attempting to connect with the flow of Adrianna's fountain pen.

Erica slid her fingers beneath the flap and tore the envelope open, gently easing the card out. The cover was a soft Impressionist painting, maybe a Monet, of two women picnicking at the edge of a lake. Inside Adrianna had written,

My Sweetest, Erica,
My greatest pleasure is the time I spend with you.
You are my soul mate and my love light.
I love you with all my heart.
Love always,
Your Adrianna xoxo

Erica blinked back the tears when she heard the distant sound of a ringing phone. A beep sounded on the answering machine, and she realized that Abby and Trina must have turned the ringer off on the bedside phone.

Erica's heart lurched as she heard Adrianna's s hesitant voice. "Hi. I haven't had the answering machine come on for a few days, so I guess this means that Abby and Trina have gone home. I really appreciate them being there with you, sweetheart. I hope you don't hate me for calling them and getting them involved."

Erica heard her pause and take a deep breath.

"How are you, Erica? I hope you're feeling better. I wish I could be there for you."

Erica heard a loud clap of thunder and heard Adrianna gasp as she quickly sat up on the edge of the bed and listened carefully.

"I don't know if you heard that, but there is quite a thunderstorm happening here. I'm up on the sixteenth floor, so I'm much closer to it than I would like to be. I've been sitting here for an hour, watching the thunder and lightning and not feeling near the fear that I usually feel when I'm in these storms alone. I realized that's because the fear I have of losing you greatly overshadows any other fear I have ever felt in my life."

Erica covered her mouth as a lump formed in her throat and tears filled her eyes.

"I knew when I began to wage this war that I had a lot to lose, but never in my wildest dreams did I think that my greatest treasure might be among the casualties."

Erica heard Adrianna pause to catch her breath.

"I also wanted to tell you that Mother Teresa called me from heaven and said ..."

Erica quietly picked up the phone. "Mother Teresa said what, Adrianna?"

Adrianna gasped at the sound of Erica's voice and whispered, "Erica."

Erica leaned back against her headboard. "I'm here, Adrianna. Now what did Mother Teresa say about me?"

479

Adrianna was speechless for a few seconds and had to swallow hard past the lump in her throat. "Mother Teresa said to tell you that you definitely have a few dents in your halo now."

Erica pulled the duvet over her legs. "Did Mother Teresa say she was disappointed in me?"

"No, darling. Nobody's disappointed in you. I pleaded your case to Mother Teresa and begged her not to revoke your special pass into heaven. I explained to her that you were unable to react any differently in this situation considering the information you had. She told me that as long as you gave me the opportunity to explain the entire story to you on Monday, then it would be up to me to decide whether you should be punished or not. She suggested sending you to the time-out corner, but I told her that the time-out corner in our house belongs to me."

Erica laughed at Adrianna's sense of humor, but unfortunately her laughter vibrated throughout her head. Erica grabbed her head and moaned softly.

"What's wrong, Erica?"

Erica groaned and covered her eyes with her hand. "I'd really like you to pull the plug on this derailed train careening through my brain."

"I'm sorry you feel so terrible."

"You should be sorry. You introduced me to that lovely German wine in the first place."

"I wish I could have been there to share the bottle with you and ease your frustration in a more loving way."

Erica hugged little Addie tight. "Stop being so damned sweet when I want to stay mad at you for a little while longer."

"Okay."

Erica took a deep breath and closed her eyes. "I can't discuss what's happened between us over the phone, Adrianna. We need to do this in person."

"Okay."

Erica frowned and felt herself float on the waves of Adrianna's sultry voice. "Quit being so soft and agreeable."

"I'm not a very good fighter, Erica. Conflict may be my professional life, but I don't enjoy it in my personal life."

Erica held the phone close. "I noticed that in your office. You didn't fight back very hard. You just stood there and took my shit. Your strength was very impressive."

"Don't be impressed, Erica. I know you don't enjoy conflict either, and your behavior in my office was appropriate to the situation. You had every right to say the things you said."

Another loud thunderclap distorted their line, and Erica heard Adrianna gasp. "Are you okay, Adrianna?"

"I'm okay. I really wish you were here to watch this incredible storm with me. It's much less terrifying when I'm with you. My nature nut would love this light show. Besides, I'm missing some valuable time in my conditioning program here. This may set me back a while in my development."

Erica smiled. "You're going to have to talk to your program coordinator about that. I hear she's a real hard-ass, so you'd better find some way to suck up to her big time before she will even consider extending your conditioning program."

Adrianna laughed. "She's not such a hard-ass, but I really do have some major sucking up to do. I'll try and think of what I can do to win my way back into her good graces."

Erica paused and toyed with Adrianna's card in her hand. "How's Teddy?"

"He's good. He's sitting right here by my feet. He really misses you and little Addie. But not as much as I miss you."

"What are you wearing?"

"I'm wearing jeans and your denim shirt."

"Bare feet?"

"Bare feet. My toes are digging into the carpet, but they told me to tell you that they miss your soft skin and gentle touch."

"I miss your gentle touch too, Adrianna."

They both sat in silence. "Thank you for the beautiful card, Adrianna. It made me cry."

"I have a feeling that I've caused you to shed many tears over the weekend. I hope to be home tomorrow evening, Erica. I just ask that you give me the opportunity to explain this whole situation. Then we can talk about where you would like to take things from there."

"That sounds fair, and Adrianna?"

Adrianna attempted to catch her breath as she answered quietly, "Yes, darling?"

"You're not going to lose me." Erica heard Adrianna's soft cry.

"I really needed to hear you say that."

"I really needed to tell you that." Erica looked over at the bedside clock. "What time is it there?"

"Midnight."

"Adrianna! Your hearing is at ten o'clock."

"Thank God! I can't wait to get this over with."

"Are you tired, Adrianna? Did you want to go to bed?"

"Sleep has not been a big priority this weekend. You have."

"I expect the best results for everyone involved tomorrow morning, so I want you to get some sleep so you can be at your best."

"This bed is so lonely without you."

"I know the feeling, darling." Erica ached to touch Adrianna. "I don't want to, but we should say good night."

"No, Erica, please don't go."

"You need to sleep, babe. You have a big day ahead of you."

"Okay."

"Stop being so damned adorable. You're making this so hard."

"I just want to thank you for picking up the phone tonight and talking to me. I can't tell you how much that means to me. Abby and Trina must have been getting tired of all my phone calls."

"They were happy to talk to you. It was my cranky behavior they were getting tired of."

"I hear they nicknamed you baby bear."

"I deserved that nickname. I was too angry or hung over to talk to you sooner."

"I understand."

"I wish I understood, Adrianna."

"You will tomorrow, Erica. I promise."

"I'm going to hold you to that promise, young lady. You have a hell of a lot of explaining to do, and I also want you to know that I ..." Erica paused briefly as tears choked her voice. "I can't wait to see you tomorrow."

"Till tomorrow, my love."

"Sleep tight, Adrianna."

"Sweet dreams, Erica, and know that I love you."

"Adrianna, do what you have to do tomorrow and know that I love you."

Chapter 28

Erica stood at her office window and stared out at the early evening shadows creeping across the South Mountain range. She admired the wispy clouds against the powder-blue sky as she watched the planes take flight in the distance from Sky Harbor Airport. The Bank of America building, Wells Fargo, and Bank One all stood proudly in downtown Phoenix to meet the endless blue sky. The Hyatt with its circle top looked like an airport control tower. The home of the Arizona Diamondbacks, Bank One Ballpark, glistened in the early evening with its roof wide open to let in the good weather. Erica's favorite building was City Hall. She loved the roof shaped like a royal crown.

Erica stepped away from the window and settled into her executive leather chair. She picked up the phone on her antique mahogany desk, punched in a number and waited.

"Hello, Carolyn. How are you?"

"Erica, I'm so glad you called. I'm much better than you are, I bet. How are you feeling?"

"Pretty beat up. I'm sorry I didn't call you sooner. Abby and Trina told me each time you called. Thank you for caring."

"Erica, you are very precious to us. It upsets me to see you and Adrianna at odds like this. If it's any consolation, Adrianna is as emotionally beat up as you are."

"I know. I talked to her last night."

"She told me. She was ecstatic to have spoken to you."

"None of this makes sense to me, Carolyn."

"I know, Erica. I have more knowledge of Adrianna's past cases, so this makes more sense to me than it would to you. I know that Adrianna wants to explain this all to you herself, so that's all I'm going to say. Especially since I promised not to interfere."

Erica laughed and leaned back in her chair.

"Just know that everything you have come to love about Adrianna is true to who she is. You can trust your heart with her, Erica. You promised me that you would not give up on Adrianna. Keep that promise, and I know you won't be disappointed."

"I love Adrianna very much, Carolyn. I just feel so detached from her professional life and what is going on right now."

"That was Adrianna's biggest fear. She never wanted you to feel that way. She can't wait to share with you this case that has consumed her professional world for the past two years."

"I can't wait either, Carolyn. This has been a brutal weekend."

"I know. I hope Adrianna gets home tonight and puts your mind at ease. I told her I want my ducks back waddling together once this case is done."

"I hope so too, Carolyn. We've been swimming upstream all weekend."

"Are you still at work?"

"Yes, I am. I'm sitting in my office."

"I won't keep you then, Erica. Stay strong. Know that we love you and I will call and talk to you tomorrow."

"Okay, Carolyn. I love you too. Please give David my love."

"I will. Good-bye, Erica."

"Good-bye, Carolyn." Erica set the phone back in its cradle and leaned her elbows on her desk. She was lost in thought about Adrianna and Michael when Abby walked into her office. Erica got out of her chair and took Abby into her arms and hugged her tight.

Erica looked into Abby's eyes. "Have you forgiven me for my bad behavior yet, Abby?"

Abby smiled into the face of the woman she had loved dearly for thirty years. "Erica, if Trina had done this to me, I would have been a hell of a lot worse than you were. I'm just glad we could be there for you."

They held each other tight. Erica was about to ask about Trina when she heard a knock at her door. She stepped toward the door and opened it wide.

Dr. Michael Thomas stood in the doorway in a charcoal-gray pinstriped suit with his arms out wide and his briefcase at his feet. "Ask me how my trip to New York was." He stepped toward Erica and gave her a big kiss on her stunned face before picking up his briefcase and moving toward Abby and taking her into his arms.

Erica was in shock as she wordlessly closed the door and stepped toward him. "What do you mean your trip to New York?"

Michael grinned at Abby then looked back at Erica. "I called your place Saturday night to tell you I was going to New York this weekend, but Abby and Trina made it quite clear that you were not in a conversational mood."

Erica looked at Abby. "You didn't tell me Michael had called or that he was going to New York."

Michael reached down for his burgundy leather briefcase and laid it flat on Erica's desk. "No, she didn't because I asked her not too. I told Abby where I was going and to let me explain everything to you myself when I got back." He clicked the briefcase open and pulled out a large manila envelope and handed it to Erica. "I finally read all the letters Adrianna sent me over the past year. If I had done that when she first wrote them to me, I wouldn't have needed to carry all this grief and anger around with me like a total fool."

Erica looked down at the envelope balanced lightly in the palm of her hands before looking back at Michael. "What did you learn from the letters, and what were you doing in New York?"

"First of all, I went to talk to Adrianna's father like you suggested. What a great guy. He has an incredibly sharp mind and flawless memory of past cases. He was well aware of Dr. MacGregor's and my malpractice cases. He said he always took a keen interest in the cases Adrianna worked on and liked to watch how she handled each case. He said he was disgusted with Adrianna for even thinking of prosecuting a physician, so Adrianna challenged him to find evidence to prove the physicians innocent of the charges brought before them. If you ask me, she was incredibly smart for challenging her father and getting his help indirectly.

"David confirmed everything that Adrianna had said about Dr. MacGregor. He was suffering from back pain and taking three different painkillers. From what David found out, he was drinking a lot heavier on his medication than Adrianna told us. He showed me copies of the complaint letters against Dr. MacGregor, and he even had a copy of the suicide note in his files. It told me all I wanted to know. He admitted to totally ignoring Hailey's complaints of abdominal pain and not ordering the proper tests that might have diagnosed her cancer sooner. After seeing all the documentation, Adrianna had every right to sue him for Hailey's death. David said he was really proud of the way Adrianna handled herself during that difficult case."

"So she was telling us the truth about Dr. MacGregor."

"Yes, Erica. Somehow I couldn't see Adrianna making all that stuff up. From the legal documents, I saw it was all the truth. Hailey's death was senseless and a horrible loss to Adrianna. I didn't want to believe her because I had loved Dr. MacGregor so much and was so angry over his death. I only wanted to believe what my memories were of him, not the person that Adrianna had painted. I didn't know that man and refused to believe that our Dr. MacGregor could have been so inhumane and inept. Well, I was as inept as he was for not investigating the truth before passing judgment on the one person who did seek the truth in this case. She wanted the truth and sought justice for the death of her lover, and she had every right to do that."

Erica set the manila envelope down on her desk and stepped closer to Michael. "Why did you go to New York? What happened there?"

"I felt like a total fool when David told me the truth about Dr. MacGregor's case. I just wanted to get out of there, but I needed to hear what David knew about my case. When I asked him, he knew that I must not have read the letters Adrianna had sent me. He asked me if I really wanted to know the truth. I told him I was finally ready. Then he shocked me. He picked up the phone and booked me a seat on the next flight to New York City. He said that if I wanted to truly learn the truth, then I needed to sit in on Adrianna's case Monday morning. He said it would be the only way I would understand Adrianna's agenda. He also told me to use the time during the flight to read Adrianna's letters before getting to New York. David booked me a room at the Mayflower Hotel where Adrianna was staying. Funny thing is my room was right across the hall from Adrianna's. Interesting coincidence, don't you think?

"Anyway, on Sunday morning I wrote Adrianna a note and slipped it under her door. In the note I said that it was a gorgeous day for a walk through Central Park if she cared to join me. I was ready to talk like a civilized human being if she had some forgiveness in her heart and some time on her hands." Michael smiled as he leaned back against the soft leather couch. "Fifteen minutes later there was a knock on my door. I opened the door and there stood Adrianna in a warm jacket. It was pretty obvious she was shocked to see me. She stood there for a few seconds before she said; 'I've got lots of forgiveness for you, Dr. Michael Thomas, but only about an hour of spare time. Will that be a good place for you and me to start?'"

"We walked through Central park for an hour and a half and talked nonstop. I'll always be grateful for that talk. Then I sat in on Adrianna's case this morning, and she was truly incredible. She blew everyone away."

Erica leaned back against her desk and rubbed her throbbing head. "Michael, I can't take this. Please tell us what happened."

"Adrianna prosecuted a bigwig lawyer from another law firm by the name of Edward Harrington. She had no intention of prosecuting me when she took on my malpractice case." Michael looked from Abby to Erica. "Apparently, information came to David Taylor from a close colleague that a big boss in a law firm had been using dirty tactics to win big medical lawsuits. David had known this Harrington for years and couldn't believe it was true. They were looking for a lawyer to investigate the allegations and wanted to hire Adrianna. David said if anyone would get to the truth it would be Adrianna. He said she would be the person for the job and said they should ask her to take on the case.

"Apparently Adrianna had her own concerns about Harrington years earlier with his dealings in medical malpractice cases but had never been able to prove anything. She even went to the other partners to reveal her concerns, and they laughed her out of their office.

Even the partners in her own law firm were not pleased with her taking on this case because these old boys seemed to enjoy a good game of golf every week. They only allowed her to do it because of the money it would bring in if she won. Regardless of the lack of support around her, Adrianna was determined to stop this bastard, and when she read my case, she saw the inconsistencies in the evidence. She did some snooping around and found that important documents had been destroyed, witnesses had been coerced, and computerized vital signs and times of events had been altered. That's why she took on my case. Adrianna is the one who stopped my case from ever getting near a courtroom or judge." Michael looked into Erica's eyes. "Adrianna wanted to prove my innocence and prosecute this bastard Harrington, and today she brought a giant to his knees."

Michael saw the shock in Erica's eyes. He reached toward Erica and squeezed her arm. "You would have been so proud of her, Erica. She stood up in a crowded courtroom and submitted exhibit after exhibit of falsified documents. She unfolded Harrington's dirty schemes right before the judge's eyes and received a standing ovation from everyone in that courtroom. It was a circus, and the judge went nuts trying to regain order."

Erica and Abby were in shock as Michael grinned from ear to ear. "After it was all over, I stepped out of the courtroom and saw Adrianna in the hallway with two other female lawyers. They were all thrilled with the outcome, and Adrianna praised them for all their hard work. I saw two older men in suits walk toward Adrianna with rage in their eyes, and she just stared them down and handed them a large manila envelope and said, 'In there you will find all of our resignations. So from this moment on, you can take our jobs in this pathetic, unconscionable law firm and shove them.'"

Erica shook her head. She could picture Adrianna saying that.

"Her young lawyers applauded, and Adrianna left those sniveling partners speechless. She turned and saw me watching her and sent her team of lawyers away. She walked up to me with her head held high, with a huge smile on her face, and said, 'Let's go home, Dr. Michael Thomas. You have patients who need you, and I have a special woman in my life who deserves an explanation and a whole lot more.'" Michael smiled broadly as he saw the pride in Erica's eyes. "She slipped her hand into mine and whisked me away to the airport with them."

Erica blinked back tears, finally understanding Adrianna's agenda. It wasn't prosecuting a prominent doctor or making partner in her law firm. It was to seek and serve justice as she always professed to do. Erica felt ashamed of herself and proud of Adrianna.

Michael stepped toward her, took her into his strong arms, and held her tight. He wiped away her tears and smiled. "Adrianna is an incredible woman, Erica. I'm so glad I got to meet her. We were on the same flight home and sat side by side and talked the whole way. She loves you so deeply. I do believe you two were made for each other. Go home to her, Erica. Let her explain in her own words. There's still so much she needs to tell you." Michael reached for the manila envelope on Erica's desk and handed it to her. "After you give Adrianna the chance to explain, read these letters. They confirm everything she has told us."

Erica gave Michael and Abby a big hug and bounded out of her office.

Abby stepped toward Michael and tugged on the lapels of his tailored suit. "Good work, detective. You should see if Adrianna needs a handsome sidekick."

✸✸✸✸

Erica stormed into her house out of breath and barely got her leather jacket off when she saw Adrianna walk toward her from the kitchen. Her eyes were brimming with tears, and the emotional strain of the past weekend showed in her walk. She looked so tiny and scared dressed in jeans and a soft cotton blouse. Erica was frozen in her spot as the sight of Adrianna's bare feet melted her soul. Erica raced forward and swept Adrianna into her arms. They held each other tight, and neither one wanted to let go. Their tears of emotional exhaustion streamed down their cheeks and merged on each other's faces.

Wordlessly, Erica wrapped her arm around Adrianna's waist and walked her into the kitchen. Erica sat her on the counter as she reached for a box of tissues and handed her several. Adrianna wrapped her legs around Erica's waist and pulled her in intimately close.

Adrianna dried her eyes and touched her fingertip to Erica's amethyst pendant. She looked up and smiled brightly. "Hi."

Erica wrapped her arms around Adrianna and luxuriated in the feel of her body as she pulled her close. "Hi there. I hear you're unemployed."

Adrianna laughed and brimmed with excitement. "Yes, I am. Isn't that great?"

"That is great. I also hear that you brought a giant to his knees today."

Adrianna's eyes narrowed suspiciously. "We really need to do something about that Dr. Michael Thomas storming into your office and telling you things that I want to tell you first."

Erica laughed and shook her head. "Adrianna, can you please explain to me what happened from the beginning because I'm in a state of shock and I really need to hear this from you."

Adrianna smiled and brushed away a stray ringlet. "I've waited for this opportunity for weeks, so it would be my absolute pleasure to explain this nightmare to you, my love.

"Edward Harrington is a corrupt lawyer. I have spent the past two years trying to uncover his deception and malicious practices. When Michael's case landed on my desk and I read through it, I couldn't believe how it showcased everything that man had been doing illegally. I finally found the opportunity to destroy the one lawyer who was attempting to destroy so many doctors."

"Why did he do this?"

Adrianna exhaled a deep breath and shook her head. "Greed, pure greed. The money in these medical cases is incredible, and that is why he did everything in his power to corrupt the evidence and win the big bucks, regardless of the bright medical careers he destroyed along the way."

"Why didn't you tell me all this before, Adrianna?"

"When I first met you, your name was vaguely familiar, but I couldn't place it. It was not until I had fallen madly in love with you that I remembered that you were listed as being present in the emergency department when that little boy was brought in. Your name was on the pre-trial list as a potential witness for the defense. Even though I proved that Harrington had tampered with the evidence in Michael's case and the case against him was thrown out, I didn't know if the judge might still call you in as a witness to the events that occurred in Harrington's trial. I knew that I could not divulge any of this information to you; otherwise, it would destroy your credibility under oath. I was not willing to jeopardize your career or integrity by giving you information you would not have obtained through normal channels. Worst of all, the lawyers involved would have tried to discredit you as a witness because you are my lover. I refused to jeopardize you under oath, so I was determined to end this case as soon as possible so you would not have to go through a horrible ordeal."

"So instead you chose to jeopardize our relationship."

Adrianna played with a ringlet at Erica's cheek. "I had to risk us to protect you, Erica. I knew in my heart that you would give me the chance to explain. I prayed that my explanation would be enough to earn me a chance to let us start again and repair any damage that had been done. When you told me what you saw in that trauma room, I knew I was on the right track. It was your love and dedication to your career that inspired me to keep going and take care of that evil man once and for all. I didn't know how else to protect you, Erica. I had jeopardized you enough by falling in love with you, so I felt responsible to shield you from the witness stand in this lawsuit. So I tried to hide the whole thing from you and lived with that fear of disclosure every day. When I stepped out of your bathroom and saw you talking to Michael, I knew that the protective bubble I had put around you had just burst.

"That day you delivered those beautiful red roses to my office, Mia and Darby realized who you were and that you were a potential witness in Michael's defense. They became well aware of the nature of our relationship when I greeted you at the elevator. I'm the one who forbids them from sleeping with anyone involved with our cases, and you go ahead and make me fall in love with you and destroy my credibility."

Erica leaned her forehead against Adrianna's. "So you did all this to protect me."

Adrianna held Erica's face in her hands. "I did all of this to protect you and Michael and all the other doctors wrongly accused of malpractice. You showed me the human side of medicine, Erica. Even I was starting to lose sight of that."

Erica was overwhelmed by all this information as she inhaled a deep breath and caressed Adrianna's cheek. She watched Adrianna's moist, slightly parted lips and looked up into her eyes.

Adrianna caressed Erica's hair and, easing the gold butterfly-shaped barrette from her ponytail, watched Erica's beautiful ringlets bounce free. She set the barrette on the counter and slowly guided Erica's face closer as their lips gently met, as if for the first time. They both moaned tenderly as Adrianna leaned closer and rediscovered the lips she loved so deeply.

Erica brushed the soft pad of her thumb across Adrianna's full, moist lower lip. She leaned closer and touched her lips to the corners of Adrianna's mouth before consuming her lips with all the intensity and passion burning in her soul.

Adrianna leaned back slightly and placed soft, moist kisses along Erica's cheek and eyes. "I missed your kisses so much."

Erica rested her cheek against Adrianna's. "I missed you and your kisses very, very much."

"I'm so sorry for everything I put you through, sweetheart."

"You did what you had to do, Adrianna. I'm so proud of you and everything you accomplished today."

"It means so much to me to hear you say that. I'm sorry that Michael had to temporarily be the scapegoat, but he was always innocent of any wrongdoing. His only downfall is his handwriting, and he has promised me that he will print his notes from now on. I explained everything to him in New York and on the plane ride home and apologized for all the grief and anger I caused him. He told me I owe him a keg of gourmet jelly beans as my punishment."

Erica laughed as she brushed away a strand of hair from Adrianna's eyes. "What's going to happen to this Edward Harrington?"

"He will go to prison for his actions. When I first disclosed his deceit in Michael's case, his firm had no choice but to suspend him and put the responsibility on me to fully investigate his wrongdoings. They hated what I was doing to their partner, but they had no choice but to find out the truth. He was their beloved partner, and they couldn't help but despise me for unveiling his dark side, regardless of how evil he was and what he was doing to destroy innocent doctors. The animosity I felt in this case seemed to be a ripple effect from the old boys in the law community that had been his buddies. Many of them were shocked by the allegations and even more shocked when the truth unfolded. My father also knew Harrington, but their relationship was purely professional. He also didn't want to believe the rumors but felt there was enough evidence to investigate the allegations. This was a really difficult case, and my father told me he felt I would uncover the truth because of the experience I had with other medical malpractice cases. His confidence meant a lot to me. I wanted to give this case my best."

"David and Carolyn must be really proud of you."

Adrianna's smile lit up her sapphire eyes. "They are. I just got off the phone with them. They were ecstatic. I told them I had some unfinished business to take care of with you and that hopefully tomorrow we could celebrate with them."

"That sounds wonderful. I really am proud of you, Adrianna. It took a lot of guts and intelligence to do what you did today. You risked your career and personal life to slay Goliath, and in the end little David stood tall with nothing lost but tears."

"It means so much to me that you feel that way."

"Did you ever doubt how proud I would be of you when this was all over?"

"No. I also never doubted your love for me."

"I'm glad, because my love for you consumed me even when I felt so angry." Erica brushed her fingertips across Adrianna's soft cheek. "It must have felt wonderful handing in all of your resignations."

"It was such an incredible feeling. I wish you could have been there to enjoy it with me."

"I wish I could have been there too, darling."

Erica wrapped her arms around Adrianna's waist and held her close. "What are your professional plans now, my little hotshot lawyer?"

"I would like to take some time off and just be your wife for a while and allow us to get reacquainted."

"I would really like to get reacquainted with my wife." Erica leaned toward Adrianna and gently united their passionate need with a kiss of hunger and recovery.

Adrianna leaned her forehead against Erica's cheek and caught her breath. "I had the most incredible phone call from my father Saturday night. He always calls me when I'm in New York because he worries about me so much. This time he called really late at night and told me all about his conversation with Michael and his search for the truth after all this time.

"He told me that for the past several months they have had several gay and lesbian clients come to his firm for different legal matters, and my dad realized that there are specific legal services that the gay and lesbian community needs. He asked me if I would join his law firm as a partner and set up a division to serve the needs of the gay and lesbian community."

"Now, that's incredible. That would be a dream come true for you to work with David and to provide for our community."

"I told my father how touched I was by his incredible offer, but I had to talk to you before I made any decisions in my life. He said he thought you might be as excited about this prospect as I was and said to think about the staff that I would like to hire to help me out. I told him I knew two unemployed young lawyers I'd like to hire, and I heard there's a nosy secretary who also resigned, all of whom I would love to hire."

"This is all so wonderful. Everybody who risked everything is going to win big in the end."

Adrianna reached up and traced Erica's lower lip. "The most amazing thing that my father said to me was that you opened his eyes to my world and my happiness. He said that he always hoped that my desire to be with a woman was just a phase and that someday I would find the right man and be happily married. He then said that his only wish for Leah and me is to have partners who loved us and cared for us. You fulfilled his dreams for me and made him realize that I could never find a better partner. He said he has never seen me so happy and so full of life as I am with you. I told him that I have never been so happy and that I truly believe I have found my soul mate." Adrianna guided Erica's face down to her and gently brushed against her lips as she heard Erica's soft moans of pleasure and kissed her with deep, probing desire.

Adrianna leaned her forehead against Erica's and toyed with the buttons on her silk blouse. "I even told my father that I would ask you if you would consider consulting in our new division to help guide gays and lesbians to proper health care." Adrianna loosened the top two buttons of Erica's silk blouse and looked at her with eyes full of love and passion. "I'm sure I could find some way to repay you for your time and expertise."

Erica loved the seductive look in Adrianna's eyes as she leaned closer and brushed her lips with soft, teasing kisses. "Do I get to choose how I wish to be paid?"

"My request line is always open to you." Adrianna took Erica's lips in a kiss of sensuous passion.

Adrianna held Erica tight and caressed her head of bouncing ringlets. "Do you fully understand everything that happened, sweetheart?"

"I fully understand what your agenda was all about and why you had to keep me in the dark."

"You believe that I never intended to make a fool of you?"

Erica remembered her raging tirade in Adrianna's office. She looked away from Adrianna's passionate eyes. "Yes. I always believed that."

Adrianna touched her chin and guided her eyes up to her. "I want you to know that I looked long and hard in New York for my conscience and realized I had it in my purse the whole time."

Erica burst into laughter and looked away in embarrassment. "I'm sorry for all the nasty things I said to you in your office. I was furious. I hurt you very badly, and I'm so sorry. I hope you can find it in your heart to forgive me."

Adrianna held Erica's face in her hands and remembered her seething rage. "I'm responsible for putting you in this impossible situation, Erica. Your anger was justified, and it was so nice to see you be human like the rest of us." Adrianna caressed her cheek. "You have nothing to apologize for, my love, and I just want you to know that I did not seduce you to eliminate you as a credible witness. I seduced you because I fell deeply in love with you and because I find you so damned irresistible." Adrianna smiled at Erica's embarrassment. "I'm the one who hurt you very deeply, Erica. I'm so sorry for everything I put you through. I never intended to put such a terrible strain on you or our relationship. I hope you can find it in your heart to forgive me. I don't ever want to see that look of anger and betrayal in your eyes again because of something I've done. I really tested your love and faith in me, Erica. I don't ever plan on doing that again. I felt sick as I felt you slip away from me and unable to do anything to pull you back."

"I do forgive you, Adrianna. I love you, and I'm so proud of you."

Erica rubbed her temple as Adrianna entwined her fingers behind her neck. "How are you feeling?"

"My stomach has really settled down, but yesterday I had a very cross mommy elephant stomping around in my head. Today it's just a playful baby elephant."

Adrianna caressed Erica's temples as she closed her eyes and luxuriated in her touch. "Can I get you something for your headache, sweetheart?"

"Nothing works. I'm sure this damned headache will go away soon."

"You, young lady, are banned from ever drinking wine without me again."

Erica dropped her face in embarrassment. "That was a really stupid thing I did."

"You were very angry and very upset, sweetheart. I feel so bad for pushing you to that depth of despair."

They held each other close as Adrianna caressed Erica's face. She brushed her hand across her strong shoulder and down her arm. "You're not wearing your bracelet."

Erica stood tall and looked into Adrianna's eyes and stepped toward the kitchen counter. She returned with the wine glass containing her bracelet. She handed Adrianna the glass and watched her smile.

"I hope you didn't plan on drinking this too?"

Erica blushed. "I took it off when I was pretty angry."

"I understand, sweetheart."

Erica slid the bracelet out of the crystal wine glass and handed it to Adrianna. "I'd really like you to help me put it back on."

Adrianna took the sparkling bracelet and easily linked it on Erica's wrist.

Erica took Adrianna's heart pendant between her fingers and touched it gently.

Adrianna reached for her and pulled her closer, leaning her lips against Erica's softly, gently. Erica's moans intensified their desire as their lips united in a passionate dance of deep love.

"I want you, Erica. I want to make love to you."

Erica smiled and wrapped her arms snugly around Adrianna. "Hang on." Erica easily scooped her into her arms and carried her into the bedroom.

Erica set Adrianna down beside their bed as they stood facing each other, staring into each other's eyes and slowly, carefully removing each other's clothing and jewelry, as if for the first time. Erica pulled Adrianna into her arms as they stood and held each other close, luxuriating in the feel of each other's soft skin. The only light in the room was the soft glow from their heart-shaped nightlight.

Adrianna guided Erica beneath the sheets and gently eased herself on top of her as they looked at each other longingly. "You feel so wonderful. I have missed you so much."

Erica brushed away a strand of hair from Adrianna's eyes. "I needed you so much this weekend, and you abandoned me and left me in my bear cave alone, aching for you."

Adrianna smiled and brushed her fingertips across Erica's naked shoulder. "Maybe I can come in your bear cave and find a way to earn your forgiveness."

Erica skimmed her fingertips down the shallow hollow of Adrianna's spine and over her shapely bottom. "Well, you'd better get to work, young lady, because you have a hell of a lot of sucking up to do."

Adrianna lowered herself to Erica's neck and luxuriated in her passionate moans of delight. "This will be my pleasure."

Chapter 29

Abby and Trina let themselves into Erica's house and called out to them to no avail. They locked the door behind them and reset the alarm before continuing their search in the kitchen. Abby turned to Trina, smiling. "Gee, babe, I wonder where they could be?"

Trina loved the mischievous gleam in Abby's eyes as she watched her place their bags of Chinese food on the counter. Abby took the newspaper from Trina, took her hand and guided her toward the master bedroom.

Abby and Trina stood in the doorway as they adjusted their eyes to the soft, dim light and saw the single pile of clothes heaped on the floor beside the disheveled bed. The bed sheet was entangled among their entwined legs and barely covering their beautiful bodies as they lay on their sides facing each other. They saw Adrianna gently trace her fingers up and down Erica's naked back as she leaned up on one elbow and smiled.

"Good evening, ladies. We heard you guys come in and knew you would eventually find us."

Abby and Trina stepped toward the bed. "Welcome home, Adrianna," Trina said.

"Thank you. It's wonderful to be home."

Erica was completely nestled into Adrianna with her eyes closed as Abby peeked down at her. "We can see that you got quite a welcome. Is the baby bear sleeping?"

Adrianna smiled and held Erica close. "No. She's just recovering."

Erica stayed snuggled into Adrianna. "When are you two ever going to learn to knock? Better yet, how about I in-service you on the use of a doorbell?"

Abby burst into laughter as she stepped closer to Trina and put her arm around her waist. "Well, Trina, isn't this a lovely welcome and a lovely sight? Paradise has obviously been restored to the Taylor-Beaumont household. Adrianna and Erica have obviously kissed and made up or made out, however you want to see it, and you and I haven't even heard her side of the story."

Adrianna kissed Erica's forehead and saw the smile crease the corner of her lips. "Uh-oh. I think we're in trouble," Adrianna whispered against Erica's ear.

Abby smacked Adrianna's hip with the newspaper. "Michael gave me this newspaper before I left work and asked me to give it to you so you can see that you made the front page of the *New York Times*. Apparently they ran a big story on the trial."

Erica opened her eyes as Adrianna reached for the newspaper in Abby's hand. "What?"

508

Abby gently pulled it out of Adrianna's reach and shook her head. "Not so fast, Ms. Taylor. On behalf of Trina and me, we would like to express our appreciation to you for sending our emotions on a nonstop roller coaster ride all weekend long."

"I guess the least I owe you both is an explanation."

Abby smacked her hip with the curled up newspaper and dropped it on the foot of the bed. "You're damn right about that. Now, get your sorry asses out of bed and come join us for Chinese food because Trina and I are hungry, and we can't wait to hear this story." Abby leaned closer and kissed both their cheeks.

Trina leaned in behind Adrianna and kissed them both. She leaned in close to their joined faces. "I love when you guys get into trouble." She took Abby's hand, and they headed toward the kitchen together.

Erica and Adrianna showered together and dressed in jeans and cotton shirts. In the kitchen, Erica admired the picture of Adrianna on the front page of the newspaper. They walked through the kitchen and found Trina and Abby setting the table in the sunroom. Adrianna walked toward them. She hugged them both as they welcomed her home. Abby stepped into Erica's arms and hugged her tight. Abby stepped back slightly, and Trina slipped into Erica's arms and hugged her. "It's so nice to see that glow back in your eyes. Now, let's go eat before the food gets cold. Besides, I'm dying to hear Adrianna's explanation." Trina stepped toward Adrianna and slipped her hand into hers. "And it had better be a good one."

509

Adrianna looked from Trina's playfully stern face to Erica. "Uh-oh." They sat together at the table and dug into the delicious dishes of orange chicken, vegetable fried rice, garlic snap peas, Buddha's delight, curry vegetables, and white rice as Adrianna told them the story from start to finish.

Abby leaned back in her chair and set her coffee mug down. "So let me get this straight. You never intended to sue Michael for medical malpractice. You were actually the one who disclosed the fact that this lawyer, Edward Harrington, had concocted some grand scheme where he falsified documents and vital signs in different cases including Michael's to win big medical malpractice law suits."

Adrianna set her glass of water down. "That's correct."

Abby leaned closer on the table. "And you couldn't tell Erica any of this till it was over because she was a potential witness in Michael's case."

"Correct again."

Abby leaned toward Erica. "Makes perfect sense to me, Erica. How could you have doubted Adrianna?"

The growl came deep from within Erica's throat as she curled up the newspaper and smacked Abby's shoulder.

Abby quickly rose from her chair and extended her hand to Trina. "I don't think I can handle any more excitement for one day. Let's go home, Trina, and hide from these exhausting women who really need to learn to communicate better."

Abby helped Trina to her feet, and they all headed toward the front door.

They hugged and kissed each other good-bye. Abby took Adrianna into her arms. "Do you really know how proud we are of you?"

Adrianna held Abby close. "Yes, I do. Do you guys really know how much I appreciated you both being here for Erica?"

"Yes, we do. Now that we have the pleasantries out of the way, repeat after me: I, Adrianna Taylor, will never, ever, ever put my dear friends through this emotional turmoil again."

Adrianna smiled sheepishly and repeated the words. Abby kissed her softly and hugged her tight. "Welcome home, Adrianna. We all missed you."

Erica and Adrianna stood together and watched Abby and Trina head for their SUV.

Abby looked back before slipping into their Toyota Sequoia. "Take care, ladies, and love each other well."

"We will, Abby. The same for both of you."

Abby waved one final time before slipping into their vehicle. She backed out of the driveway and headed for home.

Erica guided Adrianna back inside, locked the door, and reset the house alarm. She took Adrianna by the hand and walked her back to the cozy fire in the living room. She turned to face Adrianna and held both her hands. "I haven't had a cup of tea since you left."

Adrianna smiled and squeezed Erica's hands. "Neither have I, sweetheart. Why don't we get reacquainted with our nightly ritual."

"I'd really like that." Erica kissed Adrianna's forehead and guided her into the kitchen. She stood before her French walnut armoire and opened the elegantly crafted double doors. She stood in stunned silence for a few seconds before reaching in and pulling out the delicate white cat teapot. "Oh my God, Adrianna. You bought me a Duchess teapot."

Adrianna stood beside her and touched the fine bone china teapot. "I did. I found it in the Disney store in New York. You always remind me of Duchess from the *Aristocats*. You will always be my duchess, Erica."

Erica slid her hand into Adrianna's thick, dark hair and guided her closer. She gently brushed her mouth against her moist, slightly parted lips, hearing that familiar purring moan that always set her body on fire. "Thank you. It's so beautiful. Duchess will be happy to serve us tea from now till eternity."

Adrianna nodded her head as she kissed Erica gently. She touched the tip of her tongue to Erica's lower lip and felt her quick indrawn breath. "Why don't you peek inside and see what else Duchess would like to serve you."

Erica leaned back slightly and pointed at the teapot.

Adrianna smiled mischievously. "Look inside."

Erica slowly lifted the lid off the teapot and peeked inside. She looked back at Adrianna and gave her a jubilant grin. She reached deep down inside and pulled out a tiny, square, silver-wrapped box.

Adrianna took the teapot from her hands and placed it back in the armoire. She closed the walnut doors and watched Erica admire the tiny gift in the palm of her hand. She touched her cheek and looked deeply into her glistening emerald eyes. "Open your gift, sweetheart."

Erica carefully removed the red ribbons and sparkling silver wrapping paper. She placed the wrappings in Adrianna's hand and ran her thumb across the plush black velvet box. She slowly creaked open the lid of the ring box. The sight of the shimmering band of one-carat diamonds overwhelmed Erica.

Tears filled Erica's eyes as Adrianna took the ring and slipped it onto her ring finger. She gently tilted Erica's strong hand and admired the ring's beauty. Adrianna reached up and brushed her fingertips across her tear-stained face. "I love you, Erica. You are my love light, and I'm thrilled to have you as my wife."

Erica pulled Adrianna into her arms and hugged her tight. "The ring is so beautiful, babe. I just love it. I'm so happy to be your wife, and I'm so happy to have you back home with me."

Adrianna took Erica's face in her hands. "I don't ever plan on being away from you again, my love." Adrianna felt Erica's intense love and desire and ached to fill her need. She placed soft gentle kisses on the corners of her mouth and along her jaw. She brushed her lips along her neck and nipped teasingly at her ear.

Erica tilted her head and sighed deeply. Adrianna's delicate touch enflamed her burning need. She skimmed her hands down Adrianna's slender back and pulled her in tight, aching for more of her touch. She slipped her hands over the contours of Adrianna's jeans-clad bottom and felt her sway temptingly against her.

Adrianna leaned back slightly and took Erica's face in her hands. She brushed a soft kiss against her moist, slightly parted lips and stared into her bewitching eyes. "I want you so much."

Erica leaned in closer and touched her mouth to Adrianna's pillowy lower lip. "I want you like I've never wanted another woman before."

Adrianna wordlessly took Erica's hand and guided her into the sunken living room. She grabbed several overstuffed pillows and placed them before the crackling fire. She guided Erica down among the cushions and carefully straddled her thighs. She loved the alluring look in her eyes as she slid her hands along the front of her faded Levi's and traced the button with her thumbs. She slowly loosened the button and eased the zipper down, watching the denim material part. Craving that essence of her femininity, she lowered herself over Erica and placed feathery, moist kisses just above the waistband of her pastel pink panties.

Erica closed her eyes and sighed as she luxuriated in Adrianna's seductive touch. She wove her fingers into her thick, dark hair as she arched beneath her. A scorching heat burned beneath Adrianna's moist touch and surged deep between her thighs.

Adrianna adored the way Erica writhed beneath her in complete surrender. She skimmed the tip of her tongue below Erica's belly button before darting it beneath the waistband of her panties. Erica's euphoric murmurs inflamed Adrianna's sultry desire as she gripped her jeans and panties and slipped them over her raised hips. She eased herself lower and tossed her clothes carelessly aside. She leaned over Erica and guided her out of the rest of her clothes and laid her back among the cushions.

Erica laid her head on her arms and watched Adrianna slowly, teasingly remove her own clothing as the soft glow of the firelight caressed her perfect skin. Erica reached her hand out to her and guided Adrianna to lie over her.

Erica luxuriated in the gentle weight of Adrianna against her as she slowly ran her fingertips along the shallow indent of Adrianna's smooth back and over her shapely bottom. She parted her own legs and eased Adrianna down tight as she looked into her moist eyes. "I love you so much."

Adrianna loved the look of endearing warmth in Erica's emerald eyes and touched her fingertip to her full, moist lower lip. "Ti amo, my green-eyed maiden."

Erica gently took the tip of her finger into her mouth and touched it with her tongue. She sucked it gently as she watched Adrianna's yearning darken her eyes to a deep sapphire blue.

Adrianna slowly freed her moist finger and slanted her mouth over Erica's, kissing her with a hunger that would only begin to satiate their need.

She felt Erica playfully probe her with her tongue as she opened to her and allowed her the freedom to fully explore.

Adrianna was a willing captive of Erica's skillful tongue as she brushed her hand over Erica's shoulder and down her smooth chest. She skimmed her fingertips beneath the soft underside of her breast before trailing across her peaked nipple. Erica's raspy moans filled Adrianna with sizzling urgency as she eased herself down and placed soft, sucking kisses down Erica's neck and shoulder. She nipped at the

515

sensitive skin beneath her collarbone as she felt Erica squirm beneath her. Her burning, passionate desire consumed Adrianna as she touched her lips to her firm nipple, brushing her moist lips back and forth before sucking it deeply in her mouth.

Erica arched her back and cried out in euphoric bliss. She wove her fingers deeply into Adrianna's hair, burying her nipple deeper against her caressing tongue.

Adrianna let the turgid nipple slip from between her damp lips before moving to the other breast and taking the rigid nipple into her mouth and leaving it moist and hot from her tongue's caress.

Erica's pleading moans incited Adrianna's yearning as she moved slowly down to Erica's slender abdomen and planted a trail of warm, wet kisses. She touched her tongue to the sensitive skin beneath Erica's belly button and steeped her senses in her womanly scent.

Erica grabbed the pillow beneath her head and arched her neck as raucous moans of delight echoed from her throat.

Erica parted her legs wider in invitation. Adrianna gladly accepted and slipped lower between her thighs. She laid soft, moist kisses along the insides of Erica's thighs as Erica impatiently arched her hips toward her. Adrianna smiled and drew small, tight circles with the tip of her tongue all along the inside of her sensitive thigh.

Erica groaned and reached for Adrianna's face. "You're tormenting me, babe."

Adrianna kissed the palm of Erica's hand and smiled mischievously. "I was just taking my time, sweetheart, so we could get reacquainted."

Erica ran her fingers gently across the top of Adrianna's head. "God, I missed you."

Adrianna nuzzled her cheek against Erica's dark mound of curls. "I missed you so much, my darling. Let's see if we can't get further reacquainted." Adrianna tilted her head up and softly kissed Erica's hand. She kissed each finger before she leaned down and ached to meet her desperate need.

Adrianna leaned toward her dark mound and inhaled her feminine scent before dipping her tongue into her pool of wetness. She slid higher and touched her tongue to her erect essence in a light, gentle caress.

Erica released a gratifying cry as she gently thrust against Adrianna's scintillating touch. She felt a building surge of vibrating tension emanating from Adrianna's wondrous tongue and coursing throughout her entire being. She gasped for each breath as Adrianna dangled her tantalizingly before the precipice of unparalleled ecstasy.

Their rhythm and intimacy was timeless as Adrianna felt Erica's thighs tense against her shoulders. She slid her tongue lighter and lighter across her rigid center as she slipped her fingers deep within her. Erica's blissful cries inflamed Adrianna's desire to satiate her raging need as she gently thrust within her.

Erica suddenly stopped moving her hips as the tightly coiled tension began to lose its grip and ease her toward that wondrous abyss. An undeniable wave of spasms erupted from deep within and gripped at

Adrianna's fingers as Erica arched her back and shouted Adrianna's name.

Adrianna laid her face against Erica's belly and luxuriated in the astonishing release of her lover's fulfillment.

Minutes later, Adrianna felt Erica weave her fingers gently through her hair. "That was truly incredible."

Adrianna kissed Erica's belly before easing herself up and lying in her arms. She leaned up on one elbow and looked deeply into Erica's satiated, happy face as she trailed a finger across her soft breast. "It was beautiful, sweetheart. I'm really enjoying getting reacquainted."

Erica rolled Adrianna onto her back and eased herself over her. She looked into her gorgeous blue eyes and kissed her lightly, tasting their intimacy on her lips. "Lady, I plan on doing more than just getting reacquainted."

Erica leaned into Adrianna and took her lips in a ravenous kiss of uninhibited zealousness. She gave as much as Adrianna took and still craved more. Their kisses deepened and forged; aching to pull each other in to a place that only they shared.

Adrianna's writhing body shattered Erica's resolve to take her slowly as she slid her hand over the subtle hollow of her smooth hip and down her thigh. She combed her fingers through her dark V-shaped mound and felt the moisture of her arousal. She groaned her pleasure against Adrianna's full lips before slipping her fingers deep into her pool of wetness.

Adrianna arched her neck and moaned blissfully. She reached up and entwined her fingers into Erica's thick ringlets and gasped her next breath. "Oh, God, you feel so wonderful."

Erica thrust gently inside her and kissed her upturned jaw. "Oh, no, babe, it's you that feels wonderful."

Erica slipped her fingers carefully from within her and slid toward her rigid center. She caressed her in light, tight circles as she felt Adrianna's wetness surge against her finger. She stroked her into a rhythmic sea of ecstasy as she took her peaked nipple in her mouth and shamelessly devoured it.

Adrianna cried out in exultant pleasure as she rocked hard against Erica's glorious touch. She gripped Erica's shoulders tight and willed herself to hold on as the surge of torrid heat flamed from Erica's touch and threatened to consume her like an arid forest. Her fingers gripped tighter as she felt herself lose hold and slip into that sea of all-encompassing ecstasy.

A tidal wave of spasms erupted and flowed over her as she arched her neck and screamed Erica's name.

Erica kissed her parted lips as she saw the tears clinging to Adrianna's thick, dark eyelashes. She wiped away a stray tear and kissed her closed eyes. "Welcome home, my love light. Welcome home."

A Note to Readers

I have been a nurse for nineteen years. Fifteen of those years have been spent working in intensive care units. I enjoy weaving my nursing experience with my love for women as the backdrop of my story. I have been blessed to experience the beauty of love between women. It is that depth of understanding, passion and respect that I enjoy exploring through my stories.

I have always been fascinated by law and wondered what it would be like to pit a dedicated physician against a tenacious lawyer. Thus *Love Light* began to unfold in my mind. I wrote this story in 1997 and put it away for several years to work on my novels, *Tender Heart* and *Bradley Bay.* When I pulled it out again and started to read the story I fell in love with Erica and Adrianna all over again. I hope that you will enjoy them as well.

I currently live in Arizona with my partner of twelve years and our governing cats. Without

Catherine's love and support this story would never have come to life.

When you have the time, cuddle into a favorite chair and wrap yourself in a cozy blanket. Bend back the cover of *Love Light* and allow Erica and Adrianna to take you away for several hours.

Warmly;

Ana P. Corman

Tender Heart and ***Bradley Bay***, were also published by 1st Books Library. www.1stbooks.com